An Introduction to Applied Cognitive Psychology

An Introduction to Applied Cognitive Psychology

Anthony Esgate and David Groome

with Kevin Baker, David Heathcote, Richard Kemp,
Moira Maguire and Corriene Reed

Psychology Press
Taylor & Francis Group
HOVE AND NEW YORK

First published 2005 by Psychology Press
27 Church Road, Hove, East Sussex BN3 2FA

Simultaneously published in the USA and Canada
by Psychology Press
270 Madison Avenue, New York NY 10016

Reprinted 2008

*Psychology Press is part of the Taylor & Francis
Group, an Informa business*

Copyright © 2005 Psychology Press

Typeset in Century Old Style by
RefineCatch Limited, Bungay, Suffolk
Printed and bound in Great Britain by
TJ International Ltd, Padstow, Cornwall

This publication has been produced with paper
manufactured to strict environmental standards and
with pulp derived from sustainable forests.

British Library Cataloguing in Publication Data
A catalogue record for this book is available from
the British Library

Library of Congress Cataloging-in-Publication Data
An introduction to applied cognitive psychology /
Anthony Esgate & David Groome; with Kevin Baker
  . . . [et al.].
   p. cm.
Includes bibliographical references and index.
ISBN 1-84169-317-0—
ISBN 1-84169-318-9 (pbk.)
1. Cognitive psychology.   2. Psychology, Applied.
I. Esgate, Anthony, 1954–   II. Groome, David,
1946–   .   III. Baker, Kevin.
BF201.156 2004
153—dc22   2004008923

ISBN 978-1-84169-318-7

To my parents, Reg and Barbara (DG)

For Deanna and Snowball (AE)

Contents

6 Skill, attention and cognitive failure 109

11 Reading and dyslexia

Figures and tables

Figures

Tables

Figure acknowledgements

Sources for figures reproduced in this book are acknowledged as follows:

Figure 1.1   Reproduced with the kind permission of the Department of Experimental Psychology, University of Cambridge

Figure 1.2   Reproduced with the kind permission of the MRC Cognition and
Brain Sciences Unit

Figure 1.3   Reproduced with the kind permission of Ulric Neisser

Figure 3.1   Reproduced with the kind permission of David T. Lawrence of
J.C. Lawrence & Sons (photographers)

Figure 3.3   CREDIT: Popperfoto.com

Figure 3.4   CREDIT: Popperfoto.com

Figure 3.5   CREDIT: Popperfoto.com

Figure 3.6   CREDIT: Popperfoto.com

Figure 4.1   Reproduced with the kind permission of Vicki Bruce

Figure 6.2   Reproduced with the kind permission of Psychology Press

Figure 6.3   Reproduced with the kind permission of Psychology Press

About the authors

Anthony Esgate, David Groome, Moira Maguire and Corriene Reed are all lecturers in the Psychology Department of the University of Westminster, London. Kevin Baker is at the University of Leicester, David Heathcote is at the University of Bournemouth and, finally, Richard Kemp is at the University of New South Wales. The authorship of individual chapters is as follows:

Chapter 1: David Groome
Chapter 2: David Groome
Chapter 3: David Groome
Chapter 4: Richard Kemp
Chapter 5: David Heathcote
Chapter 6: Anthony Esgate
Chapter 7: Moira Maguire
Chapter 8: Moira Maguire
Chapter 9: Anthony Esgate
Chapter 10: Kevin Baker
Chapter 11: Corriene Reed

Preface

We decided to write this book because we could not find any other current titles covering the field of applied cognitive psychology adequately. There are plenty of books about cognitive psychology, but none of them deal specifically with the application of cognitive psychology to real-life settings. This seemed rather odd to us, but it probably reflects the fact that applied cognitive psychology is a relatively new science. Applied cognitive psychology has only really begun to take off as a major research area over the last 20–30 years, and even in recent times the applications of cognitive research have been relatively sparse and sometimes of doubtful value. It is only now beginning to be accepted that cognitive psychologists really do have something useful to say about real-life situations.

We have tried to collect together in this book some of the most important examples of the application of applied cognitive research. There are chapters about improving the effectiveness of your learning and exam revision, improving the accuracy of eyewitnesses, and optimising the performance of individuals working under stress and multiple inputs, such as air-traffic controllers. There are also chapters about the effects of drugs and circadian rhythms on cognitive perform-ance, and on the factors that cause errors in our decision making. These are all areas in which the findings of cognitive psychologists have actually been put to use in the real world. Being a new and developing area, applied cognitive psychology remains somewhat incomplete and fragmented, so inevitably the chapters of this book tend to deal with separate and fairly unrelated topics. One advantage of this fragmenta-tion is that you can read the chapters in any order you like, so you can dip into any chapter that interests you without having to read the others first.

One problem when dealing with a relatively new and developing area of research is that there is still no clear agreement about which topics should be included in a book of this kind. We have tried to pick out what we think are the main areas, but we are well aware that not everyone will feel that our book is comprehensive enough. No doubt there will be several topics that some of you may think should have been included in the book but which aren't. If so, perhaps you would be good enough to write to us and tell us which topics you think we should have included, and we will think about including them in the next edition. In the meantime, we hope this book will help to fill a gap in the market, and with a bit of luck we hope it will also fill a gap on your bookshelf.

I would like to close by offering my thanks to the people at Psychology Press who have helped us to produce this book, especially Ruben Hale, Dave Cummings, Lucy Farr and Kathryn Russel. They are all very talented people, and they are also very patient people.

David Groome

P.S. Trying to write a book that can be applied to real-life settings is a considerable challenge, but I would like to close by giving you one really clear-cut example of someone who succeeded in doing just this. It concerns a young man called Colin, who managed to get himself a job working behind the complaints desk of a big department store. On his first morning Colin's boss presented him with an enormous training manual, explaining that it would provide him with the solution to any complaint the customers could possibly come up with. Later that morning Colin found himself confronted by a particularly tiresome customer, who seemed to have an endless series of annoying complaints about his purchase. Remembering the advice he had received earlier, Colin picked up the training manual and used it to strike the customer an enormous blow on the side of the head. As the customer slumped to the floor dazed, Colin noted with some satisfaction that his boss had been absolutely right, as the training manual had indeed provided an effective solution to this particular complaint. As it turned out, his boss was rather less pleased with Colin's approach to customer relations, explaining to him that striking a customer was not in accordance with normal company policy. "On the contrary", Colin said, "I dealt with this complaint strictly by the book". We hope you will find ways of applying our book to situations you encounter in the real world, but hopefully not the way Colin did.

Chapter 1

Introduction to applied cognitive psychology

1.1 Applied cognitive psychology

Cognitive psychology is the study of how the brain processes information. In more everyday terms, it is about the mental processes involved in acquiring and making use of knowledge and experience gained from our senses. The main processes involved in cognition are perception, learning, memory storage, retrieval and thinking, all of which are terms that are used in everyday speech and therefore already familiar to most people. Various types of information are subjected to cognitive processing, including visual, auditory, tactile, gustatory and olfactory information, depending on the sensory system detecting it. However, humans have also developed the use of symbolic language, which can represent any other form of information. Thus language constitutes another important type of information that may be processed by the cognitive system.

All of these various aspects of cognition have been extensively studied in the laboratory, but in recent years there has been a growing interest in the application of cognitive psychology to situations in real life. This approach is known as applied cognitive psychology, and it is concerned with the investigation of how cognitive processes affect our behaviour and performance in real-life settings. It is this research which provides the subject matter of this book.

1.2 Early cognitive research

The earliest experiments in cognitive psychology were carried out over a century ago. Cognitive processes had long been of interest to philosophers, but it was not until late in the nineteenth century that the first attempts were made to bring cognitive processes into the laboratory and study them in a scientific way. The earliest cognitive psychologists made important discoveries in fields such as perception and attention (e.g. Wundt, 1874), imagery (Galton, 1883), memory (Ebbinghaus, 1885) and learning (Thorndike, 1914). This early work was mainly directed at the discovery of basic cognitive processes, which, in turn, led to the creation of theories to explain the findings obtained. New techniques of research and new experimental designs were developed in those early days that were to be of lasting value to later cognitive psychologists.

In some cases, this early research produced findings that could be applied in real-life settings, but this was not usually the main purpose of the research. For example, Ebbinghaus (1885), while investigating the basic phenomena of memory, discovered that spaced learning trials were more effective than massed trials. Subsequently, spaced learning came to be widely accepted as a useful strategy for improving the efficiency of learning and study (see Chapter 2 for more details). However, despite a few examples of this kind where research led to real-life applications, the early cognitive researchers were mostly concerned with pure research and any practical applications of their findings were largely incidental.

This approach was later challenged by Bartlett (1932), who argued that cognitive research should have relevance to the real world. Bartlett suggested that cognitive researchers should make use of more naturalistic experimental designs and test materials, bearing some resemblance to the situations encountered in real life. Bartlett's research on memory for stories and pictures was of obvious relevance to memory performance in real-world settings, such as the testimony of courtroom witnesses (see Chapter 3). His emphasis on the application of research was to have a lasting influence on the future of cognitive psychology.

1.3 Post-war developments in applied cognitive psychology

The Second World War provided a major catalyst to the development of applied cognitive psychology. The war produced dramatic improvements in technology, which placed unprecedented demands on the human beings who operated it. With the development of complex new equipment such as radar and high-speed combat aircraft, the need to understand the cognitive capabilities and limitations of

Figure 1.1 Frederic Bartlett

human operators took on a new urgency. Consequently, the cognitive performance of pilots, radar operators and air-traffic controllers emerged as an important area of study, with the general goal of maximising operator performance and identifying performance limitations to be incorporated into equipment design. In the fore-front of this new wave of applied research was the British psychologist Donald Broadbent, who had trained as a pilot during the war and thus had first-hand experience of the cognitive problems encountered by pilots. Broadbent became interested in investigating the information-processing capabilities of human beings, and more specifically their ability to deal with two or more competing perceptual inputs (Broadbent, 1958). He investigated this by presenting his participants with a different input to each ear via headphones, a technique known as "dichotic listening". Broadbent was thus able to establish some of the basic limitations of

Figure 1.2 Donald Broadbent

human attention, and he was able to apply his findings to assisting the performance of pilots and air-traffic controllers who often have to deal with two or more inputs at once. Broadbent (1980) argued that real-life problems should not only be studied by cognitive psychologists but should ideally provide the starting point for cognitive research, since this would ensure that the research findings would be valid (and possibly useful) in the real world.

1.4 Laboratory versus field experiments

Although applied cognitive research is intended to be applicable to the real world, this does not necessarily mean that it always has to be carried out in a real-world setting. Sometimes it is possible to recreate real-life situations in the laboratory, as in the case of Broadbent's research on divided attention described above. However, in recent years there has been debate about whether cognitive psychology should be researched "in the field" (i.e. in a real-world setting) or in the laboratory. Neisser (1976) argued that cognitive research should be carried out in real-world settings wherever possible, to ensure what he called "ecological validity". By this Neisser meant that research findings should be demonstrably true in the real world, and not just under laboratory conditions. Neisser pointed out the limitations of relying on a body of knowledge based entirely on research performed in artificial laboratory conditions. For example, we know from laboratory work that people are subject to a number of visual illusions, but we cannot automatically assume that those same illusions will also occur in everyday life, where such simple geometric forms are rarely encountered in isolation but tend to form part of a complex three-dimensional visual array. Neisser was not only concerned with applied cognitive research, as he felt that even theoretical research needed to be put to the test of ecological validity, to ensure that research findings were not merely created by the artificial laboratory environment.

Neisser's call for ecological validity has been taken up enthusiastically by many cognitive researchers over the last 25 years. However, as Parkin and Hunkin (2001) remarked in a recent review, the ecological validity movement has not achieved the "paradigm shift" that some had expected. One reason for this is the fact that field studies cannot match the standards of scientific rigour that are possible in laboratory studies. For example, Banerji and Crowder (1989) have argued that field studies of memory have produced few dependable findings, because the experimenter has so little control over extraneous variables. Indeed, there may be important variables affecting behaviour in real-life settings which the experimenter is not even aware of. Banerji and Crowder conclude that research findings obtained in a real-world setting cannot be generalised to other settings because the same variables cannot be assumed to apply. Although Banerji and Crowder directed their attack primarily at memory research, the same basic criticisms apply to other aspects of cognition researched in the field. In response to this attack on applied cognitive research, Gruneberg, Morris and Sykes (1991) point out that applied research can often be carried out under controlled laboratory conditions, as for example in the recent research on eyewitness testimony. It can also be argued that although field experi-

Figure 1.3 Ulric Neisser

ments may not be perfectly controlled, they are still better than not carrying out field research at all.

At first glance, the views of Neisser (1976) and Banerji and Crowder (1989) would appear to be in complete opposition to one another, but they can perhaps be partly reconciled if we accept that both views contain an important cautionary message. On the one hand, Neisser argues that cognitive research needs validation from field studies, but at the same time we must bear in mind Banerji and Crowder's caution that such field research will inevitably be less effectively controlled. One possible way to address these problems is to combine both field and laboratory research directed at the same phenomenon. This has been achieved with topics such as eyewitness testimony and cognitive interviews, both of which have been investigated in controlled laboratory experiments and in actual police work. This double-edged approach offers the possibility of comparing the findings of field studies and laboratory studies, and where we find agreement between the two types of studies we have more reason to find the results convincing.

1.5 The aims of applied cognitive psychology

There are arguably two main reasons for studying applied cognitive psychology. First, there is the hope that applied research can produce solutions to real problems, providing us with knowledge and insights that can actually be used in the real world. A second benefit is that applied research can help to improve and inform theoretical approaches to cognition, offering a broader and more realistic basis for our understanding of cognitive processes. In some cases, applied and theoretical cognitive research have been carried out side by side and have been of mutual benefit. For example, laboratory research on context reinstatement has led to the development of the cognitive interview, which has subsequently been adopted for use in police work. The application of these techniques by police interviewers has generated further research, which has, in turn, fed back into theoretical cognitive psychology. Thus there has been a flow of information in both directions, with applied and theoretical research working hand in hand to the mutual benefit of both approaches. Our understanding of human cognition can only be enhanced by such a two-way flow of ideas and inspiration.

1.6 About this book

This book offers a review of recent research in applied cognitive psychology. The early chapters are concerned with memory, starting with Chapter 2, which is about improving memory performance. Strategies such as spacing and mnemonics are considered, as well as the most recent work on retrieval facilitation and inhibition, and the chapter is intended to give the reader a wide-ranging knowledge of how to maximise their memory performance. This chapter would therefore be of interest to students who wished to improve their learning and study skills, and it would also be of value to teachers and instructors. Chapter 3 continues with the theme of memory, but here the emphasis is on everyday memory. The chapter deals with topics such as autobiographical memory, eyewitness testimony and police interviews. Once again the chapter deals with methods of maximising the retrieval of information by eyewitnesses and other individuals in real-life settings. Maintaining the theme of eyewitness testimony, Chapter 4 focuses on the identification of faces by eyewitnesses, including research on the effectiveness of police identity parades. Staying with the memory theme, Chapter 5 is concerned with working memory and its limitations. This chapter includes extensive coverage of research on the performance limitations of air-traffic controllers. Chapter 6 also deals with the limitations on human cognitive performance, but this time the focus is on the performance of skills. This chapter also deals with the cognitive factors that lead to performance errors. Chapter 7 goes on to consider how cognitive performance can be affected by biological cycles, such as circadian rhythms and the menstrual cycle. The chapter also includes research on the effects of various types of disruption of circadian rhythms, as in the case of shift work and jet-lag. Chapter 8 deals with the effects of commonly used drugs (both legal and illegal) on cognitive performance. Chapter 9 is concerned with the ways in which people make use of intuitive statistics when making judgements and decisions. Sources of error and bias in decision making are examined, with reference to real-life settings such as the making of medical decisions. Chapter 10 is concerned with the ways in which people process auditory information. It includes techniques for optimising auditory performance, and also forensic applications such as the accuracy of earwitness identification of voices and other sounds. Finally, Chapter 11 deals with reading and dyslexia, including applications in clinics, schools and workplace settings.

Topics such as memory and perception can of course be found in other cognitive psychology textbooks, but our book is quite different from most other current cognitive texts in that it deals with the application of these cognitive topics to real-life situations. Our book is concerned with cognitive processes in real life, and we very much hope that you will find its contents have relevance to your life.

Chapter 2

Memory improvement

2.1 Introduction

Most of us would like to have a better memory. The ability to remember things accurately and effortlessly would make us more efficient in our daily lives, and it would make us more successful in our work. It might also help us socially, by helping us to remember appointments and avoiding the embarrassment of forgetting the name of an acquaintance. Perhaps the most important advantage, however, would be the ability to study more effectively, for example when revising for an examination or learning a new language. Although there are no magical ways of improving the memory dramatically overnight, a number of strategies have been developed that can help us to make worthwhile improvements in our memory performance, and for a few individuals the improvements have been quite spectacular. In this chapter, some of the main principles and techniques of memory improvement will be reviewed and evaluated in the light of scientific research. I begin with a review of the most efficient ways to learn new material and the use of mnemonic strategies, and then move on to consider the main factors influencing retrieval.

2.2 Organising and spacing of learning sessions

The most obvious requirement for learning something new is practice. We need to practise to learn a new skill such as playing the piano, and we need practice when we are trying to learn new information, for example when revising for an examination. Certainly there is no substitute for sheer hard work and relentless practice when we are revising for an examination, but there are things we can do to improve the efficiency of our learning, by carefully organising the way in which we perform it.

One basic question which applies to most learning situations is whether it is better to do the learning in one large "cramming" session, or whether to spread it out over a number of separate learning sessions. These two approaches are known as "massed" and "spaced" learning, respectively, and they are illustrated in Figure 2.1.

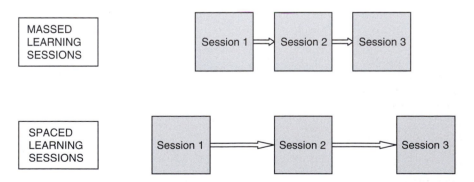

Figure 2.1 Massed and spaced learning sessions

It has generally been found that spaced learning is more efficient than massed learning. This was first demonstrated more than a century ago by Ebbinghaus (1885), who found that spaced learning sessions produced higher retrieval scores than massed learning sessions, when the total time spent learning was kept constant for both learning conditions. Ebbinghaus used lists of nonsense syllables as his test material, but the general superiority of spaced over massed learning has been confirmed by many subsequent studies using various different types of test material, such as learning lists of words (Dempster, 1987), sentences (Rothkopf & Coke, 1963) and text passages (Reder & Anderson, 1982). Spaced learning has also generally proved to be better than massed learning when learning motor skills, such as learning pursuit rotor skills (Bourne & Archer, 1956) and learning keyboard skills (Baddeley & Longman, 1978).

Most early studies of spaced learning involved the use of uniformly spaced learning sessions. However, Landauer and Bjork (1978) found that learning is often more efficient if the time interval between retrieval sessions is steadily increased for successive sessions. This strategy is known as "expanding retrieval practice" (see Figure 2.2). For example, the first retrieval attempt might be made after a 1 sec interval, the second retrieval after 4 sec, the third after 9 sec, and so on. Subsequent research has shown that expanding retrieval practice not only improves retrieval in normal individuals, but it can also help the retrieval performance of amnesic patients such as those with Alzheimer's disease (Camp & McKittrick, 1992; Broman, 2001). The same principle has also been adapted for various other real-life settings, for example learning the names of people attending a meeting (Morris & Fritz, 2002).

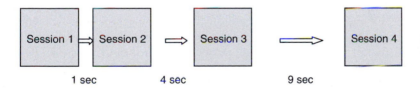

Figure 2.2 Expanding retrieval practice

Several explanations have been proposed for the superiority of spaced learning over massed learning. Ebbinghaus (1885) suggested that with massed learning there will be more interference between successive items, whereas frequent rest breaks will help to separate items from one another. A later theory proposed by Hull (1943) suggested that massed learning leads to a build-up of mental fatigue or inhibition of some kind, which requires a rest period to restore learning ability. A more recent theory, known as the "encoding variability hypothesis" (Underwood, 1969), suggests that when we return to a recently practised item that is still fresh in the memory, we tend to just re-activate the same processing as we used last time. However, if we delay returning to the item until it has been partly forgotten, the previous processing will also have been forgotten, so we are more likely to process the item in a new and different way. According to this view, spaced learning provides more varied forms of encoding and thus a more elaborated trace, with more potential retrieval routes leading to it. The encoding variability hypothesis can also help to explain the effectiveness of expanding retrieval intervals, since the time interval required for the previous processing event to be forgotten will increase as the item becomes more thoroughly learned. Schmidt and Bjork (1992) suggest that, for optimum learning, each retrieval interval should be long enough to make retrieval as difficult as possible without actually rendering the item irretrievable. They argue that the partial forgetting that occurs in between successive learning trials creates additional opportunities for learning.

Although spaced learning has been consistently found to be superior to massed learning over the long term, it has been found that during a learning session (and for a short time afterwards) massed learning can actually produce better retrieval than spaced learning, and the advantage of spaced learning only really becomes apparent with longer retrieval intervals (Glenberg & Lehman, 1980). Most learning in real life involves fairly long retrieval intervals (e.g. revising the night before an exam), so in practice spaced learning will usually be the best strategy. An interesting recent finding is that despite the general superiority of spaced learning, most people believe that massed learning is better (Simon & Bjork, 2001), because it produces better performance during the actual learning session. This temporary benefit seems to mislead individuals into making an incorrect judgement about longer-term learning strategies. Misjudgements of this kind are fairly common and are considered in more detail in Section 2.9.

Although it has been demonstrated that spaced learning sessions are usually more effective than massed learning sessions, in real-life settings this advantage may sometimes be compromised by practical considerations. For example, there are some occasions when we only have a limited period of time available for study (for example, when we have only one hour left to revise before an exam); in such cases, it may be better to use the entire period rather than to take breaks, which will waste some of our available time. Again, a very busy person might have difficulty fitting a large number of separate learning sessions into their daily schedule. A further problem is that spaced learning obviously requires more time overall (i.e. total time including rest breaks) than massed learning, and therefore may not represent the most efficient use of that time unless the rest breaks can be used for something worthwhile. Because spaced learning can create practical problems of this kind, there is no clear agreement about its value in a real-life learning setting such as a school classroom. Dempster (1988) suggests that teachers should make use of the spaced learning principle, whereas Vash (1989) argues that spaced learning is not really practicable in a classroom setting, since the periodic interruption of learning sessions can be inconvenient and can make learning less pleasant. On balance it can be argued that spaced learning is probably the best option for most simple learning tasks so long as we can fit the sessions around our other activities, but it may not be practicable in some settings such as the school classroom.

2.3 Meaning, organisation and imagery as learning strategies

One of the most important principles of effective learning is that we will remember material far better if we concentrate on its meaning, rather than just trying to learn it by heart. Mere repetition or mindless chanting is not very effective. To create an effective memory trace we need to extract as much meaning from it as we can, by connecting it with our store of previous knowledge. In fact, this principle has been used for centuries in the memory enhancement strategies known as mnemonics, which mostly involve techniques to increase the meaningfulness of the material to be learned. These will be considered in the next section.

There is now a considerable amount of experimental evidence to support the view that meaningful processing (also known as semantic processing) creates a stronger and more retrievable memory trace than more superficial forms of processing (Hyde & Jenkins, 1969; Craik & Tulving, 1975; Craik, 1977, 2002; Parkin, 1983). Most of these studies have made use of orienting tasks, which are activities designed to direct an individual's attention to certain features of the test items to control the type of processing carried out on them. For example, Craik (1977) presented the same list of printed words visually to four different groups of individuals, each group being required to carry out a different orienting task on each one of the words. The first group carried out a very superficial structural task on each of the words (e.g. Is the word written in capitals or lower-case letters?), while the second group carried out an acoustic task (e.g. Does the word rhyme with "cat"?), and the third group carried out a semantic task (e.g. Is it the name of a living thing?). The fourth group was given no specific orienting task, but was simply given instructions to try to learn the words as best they could. The participants were subsequently tested for their ability to recognise the words; the results obtained are shown in Figure 2.3.

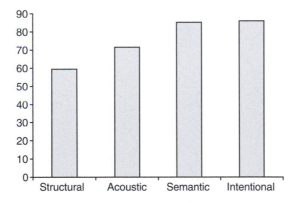

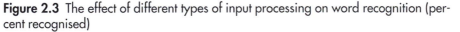

Figure 2.3 The effect of different types of input processing on word recognition (percent recognised)

It is clear that the group carrying out the semantic orienting task achieved far higher retrieval scores than those who carried out the acoustic task, who, in turn, performed far better than the structural processing group. Craik concluded that semantic processing is more effective than more shallow and superficial types of processing (e.g. acoustic and structural processing). In fact, the semantic group performed as well as the group that carried out intentional learning, even though the intentional learning group were the only participants in this experiment to make a deliberate effort to learn the words. It would appear, then, that even when we are trying our best to learn, we cannot improve on a semantic processing strategy, and indeed it is likely that the intentional learning group were actually making use of some kind of semantic strategy of their own. The basic lesson we can learn from the findings of these orienting task experiments is that we should always focus our attention on the meaning of items we wish to learn, since semantic processing is far more effective than any kind of non-semantic processing.

A number of theories have been proposed to explain the superiority of semantic processing, most notably the "levels of processing" theory (Craik & Lockhart, 1972; Lockhart & Craik, 1990; Craik, 2002). The levels of processing theory states that the more deeply we process an item at the input stage, the better it will be remembered, and semantic processing is seen as being the deepest of the various types of processing to which new input is subjected. Later versions of this theory (Lockhart & Craik, 1990; Craik, 2002) suggest that semantic processing is more effective because it involves more "elaboration" of the memory trace, which means that a large number of associative connections are made between the new trace and other traces already stored in the memory (see Figure 2.4). The result of such elaborative encoding is that the new trace becomes embedded in a rich network of inter-connected memory traces, each one of which has the potential to activate all of those connected to it. Elaborative encoding thus creates a trace that can be more easily retrieved in the future because there are more potential retrieval routes leading to it.

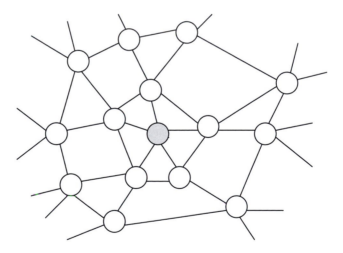

Figure 2.4 Elaborative connections between memory traces

Craik and Lockhart (1972) suggested that there are two different ways in which we can rehearse material we are trying to learn. They made a distinction between "elaborative rehearsal", in which associative connections are created with other existing memories, and "maintenance rehearsal", which involves mere repetition and therefore only serves to hold the trace temporarily in the working memory. Their original view was that elaborative rehearsal was essential for the creation of a permanent memory trace, and that maintenance rehearsal left no lasting record at all. However, more recent evidence suggests that maintenance rehearsal, although far less effective than elaborative rehearsal, can make some contribution to strengthening a memory trace (Glenberg & Adams, 1978; Naire, 1983).

One way of elaborating memory traces and increasing their connections with other traces is to organise them into groups or categories of similar items. Tulving (1962) found that many individuals will carry out such organisation spontaneously when presented with a list of items to be learned. His participants were presented with a list of words several times in different sequential orders, and were subsequently tested for their ability to retrieve the words. Tulving found that many of his participants had chosen to group the words into categories of items related by some common feature, and those who did so achieved far higher retrieval scores than those who had not organised the list of words. Tulving also noted that regardless of the original order in which the words had been presented, they tended to be recalled in pairs or groups reflecting the categories applied to them by each participant. In a similar experiment, Mandler and Pearlstone (1966) gave their participants a pack of 52 cards with a different noun written on each card. One group of participants was asked to sort the words into groups or categories of their own choosing, whereas a second group was given the cards already sorted into categories by a different person. Both groups were subsequently tested for their ability to re-sort the cards into their original categories, and it was found that the participants who had carried out their own category sorting performed this task far better than the participants who received the pre-sorted cards. From these results we can conclude that sorting and organising test items for oneself is far more effective than using someone else's system of categorisation. A further study of category sorting (Mandler, 1968) showed that retrieval improved when participants increased the number of categories they employed, though performance reached a maximum at about seven categories and fell thereafter. This finding may possibly reflect the limit on the span of working memory (i.e. the maximum number of items we can hold in conscious awareness at one moment in time), which is known to be about seven items (Miller, 1956).

Visual imagery is another strategy known to assist memory. Paivio (1965) found that his participants were far better at retrieving concrete words such as "piano" (i.e. names of objects for which a visual image could be readily formed) than they were at retrieving abstract words such as "hope" (i.e. concepts which could not be directly imaged). Paivio found that concrete words retained their advantage over abstract words even when the words were carefully controlled for their meaningfulness, so the difference could be clearly attributed to the effect of imagery. Paivio (1971) explained his findings by proposing the dual coding hypothesis, which suggests that concrete words have the advantage of being encoded twice, once as a verbal code and then again as a visual image. Abstract words, on the other hand, are encoded only once, since they can only be stored in verbal form. Dual coding may offer an advantage over single coding because it can make use of two different loops in the working memory (e.g. visuo-spatial and phonological loops), thus increasing the total information storage capacity for use in the encoding process.

It is generally found that under most conditions people remember pictures better than they remember words (Haber & Myers, 1982; Paivio, 1991; Groome & Levay, 2003). This may suggest that pictures offer more scope for dual coding than words, though it is also possible that pictures are intrinsically more memorable than words, perhaps because they tend to contain more information (e.g. a picture of a dog contains more detail than the three letters "DOG"). In fact it has also been found that people can usually remember non-verbal sounds better than words (Sharps & Pollit, 1998; Groome & Levay, 2003), though again it is unclear whether this is due to dual encoding or greater information content.

Bower (1970) demonstrated that dual encoding could be made even more effective if the images were interactive. In his experiment, three groups of participants were each required to learn a list of 30 pairs of concrete words (e.g. frog–piano). The first group was instructed to simply repeat the word pairs after they were presented, while the second group was asked to form separate visual images of each of the items. A third group was asked to form visual images in which the two items represented by each pair of words were interacting with one another in some way, for example a frog playing a piano (see Figure 2.5). A test of recall for the word pairs revealed that the use of visual imagery increased memory scores, but the group using interactive images produced the highest scores of all.

Figure 2.5 An interactive image

A recent study by De Bene and Moe (2003) confirmed the value of imagery in assisting memory, but found that visual imagery is more effective when applied to orally presented items rather than visually presented items. A possible explanation of this finding is that visual imagery and visually presented items will be in competition for the same storage resources (i.e. the visuo-spatial loop of the working memory), whereas visual imagery and orally presented items will be held in different loops of the working memory (the visuo-spatial loop and the phonological loop, respectively) and will thus not be competing for storage space.

The experimental studies described above have established several important principles which are known to help us to learn more effectively, notably the use of semantic encoding, organisation of input, and imagery. These are all principles that we can apply to everyday learning or indeed to exam revision, though it may need a little thought to devise methods of putting these principles into practice. For example, when revising for an exam it is important to focus your attention on the meaning of the material you are reading, and to try to think of any connections you can find between the new material and your previous knowledge. Sometimes you may be able to find a connection with some personal experience, which will add to the significance of the material and may also provide a visual image that you can add to the memory. Another good revision strategy is to rewrite your notes in a way that groups together items that have something in common, for example by drawing a "tree diagram" or "mind map" (Buzan, 1974) of the sort shown in Figure 2.6. Such strategies can help you to organise facts or ideas in a way that will strengthen the associative connections between them, and it may also help to add an element of visual imagery too.

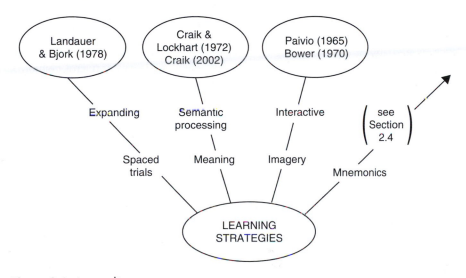

Figure 2.6 A tree diagram

Although the methods advocated above are based on sound and well-established principles, there has been relatively little scientific research on the effectiveness of specific learning and revision techniques until quite recently. Lahtinen, Lonka and Lindblom-Ylanne (1997) reported that medical students who made use of memory improvement strategies during their revision were more successful in their exams than those who did not, and the most effective strategies were found to be mind maps and summaries of lecture notes. McDougal and Gruneberg (2002) found that students preparing for a psychology exam were more successful if their revision included the use of mind maps and name lists. Memory strategies involving first-letter cues or concepts were less effective but still had some benefit, but those students who did not use a memory strategy of any kind performed worst of all. For those who seek more detailed advice on how to improve the effectiveness of learning and revision for specific types of material, Herrmann, Raybeck and Gruneberg (2002) have recently written a book devoted to such techniques.

The main principles of effective learning that have emerged from scientific research are meaningful encoding, organisation of input and the use of imagery. All of these principles can be incorporated into real-life learning strategies, such as exam revision techniques. However, these same general principles have also been used in more specialised memory improvement strategies known as mnemonics, which are strategies used to add meaning, organisation and imagery to material that might otherwise possess none of these qualities.

2.4 Mnemonics

Mnemonic strategies

It is relatively easy to learn material that is intrinsically meaningful, but we are sometimes required to learn items that contain virtually no meaning of their own, such as a string of digits making up a telephone number. This normally requires rote learning (also referred to as "learning by heart" or "learning parrot-fashion"), and the human brain does not seem to be very good as it. People have known for centuries that memory for meaningless items can be greatly improved by strategies that involve somehow adding meaning artificially to an item which otherwise has little intrinsic meaningful content, and it can be even more helpful if it adds a strong visual image to the item. Various techniques have been devised for this purpose, and they are known as mnemonics. Even if you are not familiar with that term, you have probably already made use of mnemonics when you were at school. For example, there are several popular *first-letter mnemonics* for learning the sequential order of the colours of the spectrum (which are: red, orange, yellow, green, blue, indigo, violet). Usually these colours are remembered by means of a mnemonic sentence providing a reminder of the first letter of each colour, such as "Richard of York Gained Battles In Vain" or, alternatively, that colourful character "ROYGBIV". It is important to note that in this example it is not the actual colour names which are meaningless, but their sequential order. The mnemonic is thus used primarily for remembering the sequential order of the colours. Other popular first-letter mnemonics include notes of the musical scale (e.g. "Every Good Boy Deserves Favours"), the cranial nerves (e.g. "Only One Onion To Teacher Against Four Awful Girl Visitors") and the "big five" factors of personality (e.g. "OCEAN"). For other purposes, a simple *rhyme mnemonic* may help. For example, we can remember the number of days in each month by recalling the rhyme "Thirty days hath September, April, June and November. All the rest have thirty-one (etc.)". All of these mnemonics work essentially by adding meaning to material which is not otherwise intrinsically meaningful, though a further benefit is that the mnemonic also provides a set of retrieval cues that can later be used to retrieve the original items.

The mnemonics described above have been devised for specific memory tasks, but a number of mnemonic systems have been devised which can be used in a more general fashion, and which can be adopted to assist memory in various different situations. Most of these involve not only adding meaning to the input, but also making it into a visual image. The *method of loci* involves a general strategy for associating an item we wish to remember with a location that can be incorporated into a visual image. For example, if you are trying to memorise the items on a shopping list, you might try visualising your living room with a tomato on a chair, a block of cheese on the radiator, and a bunch of grapes hanging from the ceiling. You can further enhance the mnemonic by using your imagination to find some way of linking each item with its location, such as imagining someone sitting on the chair and squashing the tomato or the cheese melting when the radiator gets hot. When you need to retrieve the items on your list, you do so by taking an imaginary walk around your living room and observing all of the imaginary squashed tomatoes and cascades of melting cheese. It is said that the method of loci was first devised by the Greek poet Simonides in about 500 B.C., when he achieved fame by remembering the exact seating positions of all of the guests at a feast after the building had collapsed and crushed everyone inside. Simonides was apparently able to identify each of the bodies even though they had been crushed beyond recognition, though cynics among you may wonder how they checked his accuracy. Presumably they just took his word for it.

Lorayne and Lucas (1974) devised a mnemonic technique to make it easier to learn people's names. This is known as the *face-name* system, and it involves thinking of a meaningful word or image that is similar to the person's name. For example, "Groome" might remind you of horses, and "Esgate" might remind you of a gate with curved (S-shaped) beams. The next stage is to select a prominent feature of the person's face and then to create an interactive image (see previous section) linking that feature with the image you have related to their name. This may seem to be a rather cumbersome system, and it certainly requires a lot of practice to make it work properly. However, it seems to be very effective for those who persevere with it. For example, the World Memory Champion Dominic O'Brien has used this method to accurately memorise all of the names of an audience of 100 strangers, despite being introduced only briefly to each one of them (O'Brien, 1993).

A variant of this method has been used to help people to learn new languages. It is known as the *keyword* system (Atkinson, 1975; Gruneberg, 1987), and involves thinking of an English word that in some way resembles a foreign word that is to be learned. For example, the French word "herisson" means "hedgehog". Gruneberg suggests forming an image of a hedgehog with a "hairy son" (see Figure 2.7). Alternatively, you might prefer to imagine the actor Harrison Ford with a hedgehog. You could then try to conjure up that image when you next need to remember the French word for hedgehog (which admittedly is not a frequent occurrence).

Figure 2.7 A hedgehog with its "hairy son" (L'Herrison)

Gruneberg further suggests that the gender of a French noun can be attached to the image, by imagining a boxer in the scene in the case of a masculine noun or perfume in the case of a feminine noun. Thus for "L'Herisson" you might want to imagine Harrison Ford boxing against a hedgehog. This may seem like an improbable image (though arguably no more improbable than his exploits in the Indiana Jones movies), but in fact the more bizarre and distinctive the image, the more memorable it is likely to be.

The keyword method has proved to be a very effective way to learn a foreign language. Raugh and Atkinson (1975) reported that students making use of the keyword method to learn a list of Spanish words scored 88% on a vocabulary test, compared with just 28% for a group using more traditional study methods. Gruneberg and Jacobs (1991) studied a group of executives learning Spanish grammar, and found that using the keyword method they were able to learn no less than 400 Spanish words, plus some basic grammar, in only 12 hours of teaching. This was far superior to traditional teaching methods, and as a bonus it was found that the executives also found the keyword method more enjoyable. Thomas and Wang (1996) also reported very good results for the keyword method of language learning, noting that it was particularly effective when followed by an immediate test to strengthen learning.

Another popular mnemonic system is the *peg-word* system (Higbee, 1977), which is used for memorising meaningless lists of digits. In this system, each digit is represented by the name of an object that rhymes with it. For example, in one popular system you learn that "ONE is a bun, TWO is a shoe, THREE is a tree, FOUR is a door", and so on. Having once learned these associations, any sequence of numbers can be woven into a story involving shoes, trees, buns, doors, and so on.

An alternative strategy for learning long lists of digits is the method of *chunking*, in which groups of digits are linked together by some meaningful connection. This technique not only adds meaning to the list, but also reduces the number of items to be remembered, because several digits have been combined to form a single memorable chunk. For example, try reading the following list of digits just once, then cover it up and see if you can write them down correctly from memory:

1984747365

It is unlikely that you will have recalled all of the digits correctly, as there were 10 of them and for most people the maximum digit span is about 7 items. However, if you try to organise the list of digits into some meaningful sequence, you will find that remembering it becomes far easier. For example, the sequence of digits above happens to contain three sub-sequences that are familiar to most people. Try reading the list of digits once again, but this time trying to relate each group of digits to the author George Orwell, a jumbo jet and the number of days in a year. You should now find it easy to remember the list of digits, because it has been transformed into three meaningful chunks of information. What you have actually done is to add meaning to the digits by making use of your previous knowledge, and this is the principle underlying most mnemonic systems. Memory can be further enhanced by creating a visual image to represent the mnemonic, so for the sequence of digits above you could form a mental picture of George Orwell sitting in a jumbo jet for one year.

Of course, the example I have just used to illustrate the addition of meaning to a list of digits represents a somewhat artificial situation, in which the list was deliberately created from a number of familiar number sequences. In real-life learning situations, you are unlikely to be so lucky, but if you use your imagination and make full use of all of the number sequences that you already know (such as birthdays, house numbers, or some bizarre hobby you may have), you should still be able to find some familiar sequences in any given digit string. This technique has in fact been used with remarkable success by expert mnemonists such as SF (an avid athletics enthusiast who made use of his knowledge of running times), as explained in the next section.

In summary, most mnemonic techniques involve finding a way to add meaning to material which is not otherwise intrinsically meaningful. This is achieved by somehow connecting it to one's existing knowledge. Memorisation can often be made even more effective by creating a visual image to represent the mnemonic. These are the basic principles underlying most mnemonic techniques, and they are used regularly by many of us without any great expertise or special training. However, some individuals have developed their mnemonic skills by extensive practice and have become expert mnemonists. Their techniques and achievements will be considered in the next section.

Expert mnemonists

The mnemonic techniques described above can be used by anyone, since any reasonably intelligent person can improve their memory if they are prepared to make the effort. However, a number of individuals have been studied who have achieved remarkable memory performance, far exceeding that of the average person.

Chase and Ericsson (1981) studied the memory performance of an undergraduate student ("SF"), who trained himself to memorise long sequences of digits simply by searching for familiar number sequences. It so happened that SF was a running enthusiast who already knew the times recorded in a large number of races, such as world records, and his own best performances over various distances. For example, Roger Bannister's time for the very first 4 minute mile happened to be 3 minutes 59.4 seconds, so for SF the sequence 3594 would represent Bannister's record time. SF was thus able to make use of his prior knowledge of running times to develop a strategy for chunking digits, as described in the previous section (see Figure 2.8).

In fact, SF had to work very hard to achieve these memory skills. He was eventually able to memorise lists of up to 80 digits, but only after he had practised his mnemonic techniques for one hour a day over a period of 2 years. Indeed, it appears that SF was not innately gifted or superior in his memory ability, but he achieved his remarkable memory performance by sheer hard work, combining a mixture of laborious practice and refinement of memory strategy. It is significant that despite his amazing digit span, his performance in other tests of memory was

21

Figure 2.8 Running times as used as a mnemonic strategy by SF

no more than average. For example, his memory span for letters and words was unremarkable, and failed to show any benefit from his mnemonic skills despite being very similar to the digit span task. In fact, even his digit span performance fell to normal levels when he was presented with digit lists that could not be readily organised into running times.

There are many other well-documented cases of individuals who have achieved exceptional memory feats, in most cases by extensive practice at memory improvement techniques. For example, Rajan Mahadevan successfully memorised the constant *pi* (used for calculating the area or circumference of a circle from its radius) to no less than 31,811 figures, though his memory in most other respects was unexceptional (Biederman, Cooper, Fox, & Mahadevan, 1992). Dominic O'Brien trained his memory to such a level that he became the World Memory Champion in 1992, and he was able to make a living by performing in front of audiences and by gambling at blackjack. He wrote a book about his memory improvement techniques (O'Brien, 1993), in which he pointed out that he had been born with a fairly average memory, and he had only achieved his remarkable skills by devoting 6 years of his life to practising mnemonic strategies.

Chase and Ericsson (1982) proposed a theory of skilled memory which suggests that memory improvement requires three main strategies:

1   Meaningful encoding: relating the items to previous knowledge.
2   Structured retrieval: adding potential cues to the items for use during retrieval.
3   Practice: to make the processing automatic and very rapid.

Their view was that any reasonably intelligent person who is prepared to practise these techniques over a long period of time can achieve outstanding feats of memory, without the need for any special gift or innate superiority. Subsequent research has largely supported this assumption. Groeger (1997) concluded that individuals with outstanding memory skills had usually achieved them through years of practice, and their memory skills did not normally extend beyond the range of the particular strategies that they had practised and perfected.

While most memory experts seem to have used mnemonic techniques to enhance an otherwise unexceptional memory, a few very rare individuals have been studied who seem to possess special memory powers. The Russian psychologist Luria (1975) studied a man called V.S. Shereshevskii (referred to as "S") who not only employed a range of memory organisation strategies, but who also seemed to have been born with an exceptional memory. S was able to memorise lengthy mathematical formulae and vast tables of numbers very rapidly, and with totally accurate recall. He was able to do this because he had the ability to retrieve the array of figures as a complete visual image with the same vividness as an actual perceived image, and he could project these images onto a wall and simply "read off" figures from them like a person reading a book. This phenomenon is known as *eidetic imagery*, an ability that occurs extremely rarely. On one occasion, S memorised an array of 50 digits, which he could still repeat with perfect accuracy several years later. S used his exceptional memory to make a living, by performing tricks of memory on stage. However, his eidetic imagery turned out to have certain drawbacks in everyday life. First, his eidetic images provided a purely visual representation of memorised items, without any meaningful organisation or under-standing of the memorised material. A second problem that S encountered was that he had difficulty forgetting the material in his eidetic images, so that he often found that his efforts to retrieve an image would be thwarted by the unwanted retrieval of some other image. In the later part of his life, S developed a psychiatric illness and he ended his days in a psychiatric hospital, possibly as a consequence of the stress and overload of his mental faculties resulting from his almost infallible memory. On the whole, S found that his unusual memory powers produced more drawbacks than advantages, and this may provide a clue to the reason for the extreme rarity of eidetic imagery. It is possible that many people are born with eidetic imagery, but that it is replaced in most individuals as they mature by more practical forms of retrieval. It is also possible that eidetic imagery may have been more common among our ancient ancestors, but has begun to die out through natural selection. Either of these possibilities could explain why eidetic imagery is so rare. Presum-ably it would be far more common if it conveyed a general advantage in normal life.

Wilding and Valentine (1994) make a clear distinction between those who achieve outstanding memory performance through some natural gift (as in the case of S), and those who achieve an outstanding memory performance by practising some kind of memory improvement strategy (as in the case of Dominic O'Brien). There were some interesting differences, notably the fact that those with a natural gift tended to make less use of mnemonic strategies, and that they frequently had close relatives who shared a similar gifted memory. However, these gifted individuals are extremely rare, and in the majority of cases an outstanding memory is the result of careful organisation and endless practice.

The study of expert mnemonists has shown us that the human brain is capable of remarkable feats of memory when rigorously trained. However, for most ordinary people it is simply not worth the years of practice to develop a set of skills that are of fairly limited use. Mnemonics tend to be very specific, so that each mnemonic facilitates only one particular task. Consequently, expert mnemonists tend to perform very well on one or two specialised tasks, but they do not acquire any general memory superiority. Another important limitation is that mnemonic skills tend to be most effective when used for learning meaningless material such as lists of digits, but this is a fairly rare requirement in real-life settings. Most of us are not prepared to devote years of our lives to becoming memory champions, just as most of us will never consider it worth the effort and sacrifice required to become a tennis champion or an expert juggler. However, just as the average tennis player can learn something of value from watching the top players, we can also learn something from studying the memory champions even though we may never equal their achievements.

2.5 Retrieval and retrieval cues

Learning a piece of information does not automatically guarantee that we will be able to retrieve it whenever we want to. Sometimes we cannot find a memory trace even though it remains stored in the brain somewhere. In this case the trace is said to be "available" (i.e. in storage) but not "accessible" (i.e. retrievable). In fact, most forgetting is probably caused by retrieval failure rather than the actual loss of a memory trace from storage, meaning that the item is available but not accessible.

Successful retrieval has been found to depend largely on the availability of suitable retrieval cues (Tulving & Pearlstone, 1966; Tulving, 1974, 1976). Retrieval cues are items of information that jog our memory for a specific item, by somehow activating the relevant memory trace. For example, Tulving and Pearlstone (1966) showed that individuals who had learned lists of words belonging to different categories (e.g. fruit) were able to recall far more of the test items when they were reminded of the original category names. It is widely accepted that the main reason for the effectiveness of elaborative semantic processing (see Section 2.3) is the fact that it creates associative links with other memory traces and thus increases the number of potential retrieval cues that can re-activate the target item (Craik & Tulving, 1975; Lockhart & Craik, 1990; Craik, 2002). This is illustrated in Figure 2.9.

These findings suggest that when you are trying to remember something in a real-life setting, you should deliberately seek as many cues as you can find to jog your memory. However, in some circumstances there are not many cues to go on, so you have to generate your own retrieval cues. For example, in an examination, the only overtly presented cues are the actual exam questions, and these do not usually provide much information. You therefore have to use the questions as a starting point from which to generate further memories from material learned during revision sessions. If your recall of relevant information is patchy or incomplete, you may find that focusing your attention closely on one item which you think may be correct (e.g. the findings of an experimental study) may help to cue the retrieval of other information associated with it (e.g. the design of the study, the author, and

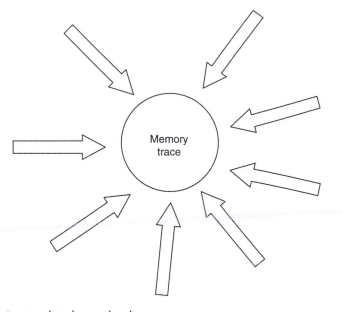

Figure 2.9 Retrieval pathways leading to a memory trace

maybe even a few other related studies if you are lucky). Try asking as many different questions as you can about the topic (Who? When? Where? Why?). The main guiding principle here is to make the most of any snippets of information that you have, by using it to generate more information through associative cueing and the general activation of related memory traces.

Occasionally, you may find that you cannot remember any relevant information at all. This is called a retrieval block, which is probably caused by a combination of the lack of suitable cues (and perhaps inadequate revision) together with an excess of exam nerves. Unfortunately, such a memory block can cause further stress, which may build up to a state of total panic in which the mind appears to go completely blank. If you do have the misfortune to suffer a retrieval block during an examination, there are several strategies you can try. In the first place, it may be helpful to simply spend a few minutes relaxing, by thinking about something pleasant and unrelated to the exam. It may help to practise relaxation techniques in advance for use in such circumstances. In addition, there are several established methods of generating possible retrieval cues that may help to unlock the information you have memorised. One approach is the "scribbling" technique, which involves writing on a piece of scrap paper everything you can remember which relates even distantly to the topic, regardless of whether it is relevant to the question or not (Reder, 1987). You could try writing a list of the names of all of the psychologists you can remember. If you cannot remember any, then you could just try writing down all the names of people you know, starting with yourself. (If you cannot even remember your own name, then things are not looking so good.) Even if the items you write down are not directly related to the question, there is a strong possibility that some of them will cue something more relevant.

When you are revising for an exam, it can often be helpful to create potential retrieval cues in advance, which you can use when you get into the exam room. For example, you could learn lists of names or key theories, which will later jog your memory for more specific information. You could even try creating simple mnemonics for this purpose. Some of the mnemonic techniques described in Section 2.3 include the creation of potential retrieval cues (e.g. first-letter mnemonics such as "ROYGBIV" to cue the colours of the spectrum). Gruneberg (1978) found that students taking an examination were greatly helped by using first-letter mnemonics of this kind, especially those students who had suffered a retrieval block.

The encoding specificity principle (Tulving & Thomson, 1973) suggests that, to be effective, a retrieval cue needs to contain some aspects of the original memory trace. According to this view, the probability of retrieving a trace depends on the amount of overlap between features present in the retrieval cues and features encoded with the trace at the input stage. This is known as "feature overlap", and it has been found to apply not only to features of the actual trace, but also to the context and surroundings in which the trace was initially encoded. There is now considerable evidence that reinstatement of context can be a powerful method of jogging the memory. For example, experiments have shown that recall is more successful when individuals are tested in the same room used for the original learning session, whereas moving to a different room leads to poorer retrieval (Greenspoon & Ranyard, 1957; Smith, Glenberg, & Bjork, 1978). The design used in these experiments is illustrated in Figure 2.10.

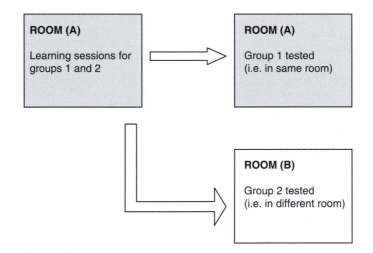

Figure 2.10 A context reinstatement experiment

Even imagining the original learning context can help significantly (Jerabek & Standing, 1992). It may therefore help you to remember details of some previous experience if you return to the actual scene. Alternatively, during an examination it may help to try to visualise the place where you carried out your revision, or the room in which you attended a relevant lecture. Remembering other aspects of the learning context (such as the people you were with, the clothes you were wearing, or the music you were listening to) could also be of some benefit. Context reinstatement has been used with great success by the police as a means of enhancing the recall performance of eyewitnesses to crime as a part of the so-called "cognitive interview" (Geiselman, Fisher, MacKinnon, & Holland, 1985; Fisher & Geiselman, 1992; Larsson, Granhag, & Spjut, 2003). These techniques will be considered in more detail in Chapter 3.

2.6 Retrieval practice and disuse

It is well known that memories tend to gradually become less retrievable with the passage of time. Ebbinghaus (1885) was the first to demonstrate this scientifically, and he suggested that memories may simply fade away as time passes, a mechanism he called "spontaneous decay". However, Thorndike (1914) argued that such decay occurred only if the trace was left unused, whereas a frequently retrieved memory trace would remain accessible. Thorndyke called this the "decay with disuse" theory. Bjork and Bjork (1992) have recently proposed a "new theory of disuse", whereby memory traces are assumed to compete with one another for access to a retrieval route. The frequent retrieval of one particular trace is assumed to strengthen its access to the retrieval route, thus making it more accessible in future, while at the same time blocking off the retrieval route to rival traces, as illustrated in Figure 2.11.

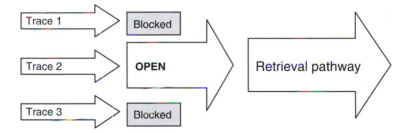

Figure 2.11 Memory traces competing for a retrieval pathway

Bjork and Bjork (1992) proposed their new theory of disuse because it was consistent with many established memory phenomena. There is a large body of evidence confirming that retrieval of an item makes it more retrievable in the future, and that active retrieval is far more beneficial than passive rehearsal (Gates, 1917; Allen, Mahler, & Estes, 1969; Landauer & Bjork, 1978; Payne, 1987; Macrae & MacLeod, 1999). There is also evidence that retrieving one item successfully can subsequently inhibit the retrieval of a rival item (Bjork & Geiselman, 1978; Anderson, Bjork, & Bjork, 1994; MacLeod & Macrae, 2001).

The most important feature of the new theory of disuse is the proposal that retrieving an item will strengthen its future retrievability, so that the act of retrieval is in itself a powerful learning event. This has important implications for learning and exam revision, since it suggests that revision techniques will be more effective if they involve active retrieval of the target items rather than merely reading them. So if you are revising for an exam, you should try to find ways of practising and testing your retrieval of the material rather than just reading it through.

A further implication of the new theory of disuse is that the retrieval of one memory trace will inhibit the retrieval of rival traces. This will normally help retrieval of the trace, so long as it is retrieved correctly during the practice session. However, if an incorrect item is retrieved by mistake, this will make the incorrect trace more retrievable and will actually make it harder to retrieve the correct item. A number of studies have demonstrated that individuals do tend to persistently retrieve their previous errors rather than learning correct items. For example, individuals who were repeatedly shown the same text passage and then tested for their retrieval of the passage continued to make the same mistakes each time, regardless of repeated exposure to the original passage (Kay, 1955; Fritz, Morris, Bjork, Gelman, & Wickens, 2000). It seems that incorrect items retrieved on the first trial are likely to continue being retrieved in subsequent trials.

One way to avoid the risk of strengthening the retrievability of incorrect items is to devise a learning strategy that will generate only correct answers and no errors (Herrmann *et al.*, 2002), a principle known as "errorless learning". For example, you should try to avoid testing yourself on material that you have not properly revised, because this may lead to retrieval errors and it will be the errors that are strengthened rather than the correct items. You could also use some means of restricting the range of possible answers so that errors are less likely, possibly by using cues or guidelines written down in advance. The "errorless learning" strategy has been found to be effective not only for students and those with normal memory capabilities, but also as a means of enhancing the learning of amnesic patients (Wilson, Baddeley, Evans, & Shiel, 1994).

2.7 Retrieval-induced forgetting

The new theory of disuse proposes that the act of retrieval leads to the strengthening of the retrieved trace at the expense of rival traces. It was hypothesised that this effect might reflect the activity of some kind of inhibitory mechanism operating in the brain, and recent experiments have demonstrated the existence of such a mechanism. It is known as "retrieval-induced forgetting" and was first demonstrated by Anderson *et al.* (1994). They presented their participants with word pairs, each consisting of a category word and an example of an item from that category (e.g. Fruit–Banana). The list contained further items from the same category (e.g. Fruit–Apple) and others from different categories (e.g. Drink–Whisky). Half of the items from certain categories (e.g. Fruit) were subjected to retrieval tests, which were repeated three times. When retrieval was subsequently tested for all of the previously untested items, it was found that the previously untested items from a previously tested category gave lower recall scores than those from a previously untested category. It was concluded that the earlier retrieval of an item from a particular category had somehow inhibited the retrieval of other items in the same category (see Figure 2.12).

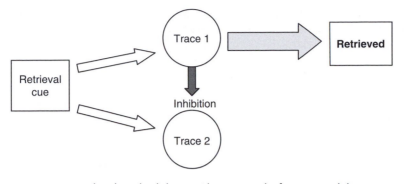

Figure 2.12 Retrieval-induced inhibition (the retrieval of trace 1 inhibits retrieval of trace 2, which shares the same retrieval cue)

The phenomenon of retrieval-induced forgetting has now been confirmed by a number of studies (e.g. Anderson, Bjork, & Bjork, 1994, 2000; Macrae & MacLeod, 1999; MacLeod & Macrae, 2001). Anderson *et al.* (2000) established that the inhibition of an item only occurs when there are two or more items competing for retrieval, and when a rival item has actually been retrieved. This supported their theory that retrieval-induced forgetting is not merely some accidental event, but involves the active suppression of related but unwanted items to assist the retrieval of the item actually required. Early experiments suggested that retrieval-induced forgetting might have a relatively short-lived effect, but MacLeod and Macrae (2001) found a significant inhibition effect lasting up to 24 hours after the retrieval practice occurred.

It is easy to see how such an inhibitory mechanism might have evolved, because it would offer considerable benefits in helping people to retrieve items selectively. For example, remembering where you left your car in a large multi-storey car park would be extremely difficult if you had equally strong memories for every previous occasion on which you had ever parked your car. A mechanism that activated the most recent memory of parking your car, while inhibiting the memories of all previous occasions, would be extremely helpful (Anderson & Neely, 1996).

The discovery of retrieval-induced forgetting in laboratory experiments led researchers to wonder whether this phenomenon also occurred in real-life settings involving meaningful items, such as the performance of a student revising for examinations or the testimony of an eyewitness in a courtroom. Macrae and MacLeod (1999) showed that retrieval-induced forgetting does indeed seem to affect students revising for examinations. Their participants were required to sit a mock geography exam, for which they were presented with 20 facts about two fictitious islands. The participants were then divided into two groups, one of which practised half of the 20 facts intensively while the other group did not. Subsequent testing revealed that the first group achieved good recall for the 10 facts they had practised (as you would expect), but showed very poor recall of the 10 un-practised facts, which were recalled far better by the group who had not carried out the additional practice. These findings suggest that last-minute cramming before an examination may sometimes do more harm than good, because it assists the recall of a few items at the cost of inhibited recall for all of the others.

Shaw, Bjork and Handal (1995) have also demonstrated the occurrence of retrieval-induced forgetting in an experiment on eyewitness testimony. Their participants were required to recall information about a crime presented in the form of a slide show, and they found that the retrieval of some details of the crime was inhibited by the retrieval of other related items. From these findings, Shaw *et al.* concluded that in real crime investigations there was a risk that police questioning of a witness could lead to the subsequent inhibition of any information not retrieved during the initial interview. However, MacLeod (2002) found that these inhibitory effects tended to subside about 24 hours after the initial questioning, suggesting that a second interview with the same eyewitness could produce further retrieval so long as the two interviews were separated by at least 24 hours.

There is some recent evidence that retrieval-induced forgetting can increase the likelihood of eyewitnesses falling victim to the misinformation effect. The misinformation effect is dealt with in Chapter 3, and it refers to the contamination of eyewitness testimony by information acquired subsequent to the event witnessed, for example information heard in conversation with other witnesses or imparted in the wording of questions during police interrogation. Saunders and MacLeod (2002) confirmed that eyewitnesses to a simulated crime became more susceptible to the misinformation effect (i.e. their retrieval was more likely to be contaminated by post-event information) following guided retrieval practice of related items. However, they found that both retrieval-induced inhibition and the associated misinformation effect tended to disappear about 24 hours after the retrieval practice, again suggesting that a 24 hour interval should be placed between two successive interviews with the same witness.

The discovery of retrieval-induced forgetting suggests the existence of inhibitory mechanisms in the brain that selectively inhibit or facilitate memories, at least for fairly short retrieval intervals (up to 24 hours). However, it is possible that there may be similar inhibitory mechanisms occuring over longer time periods, which may explain the mechanism underlying the new theory of disuse.

2.8 Clinical applications of disuse and retrieval inhibition

In addition to its applications in the field of learning and revision, the new theory of disuse and the related phenomenon of retrieval-induced forgetting may also have applications in the treatment of clinical disorders. Lang, Craske and Bjork (1999) suggest that phobic anxiety reactions can be regarded as a response to some fear-provoking stimulus which has been retrieved from memory. Lang *et al.* propose that phobias could be treated by teaching the sufferer to practise the retrieval of alternative non-fearful responses to the phobic stimulus, which should lead to the inhibition of the fear response. For example, a person who has developed a phobic fear of spiders through some earlier bad experience with a spider, could be taught to associate some more pleasant and relaxing experience with the presence of a spider. As you may have noticed, this treatment is generally similar to traditional (and very successful) methods of cognitive behaviour therapy such as progressive desensitisation, except that the emphasis is now placed on inhibiting memory retrieval rather than extinguishing a conditioned response by manipulating reinforcement.

It has also been proposed that other anxiety disorders, such as panic attacks and panic disorder, can also be understood in terms of disuse and retrieval inhibition, and may be amenable to similar techniques involving repeated retrieval of a rival memory response (Groome, 2003). Most panic attacks are triggered by some phobic stimulus or memory from the past (these are known as "cued" panic attacks), and even those cases where there is no obvious phobic trigger (so-called "spontaneous" panic attacks) are probably still set off by a stressful memory, but one that has fallen below the level of conscious retrieval. The suggested therapy therefore involves identifying the stimulus which cues a panic attack, and then carrying out extensive retrieval practice of some alternative memory response to that stimulus. A hypothetical model of this approach to anxiety disorders is shown in Figure 2.13.

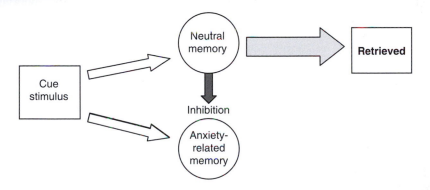

Figure 2.13 Retrieval-induced inhibition used to inhibit memory causing anxiety or panic response

Victims of severe traumatic events such as wars and earthquakes often suffer later from disturbing intrusive memories that can cause great distress for many years (Horowitz, 1976; Yule, 1999; Groome & Soureti, 2004). In fact, intrusive memories are among the most important symptoms of post-traumatic stress disorder. In accordance with the new theory of disuse and the principle of retrieval-induced forgetting, it has recently been proposed that such intrusive memories could be suppressed by the selective strengthening of competing memory traces (MacLeod, 2000; Anderson, 2001).

The suggestion that anxiety disorders can be triggered by memories stored at an unconscious level is not of course new, as this idea lies at the heart of Freudian psychoanalytic theories of neurosis. However, the Freudian view was derived from theories about the dynamic interaction of hypothetical forces within the personality, and made no direct use of memory theory as such. Freud proposed that memories could be repressed into the unconscious because they were distressing or unacceptable, but no clear explanation was ever provided for the mechanism of repression in terms of memory theory. However, Anderson (2001) suggests that the phenomenon of repression (i.e. the selective forgetting of disturbing traumatic memories) could be explained by inhibitory mechanisms activated by the retrieval of competing memories, in accordance with the new theory of disuse. For example, victims of child abuse are often unable to recall the abusive event, especially if the abuser was a close relative rather than a stranger. Anderson points out that there would be many other memories of events involving the close relative that would be in competition with the memory for the abusive incident and thus likely to inhibit its retrieval.

The discovery of memory processes such as retrieval-induced forgetting, disuse and response inhibition have opened up new possibilities in the analysis and treatment of clinical disorders. It may appear odd to consider clinical disorders in terms of memory function, but clearly these disorders must involve the memory system, so it is entirely plausible that memory processes could play a part in causing the disorder. Moreover, this new memory-based approach offers different perspectives and approaches to therapy. At first glance it might be argued that the techniques advocated are no different to those already in use, but there are actually important differences. Practising a new response may broadly resemble the established behaviour therapy technique of reinforcing a new response and extinguishing the old one, but these techniques emphasise reinforcement. In contrast, the use of retrieval inhibition involves the use of repeated retrieval to inhibit an unwanted memory trace. Again it could be argued that the uncovering of a repressed memory to change the patient's response to it resembles the techniques used by psychoanalysts for many years. However, the implications of retrieval inhibition theory are very different to the psychoanalytic view. Freudian theory suggests that the traumatic memory must be identified and brought out into the open, and the assumption is made that this process in itself will be cathartic and therapeutic. However, the retrieval inhibition approach suggests that the traumatic memory needs to be inhibited (and thus covered up), a goal which is the very opposite of that of psychoanalysis, and one which has quite different implications for therapy.

2.9 Retrieval strength, storage strength and metamemory

In their original paper introducing the new theory of disuse, Bjork and Bjork (1992) make an important distinction between storage strength and retrieval strength. Storage strength reflects how strongly a memory trace has been encoded, and once established it is assumed to be fairly lasting and permanent. Retrieval strength, on the other hand, reflects the ease with which a memory trace can be retrieved at any particular moment in time, and this varies from moment to moment as a consequence of factors such as disuse and retrieval-induced inhibition. It is therefore possible that a trace with high storage strength may still be difficult to retrieve. In other words, a trace can be available without necessarily being accessible.

There is some evidence that when individuals attempt to estimate the strength of their own memories (a form of subjective judgement known as "metamemory"), they tend to base their assessment on retrieval strength rather than storage strength. However, this is likely to be inaccurate (Bjork, 1999; Simon & Bjork, 2001), because retrieval strength is extremely variable, whereas the underlying storage strength of an item is more lasting and therefore provides a more accurate prediction of future retrieval success. For example, it has been established that spaced learning trials produce more effective long-term retrieval than massed learning trials (see Section 2.2), but during the actual learning session massed learning may hold a temporary advantage in retrieval strength (Glenberg & Lehman, 1980). However, Simon and Bjork (2001) found that individuals learning motor keyboard skills by a mixture of massed and spaced learning trials tended to judge massed trials as being more effective than spaced trials in the long term. They appear to have been misled by focusing on transient retrieval strength rather than on the underlying storage strength.

It turns out that in a variety of different learning situations participants tend to make errors in judging the strength of their own memories as a consequence of basing their subjective judgements on retrieval strength rather than storage strength (Bjork, 1999; Simon & Bjork, 2001). One possible reason for this inaccuracy is that storage strength is not available to direct experience and estimation, whereas people are more aware of the retrieval strength of a particular trace because they can check it by making retrieval attempts. In some ways, the same general principle applies to experimental studies of memory, where retrieval strength is relatively easy to measure by using a simple recall test, whereas the measurement of storage strength requires more complex techniques such as tests of implicit memory, familiarity, or recognition.

Most people are very poor at judging the effectiveness of their own learning, or which strategies will yield the best retrieval, unless of course they have studied the psychology of learning and memory. Bjork (1999) notes that in most cases individuals tend to overestimate their ability to retrieve information, and he suggests that such misjudgements could cause serious problems in many work settings, and even severe danger in some cases. For example, air-traffic controllers and operators of nuclear plants who hold an over-optimistic view of their own retrieval capabilities may take on responsibilities which are beyond their competence, or may fail to spend sufficient time on preparation or study.

In summary, it seems that most people are very poor at estimating their own retrieval capabilities, because they base their judgements on retrieval strength rather than storage strength. In any learning situation, it is important to focus on more objective measures of long-term learning rather than basing judgements of progress on the subjective opinion of the learner. This finding obviously has important implications for anyone involved in learning and study, and most particularly for instructors and teachers.

Summary

- Learning is usually more efficient when trials are "spaced" rather than "massed", especially if expanding retrieval practice is employed.
- Learning can be made more effective by semantic processing (i.e. focusing on the meaning of the material to be learned) and by the use of imagery.

- Mnemonic strategies, often making use of semantic processing and imagery, can assist learning and memory, especially for material that has little intrinsic meaning.
- Retrieval can be enhanced by strategies to increase the effectiveness of retrieval cues, including contextual cues.
- Active retrieval of a memory makes it more retrievable in the future, whereas disused memories become increasingly inaccessible.
- Retrieving an item from memory tends to inhibit the retrieval of other related items.
- Attempts to predict our own future retrieval performance are frequently inaccurate, because we tend to base such assessments on estimates of retrieval strength rather than storage strength.

Further reading

Groome, D.H., with Dewart, H., Esgate, A., Gurney, K., Kemp, R., & Towell, N. (1999). *An introduction to cognitive psychology: Processes and disorders*. Hove, UK: Psychology Press. This book provides the background to basic processes of cognition that are referred to in the present text.

Herrmann, D., Raybeck, D., & Gruneberg, M. (2002). *Improving memory and study skills: Advances in theory and practice*. Ashland, OH: Hogrefe & Huber. A very detailed and practical do-it-yourself manual about how to improve your study skills and revision techniques.

Chapter 3

Everyday memory

3.1 Introduction: memory in the laboratory and in real life

Scientific studies of memory have been taking place for well over a century, but until recently most memory research was restricted to laboratory experiments carried out under highly artificial conditions. It is only in relatively recent times that psychologists have begun to investigate memory function in real-life settings.

Early memory studies mostly involved the testing of nonsense material, following the tradition begun by Ebbinghaus (1885). But this type of test material bore very little similarity to the items that people need to remember in real-life settings. The experiments of Ebbinghaus were essentially studies of rote learning, but in real life we are very rarely required to learn meaningless items off by heart. Bartlett (1932) was very critical of Ebbinghaus's use of nonsense material, preferring to test memory for meaningful material such as stories and pictures. Bartlett found that his participants tended to remember the test material in terms of the meaning they had extracted from it. For example, they tended to remember the gist of a story rather than the exact words. Bartlett also found that the theme and meaning of the story was subjected to distortion as his participants attempted to make it fit in with their pre-existing knowledge and schemas. Thus Bartlett was able to discover new phenomena of memory that would never have emerged from studies of memory for nonsense material.

Bartlett argued for an increased emphasis on the use of more naturalistic test methods and materials for the study of memory function. This point was subsequently taken up by Neisser (1976), who argued that experimenters should not only make use of more naturalistic test materials, but that they should also carry out research in real-life settings. This plea for "ecological validity" in memory studies has led to a new interest in the study of everyday memory, and this approach has grown over the years as a body of research that is largely separate from laboratory studies and yet complementary to them. In one sense, such real-life studies provide a "reality check" for the laboratory findings, offering a chance to confirm or disconfirm their validity in the real world. Real-life memory studies can also sometimes provide knowledge that may be applied in the real world, and sometimes they can even identify memory phenomena that have not previously emerged from laboratory experiments.

As explained in Chapter 1, Banaji and Crowder (1989) argued that studies of memory carried out in the field have produced few dependable findings, due to the lack of adequate scientific control over unwanted variables. However, their criticism seems to have been somewhat premature, as many studies of everyday memory over the subsequent years have produced interesting and valuable findings, many of which are described in this chapter.

However, Conway (1991) points out that there are certain fundamental differences between everyday memory in real-life settings and memory tested in a laboratory setting. One important difference is that memory in everyday life tends to involve personal experiences, which hold considerable significance for the individual, whereas the test items typically used in laboratory experiments normally lack any element of personal interest or significance. Koriat and Goldsmith (1996) also point out that laboratory experiments usually involve quantitative measures of memory (e.g. the number of words recalled from a list), whereas in real life there is more emphasis on qualitative aspects of a memory trace. A similar point is made by Neisser (1996), who suggests that in laboratory experiments on memory participants are required to retrieve as many test items as possible, whereas in real life memory may involve more subtle motives, and both learning and retrieval tend to be more selective. For example, sometimes we may wish to recall events that will be reassuring to us, or incidents that we can use to impress other people. These motives will often result in a tendency to remember selectively rather than accurately.

All of these factors should be borne in mind as we examine the research on various types of everyday memory, starting with autobiographical memory, which is the store of memory we all have for the events and experiences of our own lives.

3.2 Autobiographical memory

Memory for the distant past

Autobiographical memory refers to our memory for the events we have experienced in our own lives. You can test some aspects of your own autobiographical memory very easily. For example, try to write down the names of all of the children in your primary school class. Better still, go and fish out an old school photograph like that in Figure 3.1 and see how many of the children you can name.

Figure 3.1 A school photograph

These tasks require you to draw upon memories that have probably remained undisturbed for many years, and yet you will probably be surprised how many names you can produce. You will also probably find that many other related memories are dragged up along with the names you recall, because of the interconnections between these related memories.

A more scientific version of this experiment was carried out by Bahrick, Bahrick and Wittlinger (1975), who investigated the ability of American adults to remember their old high school classmates. Bahrick *et al.* used a number of different types of test, including the accuracy with which individuals could recall names to match the faces in college photographs (the "picture-cueing" test) and their ability to match photos with a list of names supplied to them (the "picture-matching" test). On the picture-matching test, they found that most of their participants could still match up the names and photos of more than 80% of their college classmates even 25 years after graduation, and there was no significant decline in their performance over the years since they had graduated. Although scores did drop off slightly at longer retention intervals, they still remained above 70% despite an average time lapse of 47 years. The picture-cueing test, not surprisingly, yielded lower overall recall scores since names had to be generated by each participant spontaneously, but performance was still quite impressive and again showed relatively little decline over the years.

Bahrick *et al.* (1975) concluded that memory for real-life experiences is often far more accurate and durable than memory for items tested in a laboratory experiment. In fact, Bahrick *et al.* suggested that some of our autobiographical memories are so thoroughly learned that they achieve "permastore" status and remain intact indefinitely. This phenomenon has not generally been found in laboratory studies, where forgetting is typically found to be far more rapid. One possible explanation for this discrepancy may be the fact that (as mentioned in Section 3.1) autobiographical memories have far greater personal significance to the individual than do the test items in a laboratory experiment (Conway, 1991).

One reason for studying autobiographical memory is to find out whether it is subject to the same general principles that we find in laboratory studies of memory, and the findings of Bahrick *et al.* (1975) of a relatively permanent store of memories do indeed differ from the usual laboratory findings.

Diary studies and retrieval cues

One of the biggest problems with the testing of autobiographical memory is that we do not usually have a precise and detailed record of the events an individual has experienced during their life. This means that we do not know what type of material we can reasonably expect them to remember, and we cannot easily check the accuracy of the events they may recall. An individual may appear to remember an impressive number of events from the past in great detail, but it is entirely possible that the memories they report are incorrect. In an effort to overcome these problems, some investigators have deliberately kept detailed diaries of their own daily experiences over long periods, thus providing a suitable source of memories to be tested later, which could be checked for their accuracy.

Linton (1975) used this diary technique, noting down two or three events every day for 6 years. At the end of each month, she chose two of those events at random and attempted to recall as much as possible about them. Subsequent testing revealed that items which had been tested previously were far more likely to be retrieved later on than those which had not. This finding is consistent with the findings of laboratory studies, which have also shown that frequent retrieval of an item makes it more retrievable in future. There is a large body of evidence confirming that retrieving an item from memory makes that item more retrievable in the future, since active retrieval is far more effective than passive rehearsal of test items (Landauer & Bjork, 1978; Payne, 1987; Macrae & MacLeod, 1999). Bjork and Bjork (1992) have proposed a theory to explain this, which they call the "new theory of disuse" (see Chapter 2). The theory suggests that frequent retrieval is required to keep a memory trace accessible, and that disused items will suffer inhibition and will eventually become irretrievable.

Wagenaar (1986) used a diary technique similar to that of Linton, again recording daily events over a 6 year period. However, he took the additional precaution of recording retrieval cues, for later use. Aided by these retrieval cues, Wagenaar was able to recall about half of the events recorded over the previous 6 years. This study also revealed that the likelihood of retrieving an item depended on the number of retrieval cues available, a finding that is broadly consistent with the encoding specificity principle proposed by Tulving (1972).

Both Linton and Wagenaar noted that their recall of past events showed a strong bias towards the recall of pleasant events rather than unpleasant ones. There are a number of possible explanations for this retrieval bias. Psychoanalytic theory suggests that we tend to repress our more unpleasant memories as a form of defence mechanism, to protect us from distressing thoughts (Freud, 1938). An alternative theory is that unpleasant memories are usually acquired in stressful situations, which may tend to inhibit memory input (Williams, Watts, Mcleod, & Mathews, 1988; Hertel, 1992). A third possibility is that people prefer to think about pleasant memories when they are reminiscing about the past, so pleasant memories are likely to benefit from more frequent retrieval and rehearsal than unpleasant memories (Searleman & Herrmann, 1994).

Memory for different periods of life

Since autobiographical memory concerns the personal experiences of the individual, the usual laboratory techniques for studying memory (e.g. retrieving word lists) are not usually very appropriate, and researchers have had to develop new test methods. Autobiographical memory is sometimes tested by free recall, but more often participants are provided with a retrieval cue of some sort, which provides more control over the type of items to be retrieved. The use of old school photos would be one example of such a cue, as described above. However, the first experiments on autobiographical memory made use of verbal cues, starting with the "cue-word" technique, which was introduced in the earliest days of psychology by Galton (1879). This technique was subsequently revived by Crovitz and Schiffman (1974), who used the cue-word approach to determine whether there are certain periods in a person's life that are more likely to stand out in their memory. They found that their participants were far better at recalling events from the recent past than from the distant past, and indeed there was a roughly linear relationship between the amount retrieved from a given year and its recency. However, this study was carried out on relatively young adults. Rubin, Wetzler and Nebes (1986) found a somewhat different pattern when older individuals were tested. People in their seventies tended to recall a large number of events from their early adult years, especially events which they experienced between the ages of 10 and 30. This phenomenon is sometimes referred to as the "reminiscence bump", as it appears as a bump on the graph of retrieval over time (see Figure 3.2).

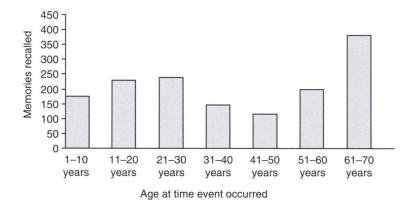

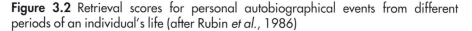

Figure 3.2 Retrieval scores for personal autobiographical events from different periods of an individual's life (after Rubin *et al.*, 1986)

One possible explanation for the reminiscence bump is that an older person may find their earlier years more memorable because they were more eventful or more pleasant, which, in turn, would have led to more frequent retrieval. Since older people tend to enjoy remembering their younger days, this frequent retrieval might help to strengthen the retrieval routes to those early memories. There is also evidence that novel experiences tend to stand out in the memory (Pillemer, Goldsmith, Panter, & White, 1988), and of course the younger stages of life involve far more of these novel experiences. Most people have fairly vivid memories for their first trip abroad, or their first date with the person they subsequently married. However, subsequent trips abroad (or remarriages) tend to lose their novelty value and thus become less distinctive.

Rubin, Rahal and Poon (1998) found that the reminiscence bump not only occurred for personal events but also for more general public events such as news items, books and academy award winners. Schulkind, Hennis and Rubin (1999) found that older individuals were also better at recognising songs that were popular in their youth rather than those from more recent times. They also rated those older songs as more emotional, which may help to explain their heightened memorability.

Chu and Downes (2000) found that odours could also act as strong cues to the retrieval of events from early life. This finding has been referred to as the "Proust phenomenon", as it reflects the observations of Proust about the evocative nature of odours (for a scientific evaluation of Proust's account, see Jones, 2001). Chu and Downes (2000) also reported a marked reminiscence bump, but noted that memories related to odours peaked at around 6–10 years of age, whereas for verbal cues the peak occurred between 11 and 25 years.

Most people have a few regrets about some of their actions as they look back on their lives, but a recent study by Gilovich, Wang, Regan and Nishina (2003) has shown that the type of regrets we feel tend to vary according to the part of the lifespan being reviewed. Gilovich *et al.* found that when people consider earlier periods of their lives, they are more likely to regret things they have not done, rather than regretting things they have done. However, when reviewing more recent actions and decisions, the opposite is usually found, and people tend to regret their actions rather than their inactions.

Infantile amnesia

Early infancy is one period of life that appears to be particularly difficult to remember. In fact, most people appear to remember nothing at all from the first 2–3 years of their lives (Waldfogel, 1948; Pillemer & White, 1989). This phenomenon is known as "infantile amnesia", and there are a number of interesting theories about its possible causes. One explanation is that the brain structures involved in memory have not completed their physical development in early infancy. However, this is unlikely to be the whole explanation, since there is clear evidence that young infants are capable of learning. Nelson (1988) found that 2-year-old children do have the ability to register and retrieve information, although their learning is considerably less effective than that of adults. It would therefore seem that there is some other reason why the memories created in the first few years of life somehow cease to be retrievable in later years.

Psychoanalysts have suggested that infancy is a period filled with conflict and guilt, which is therefore repressed as a protection against anxiety (Freud, 1905). This may be true, but it would not explain why pleasant or neutral memories are lost as well as unpleasant ones. Schachtel (1947) suggested that young infants have not yet developed adequate schemas to enable them to process and store information. Moreover, any schemas that are available in early infancy are unlikely to match up with later adult schemas, so even if any events do go into memory they will not be retrievable in adulthood. Nelson and Ross (1980) showed that very young children are able to remember general facts (i.e. semantic memory) but not specific events (i.e. episodic memory). Their earliest memories thus tend to be based on schemas and scripts for general or typical events, but not for specific episodes of their own personal lives. This could explain why we do not remember actual events and incidents from early infancy. Newcombe, Drummey, Fox, Lie and Ottinger-Alberts (2000) argue that young infants may retain implicit memories that can affect their later behaviour, but without any explicit and conscious memory of the actual episodes which led to the formation of these implicit memories. Newcombe *et al.* further suggest that a possible reason for the inability of young infants to form explicit episodic memories may be the incomplete development of the prefrontal cortex, which is known to be important in the formation of episodic autobiographical memories (Conway *et al.*, 1999; Maguire, Henson, Mummery, & Frith, 2001).

A somewhat different explanation of infantile amnesia is the suggestion of Howe and Courage (1997) that children do not develop a "sense of self" until the age of about 20 months, as indicated for example by their inability to recognise themselves in a mirror or photograph. Howe and Courage argue that this kind of self-identity may be crucial for the formation of personal autobiographical memories, which are characterised by their reference to the self.

An interesting cross-cultural study by MacDonald, Uesiliana and Hayne (2000) compared childhood recall among three different New Zealand sub-cultures. When asked to report their earliest memories, Maoris were able to report memories from earlier in their lives than NZ Europeans or NZ Asians. This finding suggests that early memory formation (or at least the tendency to report it) may be affected by cultural influences, which, in this case, might possibly be related to the heightened significance accorded by Maoris to the past.

3.3 Flashbulb memories

Memory for learning about shocking events

It has often been said that most Americans remember what they were doing at the moment when they heard the news of the assassination of President Kennedy (Figure 3.3), because it came as such a terrible shock to the entire nation. Brown and

Figure 3.3 President John F. Kennedy shortly before he was assassinated

Kulik (1977) examined this claim scientifically and found that all but one of the 80 individuals they tested were indeed able to report some details of the circumstances and surroundings in which they heard the news of Kennedy's death.

Similar findings have been reported for a range of other major news events, including the explosion of the space shuttle *Challenger* (Neisser & Harsch, 1992), the death of Princess Diana (Davidson & Glisky, 2002; Hornstein, Brown, & Mulligan, 2003) and the terrorist attack on the World Trade Center (Candel, Jelicik, Merckelbach, & Wester, 2003; Talarico & Rubin, 2003). This capacity of an important and shocking event to illuminate trivial aspects of the observer's current activities and surroundings is known as "flashbulb memory". The fact that a major news event is itself well remembered is hardly surprising, but the significance of flashbulb memory is that people are also able to remember trivial details of their own lives at the time of the event, such as where they were and what they were doing. These trivia of daily life are in some way illuminated by the simultaneous occurrence of a highly significant and shocking event, hence the term "flashbulb memory".

Does flashbulb memory involve a special process?

In an effort to explain the occurrence of flashbulb memory, Brown and Kulik (1977) suggested that a special memory process might be involved, which was fundamentally different from the mechanism involved in normal memory. This hypothesis was based on Brown and Kulik's observation that flashbulb memories appeared to be not only remarkably accurate but also immune to normal forgetting processes. This special process was assumed to be activated only by an event that was very shocking to the individual, and it was thought to create a permanent and infallible record of the details relating to that event. Brown and Kulik reasoned that such a memory process might have evolved because it would offer a survival advantage, by enabling an individual to remember vivid details of past catastrophes, which would help them to avoid similar dangers in the future.

The notion of flashbulb memory as a special process has been challenged by studies showing that flashbulb memories appear to be subject to errors and forgetting just like any other type of memory. Researchers have been able to demonstrate this by testing their participants' memories immediately after a disaster, to provide a baseline measure for comparison with later tests of flashbulb memory. For example, Neisser and Harsch (1992) tested individuals the day after the *Challenger* explosion, to establish precisely what they could recall at that initial stage. The same participants were tested again 3 years later, and a comparison of these results with the initial test data revealed that their flashbulb memories were by no means immune to forgetting over this time period. In fact, roughly half of the details recalled in the 3 year retest were inconsistent with the information recalled on the day after the crash.

A number of subsequent studies have confirmed the fallibility of flashbulb memories. The announcement of the verdict in the O.J. Simpson murder trial generated flashbulb memories in most Americans, but again these memories suffered a rapid drop in their accuracy over the months following the verdict

(Schmolk, Buffalo, & Squire, 2000). The death of President Mitterand (the President of France) was also found to produce strong flashbulb memories in French participants, but there was fairly rapid forgetting of these memories in subsequent months (Curci, Luminet, Finkenauer, & Gisle, 2001). Talarico and Rubin (2003) reported that flashbulb memories following the World Trade Center attack (Figure 3.4) showed a decline in their accuracy over the months that followed, and were in fact no more accurate and lasting than the normal everyday memories of their participants for other occasions unrelated to any kind of disaster.

Figure 3.4 The World Trade Center attack

Conway *et al.* (1994) argued that the fallibility of flashbulb memories reported in many of these studies might simply reflect a lack of interest in the key event on the part of some of the participants tested. Conway *et al.* argued that flashbulb memories might only occur in individuals for whom the event in question held particular personal significance, and more specifically for those who perceived the event as having major consequences for their own future lives. For example, many Americans would have perceived the Kennedy assassination or the attack on the World Trade Center as having major consequences for them personally, since it was clear that these events would have a major impact on life in America from that moment on. On the other hand, an event such as the *Challenger* disaster, although shocking, would probably have no direct consequences for most people's lives, so it was not entirely surprising that flashbulb effects were not so clearly found. In an effort to explore this possibility, Conway *et al.* (1994) investigated flashbulb memories for the resignation of British Prime Minister Margaret Thatcher. They discovered that the Thatcher resignation produced significant flashbulb effects in a sample of British people (for whom the event would be perceived as having important consequences), but people from other countries showed very little evidence of a flashbulb effect. Similarly, Curci *et al.* (2001) found that the death of French President Mitterand produced flashbulb memories in many French nationals, but fewer such memories in Belgian citizens, for whom there were likely to be fewer direct consequences. Other studies have confirmed that flashbulb memory tends to be related to the level of personal significance or importance which the event holds for the perceiver, as for example in a study about hearing news of the death of the first Turkish president (Tekcan & Peynircioglu, 2002) or hearing news of a nearby earthquake (Er, 2003).

Despite these findings, most studies suggest that flashbulb memories are in fact subject to normal forgetting processes and errors over time, as with other kinds of autobiographical memory. Although the available research is not conclusive, at present there does not appear to be any clear justification for regarding flashbulb memory as being fundamentally different from other types of memory. However, this is not to deny the existence of flashbulb memory. While it may involve the same basic neural processes as other forms of memory, flashbulb memory is still distinguished from other autobiographical memories by its unusual degree of vividness and detail.

Other factors affecting flashbulb memory

Neisser (1982) rejected the notion of flashbulb memory as a special process, suggesting that the apparent durability and detail of flashbulb memory could be simply a consequence of frequent retrieval. Neisser argued that a memory for a very significant event would probably be subjected to frequent review and re-telling, which would help to strengthen the memory trace. Several studies have indeed confirmed a relationship between flashbulb memory and the extent of rehearsal by the individual (Teckan & Peynircioglu, 2002; Hornstein *et al.*, 2003).

It has also been suggested that flashbulb memory could be seen as a form of context-dependent learning, but one in which a very dramatic and memorable event provides a powerful contextual cue for more trivial aspects of the occasion (Groome, 1999). For example, the rather unmemorable slice of toast you happen to be eating one morning could become extremely memorable when consumed in the context of a news report announcing the outbreak of war or the death of your country's leader. Unlike more typical examples of context-dependent memory, in this instance the major news event is serving as a context for other trivial memories, as well as being a memory in its own right. Davidson and Glisky (2002) have proposed a similar explanation, suggesting that flashbulb memory can possibly be regarded as a special case of source memory.

Some researchers have reported a relationship between flashbulb memory and the severity of emotional shock reported by individuals. Hornstein *et al.* (2003) found that flashbulb memories relating to the death of Princess Diana were greater for individuals who had been very upset by the news. However, Talarico and Rubin (2003) reported that individuals' ratings of their level of emotional shock following the World Trade Center attack predicted their confidence in the accuracy of their flashbulb memories rather than the accuracy of their retrieval.

Physiological and clinical aspects of flashbulb memory

Davidson and Glisky (2002) found that flashbulb memories following the death of Princess Diana (Figure 3.5) were stronger for younger individuals than for older individuals. It is not entirely clear why older individuals should be less prone to flashbulb memory, although this finding may possibly reflect the general decline found in the memory performance of older people. However, no relationship was found between flashbulb effects and measures of frontal or temporal lobe function, which might have been expected since these brain areas are known to be involved in context retrieval and memory storage, respectively. Davidson and Glisky speculated that the creation of flashbulb memory might be mediated by the brain's emotional

Figure 3.5 Princess Diana

centres, such as the amygdala, rather than by the brain regions involved in memory function.

Candel *et al.* (2003) investigated the flashbulb memories of amnesic Korsakoff patients in the aftermath of the attack on the World Trade Center. Despite being severely amnesic for most daily events, most of the Korsakoff patients were able to remember some information about the attack, but they did not appear to have any flashbulb memories for the details of their own personal circumstances when they heard the news of the attack.

One intriguing possibility is that the basic phenomenon of flashbulb memory may also be responsible for the occurrence of intrusive memories in certain clinical disorders (Conway, 1994; Sierra & Berrios, 2000). For example, one of the main symptoms of post-traumatic stress disorder (PTSD) is the occurrence of extremely distressing memories of some horrifying experience, which are unusually intense and vivid, and so powerful that they cannot be kept out of consciousness. Sierra and Berrios (2000) suggest that the flashbulb mechanism may be involved in a range of intrusive memory effects, including the intrusive memories found in PTSD, phobia and depression, and also possibly in drug-induced flashbacks. At present, this view is largely speculative, but if evidence is found to support it, then the mechanism of flashbulb memory would acquire a new level of importance and urgency.

3.4 Eyewitness testimony

The fallibility of eyewitness testimony

One form of memory that has particular importance in real life is eyewitness testimony. In a court of law, the testimony given by eyewitnesses is often the main factor which determines whether or not the defendant is convicted. Kebbell and Milne (1998) carried out a survey of British police officers and found that they considered eyewitness accounts to be generally quite reliable and accurate, but there is a considerable amount of evidence to suggest that eyewitness testimony is often unreliable and does not justify the faith placed in it by the courts. Reviewing such evidence, Fruzzetti, Toland, Teller and Loftus (1992) estimated that thousands of innocent people may be wrongly convicted every year on the basis of eyewitness errors and mistaken identity. Since DNA testing was introduced as a method of identifying criminals, it has all too frequently demonstrated that eyewitnesses have made mistakes. Wells *et al.* (1998) described 40 cases where DNA evidence had exonerated a suspect who had been wrongly identified by eyewitnesses, and in five of these cases the wrongly convicted person had actually been on death row awaiting execution. Yarmey (2001) concluded that mistaken eyewitness testimony has been responsible for more wrongful convictions than all of the other causes combined.

The experiments of Bartlett (1932) found that recall is prone to distortion by the individual's prior knowledge and expectations, and he warned that this effect would be likely to apply to the testimony of eyewitnesses. Research focusing more specifically on eyewitness testimony has established that eyewitnesses are indeed susceptible to reconstructive errors (Zaragoza & Lane, 1998), and Loftus and Burns (1982) have shown that eyewitness testimony tends to be particularly prone to distortion when the events witnessed involve violence, since witnesses are likely to be less perceptive when in a frightened state.

Recent research has also established that eyewitness recall of an event is vulnerable to contamination from information acquired after the event, for example mistakenly recalling things which actually originated from something suggested to them on a later occasion (Wright & Stroud, 1998; Wright, Self, & Justice, 2000). The contamination of eyewitness testimony by post-event information will be considered in the following sub-section.

Contamination by post-event information

It is now well established that eyewitness testimony is vulnerable to contamination from information received after the witnessed event, a phenomenon sometimes referred to as the "misinformation effect". In an early study of these effects, Loftus and Palmer (1974) showed participants a film of a car accident, and later asked them a series of questions about what they had seen. It was found that their answers were strongly influenced by the wording of the questions. For example, the participants were asked to estimate how fast the cars had been travelling at the time of the collision, but the wording of the question was varied for different groups of participants. Those participants who were asked how fast the cars were travelling when they "smashed into one another" gave a higher estimate of speed on average than did the participants who were asked how fast the cars were travelling when they "hit one another". They were also far more likely to report having seen broken glass when tested a week later, even though no broken glass had actually been shown.

In a similar experiment, Loftus and Zanni (1975) found that after viewing a filmed car crash, participants were far more likely to report seeing a broken headlight if they were asked if they saw "*the* broken headlight" rather than "*a* broken headlight" (again no broken headlight had actually been shown in the film). The experiment demonstrated that merely changing a single word could be sufficient to influence retrieval, essentially by making an implicit suggestion to the participants about what they should have seen.

Loftus, Miller and Burns (1978) found that eyewitness memories became increasingly vulnerable to contamination with increasing intervals between the witnessed event and the contaminating input. A possible explanation for this finding is that the original memory trace becomes weaker and more fragmented as time passes, which makes it easier for the gaps to be filled by input from some other source. In fact, there is clear evidence that eyewitness testimony (like other types of memory) becomes more unreliable with the passage of time. Flin, Boon, Knox and Bull (1992) also reported that eyewitness reports became less accurate after a 5 month delay, and although this applied to all age groups tested, they found that small children were particularly susceptible.

The ability of eyewitnesses to recall the appearance of an individual also seems to be subject to contamination effects. For example, Loftus and Greene (1980) showed that post-event information can significantly alter a witness's recall of the physical characteristics of an actor in a staged event, such as their age or their height. This contamination would be likely to have a detrimental effect on the witness's ability to provide the police with an accurate description of a suspect, or to identify that suspect at a later time. (The accuracy of eyewitness identification of individuals is covered in Chapter 4.)

A number of recent studies have shown that it is possible to inhibit the retrieval of a particular piece of information by omitting it from a subsequent post-event presentation. Again, children appear to be particularly susceptible to this effect. Wright, Loftus and Hall (2001) presented children aged 9–10 years with a video depicting a series of events (such as a drink-driving incident), and then showed them the same video again some time later with a short scene missing. The children were then asked to imagine the event or, in a second experiment, to create a story about it. Subsequent testing revealed that the children often failed to recall the omitted scene, and indeed their recall of that scene was actually made worse by their second viewing of the video, compared with controls who received no second viewing. Williams, Wright and Freeman (2002) found a similar effect when reference to a particular scene was omitted from a post-event interview. Their participants (a group of young children aged 5–6 years) were far more likely to forget a scene if it was omitted from the post-event interview.

In some circumstances, it is possible to create entirely false memories in the mind of a witness by the use of suggestion effects, especially in small children (Read, Connolly, & Turtle, 2001; Hyman & Loftus, 2002). Such false memory effects can be achieved by employing very powerful and vivid forms of suggestion, such as the use of instructions to create a detailed visual image of some imaginary scene or event. By using such techniques, it is possible to persuade some individuals to believe that they have a genuine personal recollection of an event that never actually took place.

From the findings outlined above, it is easy to see how a witness to a real-life crime might suffer contamination from suggestions contained in questions posed long after the event by a police officer or a lawyer. Another possible source of post-event contamination is the testimony reported by other witnesses. Contamination of this kind appears to have occurred in the case of the Oklahoma bombing, which provides a real-life example of the occurrence of such contamination effects.

The Oklahoma bombing

On 19 April 1995, a huge bomb exploded beside the Alfred P. Murrah Building in Oklahoma City, killing 168 innocent people and injuring more than 600 others. This was the worst act of terrorism ever to occur on American soil at that time, and it caused profound shock throughout the country. At first, there were rumours that Middle Eastern terrorists were responsible, but 2 days after the explosion an American citizen called Timothy McVeigh, who was actually a Gulf War veteran, was arrested and accused of carrying out the bombing (Figure 3.6).

Timothy McVeigh had been stopped by chance for a routine traffic offence, but his appearance was subsequently found to match descriptions given by

Figure 3.6 Timothy McVeigh, the Oklahoma bomber

eyewitnesses and with video footage captured on security cameras. McVeigh, who had connections with a right-wing anti-government racist group known as the Aryan Republican Army, subsequently confessed to the bombing. After a lengthy court case, Timothy McVeigh was found guilty of the bombing, and he was executed by lethal injection on 11 June 2001.

The Oklahoma bombing raises a number of important issues about the reliability of eyewitness testimony in real-life cases, not only for the part it played by eye-witnesses in Timothy McVeigh's arrest and conviction, but also for the apparent errors made by eyewitnesses in deciding whether McVeigh had an accomplice. The main eyewitnesses in this respect were three employees of the car body shop where McVeigh had hired the truck used in the bombing. All three claimed to have seen McVeigh (referred to at this stage as "John Doe 1") come in to hire the truck together with a second man ("John Doe 2"). The FBI spent over a year searching for "John Doe 2", but he was never found. While it remains a possibility that McVeigh may have had an accomplice, Memon and Wright (1999) suggest that the witnesses' memories were probably contaminated by a subsequent event. On the day after McVeigh's visit to the body shop, two other men had come in to hire a truck. These two men were quite unrelated to the bombing, but it is possible that the witnesses might have confused the memory of their visit with that of Timothy McVeigh. Memon and Wright point out that a further complication in this case was the apparent cross-contamination of the testimony given by different witnesses. When the three workers at the body shop were first interviewed by police officers, only one of them claimed to have seen a second man with McVeigh. The other two witnesses made no mention of a second man at this stage, but subsequently both of them came to believe that they had in fact seen two men hiring the truck. It is likely that their recall of events had been influenced by the witness who described seeing a second man with McVeigh, since the three witnesses worked together and had discussed the incident extensively among themselves.

The possibility that these two witnesses may have been victims of post-event cross-witness contamination led Wright *et al.* (2000) to conduct an experiment to test the plausibility of this phenomenon. Two groups of participants were shown a series of pictures conveying a story in which a woman stole a man's wallet. All of the participants were shown the same basic set of pictures, except for the fact that one group saw the woman with an accomplice at the start of the sequence whereas the other group saw her alone. All participants were then asked questions about the theft, including: "Did the thief have an accomplice?" At this stage, most participants recalled the version they had seen with great accuracy. Each participant was then paired off with another from the other group (who had seen a different version), and the pair were required to discuss the details of the theft and describe them to the experimenter. By this point, most of the pairs (79%) had come to an agreement about whether or not there was an accomplice, which suggests that one member of the pair must have changed their mind as a result of hearing their partner's recollection of events. Pairs were fairly equally divided about whether they agreed they had seen an accomplice or no accomplice, but further investigation showed that in most cases the direction of this effect was determined by the confidence levels of the two participants. Whichever one of the pair had the greatest confidence in their recall usually succeeded in convincing their partner that they had seen the same thing.

These experimental findings have obvious parallels with the recall of witnesses in the Oklahoma bombing case, and they confirm that cross-witness contamination and conformity do apparently occur. This phenomenon also fits in with the more general principle that eyewitness testimony is strongly affected by post-event information.

Explanations of contamination and misinformation effects

The contamination of eyewitness testimony by a subsequent input has now been clearly established by experimental studies, although the exact mechanism underlying this phenomenon remains unclear. One possible explanation is that parts of the original memory are actually replaced by the new input and are thus permanently lost from the memory store (Loftus, 1975). Some support for this hypothesis comes from the finding that when participants recalled events wrongly, an opportunity to make a second guess did not normally help them to retrieve the lost memory (Loftus, 1979). Even when presented with a choice between the correct item and an incorrect item, participants were unable to pick the correct item at beyond a chance level. However, Dodson and Reisberg (1991) found that the use of an implicit memory test would often facilitate the retrieval of some information which the eyewitness could not retrieve explicitly. This suggests that, at least in some cases, the original memory has not been totally lost but has merely been rendered inaccessible to normal explicit retrieval processes.

The mechanism causing a memory to become inaccessible could involve retrieval-induced forgetting, in which the retrieval of one memory trace inhibits the retrieval of a second memory trace belonging to the same group or category (as explained in the previous chapter). Several laboratory studies have provided evidence for the occurrence of retrieval-induced forgetting (Anderson *et al.*, 1994, 2000; MacLeod & Macrae, 2001). However, a recent study by MacLeod (2002) has confirmed that retrieval-induced forgetting also affects the retrieval of meaningful items and events such as crime descriptions, so it can also be assumed to have an effect on eyewitness testimony.

Retrieval-induced forgetting could play a part in the misinformation effect and contamination from post-event information (Loftus & Palmer, 1974; Loftus & Greene, 1980), since the strengthening of retrieval access for post-event information may possibly cause inhibition of memory traces for the original witnessed event. Retrieval-induced forgetting could also be responsible for the recent finding that witnesses tend to forget scenes that are omitted from a subsequent re-showing of the incident (Wright *et al.*, 2001; Williams *et al.*, 2002). In this case, the strengthening of rival memory traces for items included in the re-showing would be expected to inhibit the memory traces for the items omitted from the re-showing.

Children as witnesses

There is a considerable amount of evidence to indicate that small children are more prone to suggestion, contamination and memory distortion than adults (Loftus, Levidow, & Duensing, 1992). Furthermore, the accuracy of children's memories seems to be particularly susceptible to deterioration over longer retention periods. As noted earlier, Flin *et al.* (1992) found that the accuracy of children's eyewitness reports deteriorated more rapidly over a 5 month period than did those of adults. Dekle, Beale, Elliott and Huneycutt (1996) found that children are also more likely to identify the wrong person in an identity parade, although interestingly they are also more likely to make correct identifications compared with adult witnesses. These findings may therefore reflect a general tendency for children to make positive identifications more readily than do adults.

Further evidence for the high susceptibility of child witnesses to post-event contamination comes from a recent study by Poole and Lindsay (2001), in which children aged 3–8 years took part in a science demonstration. The children then listened to parents reading a story that contained some events they had experienced and some that they had not. Subsequent testing revealed that many of the fictitious events were recalled as though they had been experienced. When the children were given instructions to think carefully about the source of their memories (known as "source monitoring"), some of the older children withdrew their incorrect reports, but this did not occur with the younger children in the sample. The authors concluded that the possibility of contamination from post-event information was a serious concern with very young child witnesses, who seem to have particular difficulty in monitoring the source of a memory trace. Reviewing such studies of child eyewitnesses, Gordon, Baker-Ward and Ornstein (2001) concluded that while young children could provide accurate information under the right circumstances, they were particularly susceptible to suggestion and prone to reporting events that did not actually occur. Furthermore, Gordon *et al.* reported that there was no reliable way that even experts could distinguish between true and false memories in the testimony of small children, so particular caution is required in cases involving child witnesses.

General conclusions and recommendations

A number of lessons can be learned from the research summarised in this section, which have important implications for those who are involved in the process of obtaining eyewitness testimony. From the evidence we have so far, it is clear that the memory of a courtroom witness can easily be affected by contamination from subsequent information, which might be included in police questioning, newspaper articles, or discussions with lawyers or other witnesses. There are important lessons to be learned from these studies. In the first place, judges and juries should understand that witnesses cannot be expected to have infallible memories, and they should not place too much reliance on the evidence of eyewitness testimony alone. To minimise the risk of post-event contamination, statements should be taken from witnesses as soon as possible after the incident in question, and witnesses should be allowed to use notes when giving their evidence in court at a later date rather than relying on memory. Police interviewers should be particularly careful about their methods of questioning, and should avoid the use of leading questions or suggestions that might implant misleading information in the witness's head. Finally, there is a need for particular care when obtaining eyewitness testimony from small children, because of the difficulty they tend to have in distinguishing between real events and imagined or suggested events.

Kassin, Tubb, Hosch and Memon (2001) carried out a survey of 64 experts on eyewitness testimony, and found that there was a clear consensus view (using a criterion of 80% of the experts being in agreement) that certain findings were now supported by sufficient evidence to be presented in court as reliable phenomena. These included the contamination of testimony by post-event information, the importance of the wording of questions put to witnesses, the influence of prior attitudes and expectations on testimony, and the suggestibility of child witnesses. All of these were regarded as established phenomena that could be legitimately stated in a court of law by an expert witness in support of their case. It could be added that those involved in the legal process require a clear understanding of these established phenomena to minimise the risk of a miscarriage of justice through the fallibility of courtroom testimony.

3.5 The cognitive interview

Techniques used in the cognitive interview

Traditional police interviews were not based on scientific research. Usually, the witness would simply be asked to describe what happened, without any guidance or help of any kind. In recent years, cognitive psychologists have devised a new method of questioning witnesses based on the findings of cognitive research, an approach known as the "cognitive interview" (Geiselman *et al.*, 1985). The main techniques used in the cognitive interview ("CI") are summarised in Figure 3.7.

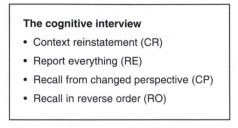

The cognitive interview

- Context reinstatement (CR)
- Report everything (RE)
- Recall from changed perspective (CP)
- Recall in reverse order (RO)

Figure 3.7 The main techniques used in the cognitive interview procedure

The first component of the cognitive interview is the CR (context reinstatement) instruction, in which the witness is asked to recall contextual details of the scene witnessed, in the hope that these may provide contextual cues that will help with the retrieval of more relevant information. The second component is the RE (report everything) instruction, in which the witness is encouraged to report everything they can remember about the incident, regardless of how trivial or unimportant it may seem. The main purpose of this instruction is again to increase the extent of context reinstatement.

Laboratory studies have shown that context reinstatement can help to elicit memories in a variety of settings (Greenspoon & Ranyard, 1957; Godden & Baddeley, 1975; Jerabek & Standing, 1992), and its effectiveness is believed to derive from the principles of encoding specificity and feature overlap (Tulving & Thomson, 1973). These findings and theories are explained in our previous book (Groome *et al.*, 1999). When applied to the task of questioning an eyewitness to a crime, the witness is encouraged to recall various aspects of the context in which the crime occurred, in addition to the crime itself. For example, the witness might be asked to describe the clothes they were wearing that day, what the weather was like, and what the surroundings were like at the crime scene. Although such contextual details may seem to be trivial and largely incidental to a crime, their retrieval can provide valuable extra cues that may jog the witness's memory for the retrieval of more central aspects of the crime itself. The interviewer may attempt to increase context recall by asking specific questions about details of the crime setting, though of course taking care not to include any information in the question that might be incorporated into the witness's memory by suggestion. The witness may also be shown photographs of the crime scene, or they may actually be taken back there. There may also be an attempt to replicate their mental state during the crime, by asking them to try to remember how they felt at the time.

There are two further components to the CI technique, namely the CP (change perspective) instruction and the RO (reverse order) instruction. In the CP instruction, the witness is asked to try to imagine how the incident would have appeared from the viewpoint of one of the other witnesses present. For example, following a bank robbery a witness who had been queuing at the till might be asked to consider what the cashier would have been likely to see. Finally, the RO instruction involves asking the witness to work backwards in time through the events they witnessed. Both the CP and the RO instructions are based on the principle of multiple retrieval routes (Bower, 1967), which suggests that different components of a memory trace will respond to different retrieval cues. Thus it is assumed that if one cue fails to retrieve the trace, then a different cue may possibly be more effective. It has been suggested (Milne & Bull, 1999) that the RO instruction may offer an additional benefit, in that it may help to prevent the witness from relying on "scripted" descriptions based on his or her previous knowledge of a typical crime or incident rather than on the actual events witnessed.

Subsequent research has led to a refined version of the original cognitive interview, known as the "enhanced cognitive interview" (Fisher, Geiselman, Raymond, Jurkevich, & Warhaftig, 1987). The main additional features of the enhanced cognitive interview are that eyewitnesses are encouraged to relax and to speak slowly, they are offered comments to help clarify their statements, and questions are adapted to suit the understanding of individual witnesses.

The effectiveness of the cognitive interview

Geiselman *et al.* (1985) carried out a scientific evaluation of the CI procedure. They showed their participants videotapes of a simulated crime, after which different groups of participants were interviewed using a cognitive interview, a traditional interview or an interview with the witness under hypnosis. Geiselman *et al.* found that the cognitive interview was in fact successful in coaxing more information from the witness than either of the other two methods. The results of this study are summarised in Figure 3.8.

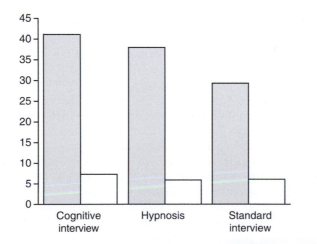

Figure 3.8 The number of correct (▨) and incorrect (☐) statements made by witnesses under three different interview conditions

Many subsequent studies have confirmed the value of the cognitive interview in eliciting more information from witnesses. In a review of 42 CI studies, Koehnken, Milne, Memon and Bull (1999) concluded that the CI procedure consistently elicits more correct information than a standard interview, for both adult and child witnesses. However, Koehnken *et al.* (1999) found that in many cases witnesses questioned by CI techniques also recalled more incorrect information than with a standard interview. This is perhaps inevitable given that the CI procedure generates an increase in the amount of information retrieved overall, and involves a lowering of the criterion for reporting information. The cognitive interview thus generates more information of any type, including both correct and incorrect facts. This is a small but significant drawback of the CI procedure, and it is important that those using the cognitive interview should take this into account when evaluating their witnesses' statements.

However, while the cognitive interview may generate a few additional errors, there is evidence that it can reduce a witness's susceptibility to misinformation and suggestion effects. For example, Milne and Bull (2003) found that using the cognitive interview made children less suggestible than children undergoing a standard interview, as they were less likely to be influenced by subsequent questions containing misleading script-related information. Holliday (2003) has also reported that using the CI procedure on very young children reduced their vulnerability to misinformation effects.

Having established the advantages of the cognitive interview in laboratory studies, Fisher, Geiselman and Amador (1990) investigated its effectiveness in real-life police work. Police detectives were trained to use the enhanced cognitive interview with real crime witnesses, and the technique was found to achieve a significant increase in the amount of information they recalled. Subsequent research has suggested that while some components of the cognitive interview seem to be very effective, others may offer little benefit. Studies of actual police work revealed that the CR (context reinstatement) and RE (report everything) instructions had been fairly widely adopted and were judged by police officers to be effective, but the CP (change perspective) and RO (reverse order) instructions were rarely used and were not considered to be particularly helpful (Boon & Noon, 1994; Clifford & George, 1996). These studies were carried out fairly soon after the introduction of the cognitive interview, when relatively few police officers had received CI training. More recently, Kebbel, Milne and Wagstaff (1999) carried out a survey of 161 police officers, and found that 96 had received formal CI training and the other 65 had not, though even in the untrained group there was some use of CI techniques. Responses from the group as a whole indicated that the cognitive interview was considered to be a useful technique among police officers, although there was concern about the increased amount of incorrect information generated, and also about the extra time required to carry out the interview. Officers reported that they made extensive use of the RE instruction, and some use of the CR instruction, but the CP and RO instructions were rarely used because they took up too much time and were not thought to be as effective.

Surveys of real-life police work provide an important indication of which CI techniques are more popular among police interviewers, but in some cases the preferences expressed by police officers simply reflected their personal preferences and time constraints. Experiments have therefore been carried out to obtain a more objective estimate of the effectiveness of the various different components of the cognitive interview. Geiselman, Fisher, MacKinnon and Holland (1986) showed the same video to four groups of witnesses, then subjected each group to a different CI procedure to test their recall. One group received the full CI procedure, a second group received only the CR instruction, a third group received only the RE instruction, and a fourth group were given a traditional interview without using any CI techniques. The retrieval scores showed a significant advantage for the full cognitive interview, with the CR and RE groups both recalling fewer items; the traditional interview proved to be the least effective. Milne and Bull (2002) carried out a similar comparative study, but this time tested all of the CI techniques, both individually and in various combinations. Their study sample included children of two different age groups as well as a group of adults, all of whom were interviewed after viewing a video of an accident. Milne and Bull found that each of the four CI instructions (i.e. CR, RE, CP, RO), when used in isolation, offered an advantage over the standard interview, though none of them proved to be any more effective than providing a simple instruction to "try again". However, the use of CR and RE instructions in combination offered a significant improvement over any of the CI instructions used alone. No significant differences were found between the child and adult groups in this study.

From these studies it would appear that some components of the cognitive interview are more effective than others. Further research is needed to clarify this issue, but based on the research reported so far, it would appear that the CR and RE instructions are more effective than the CP and RO instructions, especially when CR and RE are used in combination.

Limitations of the cognitive interview

One limitation of the CI procedure is that it does not appear to be suitable for use with very small children. Geiselman (1999) concluded from a review of previous studies that the cognitive interview was not very effective with children younger than about 6 years, and could actually have a negative effect on the accuracy of their statements in some cases. This may reflect the fact that small children sometimes have difficulty in understanding the requirements of the CI procedure. For example, Geiselman noted that small children had particular difficulty with the "change perspective" instruction, and he suggested that this component of the cognitive interview should be omitted when questioning small children. However, the cognitive interview has been found to be reasonably effective for older children, even as young as 8–11 years (Memon, Wark, Bull, & Koehnken, 1997; Larsson et al., 2003; Milne & Bull, 2003).

A further limitation of the CI procedure is that it is not very effective when very long retention intervals are involved. For example, Memon et al. (1997) carried out a study in which children aged 8–9 years were questioned on their recall of a magic show they had seen earlier. When they were tested 2 days after the show, those questioned using CI techniques recalled more correct facts than those questioned by a standard interview. However, the superiority of the CI technique completely disappeared when the children were tested 12 days after the magic show. Geiselman and Fisher (1997) carried out a review of 40 previous CI studies and concluded that while the cognitive interview had consistently generated more recalled facts than a standard interview after a short retention interval, the benefits of the cognitive interview tended to decrease at longer retention intervals. However, in most cases there were still benefits at long retrieval intervals, even though they were significantly reduced. In fact, the benefits of the CI procedure can persist over long periods, even with child witnesses. It is possible that the diminishing effectiveness of the cognitive interview with longer retention periods may be a characteristic of younger children, because studies of adults and older children appear to show more lasting CI effects. For example, Larsson *et al.* (2003) showed a film to a group of 10- to 11-year-olds and found that the CI procedure produced an improvement in retrieval that was not only found at an interval of 7 days, but was maintained after a delay of 6 months.

Another limitation of the CI procedure is that it does not seem to help with face recognition and person identification (Clifford & Gwyer, 1999). This finding was confirmed by Newlands, George, Towell, Kemp and Clifford (1999), who concluded that the descriptions of criminals generated by the cognitive interview were no better than those resulting from standard interviewing procedures, in the judgement of a group of experienced police officers. The factors involved in face recognition are taken up in Chapter 4 of this book, which is concerned with the study of eyewitness identification.

On balance, the cognitive interview appears to be a useful technique to help to increase the amount of correct information a witness is able to recall. However, the cognitive interview also has a number of serious limitations and drawbacks, which practitioners need to be aware of, notably its unsuitability for use with very young child witnesses, its reduced effectiveness at longer retention intervals, and its failure to assist with the identification of faces by eyewitnesses.

Summary

- Memory for real-life autobiographical experiences tends to be far more accurate and durable than memory for items tested in a laboratory experiment.
- Recent events and experiences are generally easier to remember than events and experiences from the distant past, but older people recall more events from their early adult years. This phenomenon is known as the "reminiscence bump".
- Early infancy is one period of life that appears to be particularly difficult to remember, and most people recall virtually nothing from the first 2 years of their lives. This phenomenon is known as "infantile amnesia".
- Most people retain very vivid and lasting memories of where they were and what they were doing at the time of hearing news of a shocking event. This phenomenon is known as "flashbulb memory".
- Although some researchers argue that flashbulb memory involves a special encoding process, this view has been challenged by the finding that

flashbulb memories are subject to errors and forgetting, as with other forms of memory.

- The recollections of eyewitnesses are not very reliable, and are responsible for the wrongful conviction of many innocent people.
- Eyewitness testimony has been found to be vulnerable to contamination from post-event information (the "misinformation effect"), and it is also susceptible to conformity effects and cross-witness contamination.
- While young children can provide accurate information under the right circumstances, they are particularly susceptible to suggestion and prone to reporting events that did not actually occur.
- The cognitive interview is a method of questioning witnesses based on the findings of cognitive research, notably the use of context reinstatement. This procedure consistently elicits more correct information than a standard interview, both in laboratory studies and in actual police work.
- The cognitive interview has a number of important limitations, notably that it is not suitable for use with very small children, it is not very effective when very long retention intervals are involved, and it does not help with face recognition.

Further reading

Gruneberg, M., & Morris, P. (1992). *Aspects of memory: The practical aspects*. London: Routledge. Contains chapters on various aspects of everyday memory, including a chapter by Fruzzetti *et al.* on eyewitness testimony.

Milne, R., & Bull, R. (1999). *Investigative interviewing: Psychology and practice*. Chichester, UK: Wiley. A detailed review of the research on the interviewing of eyewitnesses and the use of cognitive interviewing techniques.

Robinson-Riegler, G., & Robinson-Riegler, B. (2004). *Cognitive psychology*. Boston, MA: Pearson. Contains up-to date sections on autobiographical memory, flashbulb memory and eyewitness testimony.

Face identification

4.1 Introduction

On 8 March 1985, Kirk Bloodsworth of Baltimore, Maryland, USA was convicted and sentenced to death for the rape, sexual assault and first-degree premeditated murder of a 9-year-old girl. Bloodsworth's story started in July 1984 when the body of a girl who had been beaten with a rock, sexually assaulted and strangled was found in woods. The police investigation quickly identified Bloodsworth as a suspect. A total of five eyewitnesses identified Bloodsworth as the man they had seen with the girl before her death, and another person identified Bloodsworth from a police sketch produced by the witnesses. Further witnesses stated that Bloodsworth had told them he had done a "terrible" thing that would affect his marriage, and under interrogation Bloodsworth mentioned a bloody rock. Finally, there was evidence that a shoe impression found near the victim's body was made by a shoe of the same size as those worn by Bloodsworth. Bloodsworth appealed and his conviction was overturned on the basis that the police had withheld information from defence attorneys about an alternative suspect. However, Bloodsworth was re-tried and re-convicted, this time receiving two consecutive life sentences.

After an unsuccessful appeal, Bloodsworth's lawyer requested that semen stains found on the victim's clothing be analysed using the sophisticated DNA analysis techniques that had become available since the initial investigation of the crime. Fortunately, the samples had been stored and DNA analysis revealed that Bloodsworth's DNA did not match any of the evidence tested – Bloodsworth could not have been responsible for the semen found on the victim's clothing. After re-testing by prosecutors confirmed these results, Bloodsworth was finally released from prison in June 1993 and was pardoned in December 1993. Bloodsworth had served almost 9 years of a life sentence and had spent 2 years on death row awaiting execution for a crime he did not commit, but the most shocking aspect of this case is that it is not unique. This is just one of 28 such cases of post-conviction DNA exoneration detailed in a report by the US National Institute of Justice (Connors, Lundregan, Miller, & McEwan, 1996). This report provides a graphic illustration of a major theme of this chapter, and a major focus of applied psychological research in recent years – the fallibility of eyewitness identification evidence.

There is evidence that not even fame can protect you from false eyewitness identification. In the British general election held in 2001, the Right Honourable Peter Hain was re-elected to Parliament and was appointed Minister of State at the Foreign and Commonwealth Office, but 25 years earlier on 24 October 1975 he was arrested and charged in connection with a bank robbery. At the time of his arrest, Hain was well known locally as an anti-apartheid campaigner and political activist. He was also completing his PhD thesis, and on the day of the robbery drove into town to buy a new ribbon for his typewriter. While purchasing the ribbon, he was spotted by a group of children who had earlier joined in the pursuit of a man who had attempted to rob a local bank. Three of the children decided that Hain was the robber and reported the details of his car to the police, who subsequently arrested him at his home. Some of the witnesses later picked Hain out of a lineup, but not before the news of his arrest together with his photograph had appeared on the front page of many newspapers. Ultimately, Hain was shown to be innocent of all charges, but it is possible that a less eloquent and well-connected person might have been convicted for a crime he did not commit. The witnesses probably identified Hain because he appeared familiar, but he was familiar because of his public campaigning, not because they had seen him holding up a bank.

As Hain (1976) stated after his acquittal, "Once positively identified I was trapped almost as much as if I had been caught red-handed at the scene of the crime. It is tremendously difficult to dispute identification if the eyewitness is sure, and virtually impossible to challenge it directly. All one can do is challenge it indirectly, through calling other eyewitnesses or establishing an alibi. But an alibi is often very difficult to establish with absolute certainty" (p. 100).

As this case illustrates, for many years we have been aware that confident, honest and well-meaning witnesses can be completely mistaken in their identification of a suspect. However, the advent of DNA testing and the certainty that it brings has provided some insight into the scale of the problem. In this chapter, we will look at some of the recent psychological studies that illustrate the application of perceptual research to legal questions. The chapter addresses research relating to:

- identification evidence procedures;
- composite construction;
- the use of photo-identity cards.

4.2 Face-processing models

In the last few decades, a considerable amount of research has been directed towards understanding the processes involved in human face recognition. Humans are social animals who live in complex groups, and to be successful we need to identify individuals within our group. If for a moment you imagine the consequences of being unable to distinguish between your lecturers and your fellow students, you will realise just how vital this ability is. We have all made occasional recognition errors, perhaps accosting a complete stranger thinking them to be a close friend, but it is the rarity of these errors that demonstrates just how good we are at recognising familiar faces. We can recognise friends at considerable distances, under poor or changing lighting conditions, after many years of ageing and despite changes to hairstyle, facial hair or the addition or removal of facial paraphernalia such as eyeglasses. Our representation of familiar faces seems to be of such quality that it is immune to all these changes and, as a result, we often don't even notice when a close friend changes their hairstyle.

The most widely cited model of face processing is that described by Bruce and Young (1986). This model (see Figure 4.1) incorporated knowledge gained from experimental studies of normal individuals and from studying individuals with a variety of neurological deficits (Groome *et al.*, 1999). This is a useful model that predicts and explains many observations, such as the independence of the processes involved in the recognition of a familiar face and the identification of facial expressions. However, this model, like all the alternatives, focuses on the recognition of familiar faces. As such, these models are of limited value in seeking to understand why the witnesses in the cases of Bloodsworth and Hain (see Introduction to this chapter) made such serious errors of identification.

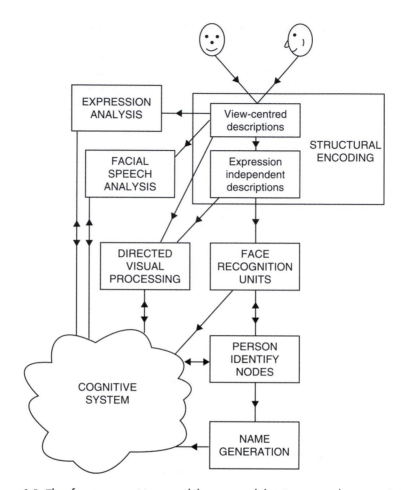

Figure 4.1 The face recognition model proposed by Bruce and Young (1986). Although this model has been very successful in helping us to understand the processes involved in the recognition of familiar faces, it is of limited value when seeking to explain the factors that can lead to recognition errors with unfamiliar faces

The explanation for these dramatic failures of recognition might lie with the distinction between our ability to process familiar and unfamiliar faces. The fact that we are very good at recognising familiar faces does not necessarily mean that we will be able to identify a previously unfamiliar face when we see it for the second time. We are so good at recognising our friends and acquaintances that we assume that if we were the witness to a crime we would easily be able to recognise the culprit in an identity parade or lineup. But the culprit will be unfamiliar, and as a result we may significantly overestimate the ability of a witness to identify the perpetrator. This distinction between our ability to process familiar and unfamiliar faces is dramatically demonstrated by some recent applied research undertaken to assess the utility of photo identity cards. This research is described later in this chapter.

4.3 Dangerous evidence: eyewitness identification

If the police investigating a crime manage to locate a witness and a suspect, they will arrange an identification procedure. Identification procedures are the mechanisms used by police to collect evidence regarding the identity of the perpetrator. The most common form of identification procedure is the lineup or identification parade, in which the suspect is placed among a number of similar-looking "foils" and the witness is asked to attempt to identify the perpetrator from the array. In the UK, the term identification *parade* is used to describe this process, which is almost always conducted "live". In the United States, the terms *lineup* or *photospread* are more commonly used to describe a process that is likely to be conducted using photographs. Regardless of the precise procedure used, juries find identification evidence very compelling and an eyewitness's positive identification of a suspect dramatically increases the probability that a jury will convict (Leippe, 1995). It is because eyewitness identification evidence is so compelling that it is also so dangerous. As we shall see, it is clear that an honest witness can be sincere, confident, convincing and quite wrong when making an identification.

Researching the factors affecting identification accuracy

The accuracy of eyewitness identification evidence has been a major focus of applied psychological research in the last three decades, with a very large number of studies employing the same basic methodology. Using this methodology, a group of "participant-witnesses" views a staged crime scene. This might be a live event that takes place in front of a class of students, or a video of a crime, or a slide show depicting a crime. After a delay that might last for a few seconds or a few weeks, the participants are then asked to attempt to identify the perpetrator in some form of identification procedure. The experimental variable under investigation might be manipulated either during the event (for example, by allocating participants to one of several lighting conditions) or during the identification procedure (for example, allocating participants to one of several different identification procedures).

An important indicator of the quality of the research in this field is the inclusion of both target-present and target-absent lineups. As we have seen, the police sometimes make a mistake and put an innocent suspect in an identification procedure, and for this reason it is vital that researchers estimate the ability of witnesses to recognise that the perpetrator is not present in the lineup. The Bloodsworth case (see Introduction to this chapter) shows us that the failure of witnesses to determine that the perpetrator is "not present" can have very serious consequences. The target-absent lineup is an experimental manipulation designed to measure the ability of the participant-witness to make this determination. In a target-absent lineup, the perpetrator (or his photograph) is not included and the parade is entirely made up of similar-looking "foils".

Meta-analytic techniques

Applied researchers have used this basic methodology to identify, and measure the impact of, variables that can affect the accuracy of eyewitness identification evidence. More recently, the results of these numerous studies have been reviewed and summarised using meta-analytic techniques. Meta-analysis represents a very significant methodological advance in psychological research in the last few decades. Over the years, many researchers have addressed similar questions – for example, the effect of the presence of a weapon on eyewitness identification accuracy. Meta-analysis combines the results of these various studies using special statistical techniques that allow us to determine the magnitude and reliability of an effect. For example, Steblay (1992) reviewed 19 studies of the effect of the presence of weapons on lineup identification accuracy and determined that there was a small but reliable effect. Witnesses who had seen a weapon were significantly less likely to correctly identify the perpetrator than witnesses who had not seen a weapon.

Meta-analytic techniques are particularly valuable in research that is applicable to the law. In many jurisdictions, a psychologist will only be allowed to act as an expert witness and inform the court of the results of relevant psychological research if he or she can first satisfy the judge that the evidence that is being presented is valid. Meta-analytic studies provide this evidence.

System variables and estimator variables

Factors that affect identification accuracy are often classified as either system or estimator variables, a distinction first proposed by Wells (1978). Wells was keen to encourage researchers to focus their attention on those variables that could be influenced by members of the criminal justice system, which Wells referred to as "system variables". For example, if we determine that the manner in which the police conduct an identification procedure affects the accuracy of the identification, then we can take action to change the procedures used and to improve the quality of future identification evidence. However, some variables are not within the control of members of the criminal justice system. For example, the knowledge that the presence of a weapon reduces the accuracy of identification evidence does not help us to improve the quality of the identification evidence. There is nothing psychologists or anyone else can do about the presence of a weapon after the fact. These variables Wells referred to as "estimator variables" – all psychologists can do is estimate their impact on performance.

Surveys of experts

Before they accept expert testimony from a scientist, in some countries a judge may also require proof that the research findings on which the evidence is based are widely accepted by scientists working in the area. This requirement is met by a different type of research – surveys of experts' opinions. These give us a very useful distillation of the opinions of experts in the field, which, in turn, are based on a thorough familiarity with the research evidence available. The findings of the latest such survey in the field of eyewitness testimony research were published in 2001 (Kassin *et al.*, 2001). The results of this survey are summarised in Table 4.1.

4.4 Factors affecting identification evidence

Identification procedures

Various different procedures are used to collect identification evidence, and these are codified to differing degrees in different countries. In the UK, Code D of the 1984 Police and Criminal Evidence Act (PACE) tightly controls all identification procedures. PACE specifies precisely the circumstances under which the various procedures can be adopted, the exact steps to be followed by the police, and the rights of the suspect. This is in stark contrast to the situation in the USA, where there is considerable variation in the procedures adopted between and even within States. Across jurisdictions, the most commonly used identification procedures include the show-up, the mugshot search and the live or photographic lineup. In the show-up, the suspect is presented to the witness who is asked whether this was the person they observed. In mugshot or photo-album identification, a witness is invited to search through police databases of known suspects. In a photographic lineup, a witness attempts to pick the perpetrator from an array of photographs that includes the suspect (who may or may not be the perpetrator). In a live or corporeal lineup, the witness attempts to pick the perpetrator from among a group of similar-looking individuals. In the USA most identifications are from photographs rather than from live lineups (Wells *et al.*, 1998), whereas in the UK the requirements of the PACE mean that almost all identifications are from live parades.

For some time it has been argued that mistaken identification is responsible for more wrongful convictions than any other form of evidence. However, it is recent advances in the science of forensic DNA analysis that have given us the clearest insight into just how dangerous eyewitness identification evidence can be. These technical developments have enabled the retrospective testing of preserved evidence, such as blood and semen samples. This process has resulted in the exoneration of a number of people who were previously convicted of serious crimes, including murder and rape. A report commissioned by the National Institute of Justice (Connors *et al.*, 1996) analysed 28 cases of so-called DNA exoneration. The report is available online (http://www.ncjrs.org) and the detailed analysis of these cases makes sobering reading. Subsequently, Wells *et al.* (1998) identified 12 additional cases of DNA exoneration, taking the total to 40. Of these 40 cases, 90% involved eyewitness identification evidence. In some cases more than one witness falsely identified the innocent suspect, and in one case five separate witnesses all falsely identified the same suspect (the case of Bloodsworth with which we introduced this chapter). We must be cautious in our interpretation of these figures. In particular, we do not know how significant the eyewitness identification evidence was to the jury in each of these cases, or what percentage of cases

Table 4.1 A summary of the findings of the survey of experts conducted by Kassin *et al.* (2001)

Topic (estimator or system variable)	Statement posed to experts	% reliable	% testify
Lineup instructions (S)	Police instructions can affect an eyewitness's willingness to make an identification	98	79
Wording of questions (S)	An eyewitness's testimony about an event can be affected by how the questions put to that witness are worded	98	84
Confidence malleability	An eyewitness's confidence can be influenced by factors that are unrelated to identification accuracy	95	79
Mugshot-induced bias (S)	Exposure to mugshots of a suspect increases the likelihood that the witness will later choose that suspect in a lineup	95	77
Post-event information	Eyewitness testimony about an event often reflects not only what they actually saw but information they obtained later on	94	83
Child suggestibility (E)	Young children are more vulnerable than adults to interviewer suggestion, peer pressures and other social influences	94	81
Attitudes and expectations	An eyewitness's perception and memory for an event may be affected by his or her attitudes and expectations	92	70
Hypnotic suggestibility (S)	Hypnosis increases suggestibility to leading and misleading questions	91	76
Cross-race bias (E)	Eyewitnesses are more accurate when identifying members of their own race than members of other races	90	72
Alcoholic intoxication (E)	Alcoholic intoxication impairs an eyewitness's later ability to recall persons and events	90	61
Weapon focus (E)	The presence of a weapon impairs an eyewitness's ability to accurately identify the perpetrator's face	87	77

Accuracy–confidence (E)	An eyewitness's confidence is not a good predictor of his or her identification accuracy	87	73
Forgetting curve (E)	The rate of memory loss for an event is greatest right after the event and then falls off over time	83	73
Exposure time (E)	The less time an eyewitness has to observe an event, the less well he or she will remember it	81	68
Unconscious transference (E)	Eyewitnesses sometimes identify as a culprit someone they have seen in another situation or context	81	66
Presentation format (S)	Witnesses are more likely to misidentify someone by making a relative judgement when presented with a simultaneous (as opposed to a sequential) lineup	81	64
Showups (S)	The use of a one-person showup instead of a full lineup increases the risk of misidentification	74	59
Description-matched lineup (S)	The more that members of a lineup resemble a witness's description of the culprit, the more accurate an identification of the suspect is likely to be	71	48
Lineup fairness (S)	The more members of a lineup resemble the suspect, the higher the likelihood that identification of the suspect is accurate	70	54
Child witness accuracy (E)	Young children are less accurate as witnesses than adults	70	59
False childhood memories	Memories people recover from their own childhood are often false or distorted in some way	68	52
Colour perception	Judgements of colour made under monochromatic light (e.g. an orange streetlamp) are highly unreliable	63	27
Stress (E)	Very high levels of stress impair accuracy of eyewitness testimony	60	50
Elderly witnesses (E)	Elderly witnesses are less accurate than younger adults	50	38
Hypnotic accuracy (S)	Hypnosis decreases* the accuracy of an eyewitness's reported memory	45	34

Table 4.1 — continued

Topic (estimator or system variable)	Statement posed to experts	% reliable	% testify
Identification speed	The more quickly a witness makes an identification upon seeing the lineup, the more accurate he or she is likely to be	40	29
Trained observers	Police officers and other trained observers are no more accurate as eyewitnesses than is the average person	39	31
Event violence (E)	Eyewitnesses have more difficulty remembering violent than non-violent events	37	29
Discriminability	It is possible to reliably discriminate between true and false memories	32	25
Long-term repression	Traumatic experiences can be repressed for many years and then recovered	22	20

Although some of the topics covered in the survey are not strictly relevant to the discussion of identification accuracy, all 30 items have been included in this table. The first column gives the topic and (in parentheses) an indication of whether this is an estimator (E) or a system (S) variable (where this distinction is not applicable, no label is applied). The third column gives the percentage of the 64 expert psychologists who stated that they thought the phenomenon was reliable enough for psychologists to present in courtroom testimony (yes/no question). The fourth column indicates the percentage who indicated that, under the right circumstances, they would be willing to testify in court that the phenomenon was reliable (yes/no question). Depending on where we choose to draw the line between what is "generally accepted" by the experts and what is not, we find that between the first 16 and 20 items are strongly supported by the experts (Kassin et al. employ an agreement level of at least 80%)

This survey was an update of an earlier survey covering mostly the same topics (Kassin et al., 1989). It is interesting to note how opinions of experts have changed between these two survey dates. One significant change is that in the 1989 survey only 83% of experts were prepared to testify about the effect of weapon focus (compared with 87% in the 2001 survey). This change probably reflects the intervening publication of a meta-analysis of the research on this topic undertaken by Steblay (1992). This suggests that the experts are sensitive to developments within the literature and are basing their judgements about these topics on the published research.

* Wording revised for clarity.

of this sort involve eyewitness identification evidence. However, as Wells *et al.* (1998) explain: "It is important to note that the 40 cases . . . were not selected because they happen to have eyewitness identification evidence as the primary evidence. Instead, these cases are simply the first 40 cases in the US in which DNA was used to exonerate a previously convicted person. Hence, the kind of evidence that led to these wrongful convictions could have been anything. The fact that it happens to be eyewitness identification evidence lends support to the argument that eyewitness identification evidence is among the least reliable forms of evidence and yet persuasive to juries" (p. 604).

Wells *et al.* (1998) estimate that each year in the USA approximately 77,000 suspects are charged after being identified by an eyewitness. They estimate that the eyewitness experts available in the USA could together cover no more than 500 cases each year, which means that well over 99% of all defendants go to trial without an expert to explain to the court the unreliability of eyewitness identification evidence. Of course, many of these accused will be guilty and there will be other evidence to support the identification. However, the analysis of DNA exoneration cases shows us that in some cases it will be this eyewitness identification evidence, perhaps together with the lack of a reliable alibi and other circumstantial evidence, that will lead a jury to convict.

Relative versus absolute judgements

A major problem with any identification procedure is the tendency for the witness to assume that the perpetrator will be present in the lineup. Sometimes the perpetrator will not be present, and the suspect detained by the police will be innocent. If the lineup consists of a total of nine people (as in the UK) and is conducted completely fairly, then our innocent suspect has an 11.1% (1 in 9) chance of being identified. However, in most cases the odds of the suspect being identified are probably much higher than this. There are several reasons for this. First, it is likely that the suspect will be a reasonable match to the description given by the witness; however, it is often the case that many of the "foils" bear very little resemblance to the perpetrator (Valentine & Heaton, 1999). Secondly, it is very easy for the procedure to be biased, either intentionally or unintentionally, in a way that increases the odds of the suspect being selected. For example, in a live procedure, the posture of parade members, their clothing, the interactions between the parade members and the police, and many other subtle cues can indicate the identity of the suspect. In a photo lineup, a major concern is whether the photographs are all comparable (showing the same view, in similar lighting and same background and size). During a live parade, a defendant will probably have a legal representative to observe the procedure, but this is not usually the case with photo identifications. However, this might not be a very significant safeguard; Stinson, Devenport, Cutler and Kravitz (1996) showed that lawyers may not be able to determine whether or not an identification procedure is being conducted fairly.

Imagine for a moment that you were a witness to a crime and that a few weeks later you were asked to attempt to identify the perpetrator from a lineup. What would you attempt to do as you looked down the line of faces? You should compare each face to your memory of the perpetrator, but it appears that many witnesses compare the lineup members to each other in an attempt to find the person who looks most like the perpetrator. This choice of strategy is crucial. If a witness attempts to identify the person most like the perpetrator, they will always identify someone, even on those occasions when the perpetrator is not present in the lineup. This relative judgement process will often therefore lead to a false identification. However, if a witness attempts to compare his or her memory of the perpetrator with each member of the lineup in turn, then this more absolute process should lead to fewer false identifications when the perpetrator is not present. Wells and colleagues (Lindsay & Wells, 1985; Wells *et al.*, 1998) developed "relative judgement theory" to describe this difference in the strategies that witnesses could adopt.

What is the evidence that witnesses do employ a relative judgement strategy? Wells *et al.* (1998) identified several sources of evidence. Some of the best evidence for this relative strategy comes from the behaviour of participant-witnesses who view a staged or video crime and then attempt to identify the culprit (see for example Wells, 1993). In these studies, the experimenter can measure the percentage of participant-witnesses who pick the culprit when he is present in the lineup and compare this with the performance of participant-witnesses who are presented with a culprit-absent lineup (one in which the photograph of the culprit has been removed and not replaced). Suppose, for example, that in the target-present lineup 50% of the participant-witnesses picked the culprit, 25% made no choice and the other 25% of choices were spread approximately evenly across the other lineup members. You might think that this indicates that half of our witnesses have positively identified the culprit. However, if we look at the figures from the culprit-absent lineup, we might find that only 30% have made no choice (the correct decision), with the remaining 70% of participants identifying one of the other members of the lineup. This tells us that most of the participants in the culprit-present lineup condition who picked the culprit would have picked someone else if he hadn't been present – this is a strong indication that the participants are picking the person most like the culprit rather than making a positive and absolute identification.

The evidence that the wording of the lineup instructions influences witnesses also suggests that they are employing a relative strategy. For example, Malpass and Devine (1981) gave witnesses to a staged act of vandalism one of two sets of instructions. In the biased group, the instructions encouraged the belief that the culprit was in the lineup – the witnesses were asked "which of these is the person you saw?" This instruction resulted in a significant inflation in the rate of false identifications from culprit-absent lineups relative to a set of instructions that emphasised that the culprit may or may not be present and which clearly explained the option of responding "not present" (78% compared to 33%). Even more subtle variations in the instructions can have dramatic effects on the rate of choosing in culprit-absent lineups. Cutler, Penrod and Martens (1987) found instructing participants to choose the member of the lineup who they believed to be the robber was sufficiently biasing to inflate the rate of choosing in culprit-absent parades to 90%, relative to unbiased instructions, which reminded the participants that the culprit might not be in the lineup. Clearly, participants are very sensitive to these subtle influences and this suggests that they are willing to choose the lineup member most like the culprit. A meta-analysis of the effects of instructions on lineup performance (Steblay, 1997) indicated that an unbiased instruction, that the culprit "might or might not be present", resulted in a reduction in the number of false identifications from culprit-absent lineups without reducing the number of correct identifications in culprit-present lineups. However, it should be noted that Koehnken and Maass (1988) argued that this effect only held for experimental studies in which the participants were aware that they were involved in a simulation. They found that when their participants believed that they were making a real identification, the nature of the instructions did not significantly affect the number of false identifications in culprit-absent lineups. Koehnken and Maass (1988) concluded, "eyewitnesses are better than their reputation" (p. 369).

Simultaneous and sequential identification procedures

Given this evidence that witnesses make the mistake of attempting a relative rather than an absolute judgement, a procedure that encourages more absolute judgements should have the effect of decreasing the number of false identifications in culprit-absent lineups without impacting on the number of correct identifications in culprit-present lineups. One such procedure is the sequential lineup procedure.

In a conventional or simultaneous identification procedure, the witness is able to view all the members at once and can look at each lineup member any number of times before making a choice. Relative judgement theory (Lindsay & Wells, 1985) suggests that it is this ability to compare lineup members to each other that encourages witnesses to adopt a relative judgement strategy. In the sequential identification procedure devised by Lindsay and Wells (1985), the witness is shown the members of the lineup one at a time and must decide whether or not each is the culprit before proceeding to consider the next lineup member. In sequential lineups, it is not possible to simultaneously compare lineup members to each other, and the witness is not allowed to see all of the members of the lineup before making a decision. This change in procedure is thought to encourage the use of a more absolute strategy where the witness compares each member of the lineup to his or her memory of the appearance of the perpetrator. In their initial evaluation, Lindsay and Wells (1985) found that the sequential and simultaneous lineups resulted in almost identical rates of correct identification in culprit-present lineups. However, when the lineup did not include the culprit, the rate of false identification was very much lower in the sequential than the simultaneous lineups (17% versus 43%). This result has since been replicated several times and the comparison of sequential and simultaneous parades was the subject of a recent meta-analysis (Steblay, Dysart, Fulero, & Lindsay, 2001), which considered the results from 30 experiments involving a total of 4145 participants. Steblay *et al.* found that participant-witnesses faced with sequential lineups were less likely to make an identification than participants who were presented with a simultaneous lineup. In the case of target-present lineups, this more cautious approach leads to a failure to identify the target (false rejection errors); however, in the case of target-absent lineups, this caution causes a reduction in the number of false identifications made. It appears, then, that the benefits of the sequential lineup in terms of increased protection for the innocent are made at the cost of an increased danger that the guilty will escape identification. However, this increased ability to identify culprits in target-present simultaneous lineups almost disappeared when Steblay *et al.* (2001) considered only the most realistic studies that involved live events, realistic instructions, a single culprit and adult witnesses who were asked to describe the perpetrator before attempting to identify him. Thus in real life the sequential lineup does seem to offer the police a "win–win" solution, with similar levels of correct identification and reduced levels of false identification relative to the traditionally used simultaneous lineup.

The most recent studies have sought to explain the reason for this advantage of sequential over simultaneous lineups. Kneller, Memon and Stevenage (2001) asked participants to identify a man earlier seen on video attempting to break into parked cars. Participants were randomly allocated to either sequential or simultaneous lineups that were either target-present or target-absent. Once they had made their decision, the participants were questioned regarding the strategy they employed. Participants who saw a simultaneous lineup were much more likely to claim to have used a relative strategy (e.g. "I compared the photographs to each other to narrow the choices") than were participants who saw a sequential lineup. However, some-what unexpectedly, absolute strategies (e.g. "His face just 'popped out' at me") were claimed by participants in both the sequential and simultaneous conditions. As Kneller *et al.* (2001) comment, "the present results would suggest that superiority in accuracy rates associated with the sequential lineups might not have been due solely to the use of absolute strategies *per se*" (p. 667).

4.5 Influencing policy

Given the accumulation of data regarding the fallibility of identification evidence, psychologists have been seeking to influence policy makers to modify procedures so as to reduce the likelihood of false convictions. The process of achieving policy change is difficult and often causes controversy among scientists who disagree about the type of recommendations that should be made. Changes to the way in which identification evidence is collected illustrate some of these difficulties.

In 1998, the executive committee of the American Psychology-Law Society solicited a report that would recommend improvements in the procedures used to conduct identification procedures. The report (Wells *et al.*, 1998), often referred to as the "Lineups White Paper", recommended four changes to the procedures then commonly used in the USA. On the basis of the available evidence, Wells *et al.* recommended:

1   The person conducting the identification procedure should not know which member is the suspect.
2   The witness should be warned that the perpetrator might not be present.
3   The fillers (the persons or photographs of persons other than the suspect) should be selected to match the witness's verbal description of the perpetrator.

4   The witness should be asked to describe his or her confidence in their identification immediately after the identification is made.

For a discussion of how these recommendations compare to the requirements of the UK regulations, see Kebbell (2000).

Given the research that has been described above, you might be surprised that the use of sequential lineups was not recommended. It is interesting to examine why each of these recommendations was made, and why the use of sequential lineups was not. The first recommendation requires that the lineup be conducted "blind". Given the evidence of the effect of biasing instructions reviewed above, the justification for this recommendation is clear. In the UK, PACE requires that an officer not directly involved in the investigation conducts the identification procedure; however, this officer will know which member of the lineup is the suspect. The White Paper recommendation is rather easier to implement in regions where lineups are usually conducted using photographs, than in a country such as the UK where they are corporeal (live). In a live parade, it is difficult to arrange things so that the officer organising the parade does not know who the suspect is, given the suspect will often be in police custody, will have a legal representative present and is allowed to specify where he or she stands in the parade.

The second requirement is uncontroversial. As Malpass and Devine (1981) demonstrated, explaining the "not present" option to witnesses reduces the number of false identifications. In the UK, PACE requires the police to tell witnesses that "the person you saw may or may not be in the parade" and that they should say if they cannot make a positive identification.

The third requirement is rather more controversial in that it requires that the fillers be matched not to the appearance of the suspect, but to the verbal description provided by the witness. The justification for this recommendation is based on research (e.g. Wells, Rydell, & Seelau, 1993) that shows that when only a few members of the lineup resemble the description provided by the witness, the rate of false identification rises relative to when all lineup members match the verbal description. Wells *et al.* (1993) argue that matching foils to the witness's verbal description rather than the suspect's appearance will result in lineups that are fair to the suspect while avoiding the witness being confronted with a line of "clones" who all look very similar to each other and to the suspect.

The fourth recommendation is that the witness's confidence in their identification decision should be recorded. This might seem surprising given that there is considerable evidence that the relationship between confidence and accuracy is at best a weak one (for a review, see Sporer, Penrod, Read, & Cutler, 1995). Put simply, a witness can be both very confident and very wrong. However, the reason for this recommendation has more to do with jurors' perception of the relationship between confidence and accuracy than the real relationship. Jurors find confident witnesses very convincing and many studies (see for example Cutler, Penrod, & Dexter, 1990) have found that mock-jurors were more likely to convict when a witness reported that she was 100% confident than when she was 80% confident. In addition, surveys have found that both the general public and groups of professionals within the legal system hold the belief that a confident witness is more likely to be accurate in his or her identification than a less confident witness (e.g. Brigham & Wolfskeil,

1983; Noon & Hollin, 1987). Finally, it has been shown that a witness's confidence in their identification is malleable and may change over time. Research has shown that it is easy to artificially inflate a witness's confidence in their identification by providing subtle clues about their performance. For example, Luus and Wells (1994) showed that if participant-witnesses who had made a false identification were led to believe that a co-witness had identified the same person from the lineup, their confidence in the accuracy of their decision increased. Thus, confidence is a very dangerous thing – it is a very poor predictor of accuracy, it is convincing to juries and subject to manipulation and changes over time. Wells *et al.* (1998) recommended that confidence at the time of the identification be recorded so a jury might at least get a true picture of the witness's confidence when they made their decision. We might not be able to convince jurors that confidence tells us little about accuracy, but we can at least reduce the impact of inflated reports of confidence.

The fifth recommendation

Wells *et al.* (1998) stated: "were we to add a fifth recommendation, it would be that lineup procedures be sequential rather than simultaneous" (p. 639). However, only four recommendations were made, and Wells *et al.* chose not to advocate sequential lineups partly because they felt that their value was not "self-evident" to the police and partly because a switch from simultaneous to sequential identification procedures would require a significant change in police practices.

This decision not to recommend the use of sequential lineups despite the evidence in favour of their use has been the topic of some debate (see for example Kemp, Pike, & Brace, 2001; Levi & Lindsay, 2001; Wells, 2001). Levi and Lindsay (2001) argued that psychologists should adopt a "best practices" approach and therefore recommend any procedure supported by the available evidence. Wells (2001) countered this argument, suggesting that a more pragmatic approach is preferable as this is more likely to achieve beneficial change in the long run.

Recent changes suggest that the more pragmatic approach might have been the appropriate one. In April 2001, the Attorney General of New Jersey issued a new set of guidelines that recommend that when possible a sequential lineup be administered by an officer who is "blind" to the identity of the suspect. At the same time, in the UK changes to the relevant parts of PACE are being made to allow the police to make use of video or VIPER (see below) parades that are inherently sequential. Thus, the change from simultaneous to sequential parades is beginning to occur.

4.6 The VIPER parade

The requirement in the UK to conduct live identification parades is an onerous one for the police. To conduct a live parade, it is necessary to assemble together at the same time and place, the suspect, his or her legal representative, a number of volunteers to act as foils and the witness. A survey by Slater (1995) demonstrated that about 50% of the identification parades attempted by UK police failed to take place because one of the parties involved (usually the witness) failed to turn up. In an attempt to tackle this problem, the police in the West Yorkshire region of the UK developed an innovative video-based identification system called VIPER (Video Identification Parade Electronic Recording; see Kemp *et al.*, 2001). At the heart of the VIPER system is a database of short video sequences of each of many hundreds of people. When a suspect is arrested, he is filmed using standard video equipment. The short video sequence shows the suspect turning his head to show the front and two side views of his face. This video sequence is then digitally transmitted to headquarters, where it is checked and compared with the database of potential foils. Several potential foils are selected and sent back to the police station where the suspect is given the opportunity to select which foils will be used and where in the lineup his own image will appear. The lineup is then recorded to videotape. The final lineup shows each of the nine members of the parade one at a time, and each is shown executing the same standard head movements. Research by Pike, Kemp, Brace, Allen and Rowlands (2000) showed that VIPER parades were much less likely to be cancelled than live parades (5.2% of VIPER parades cancelled compared with 46.4% of live parades) and that the two types of parades were equally likely to result in the suspect being chosen. Given that at the time the law required that VIPER parades could only be used in cases where it was difficult to conduct a live parade, this was a very encouraging result. It is interesting to note that VIPER parades are also inherently sequential, with each parade member being shown to the witness one at a time. Recently (2002), changes have been made to UK law, which make VIPER parades legally equivalent to live parades. As a result, police are now permitted to conduct a VIPER parade without first having to show that they could not conduct a live parade. As a result, in the UK an increasing number of identification parades will be sequential in nature.

4.7 Making faces: facial composite systems

The research described so far in this chapter clearly illustrates just how difficult it is to recognise an unfamiliar face. However, witnesses are not only asked to identify a suspect; if the police do not have a suspect, they will often ask a witness to describe the perpetrator. Here, the task for the witness is to recall and describe a face rather than to recognise it. Psychologists have known for many years that we perform better at tasks requiring recognition than recall (e.g. Mandler, Pearlstone, & Koopmans, 1969), so we might expect that a witness faced with the task of describing an unfamiliar perpetrator would struggle to produce a useful description. Let us now investigate the applied research relevant to this issue.

When a witness to a crime is interviewed by a police officer, one of the first questions asked is often "can you describe the perpetrator". A witness's description of a perpetrator is regarded as vital to an investigation and, in addition to providing a verbal description, a witness may be asked to attempt to construct a pictorial likeness. In previous decades, these likenesses were constructed by artists working with the witness. The artist would interview the witness about the appearance of the suspect and begin to sketch the face and offer alternatives to the witness. In this way the witness and artist would produce a likeness that could then be used by the police in their investigation. Although some police services still use artists in this way, most likenesses are now produced using a composite system. Composite systems allow the witness to construct a facial likeness by combining different facial features selected from a large database. The first composite system widely used in the USA was called Identikit and consisted of a number of hand-drawn components that could be combined to create a likeness. In 1971 in the UK, Penry introduced the Photofit system, which comprised a number of photographs of each of the facial features. Using these systems, witnesses were asked to browse through catalogues of features to select the eyes, nose, hairline, and so on, closest to that of the perpetrator. The composite was then constructed from the selected features and could be enhanced by the addition of hand-drawn components such as scars. I will refer to these paper-based systems as "first-generation" composite systems.

Evaluating first-generation composite systems

Two independent teams of psychologists used similar methodologies to systematic-ally evaluate these first-generation composite systems. In the USA, Laughery and colleagues (e.g. Laughery & Fowler, 1980) worked on the Identikit system, while Ellis, Davies and Shepherd (1978) evaluated the British Photofit system. Laughery and Fowler allowed participants to interact with a "target" for 6–8 min before working with either an artist or an Identikit operator to produce a likeness. The likenesses produced were rated by a team of independent judges, and compared to images produced by the artists and operators while they observed the targets directly. We would expect that the images produced by the artists or operators to be better rated than those produced by the participant-witnesses working from memory. However, what Laughery and Fowler found was that the sketches were rated as better likenesses than the Identikit images, and that while sketches pro-duced with the target in view were better than those made from memory, there was no difference in the quality of the Identikit images produced under these two conditions. This result suggests a floor effect; the quality of the Identikit likenesses was so low that it made no discernible difference if the likeness was made from memory or while looking at the target.

Ellis *et al.* (1978) reached similar conclusions regarding the utility of the Photofit system. Participant-witnesses watched a target on video before either working with an operator to produce a Photofit or making their own sketch of the face. These images were produced either from memory or with the target in view. When working from memory, the Photofit was regarded as marginally better than the witnesses' own drawings. However, the critical finding was that, as in the Laughery and Fowler study, the composite images produced with the target in view were no better than those made from memory. When the target was in view, the participant's own drawings of the target were rated as better likenesses than the Identikit images, suggesting that the police might do as well to hand the witness a piece of paper and a pencil!

The results of these and other tests of the first-generation composite systems were not favourable, and Christie and Ellis (1981) claimed that composites were no more useful than the verbal descriptions generated by witnesses.

Second-generation composite systems

The 1980s saw the introduction of several computer-based composite systems, such as FACE (Australia), Mac-a-Mug Pro (USA) and E-Fit (UK). These systems, which I will refer to as "second-generation" systems, utilise microcomputer technology to allow the manipulation of large databases of features. The use of computer image manipulation software allows these components to be combined without the distracting lines between features that characterise the first-generation systems. This is probably an important enhancement; Ellis *et al.* (1978) found that the addition of these lines to the photograph of a face significantly disrupted recognition of the face. Another important enhancement is that second-generation systems also use drawing software to allow the operator to edit and modify components and to "draw" additional components requested by the witness. Gibling and Bennett (1994) demonstrated that artistically enhanced Photofits were better recognised than unmodified composites. A less skilled operator will probably be more able to enhance a composite using a computer rather than traditional tools. In addition, some systems allow features to be individually moved and re sized within the face. This is critical, as it has been demonstrated that we are sensitive to even very small displacements of facial features (Kemp, McManus, & Pigott, 1990).

A critical deficiency of many of these systems, both first- and second-generation, is that they require the witness to select a feature in isolation from the face. For example, in the Identikit and Photofit systems, the witness searches through a catalogue of eyes looking for eyes that match their memory of the suspect. You can imagine how hard this task may be, and there is evidence that we are poor at recognising features outside the context of the whole face, an effect referred to as the "face superiority effect" (Homa, Haver, & Schwartz, 1976). Tanaka and Farah (1993) trained participants to name a series of composite faces. Once trained, the participants could easily distinguish a particular face, for example that of "Larry", from another face that was identical except for the nose. However, the same participants were less likely to be able to identify which of the two noses was Larry's when they were shown in isolation, or when the face was "scrambled" (see Figure 4.2). There is considerable evidence that we see a face as a perceptual whole and not simply the sum of its parts, a fact clearly demonstrated by Young, Hellawell and Hay (1987; see Figure 4.3). Not even a composite operator remembers a friend as someone with a number 36 nose and 12b eyes! The E-fit composite system is designed in an attempt to address these deficits. E-Fit is widely used by police in the UK and is unique in that the witness is never allowed to see features outside the context of the whole face. The operator interviews the witness using the cognitive interview (see Chapter 3) and then enters the description into a series of text screens, one for each feature. When completed, the system assembles the composite that best matches the description, inserting "average" components for any feature not described. Only at this point is the witness allowed to view the composite and to make modifications (see Figures 4.2 and 4.4 for examples of E-Fit composites).

A very different system was recently developed in Australia. ComFit was designed for use by rural police who might be an enormous distance from a computer-based composite system. Witnesses using the ComFit system work through

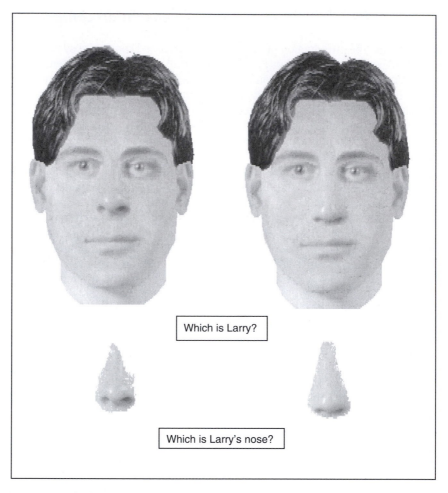

Which is Larry?

Which is Larry's nose?

Figure 4.2 Which is Larry's nose? Individuals can learn to recognise the face on the left as Larry, despite the fact that the face on the right is identical except for the nose. However, if the noses are presented outside the context of the face, it is much more difficult to recognise Larry's nose. After Tanaka and Farah (1993)

a paper catalogue of features. The selected features are listed by number and the information faxed to headquarters where the composite is assembled. The image is then faxed back to the witness who can request modifications. The evidence of the face superiority effect reviewed earlier would lead us to predict that composites produced using the E-Fit system should be better likenesses than composites assembled using the ComFit system; however, to date, no such comparison has been made.

Relatively few studies have attempted to evaluate the second-generation systems. Koehn and Fisher (1997) found that Mac-a-Mug Pro images constructed by participants 2 days after seeing a target were rated as extremely poor likenesses and

Figure 4.3 Who are these men? Even though the two pictures of these two recent US presidents are not well aligned and the join between the halves is obvious, the composite image gives a strong impression of a novel face and it is surprisingly difficult to recognise the personalities who have "donated" the top and bottom halves of the faces. The task is made slightly easier by turning the page upside-down or covering one half of the composite. After Young *et al.* (1987)

allowed other participants to pick the target out of a six-person lineup less often than would be expected by chance.

The utility of composite systems

One of the few studies to compare first- and second-generation systems was undertaken by Davies, Van der Willik and Morrieson (2000). These authors found that the E-Fit composites were measurably superior to Photofit likenesses only when constructed under rather unrealistic conditions, such as when the target was familiar to the witnesses, or when they worked from a photograph to construct the composite. However, more positively, E-Fits constructed with the target in view were better likenesses than those made from memory – a result that suggests E-fits are not prone to the floor effects that characterise Photofit composites.

Despite this slightly more positive evaluation of the E-Fit system, the very poor results of the laboratory-based evaluations would lead the police to abandon the production of composites. However, a glance at your local newspaper or television will demonstrate that composites are still widely employed as an investigative tool by the police. It would appear that the police have rather more confidence in these systems than psychologists. Some psychologists have attempted to evaluate these systems by surveying police officers involved in investigations where composites were employed, and in some cases by comparing the composite to the perpetrator once apprehended. This might seem like an obvious approach to take, but this kind of archival research is very difficult to do well. The records kept by the police are not always as complete as this approach requires, it is often very difficult for officers to estimate the investigative value of a composite to a case, and it is likely that the estimates given will be biased by many factors. Bearing these caveats in mind, what do the available surveys tell us? A survey conducted for the British Home Office (Darnborough, 1977; cited by Clifford & Davies, 1989) sought to evaluate the impact of composites on a total of 729 investigations. It was reported that in 22% of the 140 solved cases, the composites had been of significant use, while in 20% they had been of no use at all to the investigation. Bennett (1986) surveyed 512 officers who had requested Photofits. Of the 360 questionnaires returned, only 14 indicated that the crime had been solved. However, without some idea of the clear-up rate for comparable crimes in the same location at the same time, it is difficult to interpret this apparently low success rate. It is perhaps significant though, that in half of the solved cases the Photofit was judged to be a good likeness, and in three others was judged to be a fair likeness to the perpetrator. Kapardis (1997) reported an unpublished evaluation of the FACE composite system used in some Australian states. Kapardis reported that FACE led to the charging of a suspect in 19% of cases and helped to confirm a suspect in a further 23% of cases. In the cases where it was possible to compare the offender to the composite, more than half of the composites were rated 3 or higher on a 5-point likeness scale.

It is difficult to know how to interpret these figures, but it is probably fair to say that although far from spectacular, these results do suggest that composites are valuable in a small but significant number of cases. I have discussed the utility of composite systems with police composite operators in both the UK and Australia, and the almost universal view is that some witnesses are able to produce very accurate composites and that many witnesses are able to produce composites that can make a valuable contribution to an investigation. So how do we reconcile this view with the results of the laboratory studies described earlier?

There could be several explanations. It could be that it is difficult to produce a good likeness of some faces because the composite systems do not contain enough examples of each feature. There is some evidence to support this view. Distinctive faces are normally easier to recognise than "typical" or average faces (Light, Kayra-Stuart, & Hollander, 1979). It is therefore interesting that Green and Geiselman (1989) found that composites of "average" faces were easier to recognise than composites of more distinctive faces, suggesting that composite systems may lack the features necessary to construct a distinctive face. This problem has been partially tackled by the increasing size of the databases used in second-generation systems. For example, the E-Fit system has over 1000 exemplars of each facial feature. Other systems, such as FACE, also include capture facilities to allow an operator to capture a feature from a photograph of a face if the witness describes a component not available in the standard kit. However, it is important to note that a fundamental assumption behind all these composite systems is that there is a finite number of "types" of each feature. These systems assume that any face can be made if we have a large enough database. This assumption may be invalid. Alternatively, the problem may lie with the laboratory evaluations of these systems. Let us pause for a moment to consider how the police use composites. When a witness produces a composite, the police publish it together with other information, including physical description (height, weight, clothing, etc.), the time and date of the crime, and any other information such as type of vehicle driven or accent. The police hope that someone who is familiar with the perpetrator will see the image and recognise that it is a "type-likeness" of someone who also matches other aspects of the description. The police report that the people who recognise composites and inform the police of their suspicions usually know the person they name to the police. Despite what you see in fiction films, perpetrators are not usually recognised by strangers while walking down the street, but by friends, neighbours, work colleagues and relatives. Often these people will already have suspicions; the role of the composite is to raise the level of suspicion in the mind of members of the public to the point that they are prepared to pick up the telephone and contact the police.

We know that the processes involved in the recognition of familiar faces are different from those involved in the recognition of unfamiliar faces (Young *et al.*, 1985). It is important, therefore, that we evaluate composite systems using judges who are familiar with the target. Indeed, the ideal measure of composite quality is "spontaneous naming" by individuals familiar with the target. To this end, Brace, Pike and Kemp (2000) and Allen, Towell, Pike and Kemp (1998) measured the ability of a group of undergraduates to name a set of composites of famous people (see Figure 4.4). These composites were produced by participant-witnesses working directly or via an operator, and either from memory or from a photograph. The majority of the composites were spontaneously named by at least one of the judges. Relatively few incorrect names were offered and some composites were recognised by almost all participants. These results go some way to justify the confidence of the police; it is possible to produce high-quality likenesses that can be named spontaneously by judges, even without the other background information supplied by the police in a real case. However, in this study both the judges and the witnesses were familiar with the famous targets, making this a rather unrealistic task.

Thus, the latest research suggests that these systems may be rather more useful than was implied by the earlier research. There is no doubt that it is extremely difficult for a real witness to produce a high quality composite, but it seems that it can be done and that these systems can sometimes make a useful contribution to criminal investigations.

4.8 When seeing should not be believing: facing up to fraud

The results of the research on lineups and composite construction described so far in this chapter reflect the fact that we find it difficult to remember, recognise and describe unfamiliar faces. However, it has recently emerged that we even find it difficult to match images of unfamiliar faces. This is an important finding, because the task of unfamiliar face matching is one that must be undertaken by someone charged with the job of checking photo-identity documents.

The designs of coins and paper bank notes usually include an image of the face of the head of state. It is thought that this tradition originated in part in an attempt to reduce forgery, the theory being that the bearer would be more able to detect changes to the appearance of a familiar face (that of the head of state) than to other aspects of the design of the coin or note. Today, we often rely on facial images as a means of fraud protection. Driver licences, passports and many other forms of identity may include a photograph of the card's bearer. But just how effective are

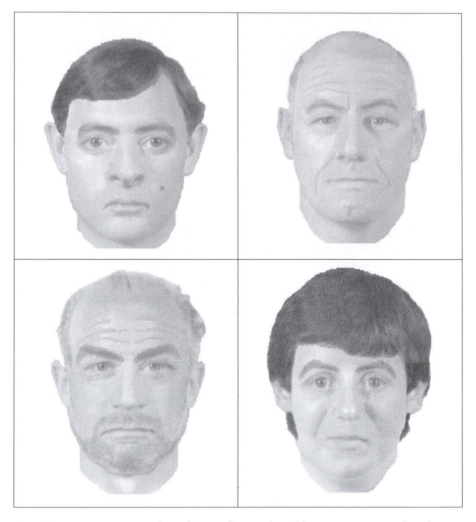

Figure 4.4 Can you name these famous faces? These likenesses were produced using the E-Fit system (Brace *et al.*, 2000). Clockwise from top left the composites represent actor Rowan Atkinson ("Mr Bean"), actor Patrick Stewart (*Star Trek*'s "Captain Jean-Luc Picard"), musician Paul McCartney and actor Sean Connery

these forms of photo ID? It is widely believed that the inclusion of a photograph of the legal bearer is a simple and effective device to prevent fraud. However, there is very little evidence to support this belief.

Kemp, Towell and Pike (1997) undertook a field experiment to assess the utility of photo credit cards as a fraud prevention measure. The study took place in a supermarket and the shop's cashiers were paid to help with the research. The "shoppers" in the study were a group of 50 students who were each issued with four real photo credit cards. The first of these cards, the "unchanged" card, showed a photo-graph of the shopper as they appeared on the night of the study. The "changed" card showed a photograph of the shopper, but showing small changes to their appearance relative to the night of the study. For example, some of the women had a change of hairstyle, with the hair worn loose for the photograph and tied back on the night of the study. These changes were modest and designed to model the natural changes in a person's appearance that might occur over the lifetime of a photo-identity card. The remaining two credit cards were designed to model attempted fraud and included photographs of persons other than the shopper. The "matched foil" card included a photograph of someone who looked similar to the shopper, while the "unmatched foil" card included a photograph of someone judged to look unlike the shopper (see Figure 4.5).

The shoppers were instructed to attempt to use these cards to purchase goods at each of six tills, and the cashiers were instructed to check the cards and decide whether to allow the transaction. In a later debriefing, the cashiers admitted that they had been more vigilant than normal, and that they had guessed that some of the photographs would be of someone other than the shopper. Despite this high level of vigilance, the results were a major surprise. It was found that the cashiers failed to identify more than half of the fraudulent "matched foil" cards and even accepted 34% of the fraudulent unmatched foil cards. In addition, when the cashiers did challenge a shopper, they often made mistakes. About 15% of the changed appearance cards were rejected by the cashiers despite being valid, and even a few of the unchanged appearance cards were rejected. Kemp *et al.* (1997) concluded that photo credit cards were unlikely to have a significant impact on fraud levels, and this research dramatically demonstrates how difficult it can be to match images of an unfamiliar face; a conclusion that has since been supported by several other studies (e.g. Bruce *et al.*, 1999).

Summary

- Identification of an unfamiliar person is difficult and error-prone.
- Honest and sincere witnesses are likely to make mistakes when asked to identify an unfamiliar perpetrator, and these errors may result in innocent people facing long terms of imprisonment.
- Psychologists have identified many variables that impact on identification accuracy, and have classified these into system and estimator variables. This research has enabled psychologists to identify changes in procedures that might reduce the rate of false identifications.
- Many psychologists are now seeking to implement changes in public policy so that the legal procedures used to collect identification evidence reflect the latest research findings.
- The difficulty in the accurate perception of unfamiliar faces is not only limited to tasks involving face recognition. Research has shown that it is also difficult to describe and construct a likeness (composite) of an unfamiliar face seen only once before. However, there is some evidence that composites can be of value to police investigations.

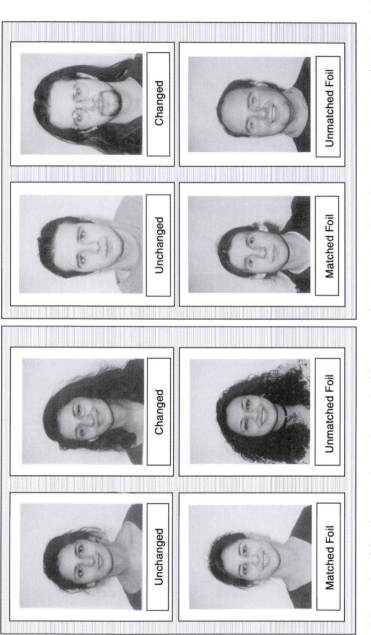

Figure 4.5 Examples of the photographs used on each of four types of credit card used by "shoppers" in the study of Kemp *et al.* (1997). Within each panel, the top left and top right photographs are of the shopper who presented the credit card. The photograph on the bottom left of each panel was included on the "matched foil" card and shows a person who was selected on the basis that they looked somewhat like the shopper. The bottom right image was used on the "unmatched foil" card and shows a person of the same sex and race but otherwise unlike the shopper. The cashiers in this study were unable to determine if the photograph on the credit card was of the shopper who presented it. They falsely accepted more than half of the "matched foil" and some of the "unmatched foil" cards, and falsely rejected several of the changed and even some of the unchanged cards

- Even the task of matching images of unfamiliar faces has been shown to be error-prone, a finding that has important implications for the use of photo-identity documents. It appears that the difficulties involved in unfamiliar face processing do not stem only from difficulties in remembering unfamiliar faces, but also from the difficulty in accurately perceiving these faces.

Chapter 5

Working memory and performance limitations

5.1 Introduction

Working memory

The term "working memory" refers to the system responsible for the temporary storage and concurrent processing of information. Working memory has been described as "the hub of cognition" because it plays a central role in human information processing (Haberlandt, 1997). Traditional approaches to the study of short-term memory focused on information storage and tended to neglect concurrent processing (Mathews, Davies, Westerman, & Stammers, 2000). As a result, early models generally ignored the function of short-term memory in everyday cognition where the processing of temporarily stored information is essential to task performance. The concept of working memory has greater ecological validity than traditional models because it can be applied to a wide range of everyday cognitive activities. Indeed, working memory appears to play an important role in comprehension, learning, reasoning, problem solving and reading (Shah & Miyake, 1999). Therefore, it is not surprising that working memory models have been usefully applied to a variety of real-world tasks, including air-traffic control, learning programming languages, industrial tasks, human–computer interaction and mental calculation. These diverse activities have been selected for discussion in this chapter to demonstrate the generality and utility of the working memory paradigm in applied research.

The Baddeley and Hitch model of working memory

The most influential model of working memory has been developed by Alan Baddeley and his collaborators (e.g. Baddeley & Hitch, 1974; Baddeley, 1986; Baddeley & Logie, 1999). In this view, the working memory system has a tripartite structure consisting of a supervisory "central executive" and two slave systems – the "phonological loop" and the "visuo-spatial sketchpad". Each of the components of working memory has limited capacity. The central executive "manages" working memory by executing a number of control processes. Some examples of executive control processes are: maintaining and updating task goals, monitoring and correcting errors, scheduling responses, initiating rehearsal, inhibiting irrelevant information, retrieving information from long-term memory, switching retrieval plans and coordinating activity in concurrent tasks. The central executive also coordinates the activity of the phonological loop and the visuo-spatial sketchpad. The phonological loop is a speech-based processor consisting of a passive storage device, the "phonological store", coupled to an active subvocal rehearsal mechanism known as the "articulatory loop" (Baddeley, 1997). It is responsible for the short-term retention of material coded in a phonological format. The visuo-spatial sketchpad retains information coded in a visuo-spatial form. In recent formulations of the model, the visuo-spatial sketchpad has been decomposed into two functionally separate components: the "visual cache", which provides a passive visual store, and an active spatial "inner scribe", which provides a rehearsal mechanism (Baddeley & Logie,

1999). Thus, both the visuo-spatial sketchpad and the phonological loop incorporate active rehearsal processes (see Figure 5.1).

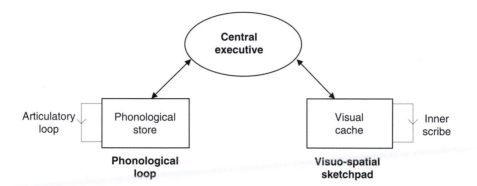

Figure 5.1 A model of working memory based on Baddeley and Logie (1999)

Individual differences in working memory capacity

One of the most important determinants of individual variation in cognitive skills is working memory capacity (Turner & Engle, 1989). Given the centrality of working memory in human cognition, we would expect individual differences in working memory capacity to manifest themselves in the performance of a range of information-processing tasks. Engle, Kane and Tuholski (1999) identified a number of empirical studies that demonstrate a relationship between working memory capacity and performance in reading comprehension, speech comprehension, spelling, spatial navigation, learning vocabulary, note-taking, writing, reasoning and complex learning. Performance in these and related tasks can be predicted by individual differences in the working memory capacities of the participants. The measure of individual working memory capacity is known as "working memory span", and several tests of working memory span have been devised (e.g. Daneman & Carpenter, 1980; Turner & Engle, 1989). All such tests involve storage and concurrent processing. For example, Daneman and Carpenter's (1980) span test requires participants to read lists of sentences. In addition to processing the sentences for meaning (the processing load), the participants are also required to recall the last word in each sentence (the storage load). Turner and Engle (1989) developed a span test in which participants are required to store words while processing arithmetic problems. In both tests, the participant's working memory span is taken to be the number of words correctly recalled.

In addition to the measures of global working memory capacity developed by Engle and his colleagues, several studies have measured individual variation in specific components of working memory (e.g. Shah & Miyake, 1996). This work has revealed that it is possible for an individual to score high on spatial working memory while scoring low on verbal working memory (and vice versa). Moreover, this approach is not confined to laboratory-based studies; it has also been applied to real-world tasks such as wayfinding in the built environment (e.g. Fenner, Heathcote, & Jerrams-Smith, 2000) and learning computer programming languages (e.g. Shute, 1991; see Section 5.2).

5.2 Working memory and computer programming

Learning programming languages

Given the importance of working memory in the acquisition of natural language (Gathercole & Baddeley, 1993), it is possible that working memory may also play a role in learning computer programming languages. Research on this question may have important educational implications. Shute (1991) argued that if we can identify the cognitive factors involved in the acquisition of programming skills, we may be able to improve the design of effective computer programming curricula, providing educators with an explicit framework upon which to base instruction. In Shute's study, 260 participants received extensive instruction in the Pascal programming language. The training consisted of three learning stages, each designed to teach one of the three different abilities involved in programming skill acquisition:

- *Understanding*: identifying the initial and final problem states, recognising the key elements of the problem and the relationship between them, and considering the operations needed to find a solution.
- *Method finding*: arranging problem elements into a solution.
- *Coding*: converting the natural language solutions from the two earlier stages into Pascal programming code.

Following the training stages, Pascal knowledge and skill were measured in three tests of increasing difficulty, each consisting of 12 problems. Test 1 required participants to identify errors in Pascal code. Test 2 involved the decomposition and arrangement of Pascal commands into a solution of a programming problem. Test 3 required participants to write entire programs as solutions to programming problems. Each participant also completed a battery of cognitive tests that examined working memory capacity, information-processing speed and general knowledge. Each category was examined in three different domains: spatial, verbal and quantitative. Quantitative working memory capacity was measured by the following tests, each of which requires the temporary storage and concurrent processing of numerical information: ABC Recall; Mental Mathematics; Slots Test. Verbal working memory capacity was measured using three tests that involved the storage and concurrent reorganisation or semantic processing of verbal information: ABCD Test; Word Span Test; Reading Span. Finally, spatial working memory was measured by tests requiring the storage and simultaneous manipulation or processing of visuo-spatial information: Figure Synthesis; Spatial Visualisation; Ichikawa. The results revealed that "the working memory factor was the best predictor of Pascal programming skill acquisition [$p = 0.001$]. With all the other variables in the equation, this was the only one of the original cognitive factors that remained significant" (Shute, 1991, p. 11).

Shute's (1991) findings appear to have implications for teaching programming languages. Indeed, Shute concluded that the importance of working memory as a predictor of programming skill acquisition suggests that instruction should be varied as a function of individual differences in working memory span. There are several ways that this might be achieved. One approach might be to adjust the informational load during training so that it is commensurate with the working memory capacity of the trainee. Other techniques might involve supplying trainees with error feedback and the provision of external working storage to reduce the internal working memory load. In practice, it is likely that an effective approach would require that several such techniques were used in combination.

Shute interpreted her results as indicating that working memory contributes to both declarative and procedural learning in computer programming. Support for this view came from a study reported in Kyllonen (1996). In this work, the performance of participants acquiring computer programming skill was examined in terms of orthogonal factors of procedural learning and declarative learning. Working memory capacity was found to account for 81% of the variance in the declarative learning factor, while no other factor had a significant effect. Working memory capacity was also found to be the most influential determinant of procedural learning, accounting for 26% of the variance on this factor. One interesting implication of these results is that the load placed on working memory by declarative information is greater than that imposed by the procedural content of the task. This may be because some procedures are partly automatised and, consequently, make less demand on working memory resources. It is worth noting that during training some of the initially declarative knowledge may become proceduralised, with the result that the load on working memory is reduced and resources are liberated for use on other components of the task.

Expert programming

The concept of working memory has also been applied to understanding the behaviour of experienced computer programmers in real-world tasks. Altmann (2001) has used a form of episodic long-term working memory or "near-term memory" to model the behaviour of expert programmers engaged in the modification of large computer programs. Altmann grounds his model of near-term memory in the SOAR cognitive architecture (Newell, 1990). Altmann argues that during inspection of the program, the programmer is presented with considerably more information than can be retained in memory. During the session, the programmer will encounter items that relate to previously encountered details. The expert programmer will be able to retrieve these details by scrolling back through the listing to their location. Retrieval is accurate even when the number of such details exceeds working storage capacity. According to Altmann, this is because each time a detail is encountered the programmer attempts to understand it by using their expert knowledge of programming. This produces an "event chunk" specifying the episodic properties of the detail (e.g. its location in the listing), which are retained in near-term memory. Thus near-term memory provides a link between external information and expert semantic knowledge with the result that key details can be retrieved when needed. In this way, expert knowledge acts as a determinant of programming expertise by "mediating access" to relevant details. In Altmann's (2001) view, expert program problem solving "depends as much on episodic detail built up in memory during task performance as it does on stable semantic knowledge brought to the task" (p. 207), and that programming environments should therefore be designed to facilitate access to relevant details in memory.

5.3 Working memory and air-traffic control

The role of working memory in the ATC task

Air-traffic control (ATC) is a complex and demanding safety-critical task. The air-traffic controller deals with transient information in a constantly changing air-traffic environment. This information must be retained in working storage for tactical use or strategic planning; as a result, performance of the ATC task is constrained by working memory limitations (Stein & Garland, 1993; Garland, Stein, & Muller, 1999). Working memory allows the controller to retain and integrate perceptual input (from the radar screen, flight strips and audio communications) while simultaneously processing that information to arrive at tactical and strategic decisions. Tactical information retained in working memory includes aircraft altitudes, airspeeds, headings, call-signs, aircraft models, weather information, runway conditions, the current air-traffic situation, and immediate and potential aircraft conflicts (Stein & Garland, 1993).

An overarching requirement of the ATC task is to maintain "separation" between aircraft (usually a minimum of 5 nautical miles horizontally). The controller must anticipate and avoid situations which result in a loss of separation (aircraft "conflicts"). The dynamic nature of the air-traffic environment ensures that this requires the execution of several control processes within working memory. One such control process involves the scheduling of actions. For example, a controller may instruct several aircraft within their sector to alter altitude or heading. It is imperative that these manoeuvres are carried out in an order that avoids the creation of conflicts between aircraft. In addition, scheduling must be responsive to unanticipated changes in the air-traffic environment, which may require schedules to be updated (see Niessen, Leuchter, & Eyferth, 1998; Niessen, Eyferth, & Bierwagen, 1999). Dynamic scheduling of this sort is an important function of working memory (Engle *et al.*, 1999). Another executive function of working memory is the capacity to process one stream of information while inhibiting others (Baddeley, 1996). Such selective processing is an important feature of the ATC task. For example, controllers reduce the general cognitive load of the task by focusing their attention on prioritised "focal" aircraft (which signal potential conflicts) and temporarily ignore "extra-focal" aircraft (Niessen *et al.*, 1999). Moreover, dynamic prioritisation is itself an important control process in air-traffic control that requires flexible executive resources.

Clearly, ATC requires controllers to make use of a great deal of knowledge stored in long-term memory. During training, controllers acquire declarative and procedural knowledge without which they would be unable to perform the ATC task. Indeed, in ATC, working memory is dependent upon long-term memory for a number of key cognitive operations, including the organisation of information, decision making and planning (Stein & Garland, 1993). The temporary activation, maintenance and retrieval of information in long-term memory are processes controlled by the central executive component of working memory (Baddeley, 1996). Thus, working memory plays a key role in the utilisation of the long-term knowledge used to interpret and analyse information emanating from the air-traffic environment.

The avoidance of air-traffic conflicts is essentially a problem-solving task and problem resolution is a key information-processing cycle in ATC (Niessen *et al.*, 1999). Working memory plays an important role in problem solving by retaining the initial problem information, intermediate solutions and goal states (Atwood & Polson, 1976). The working storage of goals and subgoals appears to be essential in a wide range of problem- solving tasks. Indeed, when the rehearsal of subgoals is interfered with, both errors and solution times increase (Altmann & Trafton, 1999). In ATC, goal management is a dynamic process because goal and subgoal priorities change as a function of changes in the air-traffic environment. In executing a plan to attain a goal, the controller may need to retain in working storage a record of the steps currently completed, and those that remain to be completed. Each time a step is completed, the contents of working memory need to be updated to record this fact. Goals and subgoals can also change before they are attained. For example, changes in the air-traffic situation can result in the removal or creation of goals and produce changes in the priority of existing goals. The management of goals is another important functional aspect of working memory and empirical studies have shown that when additional working memory resources are made available to goal management, problem-solving performance improves (e.g. Zhang & Norman, 1994).

Situation awareness

Planning and problem solving in the dynamic air-traffic environment requires that controllers have an accurate awareness of the current and developing situation (Wickens, 2000). The term "situation awareness" refers to the present and future air-traffic situation. Experienced air-traffic controllers often describe their mental model of the air-traffic situation as the "picture" (Whitfield & Jackson, 1982). The picture contains information about the fixed properties of the task and the task environment (e.g. operational standards, sector boundaries, procedural knowledge) as well as its dynamic properties (e.g. current and future spatial and temporal relations between aircraft). Thus, although some of the content of the picture is retrieved from long-term memory, working memory is involved in the retention of the assembled picture (Logie, 1993; Mogford, 1997). Moreover, the variable nature of the air-traffic environment means that the picture needs to be repeatedly updated using executive control processes in working memory.

Using a sample of experienced en-route controllers, Niessen *et al.* (1998, 1999) identified a number of "working memory elements" (WMEs) that comprise the "picture" used in air-traffic control. They found that the picture consists of three classes of WMEs: *objects, events* and *control elements*. Examples of object WMEs are incoming aircraft, aircraft changing flight level and proximal aircraft. Events include potential conflicts of a chain or crossing kind. Control elements include selecting various sources of data (e.g. audio communication, flight level change tests, proximity tests), anticipation, conflict resolution, planning and action. Control procedures select the most important and urgent WMEs, which are arranged in working memory in terms of their priority. The continuously changing air-traffic environment requires that "goal-stacking" within working memory is a flexible process.

Voice communication

Voice communication with pilots is an important element of the air-traffic control task. Via radio, the controller may convey instructions to pilots and receive voice communications from pilots. Voice communication errors can contribute to serious aviation incidents (Fowler, 1980). A tragic example is the collision between two 747s on the runway of Tenerife airport in 1977, which resulted in the deaths of 538 people and which was partly the result of a voice communication error (Wickens, 2000). Misunderstandings account for a substantial number of voice communication errors, and many of these result from overloading working memory capacity (Morrow, Lee, & Rodvold, 1993). Working memory assists speech comprehension by retaining the initial words of a sentence across the intervening words, thereby allowing syntactic analysis to be applied to the complete sentence (Clark & Clarke, 1977; Baddeley & Wilson, 1988). In addition to comprehension failures, voice communication errors can also result from confusions between phonologically similar items in working memory. For example, the callsigns BDP4 and TCG4 contain phonologically confusable characters, increasing the risk of errors relative to phonologically distinct equivalents (Logie, 1993).

Structural interference in ATC tasks

Given the importance of spatial information in the ATC task, it is likely that spatial working memory contributes to task performance. Indeed, the construction and reconstruction of the airspace traffic representation places heavy demands on spatial working memory (Logie, 1993; Stein & Garland, 1993; Wickens, 2000). One consequence of this is that concurrent manual spatial tasks (e.g. arranging and writing on flight strips) may have a disruptive effect on situation awareness (Logie, 1993; Stein & Garland, 1993). This is an example of structural interference. Structural interference occurs when two or more concurrent tasks compete for the resources of the same working memory component. Since spatial working memory can be loaded independently of phonological working storage, a concurrent verbal task is unlikely to produce as much interference as a second spatial task. Thus in air-traffic control, structural interference can be reduced by ensuring that concurrent tasks do not load the same component of working memory. For example, in the presence of an existing spatial working memory load, manual responses should, wherever possible, be replaced with vocal responses; in the absence of a spatial load, manual and vocal responses can be combined (Wickens, 2000). This has important implications for the design of the ATC interface and suggests that speech recognition technology may prove useful in reducing some of the structural interference associated with this task (Stein & Garland, 1993).

5.4 Working memory and industrial tasks

Learning industrial tasks

The role of working memory in learning industrial tasks has also been investigated by psychologists. For example, Kyllonen and Stephens (1990, Experiment 1) examined the contribution of working memory to learning a task related to electronics troubleshooting ability. In total, 120 participants were trained to understand and use electronics logic gate symbols. An earlier study conducted by Gitomer (1988) had indicated that logic gate skill was the most important determinant of electronics troubleshooting ability. Following a declarative training and testing phase, participants entered a procedural training phase in which they were required to provide solutions to logic gate problems. In addition, the working memory capacity of each of the participants was measured along with their performance on a number of cognitive ability measures, including numerical assignment, reading span, position matching, symbol reduction, word knowledge and general science knowledge. An analysis was conducted in which working memory capacity, declarative knowledge and procedural knowledge were treated as predictor factors and declarative and procedural learning of logic gates were treated as criterion factors. The results revealed that working memory capacity was the only significant predictor of declarative logic gate learning ($r = 0.74$) and procedural logic gate learning ($r = 0.73$). Working memory was also a good predictor of numerical assignment ability and reading span. Kyllonen and Stephens (1990) concluded that individual variation in logic gate learning is almost entirely due to individual differences in working memory capacity. The load placed on working memory by learning instructions can influence how well people are trained to perform industrial tasks. Marcus, Cooper and Sweller (1996) trained participants to wire simple electronic circuits. The circuits contained resistors to be wired either in parallel or in series. The working memory load generated by learning the instructions was manipulated by presenting the instructions in two different formats, either in text or in a diagrammatic form. Marcus *et al.* reasoned that the provision of a diagram would reduce the working memory load by facilitating the generation of a reductive schema. Such a schema would reduce the number of separate elements requiring working storage, thus liberating working memory resources to assist learning. The results showed an effect of instructional format (text/diagram) but only in the high difficulty task – that is, wiring the resistors in parallel. In the low difficulty task, instructional format failed to influence performance. In addition, task difficulty (parallel/series) was found to affect performance on a concurrent task in the text condition but not in the diagram condition. These results converge on the conclusion that instructional format influences working memory load in learning this task. However, it is not the case that the provision of diagrams and separate text provides an optimal instructional format. In fact, these "split source" formats appear to place a heavier cognitive load on working memory because they require trainees to mentally integrate related information from separate sources (Chandler & Sweller, 1992). When, however, text is physically integrated with related elements of a diagram, the search process is reduced and comprehension is facilitated (Sweller, Chandler, Tierney, & Cooper, 1990; Chandler & Sweller, 1992).

Multimedia training formats

Research has also indicated that the use of multimedia can provide an efficient instructional format for training industrial tasks. Presenting trainees with material in both the visual and auditory modalities can exploit the independent capacities of the verbal and visuo-spatial working memory components, effectively increasing working memory capacity (Mousavi, Low, & Sweller, 1995). Thus, although multimedia instruction is an inherently split source format, this is more than compensated for by the effective increase in capacity. In one study, participants were trained in an electrical engineering task using either conventional visual or audio-visual instructional materials. The results demonstrated the superiority of the audio-visual format when the material had a high level of complexity. To control for the possibility that this result may merely reflect a difference between the difficulty of speech comprehension and reading, trainees were required to either listen to or read instructions on electrical safety. A subsequent comprehension test revealed no significant difference between the groups, suggesting that the effect of format was the result of differences in cognitive load (Tindall-Ford, Chandler, & Sweller, 1997). Using multimedia instruction delivered by computer, Kalyuga, Chandler and Sweller (1999) trained apprentices in soldering theory. Trainees viewed diagrams that were sometimes accompanied by audio text and/or visual text. The results demonstrated that although the audio-visual format was generally superior to the visual-only format, when the audio text duplicated the visual text it impaired learning. Kalyuga *et al.* point out that this is because the duplication of information is superfluous and places an additional load on working memory. Audio-visual presentation is only effective when each modality presents differing information that can be combined to assist learning.

5.5 Working memory and mental calculation

The role of working memory in mental calculation

Mental calculation occurs in many real-world activities, ranging from "supermarket arithmetic" to technical skills used in employment and education (Hitch, 1978; Smyth, Collins, Morris, & Levy 1994). In written arithmetic the printed page serves as a permanent external working store, but in mental arithmetic initial problem information and intermediate results need to be held in working memory (Hitch, 1978). Mental calculation involving multidigit numbers requires several mental operations. Working memory is used to monitor the calculation strategy and execute a changing succession of operations that register, retain and retrieve numerical data (Hunter, 1979). Intermediate results must be retained in working storage so that they may be combined with later results to arrive at a complete solution. Mental calculation is a task that involves storage and concurrent processing and is, therefore, likely to be dependent on working memory.

Hitch (1978) provided a convincing demonstration of the involvement of working memory in mental calculation in his study of mental addition. Participants were auditorily presented with multidigit addition problems such as "434 + 81" or "352 + 279". Experiment 1 demonstrated that participants solve mental addition problems in a series of calculation stages, with the majority following a consistent strategy, for example "units, tens, hundreds". Working memory is used to retain the units and then the tens totals as partial results while the hundreds total is calculated. Hitch also found that solution times increased as a function of the number of carries required in the calculation and that carrying also loads working memory. In Experiments 2 and 3, Hitch found that effectively increasing the retention time for the "tens" and "units" totals resulted in the rapid decay of this information in working storage. The final experiment manipulated the load imposed by the retention of the initial problem information. This was achieved by allowing participants to continuously inspect varying amounts of the initial problem material. Results showed that errors increased as a function of the initial problem information load on working memory. Hitch concluded that in multidigit mental addition, working memory is used to retain both initial material and interim results.

The contribution of working memory components

Since Hitch's influential early work, a number of studies using a variety of approaches have also demonstrated the importance of working memory in mental arithmetic (Logie & Baddeley, 1987; Dark & Benbow, 1991; Ashcraft, Donley, Halas, & Valaki, 1992; Geary & Widaman, 1992; Heathcote, 1994; Logie, Gilhooly, & Wynn, 1994; Lemaire, Abdi, & Fayol 1996; McClean & Hitch, 1999; Fuerst & Hitch, 2000; Ashcraft & Kirk, 2001). Indeed, such is the extent of working memory's involvement in this task, that performance on mental arithmetic problems has been used to measure individual differences in working memory capacity (Kyllonen &

Christal, 1990). Several studies have attempted to identify the role of the different components of working memory in arithmetic. For example, McClean and Hitch (1999) had participants complete a battery of working memory tests measuring performance dependent on the phonological loop, visuo-spatial working memory or the central executive. A comparison was made between participants with poor arithmetic ability and those with normal arithmetic ability. The results revealed that while the groups failed to differ on phonological loop tests, their performance was significantly different in tests of spatial working memory and central executive functioning. McClean and Hitch concluded that spatial working memory and executive functioning appear to be important factors in arithmetical attainment. These results are consistent with studies that have shown the importance of visuo-spatial ability in the arithmetic performance of adults (e.g. Morris & Walter, 1991).

Dark and Benbow (1991) examined the working memory representational capacity of participants who scored highly on either mathematical ability or verbal ability. The results showed enhanced capacity for numerical information for the high mathematical group and enhanced capacity for words for the high verbal group. Moreover, the high mathematical ability group were found to be more efficient at representing numbers in the visuo-spatial sketchpad. Indeed, several studies point to the importance of visuo-spatial working memory in mental calculation. Ashcraft (1995) argues that in mental arithmetic the visuo-spatial sketchpad is used to retain the visual characteristics of the problem as well as positional information. This is evidenced by the fact that participants frequently "finger write" mental calculation problems in the conventional format (see also Hope & Sherrill, 1987). Visuo-spatial working memory makes a contribution to any mental arithmetic problem that "involves column-wise, position information" and "to the carry operation, given that column-wise position information is necessary for accurate carrying" (Ashcraft, 1995, p. 17).

While the visuo-spatial sketchpad appears to have an important role in mental calculation, it is unlikely to operate in isolation. Indeed, Ashcraft (1995) regards the phonological loop as also contributing by retaining the partial results generated during mental arithmetic. In support of this, Heathcote (1994) found that the phonological loop was responsible for the retention of partial results and contributed to the working storage of problem information. Heathcote's results suggested that the phonological loop operates in parallel with the visuo-spatial sketchpad, which retains carry information and provides a visuo-spatial representation of the problem. Operating in isolation, the capacity of the phonological loop may be largely depleted by the requirement to retain material in calculations involving three-digit numbers. The independent capacity of visuo-spatial working memory may be used to support phonological storage. It is worth noting that the capacity of visuo-spatial working memory for numerals is greater than the capacity of phonological working memory for their verbal equivalents (Chincotta, Underwood, Ghani, Papadopoulou, & Wresinski, 1999). Fuerst and Hitch (2000) found that mental addition was impaired by concurrent articulatory suppression (i.e. repeated vocalisation of an irrelevant word), a task known to load the phonological loop. When the problem information was made continuously available for inspection, articulatory suppression ceased to influence performance. These results support the view that the phonological loop is involved in the retention of the initial problem material.

The importance of the phonological loop was also demonstrated in Logie and colleagues' (1994) study of mental calculation. In their experiments, participants were required to mentally add two-digit numbers presented either visually or auditorily. Performance was disrupted by concurrent articulatory suppression. The results suggested that subvocal rehearsal assists in the retention of interim results (i.e. running totals), as found in previous studies (e.g. Hitch, 1980; Logie & Baddeley, 1987; Heathcote, 1994). Logie *et al.* (1994) also found that a concurrent spatial task impaired performance on visually presented problems, again suggesting that the phonological loop and the visuo-spatial sketchpad can both play a role in mental calculation.

A key finding of Logie *et al.* (1994) was that the greatest impairment of mental calculation was produced by a random generation task known to load the central executive. This result is consistent with the view that the central executive is involved in the retrieval and execution of arithmetical facts and strategies stored in long-term memory (Hitch, 1978; Ashcraft *et al.*, 1992; Heathcote, 1994; Lemaire *et al.*, 1996). Clearly, mental calculation would not be possible without the utilisation of long-term knowledge relevant to the task. The central executive appears to have a role in the retrieval and implementation of procedural and declarative arithmetical knowledge. An example of essential declarative knowledge is that mental calculation is dependent upon access to numerical equivalents (i.e. arithmetical facts) such as $7 \times 7 = 49$ or $8 + 4 = 12$. Mental arithmetic also requires procedural knowledge about calculative algorithms, for example the rule to follow when required to apply the operator $\times$ to two numbers. Having retrieved the appropriate algorithm, the central executive then applies that rule and monitors and updates the current step in the procedure. Thus, the executive is responsible for the execution of essential calculative operations, for example the execution of carry operations (Fuerst & Hitch, 2000).

Multiple working memory components

Demanding tasks like mental calculation may require multiple working memory components. Indeed, when considered together, the results from the studies discussed above are consistent with Baddeley's (1982) view that mental arithmetic may involve the deployment of a working memory group in which the central executive, visuo-spatial sketchpad and phonological loop all participate. Collectively, these findings can be explained by the "triple code model" of numerical processing proposed by Dehaene and his colleagues (Dehaene, 1992; Dehaene, Bossini, & Giraux, 1993; Dehaene & Cohen, 1995). In this model, during multidigit mental arithmetic numbers are mentally represented in three different codes. First, a visual Arabic form in a spatially extended representational medium (e.g. "592"); in this code, "numbers are expressed as strings of digits on an internal visuo-spatial scratchpad" (Dehaene & Cohen, 1995, p. 85). Second, a verbal code that is linked to phonological representations. Third, an analogical spatial representation that expresses the magnitude of numbers and contributes to approximate solutions. During complex mental calculation, all three codes operate in parallel because there is a permanent transcoding back and forth between the visual, verbal and analogical representations (see Figure 5.2). Visuo-spatial working memory is involved in the representation of the visual code and the analogical magnitude code. The phonological loop retains information coded in a verbal format. A similar view is taken by Campbell and his collaborators in their "integrated encoding complex model" (Clark & Campbell, 1991; Campbell & Clark, 1992; Campbell, 1994). They argue that there is much evidence of verbal and visuo-spatial working memory codes in numerical calculation. Their model of numerical processing "permits specific visual and verbal modes to serve as the immediate inputs and outputs of numerical operations and as the transient codes that are temporarily retained between successive operations" (Clark & Campbell, 1991, p. 219).

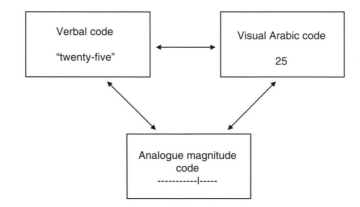

Figure 5.2 A simplified representation of Dehaene's "triple code model" of numerical processing

Working memory and mathematics anxiety

The use of the working memory model to analyse mental calculation is beginning to produce work that may have practical value. For example, Ashcraft and Kirk (2001) found that the calculation-based working memory span of participants was reduced by mathematics anxiety. The reduction in working memory capacity caused by mathematics anxiety severely impaired performance on mental addition problems. The diminution of working memory span was found to be temporary, the result of on-line processing of specifically maths-related problems. Mathematics anxiety appears to impair the efficiency of the central executive in executing procedural operations such as carrying, sequencing and keeping track in multi-step problems. Ashcraft and Kirk conclude that anxiety produces a reduction in executive processing capacity by compromising selection mechanisms, allowing intrusive thoughts and distracting information to compete for limited resources. An important implication of these findings is that interventions aimed at reducing mathematics anxiety may produce substantial improvements in the performance of maths-related tasks. Moreover, the performance of individuals with below average general working memory capacity is likely to be particularly sensitive to further decrements in capacity produced by anxiety. Therefore, it is this group that is likely to benefit most from anxiety-reducing techniques.

5.6 Working memory and human–computer interaction

Working memory errors in human–computer interaction

Interaction with computer technology is now an everyday occurrence for many people. The study of human–computer interaction is not confined to interactions with desktop computers; research on human–computer interaction encompasses the use of many different forms of information technology (Dix, Finlay, Abowd, & Beale, 1998). For example, Byrne and Bovair (1997) studied the use of automatic teller machines (ATMs) in making cash withdrawals from bank accounts. This study examined a type of systematic error known as a "post-completion error". Post-completion errors occur when the user completes their task of withdrawing cash but fails to remove their bank card from the ATM. Post-completion errors tend to happen when users have an additional step to perform after their primary goal has been attained. Byrne and Bovair found that this form of error only occurred when the load on working memory was high. In these circumstances, the presence of an additional step overloads working memory capacity. It is worth noting that the occurrence of post-completion errors led to the redesign of ATMs, with the result that they now only dispense cash after first returning the card to the user.

The ubiquity of working memory errors may also have implications for the design of telephonic communication interfaces. A common form of telephone-based interaction involves the selection of menu items in automated systems. Huguenard, Lerch, Junker, Patz and Kass (1997) examined the role of working memory in phone-based interaction (PBI) errors when using such a system. Guidelines for the design of telephone interfaces emphasise the importance of not overloading the user's short-term memory capacity. In particular, these guidelines advocate the use of "deep menu hierarchies", which limit menu structures to a maximum of three options per menu. However, Huguenard and colleagues' results indicated that deep menu hierarchies do not in fact reduce PBI errors. This is because although deep menu hierarchies reduce the storage load, they increase the concurrent processing load in working memory. In addition to its obvious practical implications, this study demonstrates how the working memory concept can provide a more accurate prediction of empirical findings than approaches that view temporary memory entirely in terms of its storage function.

Elderly computer users

Given the importance of working memory in human–computer interaction (HCI), factors that result in a diminution of working memory capacity may have a detrimental effect on the performance of computer-based tasks. Normal ageing seems to produce a decline in the processing capacity of working memory (Baddeley, 1986; Salthouse & Babcock, 1991; Craik, Anderson, Kerr, & Li, 1995) and several recent studies have examined the impact of age-related working memory decrements on performance in HCI tasks (e.g. Howard & Howard, 1997; Jerrams-Smith, Heathcote, & White, 1999; Freudenthal, 2001). Indeed, the load imposed on working memory by computer-based tasks may be a particularly influential factor in the usability of interfaces for the elderly. This may have important implications for the design of interfaces that seek to encourage the elderly to take advantage of computer technology. In pursuing this aim, Jerrams-Smith *et al.* (1999) investigated whether age-related decrements in working memory span could account for poor performance in two common tasks associated with the use of a computer interface. The results demonstrated that relative to younger users, elderly participants performed poorly in a multiple windows task that involved concurrent processing and storage. Elderly participants were also found to have smaller working memory spans than younger participants. In addition, the study examined the short-term retention of icon labels in the presence of a concurrent processing load. The results showed that under these conditions the "icon span" of younger participants was greater than that of the seniors. It was concluded that interfaces that place a considerable load on working memory (i.e. those that require considerable concurrent processing and storage) are unsuitable for many elderly users. Interfaces designed for the elderly should enable users to achieve their task goals with the minimum concurrent processing demands. Such interfaces would require sequential rather than parallel cognitive operations, thereby reducing the load on working memory.

Working memory and cognitive engineering in human–computer interaction

The application of the working memory concept to the design of interfaces for elderly users is an example of cognitive engineering. One of the earliest attempts to provide a cognitive engineering model of human–computer interaction was the GOMS (Goals, Operators, Methods and Selection) architecture proposed by Card, Moran and Newell (1983). GOMS consists of a model of the human information-processing system, the "Model Human Processor", together with techniques for task analysis in human–machine interaction situations. The Model Human Processor comprises a working memory, with visual and auditory stores, a cognitive processor, a long-term memory and perceptual and motor processors. Perceptual input from the computer interface is retained in working memory. Goals and subgoals require the execution of motor or cognitive acts known as "operators" (e.g. menu selections, keyboard commands). To realise a goal, subgoals and operators must be correctly sequenced. A sequence of subgoals and paired operators aimed at achieving a goal is known as a "method". For example, a computer user wishing to update the contents of a file may follow this method sequence: find target file (subgoal), search for target file (operator); open file (subgoal), click on file (operator); change contents (subgoal), key in new information (operator); retain amended file (subgoal), select menu item to save amended file (operator). Using selection rules, appropriate methods are retrieved from long-term memory and as each operator is executed the contents of working memory is updated.

Although GOMS is successful in modelling performance in some simple tasks, it has limited applicability to the multiple-task activities that are common in many real-world task environments. For example, in a commercial situation, a computer user may be entering information at the keyboard while simultaneously engaged in a conversation with a client. A more sophisticated architecture that is capable of handling concurrent tasks is EPIC (Executive-Process/Interactive Control) developed by Meyer and Kieras (1997). EPIC provides a cognitive architecture, which, like GOMS, has been used to model performance in HCI tasks. The working memory component of the EPIC architecture has much in common with Baddeley's model. However, there are also some important differences between the two. Although EPIC has modality-specific visuo-spatial and auditory working stores, it lacks a *general-purpose* central executive. Instead, working memory is managed by task-specific control processes (specified in terms of production rules) that update, maintain and utilise the contents of working memory to complete the task (Kieras, Meyer, Mueller, & Seymour, 1999). As an example, if a user wished to enter data in a spreadsheet, the appropriate production (essentially a GOMS "method") would be retrieved from long-term memory. Productions specify the executive operations (i.e. control processes) necessary to perform the spreadsheet task and the order in which they should be executed. Thus, in EPIC the "cognitive processor" is not a versatile general-purpose executive, rather it is pre-programmed to respond to the circumstances of a specific task. In particular, the cognitive processor is programmed to apply production rules so that when a condition is met, a production is initiated. Productions are triggered when the current contents of working memory match the production rule. In the spreadsheet example, the contents of working memory would activate the spreadsheet data entry production, which would specify all the actions necessary to achieve this goal. Several productions can operate in parallel, thereby enabling multiple-task performance (e.g. data entry combined with concurrent speech comprehension).

The EPIC architecture has been successful in modelling the performance of users in HCI tasks. Kieras and Meyer (1997) report a study in which participants were required to search for and select items from pull-down menus in a graphical user interface. Participants made their responses by pointing and clicking with a mouse and search times were recorded. Previous work had suggested that users would use a serial search strategy with the result that search times would increase linearly as a function of the number of positions the target item was from the top of the menu. In fact, search times were found to be substantially smaller than those predicted by the serial search model. The EPIC model was capable of providing an accurate prediction of the observed search times. This is because in EPIC the component processes of this task are overlapping. In particular, the menu-scanning process is controlled by a production rule that overlaps with the decision-making production rule.

EPIC provides sufficiently accurate HCI models to enable it to assist interface design in a range of real-world tasks. This architecture appears to be particularly useful in modelling tasks that involve motor responses. One reason for this is that the control of motor activity and its relation to perceptual processing is relatively well specified in its architecture. Indeed, an important addition to Baddeley's model of working memory provided by EPIC is a motor working memory. This is used to retain movement information required for ongoing interactions with the task environment (Kieras *et al.*, 1999). Human–computer interaction involves manual, ocular and verbal actions. Accordingly, in EPIC, motor working memory is divided into vocal-motor, occular-motor (for eye movements) and manual working stores.

Motor working memory in human–computer interaction

Motor memory also has an important role in an alternative cognitive architecture, ICS (Interacting Cognitive Subsystems), developed by Philip Barnard (e.g. Barnard, 1985, 1991, 1999). In addition to the motor subsystem, the ICS architecture contains nine other subsystems, each of which is associated with a different type of mental code. For example, the Morphonolexical (MPL) subsystem uses a phonological code, while the Object subsystem (OBJ) employs a visuo-spatial code. Indeed, in relation to Baddeley's model of working memory, the MPL subsystem maps onto the phonological loop and the OBJ subsystem maps onto the visuo-spatial sketchpad (Barnard, 1999). Subsystems exchange information with other subsystems and create and retain records of sensory input. Thus each subsystem has its own memory. The Body State (BS) subsystem records information relating to current body position and tactile pressure. Manual responses in HCI tasks are dependent upon the utilisation of procedural knowledge and sensory input retained in working records. When action is required, procedural knowledge in the system directs the Limb (LIM) effector subsystem (which controls the target positions of skeletal muscles) to instruct the motor subsystem to make the appropriate movement. The BS subsystem record is then updated to reflect changes in proprioceptive input produced by the movement. Clearly, complex actions require coordination of the BS, visual and LIM subsystems. In ICS, this coordination is not undertaken by a central executive; rather, it is accomplished through the exchange of information between subsystems. Thus, the system as a whole is capable of achieving the necessary coordination. In addition, the system is capable of dynamically reconfiguring itself when unexpected motor responses are required (Barnard, 1999).

Clearly, many actions in HCI tasks involve manual movement (e.g. mouse pointing and key strokes). Evidence from several studies indicates that the production and retention of hand movements involves visuo-spatial working memory (Logie, 1995). To direct a finger at a target key or point a mouse at a target icon, a motor plan must be assembled and applied (see Jeannerod, 1997). Motor plans require accurate information about the spatial location of the target relative to the initial position of the user's hand. Therefore, it is not surprising that the assembly and retention of motor plans loads the visuo-spatial sketchpad (Logie, 1995). In a relevant study, Logie, Baddeley, Mane, Donchin and Sheptak (1989) examined the performance of participants as they interacted with a complex computer game. Participants made manual responses using a joystick and the game required a high level of perceptuo-motor skill, with the result that proficient performance was dependent upon the use of accurate motor plans. While playing the game, participants engaged in various secondary tasks. After a period of extended training, results showed a pattern of selective interference. A concurrent visuo-spatial working memory task was found to impair performance on the perceptuo-motor aspects of the game but produced no impairment of its verbal components. In contrast, a concurrent verbal working memory task disrupted the verbal elements of the game but failed to impair perceptuo-motor performance. These results are consistent with the view that the processes involved in the construction or application of motor plans compete for the resources of visuo-spatial working memory.

It is worth noting that in human–computer interaction, as in most other activities, actions are not completed instantaneously. Effective and precise action is often dependent upon correctly responding to sensory feedback as the action unfolds. Jeannerod (1997) identified a number of steps involved in performing an action, each of which contains a mechanism for monitoring and correcting the action if necessary. At each step, working memory is used to enable a comparison to be made between the goal of the operation and the actual effect of the operation on the environment. Reafferent input (e.g. visual and proprioceptive feedback) indicating the current state of the action is fed into working memory and used to signal the extent of its completion (Jeannerod, 1997). Thus working memory may contribute to the accuracy of manual operations in HCI tasks by allowing correctional adjustments to be made as the action plan is implemented.

Summary

- Working memory appears to be involved in a range of tasks in which short-term storage and concurrent processing are essential to task performance.
- Many real-world tasks are dependent upon temporary information storage and simultaneous processing.
- Working memory allows long-term knowledge relating to task-specific skills to be applied to, and combined with, immediate input.
- In mental calculation, the executive component of working memory applies knowledge of calculative algorithms and numerical equivalents to the initial problem information and interim results retained in working storage.
- Dynamic task environments like air-traffic control place heavy demands on working memory resources. Such tasks present an ever-changing environment that requires dynamic scheduling of operations, and the retention, prioritisation and updating of task goals.
- Working memory contributes to situation awareness by assisting in the assembly, retention and updating of a situational mental model of the current air-traffic environment.

Chapter 6

Skill, attention and cognitive failure

6.1 Introduction

In this chapter, the development and the breakdown of skilled behaviour are considered. The nature of skill and its acquisition are first discussed followed by an analysis of the breakdown of skill under conditions of stress. One of the characteristics of skilled performance is a reduction in the requirement for conscious attention to be paid to performance as automaticity develops through practice. The example of "choking" in sports performance is used to show how a reduction in the automaticity associated with skilled performance may actually return performance to a level more characteristic of the novice. A price of automaticity is that the reduction in supervisory control that may occur when performance becomes highly routinised may result in the commission of various types of error. Techniques for the study of error are discussed and a taxonomy of error types presented. This is followed by a discussion of some of the steps that designers may take to limit the occurrence of error on the part of users of their artefacts by taking account of some of the characteristics of the human cognitive system. Finally, a real-world case study of a major mishap, an air crash, is presented in some detail. This serves to illustrate the multi-determination of such incidents by factors which include human error but which also may include factors related to design, training and organisational culture, as well as biological factors such as circadian rhythms in cognitive performance.

6.2 Skill and its acquisition

Skill may be defined as the learned ability to bring about pre-determined results with maximum certainty, often with the minimum outlay of time, of energy, or of both (Knapp, 1963). Skill contrasts with ability. The latter is usually regarded as a set of innate attributes that determine our potential for a given activity. Such potential may be developed into skilled behaviour by training and practice. Examples of skilled activities include typing, driving, playing a musical instrument, ballet dancing and playing sports. However, it should be noted that even a mundane activity such as making a pot of tea incorporates a large amount of skilled behaviour.

In the real world, most skills are cognitive-motor rather than simply perceptual-motor. That is, the operator must carry out some non-trivial processing upon incoming data and output some relatively complex motor behaviour in response. Driving, playing most sports and operating various kinds of machinery from lathes to computers are all examples of cognitive-motor tasks in this sense. Skills may be distinguished by the extent to which their output stage demands gross or fine motor control. A ballet pirouette requires finer motor control than does lifting a weight. Skills may also be distinguished by the extent to which they are primarily under open- or closed-loop control. A closed skill is one in which the entire sequence of skilled behaviour is run off in a complete and predictable manner, such as a high dive into a swimming pool, while performance of an open skill may require ongoing modifications as the action unfolds, as may be found in skilled driving.

One of the characteristics of skilled performance is the increasing ability of the performer to carry out a second activity concurrently with the main task as their proficiency increases. Thus, the novice driver needs to concentrate fully upon the driving task to be able to control a vehicle satisfactorily. The experienced driver, on the other hand, is able to converse with a passenger, operate the CD player, or carry out other secondary tasks alongside the driving task with little or no apparent disruption of either. Development of the ability to carry out a secondary task goes hand-in-hand with increasing open-loop control over behaviour. Thus the novice driver is likely to need to input control movements of the steering wheel almost continuously in response to perceived deviations from the desired trajectory if he or she is to maintain a steady course. The expert driver, on the other hand, can maintain a trajectory near effortlessly with smaller and less frequent control movements than those required by the novice (Groeger, 2000).

Acquisition of skill is characterised by gradual development with practice and a diminishing requirement for concentration. Fitts and Posner (1967) proposed a three-stage model of skill acquisition that comprises cognitive, associative and autonomous stages. The cognitive stage of a perceptual-motor skill involves the development of a motor program (Adams, 1971) as a mental representation of the skill and how to perform it. As such, this stage is likely to involve instruction by a more expert performer, verbal description, demonstration and self-observation. The second, associative, stage is an intermediate one in which an effective motor program is developed but the subtasks comprising the skilled behaviour are not yet fluent. Fluency increases with practice. Through practice, the performer learns in motor skills to rely more on feedback in the somatosensory modality than in the visual modality. Acccording to Adams' closed-loop theory, comparison of the perceptual and memory trace on each learning trial allows the performer to progressively reduce the discrepancy between them. Initially, however, comparison is under verbal-cognitive control and guided by knowledge of results or other feedback.

With growing expertise, somatosensory feedback is used for comparison, affording lower-level closed-loop control. The somatosensory sense comprises proprioception (the skin sense, or touch), kinaesthesia (awareness of the relevant orientation of body parts) and the vestibular (or balance) senses. Keele (1986) suggested that complex skills are acquired by integrating motor programs for simple movements into a more complex integrated program. An alternative view was proposed by Schmidt (1975), who employed the schema concept to integrate both closed-loop and open-loop processes in performance and learning, The theory incorporates the idea of a motor program as part of the response process but envisages a more flexible, generalised system based on schematic representations that can be used to produce varying patterns of response under different circumstances. Thus the generalised program for signing one's name would describe the lines and loops involved as an abstract code. The fact that the signature is similar whether written with a pen or with a spray gun illustrates the incorporation of local parameters, such as the shape and weight of the writing instrument, to the information encoded within the program.

With sufficient practice, the skill enters the autonomous stage in which it is largely under automatic control. Two important aspects of skill acquisition may be noted. First, while at the cognitive stage the skill may be described explicitly in terms of the (usually verbal) instructions provided by teachers, the motor program so developed depends largely upon the formation of implicit knowledge. This is as true of cognitive-motor tasks, such as those involved in process control, as it is of learning physical skills (Berry & Broadbent, 1984). Reliance on explicit rules governing skilled behaviour is therefore associated with novice rather than expert levels of performance. Secondly, the parameters governing skill acquisition, such as the pace and timing of training sessions, influence outcomes. Studies of the spacing effect (see Chapter 2) indicate that periods of practice widely distributed in time rather than massed together may be advantageous. Studies of learning to play musical instruments indicate the particular importance of practice. Sloboda, Davidson and Howe (1994) looked at acquisition of instrumental ability in a group of children at a specialist music school in the UK. With a large number of children recruited to the authors' multiple regression design, Sloboda *et al.* found that hours of practice outweighed all other variables, including parental musicality, parental social class and even musical aptitude. They concluded that expert musicians were made, not born. Factors such as parental musicality and social class may only exert an influence, they argued, via their tendency to create the conditions under which such practice would occur.

Divided attention and dual-task performance

Since skilled behaviour is required for carrying out various kinds of tasks, a definition of a task is desirable. A useful approach was provided by Wickens (1992), who observed that any task could be described in broad terms as involving four stages in a processing sequence. Initially, registration of task-relevant stimuli needs to be accomplished such that those stimuli are encoded from sensory buffer storage into working memory. Stimulus elements are chosen for encoding in this way by the processes of focused attention (see Chapter 10). Thus, in the case of the very simple piece of skilled behaviour involving computing the answer to the sum "2 + 2", the sum must first enter the individual's awareness, or working memory, as a result of focused attention to a visual or auditory presentation of the problem. Then, processes need to be carried out to compute the answer to the sum. These processes are not unique and could involve either direct look-up of the answer in memory or computation involving some arithmetic rule. With a simple problem and/or an individual skilled in mental arithmetic direct look-up may be favoured, while a harder problem or less skilled individual may favour some explicit procedure of calculation. Finally, a response needs to be output, in this case "4", which may be written, spoken or typed. This scheme is illustrated in Figure 6.1.

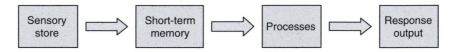

Figure 6.1 Stage model of a typical task

Wickens' (1992) analysis is useful since it enables loci for interference between two ongoing tasks to be identified at each of the four stages within the processing sequence. Thus, two tasks or subtasks may compete with one another at the level of input modality if both employ, for example, verbal or visual stimuli. At the level of memory coding within working memory, tasks may compete if both require, for example, verbal or imaginal coding. At the level of processing resources, competition for the same processing modules implicated in, for example, mental arithmetic may also give rise to interference. Finally, at the level of output, response competition may occur if both tasks require, for example, verbal or manual output. In considering task combination, the emphasis is on complete tasks rather than just the perceptual elements that are the main consideration when focused attention is discussed. Divided attention tasks may involve attending to multiple sources of perceptual input, but more usually combinations of complete tasks forming part of a repertoire of skilled behaviour are considered. While this analysis assumes two ongoing tasks, it may be noted that a single task may involve simultaneous demands at more than one of the stages in Figure 6.1. An example of this is the paced auditory serial addition or PASAT task. This requires individuals to add two numbers presented in rapid succession, then to add a third number to the last of the two previously presented. This procedure is repeated for a sequence of numbers. Competition is then created between the updating of working memory with the output to the last sum and retaining one of the addends for addition to the next incoming number. This task has been used as a laboratory and clinical simulation of divided attention, though some doubt has been cast on its validity given its strong link with arithmetic ability and training (Ward, 1997).

In a classic experiment, Allport, Antonis and Reynolds (1972) explored the possibility of interference between two tasks at the input stage. They employed the shadowing paradigm. This involves the presentation of two, simultaneous auditory messages to participants via headphones. Each headphone presents different material that could be, for example, speech, music or tones. To ensure focused attention to one of these messages, or channels, shadowing requires repeating back the input, usually speech, heard on that channel. Allport *et al.* examined the combination of shadowing with learning of words presented on the unattended channel. In keeping with other studies of shadowing, only a chance level of performance was exhibited in a subsequent recognition test of words presented on the unattended channel. However, when the experiment was repeated using the same to-be-learned words but now presented visually while the participants shadowed the attended message, subsequent recognition of those words was greatly improved. Thus, there appears to be an advantage in using different sensory modalities in two tasks if those tasks are to be combined. Allport *et al.* (1972) extended this finding to examine memory codes by comparing visually presented words to visually presented pictorial representations of those words. It is reasonable to assume that these will foster verbal and imaginal representations in memory, respectively. Pictorial representations resulted in a further gain in recognition performance consistent with the view that using different memory codes also confers an advantage if two tasks requiring those memory codes are to be combined.

Competition for processing resources in dual-task performance has been examined in a number of situations. One is driving, where use of a mobile phone while driving has been shown in some studies to be as disruptive of performance as ingestion of small amounts of alcohol. Simulator studies have indicated an increase in response times and a reduced ability to detect deceleration of a car in front (Lamble, Kauranen, Laasko, & Summala, 1999; Garcia-Larrea, Perchet, Perren, & Amendo, 2001). Garcia-Larrea *et al.* (2001) found that maintaining a phone conversation was associated with a decrease in attention to sensory inputs, as was evident from recordings of event-related potentials taken from the participants' heads. They argued that this decrease in attention to sensory inputs is characteristic of dual-task situations and is unlikely to be affected by whether conventional or hands-free telephones are used. The data from Alm and Nilsson (1994) are consistent with the view that the use of hands-free equipment has little benefit in terms of reducing performance decrements due to concurrent phone use. In another simulator study, Horswill and McKenna (1999) found that concurrent mobile phone use also made participants more likely to engage in risky behaviours such as following too close behind another vehicle. As well as having an adverse effect upon the uptake of sensory information, competition for processing resources may therefore also adversely affect the computation of risk.

One might ask why having a conversation on a mobile phone is so much more disruptive than, for example, having a conversation with a passenger in the car. A likely reason is the loss of control over the situation when having a mobile phone conversation. A passenger in the car will pick up from non-verbal cues that the driver needs to concentrate on the main task of driving at times when the latter becomes tricky. A remote interlocutor is much less likely to pick up these cues and therefore continue to make cognitively demanding conversation at a time when the secondary task needs to be shut down to devote resources to the main driving task. A cognitively demanding conversation, especially one over which the driver has little or no control in terms of dynamically adjusting his or her allocation of cognitive resources, appears to interfere with computation of speeds, distances and widths as required by the driving task, probably as a result of diminished attention to sensory inputs. Use of a mobile phone also demands other secondary tasks, such as inputting of a telephone number on the keypad, which would also tend to interfere with the main driving task.

As well as creating competition for processing resources, driving while simultaneously holding a mobile phone in order to input a telephone number or hold a conversation will also result in competition at the output level, since the same hand cannot both operate the steering wheel and hold the mobile phone. While this competition could be resolved by the use of hands-free devices, we have seen that this does little to limit more central disruption of sensory uptake. It may also affect the assembly of motor programs. In a relevant experiment, McLeod (1977) had individuals perform a manual tracking task involving the following of a contour in combination with identification of tones. Pitch of tones could be indicated either verbally or manually, the latter by pointing at response alternatives. It was found that the manual tracking task suffered more interference when responses to the tone identification task were made manually. The fact that different hands were used to carry out the tracking task and to make the pointing response indicates that response competition is not just a matter of one hand being unable to do two things at once. Rather, more central interference appears to occur where this concerns competition for the cognitive resources involved in assembling motor programs prior to manual output.

In summary, the studies described and others of a similar nature support the view that two tasks are easier to combine if they are somewhat different in terms of input modalities, required memory codes, requirements for processing resources, or requirements for response modalities. However, in the safety-critical driving task, use of a mobile phone as a secondary task is likely to result in a decrement in performance in even the most skilled operator and this may therefore be considered highly inadvisable.

Practice and the development of automaticity

Successful task combination is influenced by factors other than the amount of similarity between the tasks in terms of the demands that they make on cognitive resources. The ability to combine two tasks is greatly increased by the development of skill via practice. The difficulty of the two tasks is also relevant, as easier tasks are more readily combined than hard ones, though it should be noted that difficulty is a somewhat subjective concept, since the difficulty of a task diminishes with increased expertise on that task.

In another classic study, Spelke, Hirst and Neisser (1976) had two volunteers train extensively on an unfamiliar combination of tasks. The tasks were reading for comprehension and writing to dictation. Given that these tasks have shared requirements for processing codes (linguistic) and processing resources, a high level of interference between the two tasks would be predicted, to the detriment of both tasks. Initially, this was the case, with reading speed, handwriting and recall of comprehension passages all being adversely affected. The study, however, involved intensive daily practice and after 6 weeks handwriting, reading speed and recall were all greatly improved. After 4 months the participants could carry out an additional activity, categorising dictated words, at the same time as understanding the dictated passages. Similar studies included examination of the ability of expert musicians to sight-read at the piano while shadowing speech (Allport *et al.*, 1972) and the ability of expert touch-typists to type while shadowing speech (Shaffer, 1975). In all cases, practice resulting in expertise at the tasks produced highly successful task combination without apparent interference.

Although it is tempting on the basis of such studies to conclude that performance on sufficiently practised dual tasks may be such as to suggest that absolute limits on our ability to combine tasks may not exist, a careful analysis by Broadbent (1982) indicated that this is probably not so, since some, often quite subtle, interference may be demonstrated statistically in many cases. It is likely, then, that what is learned via practice, in addition to the implicit knowledge underlying motor programs and schemas, also includes strategies for the effective running off of motor programs in ways that minimise attentional demands. In the case of reading music or text, this would include making the most effective use of the extensive forward and backward scanning opportunities that present themselves during less demanding sections to prepare upcoming responses. Similarly, the sophisticated reader may process far larger chunks of text or music than will the novice, enabling a large amount of output behaviour to be prepared while simultaneously freeing up cognitive resources for any ongoing secondary task. The key importance of practice in the development of a skill such as playing a musical instrument was emphasised by Sloboda *et al.* (1994), who demonstrated that hours of practice was more important than any other variable in determining the level of performance achieved by school students attending a specialist music school.

The development of automaticity was simulated in studies by Shiffrin and Schneider (1977) and Schneider and Shiffrin (1977). An automatic process may be described as one that is fast, involuntary and that does not suffer any obvious interference. Its opposite is a controlled process. Responding to the colour of words in the Stroop task is an example of a controlled process, one that is slow and that suffers interference from the reading response. Reading a word in one's native language is so practised as to be automatic in most adult skilled readers. Shiffrin and Schneider's studies were based on the visual search paradigm and their participants were required to memorise between one and four target characters before searching a briefly presented display for those targets. The display also contained up to four characters including distractors. Searching a multi-character display for a single character they termed "visual search", and searching a multi-target display for multiple targets they termed "memory search". Shiffrin and Schneider claimed that the former has the characteristics of an automatic process, while the latter has the characteristics of a controlled process. Performance was compared in two conditions. In the varied mapping condition, targets and distractors were drawn at random from the same pool of letters so that a distractor could be a target on a subsequent trial and vice versa. In the consistent mapping condition, on the other hand, targets and distractors were two distinct sets of letters. It was hypothesised that under varied mapping conditions search would be effortful and serial, while in the consistent mapping condition it could be rapid and parallel (for more details of visual search tasks, see Groome *et al.*, 1999, chapter 2). Shiffrin and Schneider's (1977; see Figure 6.2) results indicate the following:

1   Negative trials (in which the target was not found) took longer than positive trials (in which the target was found) as search can be terminated sooner in the latter case.
2   Visual searches took times fairly independent of set size for consistent mapping trials, but increased near-linearly for varied mapping trials.
3   Memory search times also increased near-linearly, but more rapidly than was the case with visual search, with set size for varied mapping conditions but not for consistent mapping conditions.

Shiffrin and Schneider (1977) concluded that the varied and consistent mapping conditions do indeed have the characteristics of controlled and automatic processes, respectively. Moreover, the development of automaticity was demonstrated by having participants practise extensively on just two sets of characters, one a target set and one a distractor set. Search slowly acquired the characteristics of automaticity in that it became increasingly difficult to switch the detection rule and respond to the distractor set rather than the target set. The overlearned

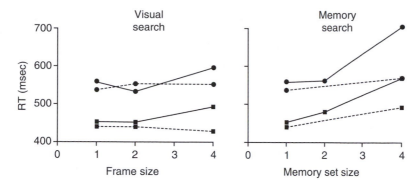

Figure 6.2 Shiffrin and Schneider's (1997) results of processing demands on response time. − − ■ − −, consistent mapping/positive trials; − ■ −, varied mapping/ positive trials; − − ● − −, consistent mapping/negative trials; − ● −, varied mapping/ negative trials

detection response therefore appeared to generate involuntary, automatic responses. As such, Shiffrin and Schneider (1977) have provided a laboratory simulation of the development of skilled behaviour via the provision of a large amount of practice. This behaviour demonstrated the characteristics of skill, namely a high level of automaticity and limited vulnerability to interference from a secondary task. The latter makes possible combination of the practised task and a secondary task.

6.3 Cognitive failure: skill breakdown

"Choking" is a situation, usually in sports, in which inferior performance occurs despite striving and incentives for superior performance (Baumeister & Showers, 1986). Typically, it occurs in professional players who are highly skilled but who suffer a massive performance decrement under the pressure of competition compared with performance in practice. To some extent, the choking phenomenon represents a procedural equivalent of blocking phenomena in declarative memory such as the tip-of-the-tongue state (Brown & McNeill, 1966).

The conditions giving rise to performance breakdown have been studied in many contexts, including stage-fright in actors (Steptoe *et al.*, 1995) and performance anxiety in musicians (Steptoe & Fidler, 1987). The phenomenon has been most thoroughly studied, however, in sport. Typically, choking occurs when performance is at a high level in practice but falls apart during competition. Often the competitive event in which this occurs is the "big one". That is, the player has performed well throughout the season, say, but in the context of a crucial competition performance declines catastrophically. This decrement may also occur within a given competitive event when the player must take a crucial action but "falls apart" under the pressure. Individual sports, such as golf or tennis, are particularly likely to give rise to choking when a key shot or point must be won.

Explanations for choking have derived from a consideration of the effects of anxiety and arousal, the effects of self-consciousness, and the effects of skill acquisition parameters on subsequent performance. The effects of anxiety on performance have been analysed in terms of the classic inverted-U relationship between arousal and performance, first suggested by Yerkes and Dodson (1908) and illustrated in Figure 6.3. On this view, there is an optimal level of arousal for a given task. This tends to be lower for a task that is relatively difficult. Elevated arousal accompanies the anxiety that results from the pressurised situation and may move the player over the maximum of the inverted-U function into a region of performance characterised by both elevated arousal and a lower level of performance. Elevated arousal is known to be disruptive of fine motor skills, so a direct, adverse impact of arousal on performance may be predictable in some cases (Schmidt & Lee, 1999). As well as being affected by anxiety, arousal may also be affected by a range of environmental variables, in particular the extent to which the environment is stimulating or non-stimulating. A non-stimulating environment may result from a requirement to perform a boring task, use of drugs such as alcohol or sedatives, or the circadian disruption attendant upon shift-work or international travel. A stimulating environment, on the other hand, may be characterised by noise, the application of threats or incentives, or the use of stimulating drugs such as caffeine. The effects of circadian rhythms and of drugs on cognitive performance are considered in Chapters 7 and 8. External factors that influence arousal are referred to as stressors and some stressors, notably nicotine and music, can act to increase or decrease arousal depending upon style of smoking (rapid shallow puffs or slow deep ones) or type of music, respectively.

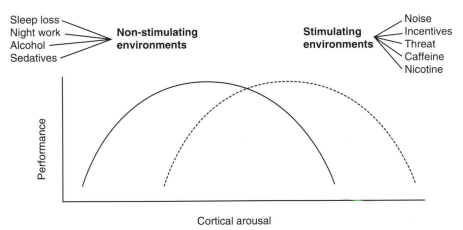

Figure 6.3 The Yerkes-Dodson law. ——, difficult task; — —, easy task

Early studies of the effects of anxiety on students' exam performances confirm its disruptive influence. Liebert and Morris (1967) found that the anxious response could be divided into a physiological component, which they termed "emotionality", and a cognitive component, which they termed "worry". The latter, but not the former, was associated with a diminution in performance (Morris & Liebert, 1970). They could not conclude, however, that worry actually causes poor performance, as both worry and poor performance could have the same origins. For example, the student may worry because he or she knows they are not adequately prepared for the exam. Multidimensional anxiety theory (Martens, Vealey, & Burton, 1990) acknowledges the cognitive and somatic components of the anxious response but also recognises a further dimension related to self-confidence. This theory also predicts that somatic anxiety will affect performance according to the curvilinear relationship expressed by the Yerkes-Dodson law. However, it posits an inverse relationship with cognitive anxiety, indicating its generally negative effect, but a positive relationship with self-confidence. Martens *et al.* provide some data to support this model.

The mechanisms underlying the negative effect of worry on performance may be explicable in terms of Easterbrook's (1959) hypothesis. This suggests that elevated arousal narrows the attentional spotlight in ways that may result in the neglect of task-relevant stimulus elements, so contributing directly to a decline in performance. In addition, anxiety may lead the player to process task-irrelevant worries, for example concerning his or her ability or preparation for the game, and perhaps also to process and worry about the uncomfortable physiological state of high arousal accompanying anxiety. Arousal control may be crucial in sports requiring fine motor control, for example snooker or golf, so that such worry may be justifiable. Given the limits of working memory capacity (see Chapter 5), however, a reduction in resources available to the task in hand is then perhaps inevitable when cognitive resources are preoccupied with these sources of worry.

A particular source of task-irrelevant worry is self-consciousness. Fenigstein, Scheier and Buss (1975) devised the Self-Consciousness Questionnaire to measure three components of the self-conscious state. These were public self-consciousness, private self-consciousness and social anxiety. The last of these, social anxiety, is a component of anxiety that generally can be assessed via standard anxiety questionnaires such as the State–Trait Anxiety Inventory of Spielberger, Gorsuch and Luschene (1970). Self-consciousness can be defined as a sense of embarrassment or unease at being the object of others' attention. Public self-consciousness is processing of the ways in which one may be seen by others and a resulting preoccupation with what others may think of one. Private self-consciousness, on the other hand, is reflection upon one's own behaviours, feelings and thoughts. As with anxiety, both public and private self-consciousness may result in distraction from the task in hand in favour of task-irrelevant cognitions concerning, for example, how one appears to others. In addition, however, private self-consciousness may lead to renewed attention to automated components of performance. This may serve as a further route by which performance can be disrupted, since highly skilled performance is at the autonomous level. Autonomous skills incorporate a high level of automaticity essential for their smooth execution. Conscious processing of skill elements in effect returns skilled behaviour to either of the earlier cognitive or associative levels where these are associated with performance that is both less fluent and less successful.

Baumeister (1984) observed that under pressure, a person realises consciously that it is important to execute a behaviour correctly. Consciousness tries to ensure the correctness of this execution by monitoring the process of performance (e.g. the coordination and precision of muscle movements); but consciousness does not contain the knowledge of these skills, so that, ironically, it reduces success. As well as being in keeping with the intuition that it is possible to "try too hard", evidence for this negative effect of pressure on performance is available from a number of areas. In terms of match statistics, a common finding from sports research is the home field advantage. This is the tendency of teams to win more often than not when playing on their home ground (Courneya & Carron, 1992). However, when a "big match" is played at home the home field advantage can actually become a home field disadvantage. Thus, the pressures resulting from playing a key match with the expectations of the home crowd in evidence all around may produce the conditions under which performance may decline. For example, in the US NBA Championships from 1967 to 1982, the first two games showed a clear home field advantage (115 wins on home soil versus 49 away wins). When the last and most crucial game of the season was played at home, however, the situation reverted to 19 home wins versus 22 away wins.

If private self-consciousness impacts performance via its effect on self-monitoring and a resulting return to novice levels of performance, then the intriguing possibility is created that players may be "innoculated" against performance breakdown under pressure if they are trained in ways that do not provide them with conscious or verbalisable rules to which they may return under pressure. This is the view that breakdown of skilled performance may be dependent upon skill acquisition parameters. That is, if explicit learning can be minimised, then the performer will have less conscious knowledge of the rules for execution of the skill and will be less able to reinvest his or her knowledge in times of stress. This possibility has been investigated by Masters (1992), who trained two groups of participants on an unfamiliar golf-putting task using either explicit (via the use of rules) or implicit instruction (without knowledge of rules). With the proviso that even implicitly trained individuals may nevertheless derive some explicit rules of their own, evidence was found to support the view that the skill of performers with a small pool of explicit knowledge is less likely to fail under pressure than that of performers with a larger pool of explicit knowledge.

Masters, Polman and Hammond (1993) defined cognitive reinvestment as a tendency to introduce conscious control of a movement by isolating and focusing on specific components of it. They subsequently developed a cognitive reinvestment scale as a hybrid of the Cognitive Failures Questionnaire of Broadbent, Cooper, Fitzgerald and Parkes (1982), the public and private self-consciousness scales of the Self-Consciousness Questionnaire (Fenigstein et al., 1975) and the rehearsal factor of the Emotional Control Questionnaire (Roger & Nesshoever, 1987). The scale demonstrated good internal consistency and reliability and was used in four studies to demonstrate that high reinvestors are more likely than low reinvestors to suffer performance breakdown under pressure. In one such study, scores on the reinvestment scale were correlated with stress-related performance ratings in squash and tennis players. This resulted in significant positive correlations of +0.63 and of +0.70, respectively. This would appear to be good evidence that cognitive reinvestment plays some part in the breakdown of skill under stress.

6.4 Skill breakdown: human error

The price of automaticity

A basic distinction may be made between errors and mistakes. Broadly speaking, an error is an appropriate action that has gone awry somewhere in its execution. A mistake, on the other hand, is a completely inappropriate action based upon, for example, faulty understanding of a situation, or faulty inferences and judgements (Kahneman, Slovic, & Tversky, 1982). Errors can be further subdivided into two classes. As well as errors *per se* (such as putting coffee into the teapot), there are also what Reason (1984a) terms "lapses". These are failures to remember something such as a word or a person's name, or failure to remember to carry out an action such as taking medicines at regular intervals. Laboratory-based studies have been devised to simulate lapses, such as those involved in the tip-of-the-tongue state (Brown & McNeill, 1966). The failure to remember to take medicines is an example of failure of prospective memory, a form of everyday memory (see Chapter 3).

Reason, Manstead, Stradling, Baxter and Campbell (1990) considered a third class of error-related behaviour that they termed "violation". Identified primarily in the context of driving, violations involve contravention of rules, laws or codes of behaviour in ways that represent a deliberate deviation from safe driving practice. Examples include drunk driving, speeding, jumping the lights, or deliberately following too near to another vehicle ("tailgating"). West, French, Kemp and Elander (1993) found a relation between violations while driving and other sorts of social violation. Reason *et al.* (1990) found that violation was more common in men than in women, in young men than in older men, and in both sexes appeared to decline with age, the latter in contrast with lapses.

An early approach to the study of error involved the use of questionnaires to assess individuals' liability to make errors, often as a function of personality. Error-proneness was considered to be a dimension of individual difference and this continues to be recognised in lay discourse concerning the "accident-prone" personality. Early studies sought to investigate the reality of this personality. Although there is some evidence in favour (McKenna, 1983), most writers now acknowledge that actual accident involvement arises not only from accident-proneness but also, and probably more importantly, from external circumstances including task demands and job design. In an attempt to link accident-proneness with personality, some investigators have examined the role of cognitive styles such as field-dependence or -independence, particularly in the context of driving. Here the suggestion would be that a more field-dependent person would have difficulty in extracting salient information, such as a road sign, from a complex scene with a resulting greater likelihood of a perceptual error and perhaps of an accident. Broadbent *et al.* (1982) developed the Cognitive Failures Questionnaire (CFQ) to assess the efficiency of distributing attention over multiple inputs under stressful conditions. The questionnaire comprises 25 items involving perceptual errors (such as not seeing a road sign), memory errors (such as forgetting someone's name) and action errors (such as bumping into things). Matthews, Coyle and Craig (1990) argued that the CFQ contained too few items to measure more than a couple of traits and suggested that these may be a generalised cognitive failure factor and another weaker factor specifically concerned with memory for people's names. While objective data linking CFQ scores to actual accident involvement is relatively weak, there is reasonably good evidence that high CFQ scorers perceive mental workload demands of task performance to be higher than do low scorers (Wells & Matthews, 1994) and that high scorers may be more vulnerable to the effects of stress (Reason, 1988).

Although the investigation of human error via individual differences has borne some fruit, the study of error has mainly employed ecologically valid methodologies that include the keeping of diaries, naturalistic observation, or the *post-hoc* study of accidents and disasters. These have given rise to error taxonomies that try to delineate the forms that errors can take. In addition, laboratory studies have been carried out to model the conditions giving rise to error.

A taxonomy of error types

Norman (1981) provided a taxonomy of error types based on the study of 1000 action slips gathered as part of a diary study. The taxonomy is presented in Table 6.1. Norman assumed that the human information-processing system is mediated

Table 6.1 Norman's (1981) classification of action slips

```
1  Slips in the formation of intention
   (a)  Mode errors
   (b)  Description errors

2  Slips that arise from the faulty activation of schemas
   (a)  Unintentional activation
           (i)  Capture errors
          (ii)  Data-driven activation
         (iii)  Associative activation

   (b)  Loss of activation
           (i)  Forgetting an intention
          (ii)  Misordering the components of a sequence
         (iii)  Leaving out steps in a sequence
          (iv)  Repeating steps in a sequence

3  Slips that arise from the faulty triggering of active schemas
   (a)  False triggering
           (i)  Spoonerisms
          (ii)  Blends
         (iii)  Thoughts leading to actions
          (iv)  Premature triggering

   (b)  Failure to trigger
           (i)  Action pre-empted
          (ii)  Insufficient activation
         (iii)  Triggering conditions failed to match
```

by many processing structures, each of which can only carry out relatively simple operations. Each of these is coupled to many other structures in what Norman termed "schemas". Norman's taxonomy is organised around three primary headings, each corresponding to a different phase in the initiation and guidance of action and each contributing to a different type of slip. These three phases are the formation of intentions, the activation of schemas and the triggering of schemas. Norman's taxonomy has the advantage of linking the idea of schemata, as the detailed control elements behind largely automatic processes occurring on all cognitive domains, with the observation that action slips take the form of organised segments of familiar behaviour (Reason, 1984b). Schemata may be triggered by a variety of agencies, including intentions, influences from neighbouring schemata, past activity and environmental circumstances.

Examples of errors in some of the categories identified by Norman (1981) are as follows (many of these examples are drawn from Norman, 1988). Mode errors arise when a system has multiple modes of operation. Although in complex systems such as aircraft it is probably inevitable that the system has multiple modes of operation, in general it is usually seen as desirable for a system not to have separate modes of operation. Examples of systems with moded and modeless operation can readily be found in different types of word processor. For example, WordPerfect 5.1 has separate entry, editing and directory scanning modes, whereas Word 2000 does not. The presence of modes in the former means that one can attempt to edit a file that one is viewing in scanning mode. Since the system does not allow one to carry out this action, it represents an error. It is, of course, necessary to come out of scanning mode and retrieve the file before editing can be undertaken. Description errors arise when an object similar to the target object becomes the target of an operation. For example, one might attempt to put the lid on the sugar bowl but instead put it on the coffee cup. This is more likely if the latter has a similar size opening to that of the former. Capture errors may occur when a frequently or recently undertaken activity captures attention. One of the examples from Norman's corpus of errors was "I was using a copying machine lately and was counting the pages. I found myself counting '1,2, . . . 9,10, Jack, Queen, King'. I had been playing a lot of cards lately".

Data-driven errors occur when an automatic response is driven by the presenting data. Again quoting from Norman's corpus, "I wanted to phone reception from the hall to find out which room to out a guest in. Instead of dialling reception I dialled the number on the door opposite". Associative errors may occur when automatic responses are generated by internal thoughts rather than the external data. For example, one may pick up the office phone and yell "come in" at it. Loss of activation errors include the kind of "losing the plot" scenario typified by going into a room for something but on entering the room finding that one has no idea what one went in there for. Further examples of loss of activation errors include the misordering, omission or repetition of components of an action sequence. For example, in making a pot of tea one may misorder the components (pour in the water before adding tea to the pot), omit steps (forget the tea altogether) or repeat steps (try to fill the kettle twice).

Spoonerisms and blends are best illustrated by speech errors. These can occur naturally or be induced experimentally in laboratory studies. Equally, thought leading to action may occur when a schema is triggered that is, however, not meant for execution. For example, in spelling my (rather unusual) surname to telephone callers, I usually expect them to be writing it down so I say the letters slowly. However, on numerous occasions I have found myself writing my own surname down on a piece of paper while doing so. Apparently the thought of someone else being enabled to write down that word is sufficient to cause me to do so myself. Premature triggering may occur when an anticipated behaviour is launched too early, as typified by the erroneous false start in competitive running.

Failure to trigger occurs when an action is not carried out. This is not the same as leaving out steps in an action sequence. This has already been discussed as a loss of activation error. Rather, failure to trigger resembles the sort of situation that occurs when one forgets to do something, for example to telephone a friend or to take medicines forming part of a course of treatment. In one such study (Wilkins & Baddeley, 1978), participants who pushed a button on a recording device four times per day to simulate taking antibiotic medication sometimes took their "medicine" at erratic spacings in time as they forgot to take the dose but then remembered and took the medicine at a later time. On some occasions, however, they appeared to be completely unaware of the fact that they had forgotten to take their medicines and no steps were taken to correct the error. Norman (1981) argues that failure to trigger may occur because an action has been pre-empted by another, because there is insufficient activation for the action to occur, or because triggering conditions failed to match. In the case of taking medicines at regular intervals, these conditions may prevail if the patient's normal routine has been disrupted by an unusual activity.

A diary study similar to that of Norman (1981) was carried out by Reason (1979) and Reason and Mycielska (1982) and involved individuals keeping diaries of known errors over an extended period. They found that slips of action were most likely to occur in highly familiar surroundings during the performance of frequently and/or recently executed tasks in which a considerable degree of automaticity had been achieved. As such, Reason (1979) regards error as the price we pay for automaticity. In Reason's error corpus, occurrence of errors was commonly associated with states of attentional "capture". Such capture could be due to some pressing internal preoccupation or to some external distraction. A large proportion of the slips (40%) took the form of intact, well-organised action sequences that were judged as recognisably belonging to some other task or activity that was frequently and/or recently executed. These they referred to as "strong habit intrusions" and could also occur as "strong emotion intrusions". Here, ongoing psychological distress would induce habits of thought likely to preoccupy the individual, making the likelihood of error greater. Finally, other types of errors could be identified in Reason's error corpus. These included place-losing errors, blends and reversals. Place-losing errors most commonly involved omissions or repetitions. These typically resulted from a wrong assessment of the current stage of the action sequence, or from an interruption. Blends and reversals appeared to result from crosstalk between two currently active schemas, either verbal or behavioural, such that the objects to which they were applied became partially or completely transposed.

Reason (1979) proposed a taxonomy of error types that is very similar to Norman's though uses different terminology. He referred to storage failures, test failures, subroutine failures, discrimination failures and programme assembly failures. This view is, however, readily assimilated within Norman's. For example, discrimination failures can lead to errors in the formation of an intention, and storage failures for intentions can produce faulty triggering of active schemas. Reason (1990) went on to propose two primitives of the cognitive system that he termed "frequency gambling" and "similarity matching". Frequency gambling results in erroneous responding in which frequently or recently executed behaviour takes precedence. Similarity matching occurs in situations in which attention is captured by a few salient features of a stimulus, resulting in the activation of incorrect schemas. Esgate and Reason (unpublished) illustrated error-related phenomena based on these primitives in the declarative domain, using biographical information about US presidents as the domain to be recalled. A study of a similar nature was carried out by Hay and Jacoby (1996), who argued that action slips are most likely to occur when the correct response is not the strongest or most habitual one and attention is not fully applied to the task of selecting the correct response. They tested this prediction by having participants complete paired associates of the form knee–b_n_. Based on previous pairing trials, the correct response could be either the strongest response (e.g. bend) or not the strongest response (e.g. bone). Participants had 1 or 3 sec to respond. Error was more likely when the responses were both not the strongest associate, and the response had to be made quickly.

Rasmussen (1982) proposed a distinction between rule-based, skill-based and knowledge-based behaviour that has proved very influential in the area of human error. On this account, skill-based behaviour is sensory-motor performance, guided by intention, which proceeds smoothly and in a highly integrated fashion while being minimally under the control of conscious attention. Since slips of action are most likely to occur when action has become automated and no longer requires conscious control, errors occurring at the skill-based level will be slips and lapses rather than mistakes or violations. In contrast, errors made at the rule-based or knowledge-based levels are more likely to be mistakes – errors of planning or of judgement. Rule-based behaviour is governed by rules that are either stored in memory or made available through explicit instructions or protocols. Rule-based mistakes there arise through failures of interpretation or comprehension of the situation. Knowledge-based behaviour is based on the operator's knowledge of how the system works and of its current state, and on the decisions made in that light. Mistakes may therefore arise at the knowledge-based level either because the operator's knowledge of the system is inaccurate or incomplete, or because he or she is overwhelmed by the complexity of the information available. The latter can occur as a result of inexperience or of excessive workload.

One of the main differences between errors and mistakes is the ease with which they can be detected. Slips can be detected relatively easily, while mistakes may often go unrealised. Reason (1990) compared error frequencies and detections for skill-based slips and lapses and knowledge-based mistakes in three different published studies. Overall, skill-based errors accounted for 61% of the total number of errors, rule-based mistakes for 27% and knowledge-based mistakes for 11%. In contrast, the detection rate was 86% for skill-based errors, 73% for rule-based mistakes and 70.5% for knowledge-based mistakes. So although most errors and mistakes are detected, slips and lapses appear to be more readily detected than mistakes.

Laboratory-induced errors

Reason (1984a) identified induced speech errors, induced memory blocks and place-losing errors as examples of the type of error that can be induced fairly readily in the laboratory. Speech errors can be induced using the method of competing plans. Participants can be induced to make predictable and involuntary speech errors if they are both given two competing plans for one utterance and they are denied sufficient time to sort out these utterances. Called spoonerisms of laboratory-induced predisposition, or SLIP, the technique typically involves presenting word pairs to participants one at a time for about 1 sec each. Participants read these pairs silently with the exception of certain cued targets designed to resemble more closely the phonology of the desired spoonerism than the intended target. For example, the target "darn bore" is expected to spoonerise into "barn door" if preceded by pairs in which a word starting with a "b" is followed by one starting with a "d" (for example, ball doze, bash door, bean deck). It has been found that some 10–30% of responses will spoonerise. Reason (1984a) argues that SLIP-type errors reflect the fact that speech errors, in common with action slips, may occur when attention has been "captured" by something else. However, in keeping with work on perceptual defence and subliminal perception, salacious spoonerisms (e.g. from "fuzzy duck") are rather harder to produce than are their non-salacious equivalents, suggesting that some part of attentional resources is usually held in reserve to guard against socially damaging errors.

The study of memory blocking dates from the work on tip-of-the-tongue states conducted by Brown and McNeill (1966), in which definitions of low-frequency words were given to participants who were then able or unable to produce the actual word. Those unable to produce the word in some cases had a strong feeling of knowing that they knew the word. It was "on the tip of their tongue". In such cases, participants were found nevertheless to be able to provide a lot of information about the word's orthography (e.g. length, first letter) and phonology (e.g. what it sounds like). Blocking in episodic and semantic memory has been reviewed by Roediger and Neely (1982). Lucas (1984) tested the hypothesis that memory retrieval could be blocked by strong-habit intrusions, as was suggested in the case of action slips. In the case of actions slips, a strong habit intrusion is an action frequently and/or recently carried out. The parallel of this in the case of verbal memory is word frequency. Consistently with her hypothesis, Lucas found that the greatest incidence of blocking occurred when cues were presented immediately after high-frequency, semantically related priming words. Orthographically related words also delayed recall of targets slightly.

Place-losing errors were also identified by diary studies. Typically, these involved unnecessary repetitions of previously completed actions, omission of part of an action sequence, or blanks. Lucas (1984) attempted to model these place-losing errors experimentally by having participants recite multiplication tables and then interrupting them at key points with a requirement to carry out an arithmetic calculation. Place-losing errors were induced in 19% of participants, with some making such errors on up to 50% of trials. Of these errors, 42% were omissions and 26% repetitions. Blanks occurred on the remaining trials with, in some cases, participants being unable to recall even which table they were reciting. Similar results were obtained by Wing and Baddeley (1980) in their examination of slips of the pen in exam scripts. In addition, Rabbitt and Vyas (1980) found that the elderly are much more prone than young people to place-losing errors, especially when required to keep track of several conversations at social gatherings.

An experimental task that readily demonstrates laboratory-induced error is the oak–yolk task (Reason, 1992). Participants are asked questions like those presented in Table 6.2. Many participants respond to the final questions with the word "yolk". The correct answer is of course "albumin". The effect of the preceding questions is to build up a response set such that participants respond on the basis of rhyming rather than meaning. "Yolk" is a common and easily retrieved word, in contrast to "albumin", and was given as the answer by some 85% of participants.

Table 6.2 The oak–yolk task

1	What do you call the tree that grows from an acorn?	(oak)
2	What do you call a funny story?	(joke)
3	What sound does a frog make?	(croak)
4	What is Pepsi's major competitor?	(Coke)
5	What is another word for cape?	(cloak)
6	What do you call the white of an egg?	?

Source: Reason (1992).

6.5 Minimising error through design

One of the contentions of Norman (1988) is that error arises as much through bad design of the artefacts that people have to make use of as it does through failings of the human cognitive system. A consideration of the error forms identified in Norman's taxonomy suggests a number of ways in which such errors can be minimised by astute design. Such recommendations may then be regarded as principles of good design and an entire discipline, ergonomics, is concerned with the production of such recommendations and principles. One such guideline would be the need to avoid having separate modes of operation within a system whenever possible. Having modes will result in confusion as to which mode the system is in at any given time, especially if the system changes between modes automatically. Moreover, when a device has separate modes of operation, the operator will become familiar with one mode but is likely to need to refer to the manual whenever he or she needs to use the less familiar one.

Description errors, or errors based on similarity matching in Reason's (1990) terminology, may be minimised by having objects requiring similar actions all having different shapes or colours. This is evident in the design of motor cars, in which the covers for receptacles for oil, water, petrol, brake fluid, and so on, are all of different shapes, sizes and colours. In addition, some will be screw top, others bayonet fitting, still others simple push down. Moreover, since putting petrol into the wrong receptacle would have serious consequences, the petrol cap is located well away from the others at the back of the vehicle.

Capture errors, which correspond to Reason's (1990) frequency gambling, may be minimised by building in a requirement for a second confirmation that an action is as indicated. Since such responding is based on the build-up of fast, automatic responding, merely slowing down responding may avert an error. For example, in computer use, when deleting several files one after the other, you may find that you have inadvertently deleted one that should be kept. Having a requirement for a second confirmation slows down the operator so that conscious, controlled processing may take over to cancel the delete operation. Thus a dialogue box such as that shown in Figure 6.4 may be employed.

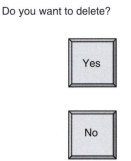

Do you want to delete?

Yes

No

Figure 6.4 Computer dialogue confirmation box

An alternative approach to prevent inadvertent deletion is to make use of the "waste-bin" facility found on many computer "desktops". This is a holding area in which deleted material is kept until the bin is emptied. Since emptying the bin is a second task, this also effectively slows down the operator and has the added benefit that the deleted material may be held in the bin, and therefore kept available for retrieval, for an indefinite period.

Norman (1988) suggests some further ways in which design may limit the commission of error. For example, in making use of a novel artefact, say a telephone or can-opener of a type not encountered before, the available options appear to be to retrieve from memory some appropriate schema for its use, to read the instructions, or to figure out from first principles how it works. Norman argues that none of these is particularly efficient, since all of them may be subject to error. Thus, an inappropriate schema for use may be instantiated as a result of, say, similarity matching. Moreover, people are notoriously unwilling to read instructions and/or follow them (Wright, 1981). The use of icon-based instructions may do little to improve the readability or comprehensibility of instructions. Finally, figuring out from first principles how the artefact works may result in a completely inappropriate mental model that will inevitably lead to the commission of mistakes.

Norman (1988) argues that a much better approach is to make use of Gibson's (1979) notion of affordances. These are something that a stimulus provides directly to the perceiver as a cue to its use. For example, chairs afford sitting – nobody is likely to have to read a manual to work out how to sit on a chair. Taking door handles as an example, Norman (1988) finds numerous examples of handles that are so inappropriate that they scream "push me" to the user when in reality a pulling action is required. Typically, the door is then equipped with a verbal instruction (in the shape of the word "PULL") to elicit the correct response. Norman argues that any such use of verbal instructions is an admission of failure. If sufficient attention were paid to the design of door handles in terms of affordances, then such verbal instructions would be redundant.

Affordance contributes to ease of use and may be increased by paying adequate attention to stimulus–response compatibility. That is, the spatial relationships between objects and operations should be transparent. A good example of this is the design of cooker hobs. Figure 6.5 (from Norman, 1988) shows a number of arrangements of controls and burners of increasing ease of use.

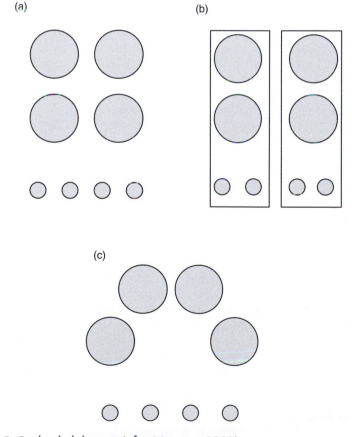

Figure 6.5 Cooker hob layouts (after Norman, 1988)

In Figure 6.5(a), there are a theoretical 24 (i.e. $4 \times 3 \times 2$) possible ways of linking controls to burners, though some are probably more likely than others. One way of dealing with this much uncertainty is to make use of some sort of redundant coding, such as colour or a verbal label ("back right"). Alternatively, a visual key could be placed by each control to indicate which burner it operates. However, Norman (1988) argues that such redundant coding is rendered unnecessary by good design. Thus, the simple grouping arrangement in Figure 6.5(b) reduces the number of possible arrangements, and therefore uncertainty, by a factor of 6 from 24 to 4. The spatial arrangement in Figure 6.5(c) is an example of a possibility that reduces the uncertainty – and therefore any need for redundant coding – completely, since the spatial arrangement makes it entirely evident which control operates which burner. Opportunities for error are therefore minimised by such arrangements. Moreover, responding will also be quicker, as the need to process redundant information has been eliminated, and this enhances the safety of the system.

Similar compatibility relations may be built into the design of vehicles. For example, the author owns a motorcycle in which the switch to operate the indicators, which indicate turning left or right, moves up and down. This simple incompatibility imposes a requirement for learning (e.g. up = right), creates a possibility for error, and may increase the possibility of an accident if the operator has to look down to read the verbal label at each end of the switch at a crucial time. In effect, the design imposes an unnecessary requirement to translate between two representational systems (up–down and left–right). In motor cars, the problem is resolved by good design. Stalks to operate indicators within a vehicle typically move in the direction of the steering wheel. Thus when wishing to turn left, if the stalk is on the left of the steering wheel you will move it down with your hand and if it is on the right you will move it up. This movement is completely compatible with the planned movement of the steering wheel and therefore demands minimal attention, minimal learning and provides few opportunities for the commission of error.

Compatibility may be further enhanced if the designer adheres to population stereotypes. These are evident in the tendency of certain actions to have culture-specific meanings. For example, if a rotary control moves clockwise or a linear control to the right, then this is usually taken to imply an increase in the parameter in question, for example an increase in volume if sound equipment is being operated. Safety-critical rotary controls of this kind, such as gas or water taps, actually move in the opposite direction from that expected under the population stereotype precisely to avoid tampering by children who are likely to assume the population stereotype. A further type of compatibility is termed "cognitive compatibility". This is compatibility at the level of mental models of a task and the model that may be built into the work system. The issue is most apparent when making use of a computer-based work system. Where incompatibilities exist between the two representations, knowledge-based mistakes may occur and be very difficult to detect. An example may be when a conventional working system has been computerised. Human understanding of the task deriving from experience of the former may not provide an accurate understanding of how the task is carried out in the latter work system.

In many psychological accounts of error, for example in the work of Reason (1990), the impression is created that errors, accidents and disasters are largely or entirely the result of the cognitive processes that give rise to error. A further layer of social psychological influence may be overlaid on top of this. For example, in the case of road traffic accidents, Reason *et al.* (1990) emphasise the role of violations. In his analysis of the Chernobyl nuclear power plant disaster in the former Soviet Union in 1985, Reason (1987) emphasises the social psychological phenomenon known as "groupthink". While both the cognitive psychology of error and social psychology are clearly important, other writers such as Norman (1988) argue that in very many cases the blame for errors, including errors that may have tragic consequences, may be laid at the door of poor design. Baker and Marshall (1988), in their response to Reason's (1987) account of the events at Chernobyl, make precisely this point and assert that the importance of design factors may be underplayed in Reason's analysis. Other factors, such as time of day, are often implicated in major disasters. Very many such disasters (e.g. Chernobyl, Bhopal, Piper Alpha) have occurred during the early hours of the morning. At such times (see Chapter 7), circadian rhythms in the cognitive performance of operators are likely to have their most pronounced effects.

6.6 A case study of "human error"

The following case study, of the Kegworth air crash, tries to illustrate the interacting nature of the factors contributing to a major disaster. These range from human error to poor design, and from inadequate training to organisational culture. The case is of British Midlands Flight BE92, a shuttle from Heathrow to Belfast, both in the UK, on 8 January 1989. This aircraft came down on a motorway outside of Birmingham, UK, as it attempted to make an emergency landing at its home airport of Castle Donnington following an emergency shutdown of one engine due to excessive engine vibration. However, the pilots shut down the wrong engine, leaving the faulty one to struggle and finally become useless during the descent. The accident was largely blamed upon the actions of the pilots – that is, on "human error".

British Midlands Flight BE92 was piloted by one of the airline's most experienced men, Captain Hunt, along with First Officer McClelland. The aircraft was a brand new Boeing 737-400. According to transcripts made from the cockpit voice recorder recovered after the crash, all was going well as the plane climbed to its cruising altitude through 28,000 feet. At this point, shuddering in the airframe alerted the pilots to a malfunction in one of the engines that was initially thought to be an engine fire, particularly as some smoke appeared to enter the cockpit. A rapid scanning of the cockpit displays indicated that it was the right-hand engine that was malfunctioning and the captain gave the order to throttle it back. This appeared to solve the problem, since the shuddering and smoke disappeared. The engine was therefore shut down completely, the aircraft was levelled at 30,000 feet, and air-traffic control clearance was sought for an emergency landing at Castle Donnington, British Midland's UK base. For the next 20 min the aircraft flew normally to its new destination.

Sadly, however, the decision to close down the right-hand engine was a fateful one, since this engine was entirely normal. Closing it down had, however, eliminated the presenting problems of vibration and smoke and the pilots quite reasonably therefore assumed that they had completely solved the problem and were flying on a normally functioning engine. However, the reasons for the apparent elimination of the presenting problem were not clear to the pilots, since these resulted from technical systems within the aircraft that the pilots had not been fully informed of. In particular, when the faulty left-hand engine started to malfunction, the thrust-balancing system needed to keep the engines of a twin-engined jet in balance so that the aircraft could fly in a straight line, pumped more fuel into the faulty engine causing it to surge and produce smoke. With the healthy right-hand engine shut down, the balancing system was disengaged and the aircraft could fly normally in undemanding level flight and descent. However, the faulty left-hand engine was to suffer a catastrophic failure during the stresses imposed by the manoeuvres leading to landing. This left the aircraft without sufficient power to reach the airport, coming down just short of it on the motorway. Thirty-nine people died on impact and nine more died later of their injuries. Many others were injured, including the captain who subsequently became a wheelchair user. Captain Hunt was subsequently retired on health grounds, while the first officer was sacked.

At the time, however, the pilots' decision to close the healthy right-hand engine appeared an entirely rational and correct course of action. Throttling back the right-hand engine eliminated the problem and it was reasonable to therefore conclude that that engine must be at fault so should be shut down. Moreover, the aircraft subsequently flew entirely normally. Very few pilots in that position would have had reason to doubt their actions. The situation was compounded by some deficits in training on the brand new aircraft, for which a simulator was not even available in the UK. This almost certainly contributed to the pilots' evident lack of understanding of the engine thrust-balancing system. In addition, cultural factors within the working system compounded the problem. Although it is clear in retrospect that the pilots were in error, many passengers and members of cabin crew had seen sparks fly from the left-hand engine and knew that this one must be faulty. The captain even announced over the public address system that the right-hand engine had been shut down. Surviving passengers, when interviewed subsequently, rationalised this to themselves by, for example, concluding that the pilots labelled left and right differently from themselves, for instance basing their labelling on how the engines would appear to them if they reversed their position in the cockpit. This reluctance to challenge high-status professionals has contributed to other disasters. For example, in the Potomac crash in the USA, in which an aircraft with iced wings came down in the Potomac River, members of cabin crew who had seen the ice on the wings before take-off had been unwilling to bring this to the attention of the pilots who, they assumed, must be aware of the problem (Norman, 1988). This situation has been termed the "two-cultures" problem and organisational analysts within airlines now recommend different ways of working, with integrated aircraft management systems taking the place of old-style rigid division of labour between pilots and flight attendants.

The two cultures may extend even into the cockpit: reluctance on the part of a first officer to challenge his captain may have contributed to the Tenerife crash of 1977, the world's worst non-intentional air disaster, which was caused by the captain commencing his take-off run prematurely. Similar considerations apply to

KoreanAir Flight 007 from Seoul, which strayed into the airspace of the former Soviet Union in 1983 and was shot down. Here organisational factors contributed to the extent that pilots had been told that any flights returning to Seoul would result in the pilots been punished. The airline had had a spate of flights returning due to difficulties with reprogramming the inertial navigation system while in flight. Clearly, the inertial navigation system had some design flaws (Norman, 1988), but in this case the organisational culture that punished "failure" resulted in the pilots trying to cover up their difficulties by continuing with the flight even though the navigation instrument was in error. The result was an infringement of Soviet airspace and the shooting down of the aircraft with the loss of all on board.

In addition, poor ergonomics contributed to the crash of British Midlands Flight BE92. In fact, a very small engine vibration indicator, placed outside of the pilots' area of focal attention, clearly indicated that it was the left-hand engine that was suffering undue vibration and was in distress. However, the position and size of this instrument, as well as the fact that the computer display used was very much harder to read than the conventional dial-and-pointer version that it replaced, meant that under conditions of stress in which focal attention was reduced (Easterbrook, 1959), the pilots completely ignored this key piece of information. In the computer-generated displays, cursors only one-third the length of the old-fashioned needles were positioned outside of horseshoe-shaped dials and subsequent studies have shown that the result takes much longer to read than do the old-fashioned needles-and-dials. Moreover, in earlier aircraft the engine vibration indicator was seen as unreliable in the extreme, to the point that pilots were actually allowed to fly with the instrument disconnected. In this case, however, the instrument was highly reliable and if attention had been paid to it, the accident could have been averted. However, in addition to its poor placing, small size and low readability, the instrument had no out-of-range red warning area. Nor did it have a warning light or tone to grab the pilots' attention, despite the fact that less important instruments were so equipped. Moreover, inadequate training on the new aircraft meant that the pilots were as unaware of the importance of this instrument as they were of the operation of the thrust-balancing system.

In fact, the conversion course for the pilots upgrading from the 737-300 to 737-400 aircraft consisted only of a one-and-a-half day slide show lecture followed by a multiple-choice test. No simulator was available in the UK at the time and pilots were expected to gain familiarity with the aircraft on routine flights alongside experienced captains, although this was standard practice in the industry and fully in accordance with the aircraft manufacturer's guidelines. One of the selling points of the aircraft was that pilot training would be minimal on account of the high compatibility between the conventional technology predecessor and its computerised replacement, the difference being only that the latter employed computer-generated displays for ease of communication with the aircraft's on-board computers. The pilots were thus placed in a condition of low cognitive compatibility. Moreover, a simple arrangement such as a tail-fitted camera to allow engine visibility would have enabled the pilots to easily see which engine had produced smoke. The fitting of such cameras had been recommended following an engine fire on the ground at Manchester Airport in the UK 4 years earlier. However, this had not been acted upon.

Of course, there would have been no crash had the engine of British Midlands Flight BE92 not failed. In fact, this was a new engine, an upgrade of an earlier model to produce the extra power needed by the bigger plane. This upgraded engine had not been tested at altitude and under those conditions it exhibited an aerodynamic phenomenon known as flutter and it was this that gave rise to the engine malfunction and accident. Faults had therefore occurred during the design and testing stage of the hardware long before the pilots even got their hands on the plane. Shortly after the Kegworth crash, two more aircraft suffered identical engine failures and afterwards the engine type was withdrawn from service.

Given the number of factors contributing to the crash of British Midlands Flight BE92, then, blaming the pilots for "human error" seems little more than a case of blaming the victim. The performance of a pilot or other system operator can only be a function of the training and equipment that he or she is provided with. If training does not equip the pilot to cope with the situations encountered or if the equipment is not as easy to use as it should be, then can this really be called human error? And are the oversights on the part of the engine manufacturer not also examples of human error? The tendency to attribute blame to the last two people to touch a system before an incident occurs ignores the role of everyone else from designers onwards in the creation, maintenance and operation of that system.

Summary

- Practice at a skilled activity results in a high level of automaticity that frees up attentional resources, so as to leave the performer able to allocate cognitive resources to a concurrent secondary task that may then be carried out successfully.
- Under certain circumstances, undue attention may be paid to a highly skilled, routinised activity in ways that disrupt the flow of that activity. This has been illustrated by the phenomenon of "choking" in sports performance.
- While under automatic control, skilled activity may run off without adequate supervisory control and this may result in various types of errors.
- Errors are not random events but take predictable forms that can be summarised in error taxonomies.
- Due attention to the ergonomics of a work system can limit the possibilities for human error.
- The case study of a major air crash has illustrated how the role of human error may be overstated and can, in the worst case, be used simply as a way of blaming the victim.
- Most human errors are detectable and detected, and well-designed working environments are sufficiently forgiving to enable recovery from such errors to take place.
- An incident may have a long aetiology stretching back as far as the design and testing of hardware, and this may exert its effects long before human operators may have had opportunities to make errors.

Further reading

Moran, A. (2004). *Sport and exercise psychology*. Hove, UK: Routledge. An excellent sports psychology textbook offering an authoritative account of choking written by an expert in the field.

Norman, D. (1988). *The psychology of everyday things*. New York: Basic Books. An absolute classic: the definitive account of relationships between error and design and a perfect example of how profundity can be combined with accessibility.

Noyes, J. (2001). *Designing for humans*. Hove, UK: Psychology Press. An up-to-date textbook of ergonomics describing good design practice for the minimisation of error.

Reason, J. (1990). *Human error*. Cambridge: Cambridge University Press. Reason's view of error presented as a final synthesis of decades of his own work in the area.

Further reading

Chapter 7

Biological cycles and cognitive performance

7.1 Introduction

Cyclicity characterises nature. For most organisms, physiological process and behavioural activity are organised into cyclic patterns. These patterns provide timetables for biological and behavioural events allowing for effective organisation of these events. Cycles ensure that important activities such as searching for food, sleeping and mating take place at optimal times. Given this temporal organisation of activities, it is essential that applied cognitive psychologists take account of the relationship between these cycles and cognitive and work performance. Is memory affected by time of day? How does working at night affect performance? Is a woman's cognitive performance affected by her menstrual cycle phase? These are the kinds of questions that we will address in this chapter. Two major human cycles will be considered. The first is the circadian rhythm or the 24 hour sleep–wake cycle. It takes its name from the Latin *circa* (about) and *diem* (a day). The second is the menstrual cycle. This is an ultradian (more than 24 hours) rhythm of approximately 30 days. This rhythm regulates ovum (egg) maturation and release in humans.

The range of biological cycles is vast – from the pulsatile secretions of hormones to breeding cycles and life cycles. Cycles govern the timing of biological events: effectively, they provide timetables for both internal physiological processes, such as hormone secretion, and active behaviours, like hunting and migration. The cycles themselves are controlled by oscillations and the frequency of these oscillations determines the time course or period of the cycle. The period is the time taken to complete a single cycle. For example, the human menstrual cycle is controlled by a low-frequency oscillator, as the time course for ovum (egg) maturation and release is relatively long. However, this low-frequency rhythm is underpinned by the high-frequency rhythms of the individual hormones (Dyrenfurth, Jewelewicz, Waren, Ferin, & Vande Wiele, 1974).

Biological cycles are not simply fluctuations in biological processes to maintain homeostasis, though this is clearly an important role: "they represent knowledge of the environment and have been proposed as a paradigmatic representation of and deployment of information regarding the environment in biological systems: a prototypical learning" (Healy, 1987, p. 271). Oatley (1974) considered that the ability to organise biological oscillations into rhythms allowed the effective timetabling of biological functions, providing "subscripts" for internal processes. You can think of biological cycles as a very effective and primitive form of learning: information about the external environment is represented internally and this information is used to organise behaviour in an adaptive way.

7.2 Circadian rhythms

In the following sections, we will consider the nature of circadian rhythms and their regulation. There are well-documented time-of-day effects on many aspects of cognitive performance. This research will be reviewed and discussed. Finally, we will consider circadian desynchrony (jet-lag and night-work) and the implications of this for performance.

The circadian rhythm is the best studied biological cycle (Figure 7.1). Circadian rhythms have been observed in a wide range of behaviours, from processes at the level of individual cells to information processing and mood. The circadian rhythm is adaptive and may be traced to early dependence on the sun as a source of energy. Organisms adapted to the cyclic fluctuations of this energy source and so their cells developed a temporal organisation (Young, 1978). This temporal organisation ensured that activities important for survival took place at the right time of day or night.

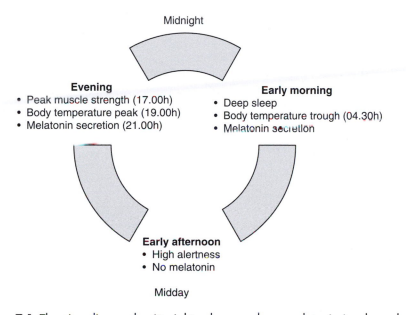

Midnight

Evening
• Peak muscle strength (17.00h)
• Body temperature peak (19.00h)
• Melatonin secretion (21.00h)

Early morning
• Deep sleep
• Body temperature trough (04.30h)
• Melatonin secretion

Early afternoon
• High alertness
• No melatonin

Midday

Figure 7.1 The circadian cycle. At night, when we sleep, melatonin is released and body temperature falls, reaching a trough at about 04.30 hours before gradually rising again. Light helps to inhibit melatonin secretion, which stops in the morning, helping us to wake. Motor coordination and reaction time are best during the afternoon. By about 17.00 hours, muscular and cardiovascular efficiency are at their best and body temperature peaks soon after. Melatonin release begins again in the late evening, promoting sleepiness, and body temperature begins to fall

A two-oscillator model of the human circadian rhythm is generally accepted. The circadian rhythm is closely linked to both arousal (indeed, sleep is usually taken as the lower point on the arousal continuum) and temperature. The daily temperature rhythm rises to a peak in the afternoon and begins to fall again, reaching its lowest point, or trough, between 04.00 and 05.00 hours. While the temperature and arousal rhythms are related they are not synonymous, and one cannot be used as an index of the other (Asso, 1987). Monk (1982) and Monk *et al.* (1983) suggest an arousal Rhythm A (controlled by the Type 1 oscillator) that is parallel to the temperature rhythm and an arousal Rhythm B (controlled by the Type 2 oscillator) that is parallel to the sleep–wake cycle. Normally, these two rhythms are synchronised, but can become desynchronised, especially when the clock is allowed to "free-run" – that is, when it is not synchronised to 24 hours by light and/or other cues. The relative influence of a particular oscillator depends on the task. By inducing desynchrony between the two oscillators, Monk *et al.* (1983) found that simple manual dexterity tasks were influenced by the temperature rhythm oscillator, whereas more complex cognitive tasks were affected by the sleep–wake cycle.

The hormone melatonin, secreted by the pineal gland, also seems to play a role in regulating the sleep–wake cycle. Melatonin is released mainly at night and is probably important in promoting sleep (see Figure 7.2). Its release is inhibited by

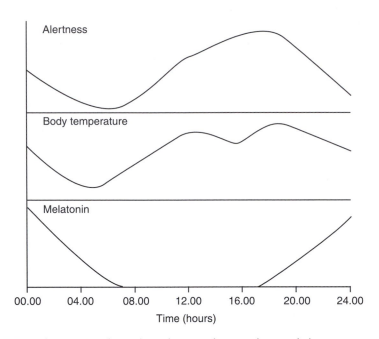

Figure 7.2 Melatonin is released predominately at night. Levels begin to rise during early evening and fall again as dawn approaches. Body temperature decreases through the night, reaching a trough at about 04.30 hours, before rising again throughout the day, peaking in the early evening. Alertness increases from early morning on, reaching a peak in the morning and another in the afternoon. Alertness then decreases from evening on, reaching its lowest in the early hours of the morning, which can be a problem for those working night-shifts

light and this seems to help people to wake up in the morning. Melatonin may be useful in treating insomnia and other sleep difficulties. Experimental studies have shown that it can advance or delay the circadian clock depending on when it is taken. Research is currently exploring the possibilities of using it to reduce or prevent jet-lag (Waterhouse, Reilly, & Atkinson, 1997).

There are individual differences in circadian rhythms. Individuals differ in the time of day when their physiological and psychological activity peaks. Horne and

Ostberg (1977) devised a questionnaire to measure circadian typology. On the basis of their responses, individuals can be categorised as either morning or evening types. Circadian typology is related to circadian fluctuations in various measures such as vigilance and other cognitive tasks (Adan, 1993).

Entrainment

Most biological cycles are believed to be endogenous – that is, they are believed to be in-built features of organisms. Of course, biological cycles may be affected by exogenous variables, such as light, but these act to entrain the cycles, rather than cause them. Entrainment refers to the synchrony of biological clocks. Light entrains the circadian rhythm to about 24 hours, whereas in the absence of the normal variations in light across the day, the "free-running" circadian rhythm is about 24½ hours. Light, in this case, acts as a *zeitgeber*, or time-giver. The circadian rhythm has been studied extensively in the fruit fly. If the fly is kept in darkness, it shows an activity rhythm of about 23½ hours; exposure to normal daily light acts to entrain this to 24 hours. In humans, too, the "free-running" clock is not set at 24 hours. In 1962, Michel Siffre lived alone in a dark underground cave for 61 days and had no exposure to natural light and no other time cues such as a watch or a radio. He did have a field telephone that he could use to contact his collaborators. Every time he woke, ate, went to bed, and so on, he telephoned through so that his collaborators could note the time at which these activities occurred. This enabled them to map his patterns of activity and rest. Through this monitoring it was found that his day had lengthened from 24 hours to about 24½ hours, and his "days" had fallen out of synch with people on the surface. Indeed, when Siffre emerged from the cave he thought that the date was 20 August. In fact, it was 14 September, so he had subjectively "lost" almost a month. Other work in controlled chronobiology (chrono refers to time) laboratories has confirmed that the free-running clock in humans has a period of about 24½ hours. So, the intrinsic circadian rhythm is "set" to 24 hours by light, though for humans other *zeitgebers*, such as social activity, are also important and may even be more important (Healy, 1987).

Circadian clocks

Within an individual, the oscillators controlling different biological rhythms become entrained or synchronised. The 24 hour sleep–wake cycle has been proposed to account for this entrainment of many rhythms (Asso, 1981). Work with mammals, in particular rats, suggests that the oscillator controlling the circadian sleep–wake cycle is located in the suprachiasmatic nucleus (SCN) of the hypothalamus. The location of the hypothalamus is shown in Figure 7.3. There are extensive connections from the retina to the SCN supporting the notion that light is the primary *zeitgeber* for this cycle. So, the SCN processes the information about light and sends this to other parts of the nervous system so that they can regulate activity. Lesions of the SCN have been found to abolish the sleep–wake cycle in rats. Although the cycle is eliminated, the total amount of sleep remains the same, suggesting that

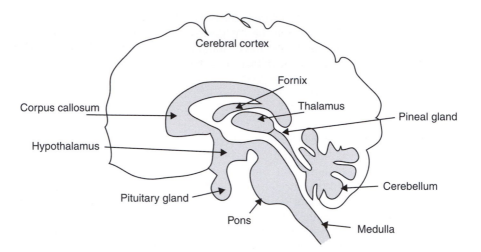

Figure 7.3 Location of the hypothalamus and the pineal gland in the human brain. The suprachiasmatic nucleus is a small nucleus of cells in the hypothalamus and contains the "circadian" clock. The pineal gland secretes the sleep-promoting hormone melatonin

the SCN does not control sleeping and waking states but rather organises these behaviours into cycles.

The circadian rhythm seems to be controlled by a number of genes that regulate the release of particular proteins. These genes were originally identified in the SCN, but later research showed that they are present throughout body tissue. So, although the SCN can be considered the master clock and master timetabler, peripheral clocks exist and these can sometimes function independently of the clock in the SCN (Wright, 2002).

7.3 The circadian rhythm and performance

Given that most human physiological functions show circadian rhythms, it comes as no surprise to learn that rhythms have also been observed in cognition. Time-of-day effects have been observed in many aspects of human performance. Tasks that require inhibition of particular responses are particularly sensitive to time of day (Wincour & Hasher, 1999). Performance seems to be related to both the temperature rhythm and the arousal rhythm, with the temperature rhythm affecting fairly basic psychomotor performance and the arousal rhythm affecting more complex cognitive tasks (Monk *et al.*, 1983), as discussed earlier. Strategy is the element of performance most likely to be affected by arousal (Asso, 1987).

Time-of-day effects have been noted in vigilance (e.g. Casagrande, Violani, Curcio, & Bertini, 1997). Craig, Davies and Matthews (1987) reported perceptual efficiency to be lower in the morning than in the afternoon. They also investigated visual discrimination and found that efficiency decreased across the day while speed increased. A similar pattern in visual identification was reported by Craig and Condon (1985), who noted a speed–accuracy trade-off across the day. These performance rhythms seem to be related to arousal level and it is strategy, rather than overall performance, that is affected.

Daily fluctuations have been also reported in relation to information-processing strategy. This has been well investigated in relation to the processing and comprehension of written material. In the morning, a fairly superficial verbatim strategy tends to be adopted, focusing specifically on the text as it is written. In the afternoon, there seems to be a shift towards a more elaborative processing strategy, integrating the material with stored knowledge (Lorenzetti & Natale, 1996). These strategies are adopted spontaneously and the effects of time of day appear to be eliminated if the experimenter gives specific instructions to adopt a specific strategy (Lorenzetti & Natale, 1996).

Evidence regarding memory is more mixed. For example, Folkard and Monk (1980) found no evidence of time-of-day effects on retrieval of information from long-term memory. Some evidence suggests that circadian rhythms in performance may be related to age, and ageing does seem to be associated with changes in circadian rhythms (Wincour & Hasher, 1999). For older people arousal and activity tend to be greatest in the morning, and there is evidence that memory performance is best in the morning and declines in the afternoon. Indeed, work with rats has demonstrated that the cognitive performance of old, but not young, rats is likely to be affected by time of day of testing (e.g. Wincour & Hasher, 1999). Ryan, Hatfield and Hofstetter (2002) examined the effects of time of day and caffeine on the memory performance of adults aged 65 and above. They found that memory performance declined from morning to afternoon for the placebo group, but no decline was seen for the experimental group, who had received caffeine. Caffeine is a stimulant that reliably increases arousal, suggesting that the change in performance is mediated through changes in the general level of arousal.

Despite being explained in terms of arousal, daily rhythms in performance do not seem to be clearly predicted by subjective measures of arousal. Owens *et al.* (1998) had 24 female volunteers participate in a 6–7 day trial. They went to bed at midnight and woke at 08.00 hours and were required to complete a battery of tests every 2 hours. Mood, reaction time and memory performance were assessed. It was found that alertness was a reasonably good predictor of simple perceptual-motor performance, but was much less good at predicting other performance measures. Casagrande *et al.* (1987) also reported little consistency between objective measures of performance across the day and self-reported fatigue and energy.

The timing of meals is an important social *zeitgeber* for humans, and for many people meals follow a regular daily pattern. The effects of meals on performance have been studied and the "post-lunch dip", whereby performance tends to decline after lunch, is well documented. Some aspects of performance seem to be more sensitive to this than others. For example, Smith and Miles (1986) found that both reaction time and attention were impaired by lunch, but movement time and concentration were not. It is likely that these performance decrements are due to a combination of factors, including arousal and size and nutritional content of the meal. It is also important to bear in mind that time-of-day effects may be due to fatigue and changes in motivation. The effects of fatigue on performance are well documented and are addressed below. Fatigue and the circadian rhythm are very closely intertwined and it can be difficult to distinguish between their effects (Dodge, 1982).

Time of day is an important variable to be controlled in laboratory studies. If you are conducting a repeated-measures study, it is essential to test participants at approximately the same time of day on successive trials to ensure that any observed differences are not simply artefacts of time of day. Indeed, it is useful to test all participants at roughly the same time of day (e.g. early morning or late afternoon). For example, time of day has been shown to interact with impulsivity/extraversion. In the morning, extraverts perform better under high stress conditions and introverts under low stress conditions. This pattern is reversed in the evening (Matthews and Harley, 1993).

7.4 Circadian disruption

The circadian rhythm can be disrupted. Two of the most important sources of disruption in everyday life are shift-work and jet-lag. Both of these have important implications for cognition and performance, particularly in applied settings such as healthcare, industry and aviation.

Jet-lag

Jet-lag causes disruption of the circadian rhythm. Flying through a number of time zones (east to west or vice versa) means that when the passengers emerge at their destination, they are exposed to a new and different light–dark cycle and their circadian clocks must adjust to this new cycle (see Table 7.1). Furthermore, all the other clocks in the body (peripheral clocks) must also readjust and they do this at different rates, so there may be a good deal of internal desynchronisation.

Table 7.1 The time and date in cities across the world

Honolulu	Los Angeles	New York	London	Cairo	Delhi	Tokyo	Auckland
7 am 10 May	10 am 10 May	1 pm 10 May	6 pm 10 May	8 pm 10 May	10.30 pm 10 May	2 am 11 May	5 am 11 May
			GMT: 5 pm				

Someone leaving London at 6 pm on 10 May to fly to Auckland would arrive about 24 hours later (approximate length of direct flight). Her body clock would "think" it was 6 pm on 11 May, whereas in fact it would be 5 am on 12 May; rather than early evening it would be early morning. Her clock has to readjust to this new time. *Note*: British summertime is one hour ahead of Greenwich mean time (GMT).

Flying north to south or vice versa does not cause jet-lag as there is no change in the light–dark cycle.

While deeply unpleasant and disruptive for all travellers, jet-lag is a particular problem for pilots and cabin crew. Some research has suggested that jet-lag can lead to errors and accidents (Waterhouse *et al.*, 1997). Jet-lag manifests itself in a wide range of symptoms such as tiredness, insomnia or sleeping at inappropriate times, headaches, indigestion, bowel problems, loss of concentration, other cognitive difficulties, mood disturbance and headache. Symptoms are worse the more time zones have been crossed and travelling east produces more jet-lag than travelling west (Figure 7.4). The symptoms usually disappear after a few days, although it can take up to 5 or more days in the case of travelling nine or more time zones (Waterhouse *et al.*, 1997).

Travelling west, phase delay, so less jet-lag

Travelling east, phase advance, so more jet-lag

Figure 7.4 Flying east necessitates a "phase advance", so the timing of activities such as eating, sleeping, and so on, is brought forward. This tends to produce more jet-lag than flying west, which involves a "phase delay" or pushing back the onset of activities

As yet, there is no widely available treatment or prevention for jet-lag, though a good deal of research is currently devoted to developing them. Symptoms can be minimised though. Travellers should avoid becoming dehydrated during the flight: drink plenty of water and avoid alcohol or keep it to a minimum. On long journeys, stopovers can help the process of readjustment and reduce the jet-lag experienced at the final destination. While flying, you should sleep only when the time coincides with night at the destination and carefully plan your activities on arrival.

Shift-work

In many ways shift-work is similar to jet-lag, but in this case exposure to circadian desynchronisation is chronic. While night workers work, their temperature rhythms and melatonin release are telling them to sleep. So even if the worker manages to sleep during the day (adjusting the sleep cycle), many core functions will still be out of synch with the worker's patterns of activity. This is further complicated by the fact that other activities such as eating and social activities may reset peripheral clocks and promote internal desynchronisation (Wright, 2002). The shift-worker will also be out of synch with the rhythms of his or her family life, such as meal times, and adapting to these rhythms on days off further complicates this.

Shift-work is strongly associated with sleep disturbances and fatigue is often a problem. Shift-workers have been found to suffer elevated levels of both acute infections, such as colds, and more serious health problems. Some of these problems may be due to a decreased immune response caused by sleep deprivation. These problems are primarily associated with night shifts, as there is little evidence to suggest that moving from day to evening working in a shift pattern is disruptive (Gold *et al.*, 1992). Gold *et al.* (1992) questioned 635 nurses about their shift patterns, sleeping patterns and sleep quality, use of sleeping aids, accidents, mistakes and "near-misses". They found that those who rotated shifts or worked nights got less sleep than those who worked days/evenings, and they were also more likely to report poor sleep quality. Approximately a third of them had "nodded-off" while working and those who worked rotating shifts were twice as likely as those on days/evenings to report an accident or error. Rosa and Bonnet (1993) examined the consequences of moving from an 8 hour, 5–7 day shift schedule to a 12 hour, 4 day one. After 10 months, general performance and alertness had deteriorated. Participants also slept less and this was associated with poorer mood.

Although it appears impossible to eliminate shift working in many occupations, such as nursing, some measures can be taken to reduce the ill effects. There is no perfect shift schedule and circadian disruption will always occur if working nights. Moreover, individual differences mean that the best schedule for one person may not suit another as well. Research findings have been applied to try to design best compromise shift schedules that minimise ill effects. Generally, it is recommended that people do not spend much time on the night shift to avoid adjustment to it and consequent readjustment to normal time on other shifts and days off. However, it is also recommended that shifts do not rotate too quickly, and some experts have suggested that permanent night shift is preferable to rotating night shift. Rotating shifts should be delay shifts, rather than advance ones. In a delay shift the worker has a later starting time for the new shift than for the old one (e.g. old shift 06.00–14.00 hours, new shift 12.00–20.00 hours), whereas in an advance shift the new start time is earlier than the old one (e.g old shift 12.00–18.00 hours, new shift 06.00–12.00 hours). Advance shifts seem to cause more problems than delay ones, just as travelling east (phase advance) produces more jet-lag than travelling west (phase delay). Prophylactic naps may also be beneficial. Bonnefond *et al.* (2001) examined the effects of a short nap during the night shift using a sample of 12 male volunteers who worked night shifts at an industrial plant. The men were allowed to take 1 hour naps every night shift in a nearby bedroom. The men themselves organised a napping rota. They were studied for 1 year to allow for adjustment to the new regime. Levels of vigilance were increased and napping produced greater satisfaction with the night shift and quality of life in general. The beneficial effects of caffeine on performance may be particularly noticeable when an individual is tired (Lorist, Snel, Kok, & Mulder, 1994) and caffeine has been shown to improve alertness during night work, when taken at the beginning of a shift. Bonnet and Arnaud (1994) examined the effects of both a 4 hour nap and caffeine on the performance of sleep-deprived participants. They found that those participants who had had caffeine maintained roughly baseline levels of performance and alertness across the night, whereas those in the placebo group showed significant deterioration in their performance. These findings demonstrated that the combination of a nap and caffeine was significantly more beneficial in terms of maintaining performance and alertness than a nap alone.

Fatigue and performance

Many of the problems discussed above are either largely caused, or complicated, by fatigue. The effects of fatigue on performance are detrimental, and indeed fatigue is a major cause of accidents through human error. It is estimated that up to 20% of accidents on long journeys are due to drivers falling asleep at the wheel. Corfitsen (1994) conducted a roadside survey of 280 young male night-time/early morning drivers. The men rated how tired/rested they felt and this corresponded well with a measure of visual reaction time: tired and very tired drivers had slower reaction times than rested drivers. Reaction time is an important component of driving and it is a cause for concern that almost half of the night-time drivers rated themselves as tired. A later study (Corfitsen, 1996) demonstrated that tiredness was an important additional accident risk factor among young male drivers under the influence of alcohol: those who had been drinking were more likely to be tired and to be more tired than sober drivers. In the UK, recent public health campaigns have focused on preventing driving when tired or ill and a number of high-profile accidents have focused awareness on this. It is crucial that drivers who feel tired stop and have a rest. Some factors may help to ameliorate the effects of tiredness. A study of truck drivers doing long round trips suggested that lone drivers experienced more fatigue and performance impairments than those who drove as part of a crew (Hartley, Arnold, Smythe, & Hansen, 1994). Lieberman, Tharion, Shukitt-Hale, Speckman and Tulley (2002) subjected US Navy SEAL trainees to 72 hours of sleep deprivation and assessed performance on a battery of cognitive tests, mood and marksmanship. Participants were allocated to one of three caffeine conditions: 100 mg, 200 mg or 300 mg. Caffeine was found to improve vigilance, reaction time and alertness in a dose-dependent fashion, but had no effect on marksmanship. Nevertheless, while caffeine can ameliorate some of the effects of fatigue, it should not be relied on as a "cure" for extreme tiredness. It is simply not safe to drive or operate machinery when very tried.

7.5 The menstrual cycle

In the following sections, we will consider the physiological basis of the menstrual cycle and briefly consider the history of menstrual cycle research. It must be emphasised that this research is, and has been, conducted in particular sociocultural contexts and has always had political implications. It is important to appreciate the methodological difficulties that complicate this research and we devote a section to discussing these. Research examining the effect of the menstrual cycle and the effects of sex hormones on cognition and performance is then reviewed.

The biology of the menstrual cycle

The menstrual cycle is experienced by most healthy women between the ages of about 12 and 50. The typical cycle lasts 28–32 days, though there is considerable variability both within and between women. Two oscillators control the menstrual cycle: the ovaries, which release ova (eggs) in a cyclic pattern, and the hypothalamic–pituitary system, which provides feedback via hormones (Yen, Vandenberg, Tsai, & Parker, 1974). Of course external events, such as stress, can influence the rhythm through affecting hormonal actions (Cutler & Garcia, 1980). A typical cycle can be divided into five distinct phases distinguished by hormonal and physiological events. These are the result of a feedback relationship between hormones released from the pituitary gland and hormones released by the ovary (estrogens) (see Figure 7.5).

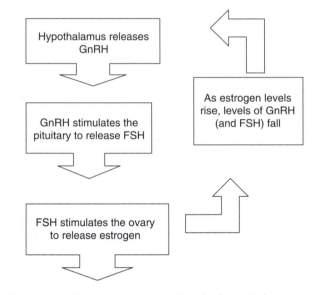

Figure 7.5 The menstrual cycle is regulated by the hypothalamic–pituitary–ovarian axis. The hypothalamus releases gonadotrophin-releasing hormone (GnRH). On reaching the pituitary, it triggers the release of follicle-stimulating hormone (FSH). FSH stimulates the ovary to secrete estrogen. Levels of estrogen and FSH are regulated through a negative feedback loop. Increasing estrogen inhibits further release of GnRH from the hypothalamus. So, as estrogen levels rise, FSH levels fall

The following description is based on a standardized 28 day cycle, with day 1 referring to the onset of menses (bleeding) (Figure 7.6):

- *Menstrual phase (days 1–5).* The uterus contracts and this causes the lining (endometrium) to be shed as menstrual blood. The preceding premenstrual drop in hormones triggers the release of a hormone called gonadotrophin-releasing hormone (GnRH) from the hypothalamus. This, in turn, causes the

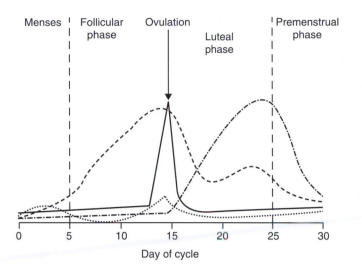

Figure 7.6 Levels of estrogen (– – – –), progesterone (–·–·–), follicle-stimulating hormone (· · · ·) and luteinising hormone (——)

pituitary gland to release follicle-stimulating hormone (FSH). FSH promotes maturation of the ovarian follicle from which the ovum is later released.

- *Follicular phase (days 6–12)*. FSH stimulates the ovaries to release estrogens and this causes the lining of the uterus to thicken. The pituitary begins to secrete lutenising hormone. Levels of estrogen begin to rise sharply and as they do levels of FSH fall (negative feedback loop).

- *Ovulatory phase (days 13–15)*. Levels of luteinising hormone reach a peak causing an ovum to be released from one of the ovaries. This is then carried to the uterus via the fallopian tube.

- *Luteal phase (days 16–23)*. Hormonal actions cause the now empty follicle to become a corpus luteum and secrete the hormone progesterone. This blocks further release of FSH and so prevents the development of more ova. Progesterone levels continue to rise to further prepare the endometrium for pregnancy. If fertilisation does not take place, then estrogen, in interaction with prostaglandins, causes the corpus luteum to disintegrate. If fertilisation does occur, the placenta begins to secrete human chorionic gonadotrophin (HCG), which prevents this happening. It is this hormone, HCG, that is detected in a pregnancy test.

- *Premenstrual phase (days 2–28)*. The disintegration of the corpus luteum triggers a sharp decline in levels of estrogen and progesterone and the thickened wall of the uterus begins to disintegrate. It is shed and the menstrual phase begins again.

Of course, the example given above is an idealised one and many women experience typically longer or shorter menstrual cycles. The length of cycle experienced by an individual woman also varies. Variations in the length of the cycle are often caused by external events delaying ovulation. The same events after ovulation usually do not affect the timing of the cycle (Asso, 1983). Anovulatory cycles (cycles in which ovulation does not occur) are also fairly common, particularly in girls and younger women.

The menstrual cycle in context

The menstrual cycle, and menstruation in particular, must be considered within the sociocultural contexts in which they occur. Menstruation is culturally defined in very negative terms (e.g. Ussher, 1989; Walker, 1997; Heard & Chrisler, 1999), though the experience for many women is little more than a minor inconvenience. Discourses of menstruation are predominantly negative and often medicalised, focusing on pain, inconvenience, embarassment and distress.

Negative representations of menstruation have a long history. Menstruation has been considered to make women "mad" or to drain energy and mental resources, yet not menstruating has also been considered a source of madness (Walker, 1997). Menstrual cycle research has its origins in the nineteenth-century growth of scientific authority. Many scientists directed their interest to the nature of the differences between men and women (with men usually being seen in a much more positive light). Most of this work focused on biological differences, principally women's reproductive capacity, of which the menstrual cycle is an obvious marker. There is an extensive literature examining the menstrual cycle from a psychological point of view. This body of research has two main foci. The first is the relationship between the cycle and women's cognitive abilities and work performance. There is still a very powerful though unsupported belief that women's abilities are somehow impaired by or before menstruation. This is usually explained in terms of hormonal actions. This research will be addressed here. The second focus is on the relationship between the menstrual cycle and women's moods, particularly premenstrually. Again, relationships between mood and menstrual cycle phase are explained in terms of hormonal actions. Much of this work is concerned either directly or indirectly with premenstrual syndrome, which is a very controversial concept. Unfortunately, a discussion of this research is outside the scope of this chapter and interested readers are referred to Walker (1997) and Ussher (1989). Taken together, both strands of research have traditionally assumed that "hormones" negatively affect women's intellectual functioning and moods. This is sometimes referred to as the "raging hormones hypothesis" and the research evidence does not support it.

7.6 Studying the menstrual cycle

Walker (1997) has identified three key traditions in psychological menstrual cycle research: mainstream, liberal feminist and postmodern. The mainstream approach applies traditional positivistic research methods (experiments, quasi-experiments, correlational studies) to the study of the effect of the menstrual cycle on particular variables, such as memory or work rate. So the menstrual cycle is used as an independent variable to observe the effects on the dependent variables (e.g.

memory), and often it is these dependent variables that are of interest to the researcher, rather than the menstrual cycle *per se*. The liberal feminist approach is concerned with challenging negative assumptions around the menstrual cycle, such as the assumption that women are cognitively impaired premenstrually. Much of this research uses positivistic methods to challenge traditional methods, assumptions and findings. Research from this approach has been important in challenging biased methods and conclusions and facilitating greater methodological rigour (e.g. in questionnaire design). The postmodern approach focuses on the menstrual cycle itself and is concerned with understanding women's experiences and exploring the discourses around menstruation. Most of this research is conducted from a feminist perspective and qualitative methods of inquiry are used. Most of the research that will be considered in this chapter comes from mainstream and liberal feminist traditions.

Methodological issues

Menstrual cycle psychology is an area fraught with methodological difficulties (see Table 7.2). The researcher cannot manipulate menstrual cycle phase, so cannot randomly allocate women to an experimental condition. Therefore, studies that examine some aspect of performance across different cycle phases are quasi-experiments and fundamentally correlational in nature. This makes inferences about causation problematic – while many researchers interpret their findings in terms of hormonal changes "causing" or mediating an observed change in performance, this cannot be unequivocally established. Many of these quasi-experimental studies interpret their findings in terms of hormonal or other physiological changes, yet observed changes may be the result of culturally mediated emotional changes, or other factors such as expectations.

Table 7.2 Key methodological difficulties in menstrual cycle research

- Difficult to establish causation – studies tend to be correlational
- Problems accurately designating menstrual cycle phase
- Definition of phase varies
- Aggregating data across menstrual cycles and across women can be problematic
- Sampling – only some cycles are studied
- Problems with some measures used, especially in research on mood

The accurate designation of menstrual cycle phase poses difficulties. The most common method is simply by counting the number of days from the last menstrual period. The period from ovulation to menstruation is set at 14–16 days, so if the date of the next onset of menstruation is obtained, then phase designation can be checked. However, this can be unreliable, particularly with small samples. Gordon, Corbin and Lee (1986) tested the hormone levels of 24 women on days 2–3, 10–12 and 20–24. Analysis revealed that almost half of the women tested were not in the expected phase. Methods such as basal body temperature or examination of vaginal mucus can be used, but many participants find these troublesome or distasteful. Levels of estrogens and progesterone and other hormones can be measured, which is useful, but it can be very time-consuming and expensive with large samples. It is important to note that levels of hormones in the periphery (assessed via blood or urine) tell us little about the activity of those hormones in the central nervous system (Broverman *et al.* 1981), and this is important if the research is concerned with the effects of hormone concentrations on central nervous system functioning. There is also a great deal of inconsistency in menstrual cycle phase definition across different studies. The number of cycle phases used by researchers has varied from 2 to 14 (see Walker, 1997). Definitions of intermenstrual and premenstrual phases can differ between studies. So, for example, one study might compare delayed recall performance pre- and post-ovulation, while another might examine performance at menses, mid-cycle and premenstrually, and yet another might track performance across five phases. These differences make it difficult to compare findings from different studies.

Menstrual cycle phase is fundamentally a within-subject concept. It makes little sense to use between-subjects designs that compare many women, all in different menstrual phases. While most work now tends to involve within-subject designs, these are not without their own problems. Unless all women are tested for the first time during the menses (and this could produce order effects), data collection will be spread over more than one menstrual cycle. This is problematic, as cycles differ both between and within individual women, for example some may be anovulatory. There are also individual differences in menstrual cycle experiences. Therefore, while research shows that on average women do not experience cycle-related changes in cognitive performance, for some women performance may be better or worse at particular cycle phases. Walker (1997, pp. 119–123) discusses the problems of aggregating data across women and cycles. Together with colleagues, Walker asked a sample of 109 women to rate their mood every day for at least two menstrual cycles. The results demonstrated an effect of menstrual cycle phase, with mood being poorest premenstrually. Yet when she examined the data at an individual level, Walker found a great deal of variation. Some women showed very little change, some had more positive mood premenstrually and some had more negative mood premenstrually. The patterns of change reported also differed between cycles, so a woman might report negative premenstrual experiences in one cycle but not in another.

Sampling is also an issue. Many women are excluded from this research if they have irregular or very long or short menstrual cycles, so not all cycles are studied (Walker, 1997). Furthermore, much menstrual cycle research uses university students or clinical samples of women who report, or have been diagnosed with, menstrual problems or premenstrual syndrome. This has clear implications for the generalisability of findings.

There are also issues around the measures used. Most work on perception and cognition uses standard measures of performance; however, the sheer range of dependent variables used in research can make it difficult to compare findings. The problem is acute in the case of research on the menstrual cycle and mood. Since the 1950s, questionnaires have been used widely to measure mood at different phases of the menstrual cycle. A key problem is that many of these instruments only allow women to rate negative states and this may not reflect women's experiences. The Menstrual Joy Questionnaire (Delaney, Lupton, & Toth, 1987) was developed as a feminist critique of these measures and demonstrated that when women are presented with positive statements about menstruation, they will endorse these too.

Most early questionnaire studies were retrospective. Retrospective studies require women to complete questionnaires based on their last menstrual cycle, or their typical menstrual cycle. These have been heavily criticised for priming reporting of stereotypical expectations rather than actual experiences. Parlee (1974) noted a report bias in relation to the widely used Menstrual Distress Questionnaire (Moos, 1968). This study was particularly influential in promoting a shift from retrospective to prospective measures. Women tend to report more distress and premenstrual symptoms in retrospective rather than prospective questionnaires (Asso, 1983; Ussher, 1992), suggesting that negative cultural expectations may be incorporated into women's self-schemata.

However used, the questionnaires themselves may prime reporting of particular experiences. Chrisler, Johnston, Champagne and Preston (1994) found that the title of the Menstrual Joy Questionnaire primed positive reporting of menstrual symptoms. Aubeeluck and Maguire (2002) replicated the experiment, removing the questionnaire titles, and found that the questionnaire items alone also produced positive priming.

7.7 The menstrual cycle and performance

The menstrual cycle and arousal

There have been many investigations of the relationships between gonadal hormones and nervous system arousal. Gonadal hormones are sex hormones released from the gonads (i.e. estrogens and testosterone). The evidence remains somewhat inconclusive, but it is reasonable to assume some relationship. A multi-dimensional view of arousal is generally accepted: the central nervous system (CNS) and the autonomic nervous system (ANS) have been shown to vary independently. Estrogens are known to enhance CNS adrenergic activity, while progesterone tends to have a deactivating effect (e.g. Broverman et al., 1981; Asso, 1987; Dye, 1992). Klaiber, Broverman, Vogel, Kennedy and Marks (1982) studied a sample of female nurses and found that CNS adrenergic functioning was reduced in the premenstrual phases of the cycle relative to the pre-ovulatory phases. The general conclusions are that the pre-ovulatory rise in estrogen is paralleled by an increase in CNS arousal. After ovulation, the arousing effects of estrogen are mediated by the rise in progesterone levels leading to a relative decrease in arousal. However, other hormones and neurotransmitters are involved and the interrelationships are not straightforward (Dye, 1992). With regards to the ANS, Broverman et al. (1981) reported greater ANS arousal premenstrually. Dye (1992), using a combination of objective and subjective measures, also reported greater ANS arousal premenstrually. Of course, most of this evidence has involved comparing various indices of arousal at different points in the menstrual cycle, so is correlational in nature (Ruble, Brooks-Gunn, & Clark, 1980).

Sensation and perception

Sex differences exist in various aspects of sensory functioning, suggesting that hormones do influence sensation (Baker, 1987); most of this research assumes that any cyclic variations in sensory performance are due to either direct or indirect hormonal action. Some of this research is concerned with examining the extent to which sensory changes may be responsible for variations in more complex performance measures, such as reaction time. Gonadal hormones may affect sensation through two mechanisms (Gandelman, 1983): first, *directly*, through acting on peripheral structures (e.g. the eye); secondly, *indirectly*, through influencing CNS processing of stimuli.

Changes in sensory function across the menstrual cycle have been reported, often suggesting an ovulatory peak in sensitivity (Parlee, 1983). Both visual acuity and general visual sensitivity have been reported to be highest mid-cycle (Parlee, 1983). Menstrual cycle rhythms have also been reported in various visual phenomena, such as the McCollough effect (Maguire & Byth, 1998), the spiral after-effect (Das & Chattopadhyay, 1982) and the figural after-effect (Satinder & Mastronardi, 1974). These rhythms probably reflect cyclic variations in CNS arousal.

Doty, Snyder, Huggins and Lowry (1981) reported a mid-cycle peak in olfactory (smell) sensitivity; this probably reflected CNS changes rather than a local effect of gonadal hormones. Menstrual cycle variations in taste and taste detection thresholds have also been reported. Wright and Crow (1973) found menstrual cycle variations in sweet preferences. Following a glucose meal, sugar solutions are judged to be less pleasant than normal, but this shift is slowest at ovulation. There is conflicting evidence regarding sensitivity to pain, but Parlee (1983) examined the evidence and suggested that there is a trend towards decreased sensitivity to pain in the premenstrual phase relative to other phases.

Cognitive performance

Much research effort has focused on investigating changes in cognitive performance across the menstrual cycle. A good deal of this research was motivated by the desire to find evidence of paramenstrual debilitation (Richardson, 1992; Sommer, 1992) – that is, poorer performance around the time of a woman's period. The term "paramenstrum" refers to both the premenstrual and the menstrual phases. There is a widespread belief that women experience cognitive debilitation during the paramenstrum and that this is caused by hormonal changes. Richardson (1992) and others have argued that any cognitive variations could be the result of culturally mediated emotional changes rather than hormonal changes. A literature bias has existed in this field, as many of the studies showing no differences were simply not published (see Nicolson, 1992). Several reviews of the literature (e.g. Asso, 1983; Sommer, 1992; Richardson, 1992; Walker, 1997) have concluded that there is no evidence of a premenstrual or menstrual decrement in cognitive performance. Indeed, performance may be improved as women compensate because they expect poorer performance. Yet the stereotype of paramenstrual debilitation remains very strong.

Asso (1987) reviewed studies that suggested that where there was variability in strategy, rather than overall performance, with a trend towards speed pre-ovulation and accuracy post-ovulation. For example, Ho, Gilger and Brink (1986) investigated performance on spatial information processing. They found that the strategy used varied across the cycle, but actual performance remained constant. Hartley, Lyons and Dunne (1987) investigated memory performance at three phases of the menstrual cycle: menses, mid-cycle and premenstrually. They found no differences in immediate and delayed recall between these phases. Speed of verbal reasoning on more complex sentences was found to be slower mid-cycle relative to the other phases. However, Richardson (1992) found no effect of menstrual cycle phase on memory performance.

Figure 7.7 summarises the research findings on the relationship between menstrual cycle phase and (1) arousal, (2) sensation and perception, and (3) cognitive performance.

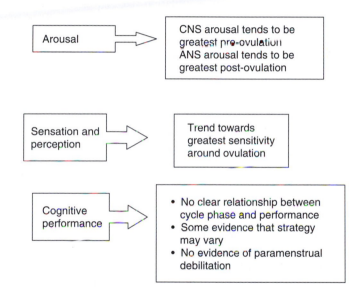

Figure 7.7 A summary of research findings on the relationships between menstrual cycle phase and (1) arousal, (2) sensation and perception, and (3) cognitive performance

7.8 A role for gonadal hormones in cognition?

Most of the research considered above was concerned with the effects of menstrual cycle phase (particularly the paramenstrum) on performance. Much of it was based on assumptions of paramenstrual debilitation or was concerned with refuting these. While many of the researchers explained observed changes in terms of the action of particular hormones, the focus of the research was not hormonal *per se*, but was explicitly concerned with potential effects of menstrual cycle phase on performance. Another strand of research has been directly concerned with exploring the effects of the gonadal hormones on cognitive function. This work has examined the effects of these hormones in both men and women in the hope of discovering more about the neurochemistry of cognition.

Broverman, Klaiber and Vogel (1980) proposed that the gonadal hormones play a functional role in cognitive processing in both women and men, via their actions in the central nervous system. They proposed that the gonadal hormones act as adrenergic agonists (increase adrenergic activity and so general arousal) through regulation of the enzyme monoamine oxidase. Adrenergic stimulants facilitate the performance of automatised tasks and impair the performance of perceptual restructuring tasks. Automatised tasks are simple, repetitive and highly practised, whereas perceptual restructuring tasks require people to inhibit their automatic response to obvious features of a task in favour of less obvious features (e.g. the embedded figures test). So, according to this theory, individuals with high levels of sex-appropriate gonadal hormone stimulation (i.e. estrogen in women and testosterone in men) would tend to have a strong automatisation style. Broverman *et al.* (1980) found that males with greater sensitivity to testosterone were better at automatisation tasks than perceptual restructuring tasks and vice versa. These predictions were further tested across the menstrual cycle (Broverman *et al.,* 1981). It was hypothesised that automatisation performance would be best when estrogen levels were high and unopposed by progesterone – in the follicular and ovulatory phases – and that perceptual restructuring performance would be better in the luteal phase. These predictions were supported on three out of four of the subtests, but only when anovulatory cycles were excluded and testing strictly coincided with the pre-ovulatory estrogen and post-ovulatory progesterone peaks. Other researchers have failed to support some of the predictions of this theory (e.g. Richardson, 1992).

Other work has been more successful in demonstrating a relationship between gonadal hormones and cognitive performance. Reliable sex differences exist in some aspects of cognitive performance (see Table 7.3). For example, on average, women show a slight advantage in verbal ability and men a slight advantage in spatial ability. Of course, even where sex differences do occur, there is a great

Table 7.3 A list of cognitive tasks that show small but reliable differences between the sexes

Female advantage cognitive tasks	Male advantage cognitive tasks
• Ideational fluency	• Mental rotation
• Verbal fluency	• Perception of the vertical and horizontal
• Verbal memory	• Perceptual restructuring
• Perceptual speed	• Mathematical reasoning
• Mathematical calculation	• Target-directed motor performance
• Fine motor coordination	

Source: Kimura (1996, 1992).

deal of overlap – the differences between any two women or any two men are greater than the average difference between the two sexes. Drawing on evidence from animal work, Elizabeth Hampson and Doreen Kimura have suggested that it is these sexual differentiated tasks that may be influenced by levels of gonadal hormones, rather than the many aspects of cognitive performance that are "gender neutral". They have investigated extensively changes in cognitive performance at different stages of the menstrual cycle in an attempt to determine the effects of variations in estrogen and progesterone (e.g. Hampson & Kimura, 1988; Kimura & Hampson, 1994). This research is very much within the "mainstream" tradition: the menstrual cycle is not the focus of interest, hormone levels are; menstrual cycle phases are selected on the basis of their hormonal profiles. So the menstrual cycle is used as a research tool rather than being the focus of interest. In contrast to much menstrual cycle research, they did not focus on the paramenstrum, but compared performance in phases when circulating hormone levels were high and low. They used only tests that show reliable (though small) average sex differences, arguing that we would not expect sex neutral cognitive abilities to be influenced by sex hormones.

Hampson and Kimura tested women at two cycle phases: mid-luteal, when estrogen and progesterone levels are high, and the late menstrual phase, when levels of both are low. They found that manual dexterity (female advantage task) was better mid-luteally, while performance on the rod and frame task (male advantage) was worse (Hampson & Kimura, 1988). Other studies have supported these findings. Hampson (1990) reported that verbal articulation and fine motor performance (female advantage) were best in the luteal phase, while performance on spatial tasks (male advantage) was best during the menstrual phase. To separate the effects of estrogen and progesterone, they conducted further studies (see Kimura & Hampson, 1994) comparing performance shortly before ovulation (high estrogen, no progesterone) and during the menstrual phase (very low estrogen and progesterone). They again found that performance on female-advantage tasks was better pre-ovulation and performance on male-advantage tasks was worse. Thus high levels of estrogens improved performance on female-advantage tasks, but impaired performance on male-advantage tasks (Figure 7.8). Other work has examined cognitive ability in post-menopausal women receiving estrogen therapy (see Kimura & Hampson, 1994). The authors found that motor and articulatory abilities were better when the women were receiving the therapy, though there were no differences on some perceptual tasks.

The research of Kimura and Hampson was also extended to men. Seasonal variations in testosterone have also been reported in men. Levels of testosterone tend to be higher in the autumn than in spring (in the northern hemisphere). Men's spatial performance was better in spring than autumn. While this may seem counterintitutive, it appears that there are optimum levels of testosterone for spatial ability and that these are higher than those present in a typical woman, but lower than those present in a typical man (see Kimura & Hampson, 1994) (Figure 7.9).

There is empirical support for these findings (e.g. Hausmann, Slabbekoorn, Van Goozen, Cohen-Kettenis, & Guentuerkuen, 2000). On the other hand, Epting and Overman (1998) failed to find a menstrual rhythm in sex-sensitive tasks. So while

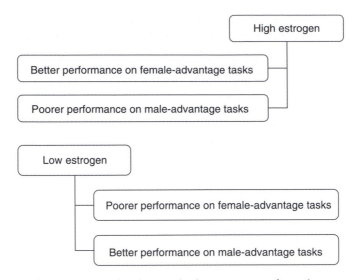

Figure 7.8 When estrogen levels are high women perform better on female-advantage tasks and worse on male-advantage tasks, and vice versa when estrogen levels are low (Hampson & Kimura, 1988; Kimura & Hampson, 1994)

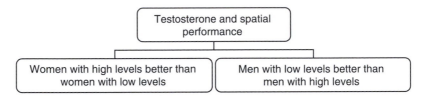

Figure 7.9 There appears to be an optimal level of testosterone for performance on spatial tasks that is higher than that typically found in women and to the low end of that typically found in men (Kimura & Hampson, 1994). Women with high levels of testosterone tend to perform better on spatial tasks than those with low levels of testosterone, whereas the opposite is true for men

there is some evidence to suggest that gonadal hormones may affect cognitive processes, in both sexes, many questions remain. Much of this research still has not ruled out potential cognitive or social effects. Another problem is the nature of the changes: if they are very subtle, they may simply not be detectable on standard measures of performance. Yet if this is the case, it suggests that these changes may simply be trivial fluctuations of little or no significance.

7.9 Work performance

Given the strong stereotype that women's work and academic performance is negatively affected by menstruation, it is not surprising that a good deal of research has been devoted to this. Dalton (1960, 1968) reported that schoolgirls' academic performance was poorer before and during menstruation; however, these findings were not statistically analysed and are generally discounted. Work with university students has failed to demonstrate an effect of menstrual cycle phase on exam performance (e.g. Richardson, 1989). However, students of both sexes do seem to believe that women's academic performance can be disrupted premenstrually and menstrually (Richardson, 1989; Walker, 1992).

Work performance is difficult to define and measure, particularly when potential variations may be small. A great deal of research has focused on the menstrual cycle and performance in industrial work, but most of this was conducted before 1940. Since then, there has been little research that has examined work output or performance across the menstrual cycle. A good deal of recent work is concerned with the relationship between particular occupations or job stress and menstrual symptoms, while other work is explicitly concerned with premenstrual syndrome in the workplace.

There is no evidence that the work performance of women suffers premenstrually or during menstruation. Farris (1956) analysed the output of pieceworkers (paid per unit of work completed) and found that output was greatest mid-cycle and premenstrually. Redgrove (1971) similarly found that work performance was best premenstrually and menstrually in a sample of laundry workers, punchcard operators and secretaries. Black and Koulis-Chitwood (1990) examined typing performance across the menstrual cycle and found no changes in either rate or number of errors made. Overall, the research evidence suggests that, as in the case of women's cognitive performance, work performance is not impaired before or during menstruation.

Beliefs about performance

Empirical research provides little support for the notion that women's ability to think and work is impaired during the paramenstrum, yet this belief remains firmly entrenched. Expectations are likely to be important mediators of performance and, as discussed earlier, expectations of poor performance may lead women to make efforts to compensate.

Ruble (1977) conducted a classic experiment to examine the effect of menstrual expectations on reporting of symptoms. Student volunteers participated in the experiment about a week before their periods were due. They were told that a new method of predicting menstruation onset had been developed and involved the use of an electroencephalogram (EEG). Participants were hooked up to the EEG but it was not actually run. One group of women was told that their periods were due in a couple of days, another group told their periods were due in 7–10 days and a third group was given no information. Those who were told that their periods were due in a couple of days reported significantly more premenstrual symptoms than those in the other groups. This study clearly demonstrated the importance of menstrual-cycle beliefs in mediating reports and behaviour (Figure 7.10).

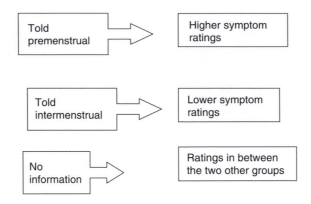

Figure 7.10 Manipulation of women's beliefs about their menstrual phase (Ruble, 1977). All the women were due to menstruate 6–7 days after the study (based on menstrual history taken before the study). The women were allocated to one of three groups. One group was told that they were premenstrual, a second group that they were intermenstrual and the third group was provided with no information. The premenstrual group reported more premenstrual symptoms, especially water retention, change in eating habits and pain. The intermenstrual group reported the least symptoms and the "no information" group reported intermediate symptoms

Summary

Circadian rhythms

- The circadian rhythm organises physiological and behavioural activity.
- The rhythm is endogenous and is entrained to 24 hours by light and social *zeitgebers*.
- Circadian rhythms have been reported in a wide range of performance measures, and strategy is the aspect most likely to be affected.
- Circadian desynchrony (e.g. jet-lag and shift-work) has deleterious effects on cognition and performance.
- The effects of time of day and circadian desynchrony are complicated by fatigue and other factors.

Menstrual cycle

- The human menstrual cycle is an ultradian rhythm that can be divided into distinct phases based on hormonal profiles.
- Menstrual rhythms have been observed in sensation and some basic perceptual processes.
- The stereotype of paramenstrual debilitation is very strong, but is *not* supported by the empirical evidence: there is no evidence that women's

abilities to think, study or work are affected negatively before or during menstruation.

- A menstrual rhythm (*not* paramenstrual debilitation) has been observed in some female-advantage tasks.
- Gonadal hormones may affect certain aspects of cognitive function, rather than overall performance, in both sexes.
- Any observed effects may be social or cognitive, rather than hormonal.
- There are methodological problems involved in investigating the menstrual cycle.

Further reading

Richardson, J.T.E. (Ed.) (1992). *Cognition and the menstrual cycle*. New York: Springer-Verlag.

Rosenweig, M., Leiman, A., & Breedlove, S. (1998). *Biological psychology* (Chapter 14). Sunderland, MA: Sinauer Associates.

Walker, A.E. (1997). *The menstrual cycle*. London: Routledge.

Waterhouse, J., Reilly, T., & Atkinson, G. (1997). Jet-lag. *Lancet, 350*, 1609–1614.

Wright, K. (2002). Times of our lives. *Scientific American, 287*, 41–47.

Chapter 8

Drugs and cognitive performance

8.1 Introduction

Drugs are substances, natural or synthetic, that produce physiological changes (though not all substances that have physiological effects are drugs). In the case of drugs used in the treatment of disease, these changes act to improve health or reduce pain. Many drugs, including drugs of addiction, have psychoactive effects – that is, they produce changes in mood, cognition and experience. Psychopharmacology is the study of the effects of drugs on the nervous system and behaviour.

Drugs affect behaviour by altering activity at nervous system synapses. A synapse is the place where messages pass from one neuron to another. Chemicals known as neurotransmitters pass the messages from neuron to neuron. Drugs achieve their effects by altering the activity of one or more of these neurotransmitters, either directly or indirectly (Figure 8.1). A drug can act as an agonist and increase the action of a given neurotransmitter. Alternatively, a

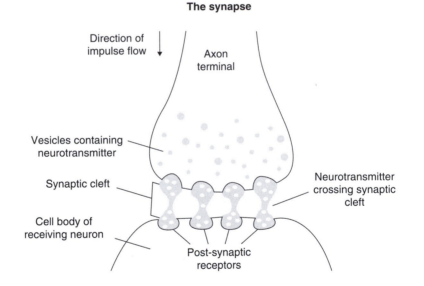

The synapse

Direction of impulse flow

Axon terminal

Vesicles containing neurotransmitter

Synaptic cleft

Neurotransmitter crossing synaptic cleft

Cell body of receiving neuron

Post-synaptic receptors

Drugs can alter:

Pre-synaptic events, e.g.
- processes in axon
- synthesis of neurotransmitter
- storage of neurotransmitter
- release of neurotransmitter

Synaptic cleft and post-synaptic events, e.g.
- inactivation/re-uptake mechanisms
- activation of receptor molecules
- activity of second-messenger systems

Figure 8.1 Drugs can affect the ways in which neurons communicate, either directly or indirectly. They can alter pre-synaptic processes, processes at the synaptic cleft and post-synaptic processes

drug can act as an antagonist and decrease or block the activity of a particular neurotransmitter.

Psychoactive substances have been used throughout human history and drug misuse and abuse is a major social problem. Most addictive drugs stimulate the release of the neurotransmitter dopamine, particularly in an area of the forebrain called the nucleus accumbens, which forms part of the brain reward system (Figure 8.2). Dopaminergic pathways (systems of neurons that use dopamine as a neurotransmitter) are important in reward and increased dopaminergic activity seems to play an important part in the reinforcing effects of these drugs (Altman *et al.*, 1996). Nonetheless, people differ in their vulnerability to drug abuse, with biological factors, personal characteristics and wider social factors all playing their part. Most drugs of abuse are currently illegal in Europe, yet alcohol and nicotine, which are legal, arguably claim the greatest social costs.

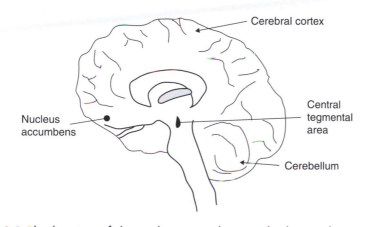

Figure 8.2 The location of the nucleus accumbens in the human brain. Both the nucleus accumbens and the ventral tegmental area form part of the reward system for all drugs. Dopaminergic neurons in the ventral tegmental area project to the nucleus accumbens and other areas of the forebrain. This pathway is part of the medial forebrain bundle and is a critical part of the brain reward system

This chapter is concerned with the effects of both the legal "social" drugs and illegal drugs on cognitive performance. These effects are of interest to cognitive psychologists for several reasons. First, drugs can be used as research tools to manipulate the activity of particular neurotransmitters and examine the effects on cognition. In this way, drugs can tell us much about the biological basis of cognition. Secondly, since the majority of people use drugs such as caffeine on a daily basis, it is important for students of applied cognition to understand if, how and when these substances affect performance. This research can also help us to understand why people use drugs like nicotine and caffeine.

The social drugs

The term "social drugs" refers to caffeine, alcohol and nicotine – substances that are legal and used routinely by people in everyday life. Most people use or have used at least one of these. People drink coffee and alcohol and smoke for many different reasons. These behaviours have important social dimensions: many of us relax and meet friends over a coffee or a drink. The use of caffeine is rarely harmful and the majority of people use alcohol sensibly. Smoking and other nicotine use (e.g. chewing tobacco) is always harmful and smoking is the biggest single cause of preventable deaths in Europe and the USA. Most smokers report that they want to stop smoking, but this can be very difficult. Smoking has important social dimensions and is a complex behaviour that is used by smokers in different ways and to fulfil different needs (Graham, 1994; Collins, Maguire, & O'Dell, 2002). However, there is a good deal of evidence to suggest that behaviours such as drinking coffee and smoking may be partly maintained because of the effects they have on cognitive performance.

Illegal drugs

Illegal drugs include cannabis, heroin, cocaine, amphetamines and ecstasy, and all have the potential to be abused. Drug abuse is a major social problem in most Western countries and is strongly associated with crime. A small minority of people use these drugs and recreational drug use is higher among young people than other age groups. The 2001–2002 British Crime Survey estimated that 12% of all 16- to 59-year-olds had used illicit drugs in the last year and 3% of this group had used a Class A drug (Aust, Sharp, & Goulden, 2002). Among 16- to 24-year-olds in England and Wales, 29% have used illegal drugs in the past year and 18% in the past month. Cannabis is the most commonly used drug, followed by amphetamines, ecstasy and cocaine. Heroin and "crack" cocaine were used by about 1% of young people in England and Wales in 2000. Illegal drug use is strongly associated with criminal activity and the negative social and health effects are well recognised. There is increasing concern about potential neurological damage caused by drug use.

8.2 Caffeine

Caffeine is the most widely used psychoactive substance in the world (Gilbert, 1984). It competes with the inhibitory neuromodulator adenosine (a neuromodulator is a substance that can affect the action of a neurotransmitter) and this action increases arousal. Caffeine is an adrenergic stimulant and acts as an agonist for a group of neurotransmitters called the catecholamines (dopamine, noradrenaline and adrenaline). In everyday life, caffeine is usually taken in the form of coffee and tea, but is also found in chocolate and many over-the-counter remedies for headaches, colds and flu (Figure 8.3). A mug of instant coffee contains about 70 mg of caffeine.

Figure 8.3 Common dietary sources of caffeine. Caffeine is found in beverages such as coffee, tea and cola. It is also found in chocolate and many over-the-counter remedies for headaches, colds and flu

Caffeine increases arousal in both the autonomic and central nervous systems. It reaches maximum blood plasma levels around 30 min after ingestion. It increases heart rate and blood pressure, causes constriction of blood vessels in the brain and can cause diuresis and gastric irritation. Under normal conditions, caffeine has a half-life of between 3 and 6 hours; however, this is affected by a number of variables including tobacco, which reduces the half-life (Arnaud, 1984), and menstrual cycle phase (Arnold Petros, Beckwith, Coons, & Gorman, 1987).

Heavy users of caffeine sometimes report withdrawal symptoms after ceasing use. The most common of these are fatigue and headaches, but some people also experience anxiety, nausea, weakness and depression (Griffiths & Woodson, 1988). Streufart *et al.* (1995) examined caffeine withdrawal in 25 managers who were heavy caffeine consumers (mean daily intake was 575 mg). After 36 hours of abstinence, their performance in managerial simulations had significantly declined. This, and other evidence, suggests that people can become dependent on caffeine and suffer withdrawal symptoms.

The effects of caffeine on cognitive performance

Caffeine has been shown to facilitate performance on vigilance tasks, simple and choice reaction times, letter cancellation, tapping, critical flicker fusion thresholds, and some aspects of motor performance (for a review, see van der Stelt & Snel, 1998). Lorist (1998) has examined the effects of caffeine using an information-processing approach. This approach divides human information processing into three stages: input processes (transforming perceptual input), central processes (further processing that is reliant on memory systems) and output processes (response). Lorist concluded that caffeine has selective effects on perceptual input, helping to direct attention towards spatial features of the input. Caffeine appears to have a limited effect on the higher processes in the central stage, with the exception of short-term memory. There is no evidence that caffeine affects output preparation, though it may help to maintain an optimal level of motor readiness and may also influence the output processes that occur after the response has been prepared.

Reaction time

Many studies have shown that caffeine improves both simple and choice reaction time. Kerr, Sherwood and Hindmarch (1991) found that choice reaction time was facilitated by caffeine and that this was largely due to effects on the motor component of the response. Lieberman, Wurtman, Emde, Roberts and Coviella (1987) reported positive effects of low and moderate doses of caffeine on vigilance and choice reaction time.

Where improvement is found, it is generally in the form of a decrease in time taken to respond (increased reaction time), rather than an increase in accuracy. It seems that caffeine can improve the perceptual input and motor output aspects of these tasks rather than the cognitive, or response choice, aspects (van der Stelt & Snel, 1998). Nonetheless, the picture is far from clear, as about half of the studies conducted have failed to find an effect of caffeine (van der Stelt & Snel, 1998).

Memory and learning

Again there is no clear consensus regarding the effects of caffeine. Several studies have reported beneficial effects of caffeine on recall (e.g. Arnold *et al.*, 1987); others have either found no effects or detrimental effects (e.g. Loke, 1993). Warburton (1995) reported beneficial effects of low doses of caffeine on problem solving and delayed recall, but not on immediate recall or working memory. Using a low 40 mg dose (about the amount in a cup of tea), Smith, Sturgess and Gallagher (1999) reported no effect of caffeine on free recall, but it did increase speed of response in a delayed recognition memory task. Kelemen and Creeley (2001) found that a 4 mg/kg dose of caffeine facilitated free recall, but not cued recall or recognition memory. Miller and Miller (1996) reported that 3 and 5 mg/kg doses of caffeine improved learning, but Loke, Hinrichs and Ghoneim (1985) found no effect of similar doses. Therefore, although a good deal of evidence suggests that acute doses of caffeine can improve learning and memory, other evidence suggests that caffeine either has no effects or tends to impair memory. Possible reasons for this equivocal picture are discussed later under "Methodological issues".

Some recent work has focused on the effects of habitual caffeine use on cognition.

A positive relationship between habitual caffeine intake and both memory and reaction time has been reported (Jarvis, 1993). Hameleers *et al.* (2000) investigated this further using a large sample of 1875 adults. Controlling for demographic variables, they found that caffeine intake was positively associated with performance in a delayed recall task and faster reaction time. There was an inverted-U relationship between caffeine consumption and reading speed: increased speed was associated with increasing caffeine intake up to five units of caffeine; thereafter the relationship was negative. There was no relationship between caffeine consumption and short-term memory, planning, information processing or attention. More research is needed to clarify the cognitive effects of habitual caffeine consumption.

Attention and alertness

The effects of caffeine on the Stroop effect are not clear: positive, negative and null findings have been reported. Evidence regarding the effects of caffeine on divided attention is similarly inconsistent (see van der Stelt & Snel, 1998). Smith *et al.* (1999) examined the effects of 40 mg doses on tests of focused attention and categoric search. They found that caffeine improved response time in both cases, but had no effect on accuracy, stimulus encoding or organisation of response.

The beneficial effects of caffeine on alertness are well documented (e.g. Lieberman, 1992; Smith, 1998) and a decrease in alertness is often reported as a symptom of caffeine withdrawal. There is some controversy about whether the effects of caffeine are true effects *per se* or whether caffeine simply increases arousal or performance to a more optimum level. James (1994) has suggested that positive effects of caffeine in laboratory experiments may be due to an alleviation of caffeine withdrawal. This position is not supported by studies in which positive effects have been documented in animals who have never received caffeine before. Positive effects have also been reported after very short "washout" periods (Smith, 1998). Washout periods are used to control for pre-experimental caffeine consumption. Participants are asked to abstain from all caffeine, and usually alcohol and tobacco as well, for a given period of time before the experiment begins. So the shorter the washout period, the less likely it is that a participant is in a state of caffeine withdrawal. This evidence suggests that the beneficial effects of caffeine are "true" effects rather than simply alleviation from withdrawal. There is also the possibility that the benefits people report from drinking coffee and tea have non-pharmacological components; for example, the act of drinking a cup of coffee itself may be beneficial. However, while this may be important in everyday life, it is unlikely to explain the effects reported in experimental studies, as positive effects have also been found when caffeine is administered in tablet form. Moreover, Smith *et al.* (1999) compared the effects of a single 40 mg dose of caffeine administered in different forms: tea, coffee, cola, tap water and sparkling water. They found that the effects of caffeine were independent of the type of drink in which it was administered and stated that "The overall conclusion is that caffeine is the major factor related to mood and performance changes induced by caffeinated beverages" (p. 481).

Caffeine and low arousal

Undoubtedly caffeine has beneficial effects on performance in low arousal conditions. Attention often decreases in the early afternoon and this is called the "post-lunch dip". Smith, Rusted, Eaton-Williams, Savory and Leathwood (1990) found that caffeine removed this "dip" in a sustained attention task. Caffeine has also been shown to sustain performance during prolonged work and to enable those with colds to compensate for impaired performance on a reaction time task (Smith, 1998). Brice and Smith (2001) concluded that the beneficial effects of caffeine often observed in the laboratory mirror effects in real-life situations.

Sleep loss reliably produces decrements in performance. Caffeine has been shown to improve alertness during night-work, when taken at the beginning of a shift. Bonnet and Arnaud (1994) examined the effects of both a 4 hour nap and caffeine on the performance of sleep-deprived participants. They assigned male volunteers to either a caffeine or placebo group. Participants in both groups were given tablets that contained either caffeine (caffeine group) or no active ingredient (placebo group). All participants had baseline data taken in the morning, after a normal night's sleep. Later that day, they took a 4 hour nap (16.00 to 20.00 hours). This was followed by 27 hours of alternating performance and mood tests, breaks and observations. Those in the caffeine group maintained roughly baseline levels of performance and alertness across the night, whereas those in the placebo group showed significant deterioration in their performance. These findings demonstrated that the combination of a prophylactic nap and caffeine was significantly more beneficial in terms of maintaining performance and alertness than a nap alone (Figure 8.4).

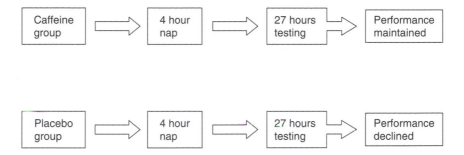

Figure 8.4 Bonnet and Arnaud (1994) found that caffeine can enable sleep-deprived individuals to maintain baseline levels of performance

Methodological issues

When caffeine has been found to improve performance, it has generally been assumed that this facilitation is due to caffeine increasing arousal to a more optimal level. However, the evidence regarding caffeine's effects on cognition and behaviour is equivocal, with studies reporting positive, negative and null findings. This is largely due to the problems in comparing studies (Lieberman *et al.*, 1987; van der Stelt & Snel, 1998). The research on caffeine (and the other social drugs) can take several approaches. Some studies focus on caffeine deprivation, others are concerned with the effects of particular doses of caffeine or dose–dependence relationships, while some researchers use caffeine as a tool to manipulate arousal. The doses used in studies range from approximately 30 to 600 mg: this is a massive range. Some use a single dose, while others provide doses relative to body size (mg/kg). There is also considerable variation in design and control measures, such as washout periods and time of day. Participant variables are important; for example, smoking and menstrual cycle phase/oral contraceptive use both affect the half-life of caffeine and a number of studies have failed to control for these factors. Some evidence also suggests that personality variables, especially impulsivity, may interact with caffeine (e.g. Arnold *et al.*, 1987; Anderson, 1994). To further complicate matters, the range of dependent variables that has been studied is enormous, making comparisons even more difficult (Koelega, 1998). These problems can also be seen in the study of the other social drugs. There is a need for greater standardisation of procedures and tasks to facilitate study comparisons and achieve a greater understanding of the effects of caffeine on human cognition, performance and mood (see Table 8.1).

Table 8.1 Summary of the inconsistencies in evidence for the effects of caffeine on cognition and performance

- Research question and focus
- Dosage
- Control measures, such as washout periods and time of day
- Participants – age, gender, smoking status, etc.
- Dependent variables

Conclusions

The picture regarding the effects of caffeine on cognition is very inconsistent, with some studies reporting beneficial effects, some no effects and others detrimental effects. A good deal of this inconsistency seems to be due to the wide range of methodologies used, which renders comparisons difficult. However, on the basis of the evidence, we can conclude that caffeine does affect human cognition and performance, generally in a positive way, and these benefits may underpin the use of coffee and tea in everyday life. Indeed, some have argued that caffeine can be viewed as a cognitive enhancer (e.g. White, 1998). Specifically:

- Caffeine tends to reduce performance decrements under suboptimal conditions (e.g. fatigue, hangover, colds and flu).
- Caffeine facilitates alertness.
- Cognitive tasks involving "speed" rather than "power" may be particularly sensitive to caffeine.

- Caffeine reliably improves vigilance performance and decreases hand steadiness.
- Beneficial effects of caffeine can be observed even at low doses (<40 mg).

Caffeine, therefore, may achieve its effects through indirect and direct mechanisms. Indirectly, caffeine may affect a general arousal factor, particularly under suboptimal conditions. Caffeine may also affect a specific speed or efficiency factor and this would make some aspects of cognitive performance more sensitive to caffeine than others.

8.3 Alcohol

Alcohol has been used since the beginning of human history. One of the first recorded mentions of alcohol is that of wine, on an Egyptian papyrus dated to 3500 B.C. In the UK, approximately 92% of men and 86% of women drink alcohol, at least occasionally. Although the majority of people use alcohol sensibly, the misuse and abuse of alcohol is a major social problem: in 2002, the charity Alcohol Concern estimated the costs of alcohol misuse to be £3 billion pounds in the UK. Alcohol is implicated in around 30% of all road accidents, and is directly responsible for around 5000 – and implicated in around 33,000 – deaths per year in England and Wales alone (*The Guardian*, 28 February 2002). There is increasing concern about the numbers of young people who drink heavily and/or binge drink.

Public health authorities recommend safe drinking levels. In terms of volume, it is recommended in the UK that women drink no more than 14 units per week and men no more than 21 units. In the UK, a unit is defined as 8 g (10 ml) of pure alcohol. A unit equals a typical glass (125 ml) of wine, UK pub measure of spirits or a half pint of standard strength beer (Figure 8.5).

Figure 8.5 A unit of alcohol is the amount in a standard glass of wine (125 ml), a UK pub measure of spirits or a half pint (~ 260 ml) of standard strength (3.5–4.0%) beer or cider. Bear in mind that many beers and ciders are stronger than this, so that half a pint of a strong lager contains more than one unit. Alcopops typically contain 1.5–1.7 units, depending on the brand, though some may be stronger

More recently, there has been a focus on safe drinking practices rather than total weekly consumption, as it is increasingly being recognised that binge drinking is harmful. The UK Department of Health now recommends daily benchmarks, rather than weekly limits. These are 2–3 units for women and 3–4 units for men. People are advised not to drink heavily on a single occasion and a number of alcohol-free days each week are recommended.

Alcohol enters the circulation quickly and is absorbed in about 2 hours. It has wide-ranging effects on the central nervous system (CNS) and is classified as a depressant: it tends to depress CNS and behavioural activity. It affects the action of the neurotransmitters GABA and glutamate. In common with other addictive drugs, alcohol stimulates the release of the neurotransmitter dopamine from the nucleus accumbens. This is an important source of positive reinforcement that acts to maintain drinking. At low and moderate doses, alcohol reduces anxiety (anxiolytic effect) and this seems to be an important source of negative reinforcement (the removal of anxiety reinforces the drinking behaviour).

The effects of alcohol on cognition

In general, alcohol has been shown to impair cognitive and psychomotor performance. Heavy alcohol consumption is associated with severe cognitive impairments. A good deal of research has focused on the effects of social drinking, but the definition of this can be problematic. The World Health Organisation has defined social drinking as an alcohol intake of 120 mg (1.5. units) of ethanol per day, yet some researchers use lower limits. For example, Zeef, Snel and Maritz (1998) defined social drinking as an average intake of 80–120 mg/day. Most experimental work has focused on the acute effects of various alcohol doses on the performance of social drinkers or problem drinkers/alcoholics, and a good deal of work has compared the performance of alcoholics and controls. More recently, work has begun to examine the effects of chronic alcohol exposure in social drinkers.

Reaction time

The effects of alcohol on reaction time have been well researched and it is clear that alcohol does impair reaction time. This impairment is mediated through central cognitive processes rather than peripheral motor processes (e.g. Kerr *et al.*, 1991). Alcohol also impairs both visual pattern recognition and visual attention. Nonetheless, some studies have found no effect of alcohol on performance (e.g. Kerr & Hindmarch, 1991) and some have even reported improvements.

Methodological issues

The fact that individuals vary greatly in their response to alcohol, and in their habitual alcohol consumption, may be partly responsible for the contradictory findings. There are differences between individuals in the effects of alcohol; for example, a given dose of alcohol tends to have more of an effect on a woman than on a man of the same weight as men's bodies contain more water and water tends to dilute the alcohol. Other factors include age, body size and composition, genetics and habitual alcohol consumption. A given individual may also have a different response to alcohol at different times and this may depend on stomach contents, time of day, mood, hormonal levels and factors such as stress, expectancies, state of health and the current circumstances (Table 8.2).

Table 8.2 Factors determining the effect a given dose of alcohol will have on an individual

- Genetics
- Gender
- Age
- Body size and composition
- Habitual alcohol consumption
- State of health
- Mood and expectancies

As in the case of caffeine, the range of methodologies used by researchers further complicates the picture. Studies vary in terms of participants, alcohol doses, methods of administration and controls used. A vast range of dependent variables has been studied and these tasks differ in terms of length and complexity. There is also a preference for reporting significant findings and this may result in a literature bias: studies that report a significant effect of alcohol may be over-represented in the literature. Furthermore, alcohol may affect performance in different ways on different tasks. Some have suggested that alcohol has a biphasic effect on performance, with low doses enhancing performance and larger doses impairing it (e.g. Kerr & Hindmarch, 1998; Streufert & Pogash, 1998).

Many authors have suggested that the effects of alcohol on performance become more detrimental as performance becomes more complex, though it is difficult to draw firm conclusions as the definition of "complex" can vary between studies. A number of studies have shown alcohol to impair memory; however, low doses of alcohol may actually improve performance by reducing anxiety (Streufert & Pogash, 1998). Lamberty, Beckwith and Petros (1990) found that alcohol administered post-trial actually improved the recall of prose passages. Streufert and Pogash (1998) have emphasised the need to examine the effects of alcohol on real-life complex tasks, outside the laboratory.

Alcohol and driving performance

The effects of alcohol on driving ability have been well investigated, as alcohol is implicated in at least 30% of UK road accidents. Currently, the alcohol limit in the UK and the Republic of Ireland stands at 80 mg alcohol per 100 ml blood, while in most other EU countries it is 50 mg per 100 ml.

Studies have tended either to focus on the effects of alcohol on tasks that assess components of driving such as coordination, complex reaction time and divided attention, or they have used driving simulators. Research has clearly demonstrated that alcohol impairs the components of driving behaviour (e.g. Kerr & Hindmarch, 1998). It disrupts behaviours that are crucial in vehicle control, like brake reaction time and steering. These impairments can be seen even at moderate and low doses of alcohol (Kerr & Hindmarch, 1998).

Alcohol also increases the likelihood that a driver will take risks (Burian, Ligouri, & Robinson, 2002). Furthermore, it produces a narrowing of attention so that individuals tend to focus on the key components of a task, like steering, at the expense of other aspects, such as road awareness. Thus people driving under the influence of alcohol often deny that their performance is harmed. The narrowing of attention to one or two components of driving leads to a subjective feeling of competence that is very much at odds with the objective reality: driving performance is always impaired after alcohol consumption (Figure 8.6). Even at a blood alcohol concentration (BAC) of 50 mg per 100 ml, which is lower than the current UK legal limit, driving ability is impaired (Kerr & Hindmarch, 1998). A driver with a BAC of 40 mg per 100 ml has doubled his or her risk of an accident compared with a driver who has not had a drink. The risk becomes progressively greater as BAC increases.

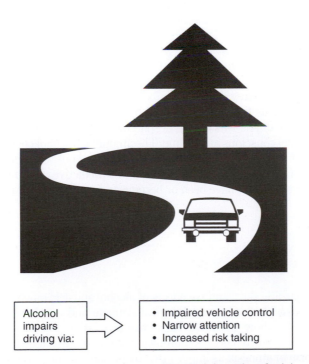

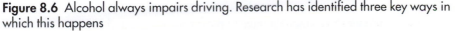

Figure 8.6 Alcohol always impairs driving. Research has identified three key ways in which this happens

175

Effects of chronic alcohol consumption

The majority of people in Western societies drink at least occasionally and moderate alcohol consumption has been linked to beneficial health outcomes, including a decreased risk of heart disease. Excessive use of alcohol is associated with cognitive deficits and neurological damage, but it is not clear when social drinking can become harmful. The picture is further complicated by the fact that definitions of social drinking, alcohol abuse and alcoholism are not stable and have changed over time, differ between countries and are used in different ways by researchers.

In 1971, Ryback proposed the continuity hypothesis, which held that there is a continuum of negative alcohol effects from small, often undetectable cognitive deficits in social drinkers, to alcoholic dementia and Korsakoff's syndrome. These effects are the result of alcohol-induced brain damage. Others have suggested that small amounts of alcohol do not cause damage and that it is the consumption of large volumes of alcohol in a single sitting (binge drinking) that is responsible for brain damage (see Nichols & Martin, 1998).

Several studies have attempted to correlate the amount or pattern of alcohol consumed with performance on a range of neuropsychological measures. The findings have been very inconsistent and research has failed to demonstrate a clear relationship between social drinking and cognitive impairment. It may be the case that any impairments are too small to be detected by standard cognitive measures, though this hypothesis is difficult to test. Parker, Parker and Brody (1991) have suggested that the effects of alcohol may be determined by the frequency of drinking. Reviewing the evidence on social drinking and memory, Nichols and Martin (1998) concluded that people who are heavy social drinkers and/or binge drink are at risk of cognitive impairment.

Certainly, a single episode of heavy drinking can have deleterious effects on memory. Episodes of heavy drinking can be associated with blackouts. When sober, an individual who has had a blackout will be unable to remember details of what happened when he or she was drunk, despite the fact that he or she will have been (or appeared to be) conscious at the time. The amount of alcohol consumed prevents the formation of memories (Victor, 1992). Blackouts are not well understood at any level. They are a feature of alcoholism and may be predictive of it, but they can also occur in people who never have been or become addicted to alcohol (Victor, 1992).

Alcohol abuse

The picture regarding the cognitive effects of alcohol abuse is much clearer. Alcohol abuse is associated with clear neurological damage and cognitive deficits. Sober alcoholics reliably show cognitive impairments relative to controls. Alcoholism can also lead to neurological syndromes including Korsakoff's disease. This disease is a form of amnesia usually caused by alcoholism; however, it is essentially a nutritional disease that is secondary to alcoholism. Thiamine deficiency resulting from poor diet causes damage to the diencephalon, and in particular to the mamillary bodies. Korsakoff's is characterised by both reterograde and anterograde amnesia (Victor, 1992). Patients have great difficulty acquiring new information, such as the name of their doctor, though short-term memory is usually preserved. There may be impairments in other cognitive functions, but these are minor in comparison to the memory deficit. The condition can be treated via administration of thiamine and resumption of a normal diet. If the disease is treated early the patient has a good chance of recovery, but once the amnesia is established only a small proportion recover fully and up to 20% show no improvement at all (Victor, 1992).

Conclusions

Acute doses of alcohol tend to have detrimental effects on performance. Alcohol abuse is associated with severe cognitive impairments. The majority of those who use alcohol do not abuse it, yet the effects of social drinking on cognition are not well understood and it is not clear at what level social drinking becomes harmful. Certainly, recent evidence suggests that drinking patterns are at least as important as volume drunk. There is a clear need for more research in this area.

Overall, we can conclude that:

- Alcohol tends to affect performance negatively, especially on complex tasks.
- Alcohol always impairs driving performance.
- Alcohol consumption can lead to concentration on main skill components to the detriment of secondary ones.

8.4 Nicotine

Nicotine is an alkaloid and is the key active ingredient in tobacco. Tobacco is most commonly smoked in the form of cigarettes, but can also be smoked in cigars and pipes or chewed (chewing tobacco and paan). The 1988 US Surgeon General's Report (USDHHS, 1988) classified nicotine as an addictive substance and drug of abuse for the first time. It is now generally accepted that nicotine is addictive and largely responsible for the tenacity of the smoking habit, although there are a small number of dissenting voices.

Smoking remains the biggest single cause of preventable death in the UK. It is estimated to kill 120,000 people a year and is responsible for 30% of UK cancer deaths (Department of Health, 1998). Smoking rates have declined steadily since the 1970s and smoking is a minority activity; currently, 29% of UK adults are smokers.

Nicotine acts as an agonist for the neurotransmitter acetylcholine. There are two kinds of receptor for acetylcholine, the muscarinic and the nicotinic. Nicotine acts as an agonist at the nicotinic receptor, hence the name. Cholinergic systems (systems of neurons that use acetylcholine as a neurotransmitter) are extremely important in cognition (e.g. Levin, 1992). Cholinergic agonists (e.g. hyoscine, nicotine) tend to improve cognitive performance, while cholinergic antagonists (e.g. scopolamine, mecamylamine) tend to impair it (Levin, 1992).

Alzheimer's disease is also associated with a decline in cholinergic activity (Perry *et al.*, 1986). This and other observations led to the cholinergic hypothesis of cognitive decline: age-related cognitive decline is the result of a decline in CNS cholinergic activity, often due to the death of cholinergic neurons, particularly in the basal forebrain. The picture, however, is not straightforward and cholinergic decline is not understood in the context of other brain changes associated with ageing (Gallagher & Colombo, 1995).

Nicotine and cognition

Given the above, we would expect nicotine to improve cognitive performance. The evidence does seem to support this: acute doses of nicotine tend to enhance performance on a range of cognitive tasks in humans and animals (see Pritchard & Robinson, 1998, for a review). A vast body of experimental work has examined the effects of nicotine on cognition and performance. This work has two main foci. The first is to use nicotine as a tool to examine the role of nicotinic cholinergic systems in cognition. Much of this work also aims to find treatments for cognitive deficits, particularly Alzheimer's disease. The second major focus is to try to understand why people smoke and to develop pharmacological and behavioural aids to smoking cessation.

Studies of the effects of nicotine on humans are complicated by the fact that some people smoke and others do not. Smokers self-administer nicotine on a regular basis and smoking is a particularly effective method of drug administration, allowing fingertip control of dosage (Figure 8.7). The amount of nicotine a smoker receives depends on the number of puffs taken and the depth of inhalation. Therefore, it is difficult to infer the extent of tobacco dependence on the basis of number of cigarettes or strength of cigarettes smoked. When smoked in the form of tobacco, nicotine enters the circulation quickly and reaches the central nervous system in approximately 10 sec (Le Houezec, 1998).

Smoking
- Fingertip control of dosage (no. puffs, depth of inhalation)
- Large alveolar surface area in lungs allows nicotine to be absorbed into the bloodstream quickly and directly

Figure 8.7 Smoking is a particularly effective means of drug administration, allowing the user to control the amount of drug taken and ensuring that it enters the circulation quickly

It is difficult to compare the effects of nicotine in smokers and non-smokers for two key reasons. Smokers represent a self-selected population and may differ from non-smokers in other ways. The effects of an acute dose of nicotine will be different in smokers and non-smokers because smokers have had chronic exposure to nicotine, while non-smokers have not. Animal studies do not suffer from these problems and a good deal of experimental work has examined the effects of nicotine on the cognitive performance of laboratory animals.

Animal studies of the effects of nicotine on cognition

Several studies have reported that nicotine facilitates learning and memory in animals (Levin, 1992). On the other hand, some studies have found negative or no effects of nicotine. A number of factors may account for these conflicting findings: variations in dose of nicotine; genetic characteristics of the animals used; individual differences in sensitivity to nicotine; variations in cognitive task; and level of training.

Levin and Torry (1996) reported that acute doses of nicotine improved the memory performance of aged rats, although there was no effect of chronic administration. Some animal work has examined the effects of chronic nicotine administration. Levin and colleagues (see Levin, 1992) trained rats on a radial-arm maze that required them to rely on working memory. After training, some of the rats were implanted with pellets that released nicotine throughout the day. The rats that were implanted with nicotine showed significantly greater improvement in task performance than the control group over a 3 week period. This improvement began in the second week and persisted to the end of the study. The rats did not develop tolerance to the enhancing effects of nicotine: the improvement was maintained throughout and the enhancement persisted for some time after withdrawal.

Human studies

As discussed earlier, it is difficult to compare the effects of nicotine in smokers and non-smokers. Many studies have compared the effects of nicotine (delivered through smoking) in abstinent and non-abstinent smokers. Overall, the evidence demonstrates that smoking after a period of abstinence improves performance on a wide range of cognitive tasks in smokers (e.g. Pritchard & Robinson, 1998). Three hypotheses have been proposed to account for this. The nicotine resource model holds that the gains in performance are due to the beneficial effects of nicotine *per se* – that is, nicotine acts to improve performance. The deprivation reversal model purports that gains in performance represent the alleviation of withdrawal symptoms that impair performance, rather than true gains. The combination hypothesis proposes some combination of the two (see Figure 8.8).

Different research designs have been employed to test these hypotheses. The effects of nicotine in non-abstinent smokers have been studied, as these smokers are not in a state of withdrawal. Researchers have also used non-smokers as a control group to observe the effects of nicotine on people who cannot suffer from nicotine withdrawal. Obviously, it would be unethical and inappropriate to ask non-smokers to smoke and the effects of smoking on a non-smoker would differ to those on a smoker. To overcome this problem, researchers have administered nicotine in different ways: in tablet form, transdermally (patches) and via nasal

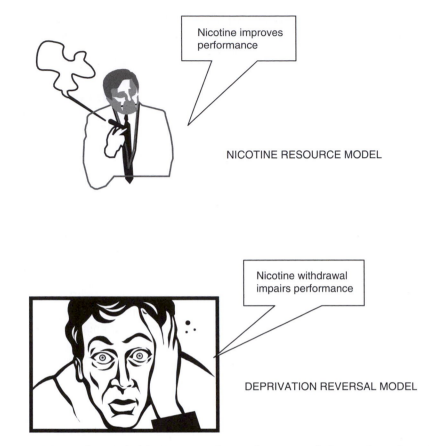

Figure 8.8 Smoking reliably improves the performance of deprived smokers. The nicotine resource model holds that this improvement is a genuine benefit of nicotine, whereas the deprivation reversal model suggests that there is no improvement, rather nicotine alleviates the impaired performance associated with the withdrawal. The combination hypothesis suggests that the effect is due to some combination of the two

sprays. A problem is that different administration methods produce different pharmacokinetic profiles. For example, when nicotine is administered orally in the form of tablets, the swallowed nicotine undergoes metabolism in the liver before entering the circulation, resulting in much slower absorption than via smoking. Smoking and nicotine nasal sprays have very similar pharmacokinetic profiles, with nicotine reaching peak plasma levels quickly before declining (known as the nicotine "spike").

Reaction time

Smoking has been shown to both improve reaction time and decrease errors (see Pritchard & Robinson, 1998). Nonetheless, some studies have found smoking to impair reaction time (e.g. Frankenhauser, Myrsten, & Post, 1970). The rapid visual information-processing (RVIP) task is a form of choice-reaction time task that has been studied extensively in relation to smoking and nicotine.

Rapid visual information-processing task

The RVIP task consists of the fast presentation of a series of digits on a computer screen or other visual display unit. Participants are required to press a response key when they detect three consecutive odd or even numbers. Performance can be assessed using three measures: the number of correct responses, the average time taken to respond to a target (reaction time) and the number of errors made. Wesnes and Warburton (1983) found that smoking improved both speed and accuracy. A later study obtained the same effects using nicotine tablets (Wesnes & Warburton, 1984). Smoking while actually doing the RVIP task has been shown to improve both accuracy and reaction time (Revell, 1988). However, Wesnes and Revell (1984) failed to find an effect of nicotine (1.5 mg tablets) on RVIP in non-smokers, although they attributed this to methodological issues and suggested that oral doses of nicotine in that range might improve performance only if that performance has already been depressed by factors such as fatigue.

Learning and memory

Evidence regarding the effects of nicotine on short-term memory is inconsistent. A number of studies have reported that nicotine increases speed of short-term memory scanning (e.g. Sherwood, Kerr, & Hindmarch, 1992), but not accuracy. Williams (1980) also reported that smoking increased short-term memory errors in smokers who had refrained from smoking overnight.

The picture is similarly inconsistent regarding long-term memory and learning. Much animal work has suggested that nicotine facilitates learning on a wide range of tasks. Nicotine delivered through smoking or other routes has been reported to improve performance on a number of learning tasks, including free recall, paired-associate learning, serial recall, retention of nonsense syllables and recall of prose (see Pritchard & Robinson, 1998, for detailed review). Some evidence also suggests that smoking after learning improves recall (e.g. Mangan & Golding, 1983). Despite this, several studies have found no effects or negative effects of nicotine on learning and memory.

Little work has focused on cognitive strategy or style, rather than overall performance. Algan, Furedy, Demirgoren, Vincent and Pogun (1997) found that smoking affected problem-solving strategies in women, but not men. In contrast, smoking improved the speed and accuracy of performance on a verbal task for men only. Further research is clearly needed in this area.

Attention

Smoking and nicotine gum have been shown to improve both visual and auditory signal detection. Nicotine also tends to reduce the drop-off in vigilance performance that occurs over time – that is, it reduces performance decrements in prolonged tasks.

The effects of nicotine/smoking on the Stroop effect have been well investigated. Nicotine gum has been reported to reduce the amount of interference (i.e. the size of the effect) (Provost & Woodward, 1991). However, some researchers have failed to find any effects of nicotine on the Stroop task (e.g. Parrott & Craig, 1992), although Pritchard and Robinson (1998) suggest that this may have been due to an insufficient number of trials.

Several researchers have suggested that attention mediates the effects of nicotine on learning and memory so that facilitation memory performance may be, at least partly, the result of improved attention. There is some evidence to support this, but it is clear that nicotine also affects information processing (e.g. Warburton & Wesnes, 1984).

Implications for theories

There is evidence to support both the absolute facilitation hypothesis and the withdrawal hypothesis; however, there is not unequivocal support for either. Pritchard and Robinson (1998) concluded, on the basis of findings with non-abstinent smokers, occasional smokers and non-smokers, that nicotine can and does facilitate cognitive performance. However, this does not rule out additional effects of withdrawal and they point to the need for more empirical investigation of the combination hypothesis.

Arousal modulation models of smoking maintain that smokers smoke to maintain preferred or optimal levels of arousal, performance and mood. This seems to be largely supported by the evidence reviewed on smoking and cognition. However, many questions still remain unanswered. It is generally assumed that any performance gains after smoking are due to the action of nicotine, yet there is no hard evidence to support this and few studies have measured actual intake or blood levels (Le Houezec, 1998). Tobacco contains many active ingredients and few have been studied in relation to humans. Moreover, smoking is a complex behaviour and non-pharmacological aspects of smoking could be responsible, or at least partly responsible, for the observed improvements in performance. It is also unclear whether the beneficial effects of nicotine on cognition are due to actions on specific processes like short-term memory or attention, or to more general actions on arousal (see Le Houezec, 1998). The modulating effects of smoking on cognitive performance may be important inducements for smokers to continue smoking. These effects are short-term gains that may be weighed positively against long-term health risk. It is important to understand the role of these effects in maintaining the smoking habit, yet most laboratory studies have used acute doses of nicotine despite the fact that smoking is characterised by chronic nicotine use. The effects of long-term chronic nicotine exposure on cognition have not been well investigated. Moreover, it must be remembered that smoking is a complex behaviour: there is more to smoking than nicotine. Physiological, cognitive, personality and wider social variables have all been implicated in recruitment, maintenance, cessation and relapse. We need to acquire a deeper understanding of the non-pharmacological effects of smoking on cognitive performance.

Conclusions

The effects of nicotine on cognitive performance are generally positive, though some studies have reported negative or no effects. Smoking reliably improves the performance of abstinent smokers and it is unclear whether this is due to facilitation, alleviation of withdrawal, or a combination of both. Overall, we can conclude that:

- The effects of nicotine on cognition are generally positive.
- Smoking reliably improves the cognitive performance of abstinent smokers.
- It is not clear whether performance gains are the result of absolute facilitation, relief from withdrawal, or some combination of both.
- The effects of nicotine/smoking on cognition probably play a part in maintaining the smoking habit, but other factors are also important.

8.5 Interactive effects of the social drugs on cognition

In everyday life, the social drugs are used in combination. Smokers tend to smoke more while drinking coffee and alcohol (Istavan & Matarazzo, 1984). Alcohol and caffeine are consumed together in the form of mixed drinks (e.g. vodka and cola) or liqueur coffee, and of course people use coffee to help "cure" a hangover. Surprisingly, this is a very under-researched area – little is known about the interactive effects of the social drugs.

Alcohol and nicotine

Alcohol is reliably associated with increased cigarette consumption (Istavan & Matarazzo, 1984); indeed, most smokers report smoking more than usual when drinking alcohol. There is some evidence that nicotine may help to counteract performance deficits resulting from low doses of alcohol, particularly on simple tasks (Kerr & Hindmarch, 1998). However, the picture is not clear-cut. Studies have reported antagonistic, synergistic, null and mixed effects of this combination on cognitive performance (see Kerr & Hindmarch, 1998).

Alcohol and caffeine

Caffeine is often used as a cure and can counteract effects of very low doses of alcohol (e.g. Pihl *et al.*, 1998). Caffeine may reduce the absorption of alcohol, but there is no clear evidence of caffeine as a "cure" for over-indulgence in alcohol. Certainly, the evidence does not suggest that caffeine can be used to counteract the negative effects of drinking on performance (Koelega, 1998). The doses used may be important: certain doses of caffeine may act synergistically with alcohol to impair performance and others antagonistically to counteract the alcohol-related decrements (Oborne & Rogers, 1983).

Nicotine and caffeine

Very few studies have examined the interactions between nicotine and caffeine, despite the fact that they are frequently used together in everyday life. Smokers are more likely to be coffee drinkers than non-smokers and they tend to consume more coffee. The relationship is unlikely to have a pharmacological basis, as studies have demonstrated that, in smokers, caffeine intake does not affect the level of smoking (e.g. Lane & Rose, 1995). Both nicotine and caffeine have been shown to improve performance, but these effects do not seem to be additive: nicotine and caffeine together do not produce a greater effect than either substance alone (Kerr *et al.*, 1991).

Conclusions

There is a real shortage of research in this area. It is difficult to draw firm conclusions on the basis of existing research, as studies cannot easily be compared due to differences in methodologies. There is a need for more standardization in terms of design and dependent variables to facilitate comparisons (Koelega, 1998).

8.6 Cannabis

Cannabis is derived from the plant *Cannabis sativa*. It is usually taken in the form of dried leaves and female flower heads, or the resin secreted by these. It can be eaten, but is more usually smoked in the form of a cannabis cigarette, or joint, often mixed with tobacco, or in a pipe. It is the most commonly used illegal drug in Europe and approximately 10% of UK adults aged 16–59 years have used it in the past year (Aust *et al.*, 2002) (see Table 8.3).

Table 8.3 Rates of adult lifetime, previous year and previous month use of cannabis in England and Wales in 1998

16–24 year olds	*25–34 year olds*	*35–44 year olds*
• 44% have used cannabis at least once in their lives	• 34% have used cannabis at least once in their lives	• 23% have used cannabis at least once in their lives
• 26% have used it in the past year	• 13% have used it in the past year	• 26% have used it in the past year
• 17% have used it in the past month	• 7% have used it in the past month	• 17% have used it in the past month

Source: Drugscope (2000).

The active ingredients are carbon alkaloids known as cannabinoids. The most important of these is delta-9-tetrahydrocannabinol (D9-THC), which is responsible for most of the effects of cannabis. These effects include enhanced perception, happiness, drowsiness, concentration and memory problems. As in the case of nicotine, smoking is a very effective method of drug delivery: a high proportion is absorbed and the effects are felt within seconds. The human body has natural (endogenous) receptors for the cannabinoids. The CB1 receptors are found in the CNS, particularly in the hippocampus, cerebellum and striatum (Ameri, 1999). The CB2 receptors are found on the cells of the immune system. Cannabis also triggers release of dopamine from the nucleus accumbens, which probably accounts for the reinforcing nature of cannabis use.

Cannabis has long been used for its medicinal properties. Glaucoma (high pressure inside the eyeball) has been successfully treated with cannabis, it prevents vomiting (anti-emetic) and has been used to treat the nausea that is often a side-effect of chemotherapy (McKim, 1997). Baker *et al.* (2000) demonstrated that THC could control tremor in an experimental model of multiple sclerosis, supporting the anecdotal reports of patients. Over the past few years in the UK, there has been increasing debate about whether cannabis should be decriminalised. From the end of January 2004, cannabis will be reclassified from a Class B to a Class C drug in the UK, but will remain illegal.

Cannabis and cognitive performance

Two main designs are employed in this research: examining the effects of acute doses of cannabis (smoked or eaten) on performance or comparing the performance of cannabis users and non-users. Kurzthaler *et al.* (1999) reported impairments in motor speed and accuracy immediately after smoking a cannabis joint. There is little evidence that cannabis use affects perception and sensory thresholds; however, it does seem to cause distorted time perception, with users perceiving time passing very quickly (McKim, 1997). Many studies have reported impairments in users relative to non-users. Cannabis does impair attention and heavy users are reported to have problems focusing attention, ignoring irrelevant information and are easily distracted compared with controls (e.g. Solowij, 1995). Cannabis users have also been found to be slower on perceptual-motor tasks than non-users (Varma, Malhotra, Dang, & Das, 1988).

Memory

Cannabis has been repeatedly shown to impair memory, particularly short-term memory. Schwartz (1991) reported impaired visual and auditory short-term memory in cannabis-dependent teenagers relative to controls. Millisaps, Azrin and Mittenberg (1994) examined memory in cannabis-abusing teenagers and found it to be significantly impaired relative to general intellectual level. These negative effects are assumed to result largely from the effects of cannabis at the CB1 receptors in the brain, particularly in the hippocampus. There is also evidence that the cannabinoids can act as neurotoxins and cause cell death (Ameri, 1999). Rodgers *et al.* (2001) developed a website to evaluate the effects of drug use on self-reports of memory ability. Memory was assessed using the Prospective Memory Questionnaire and the Everyday Memory Questionnaire. Cannabis use predicted everyday short-term cognitive problems, while ecstasy use predicted long-term memory difficulties that seem to be the result of problems in retrieval and storage.

It is unclear whether the effects of cannabis are persistent and irreversible. Several authors have suggested that cannabis-related deficits persist even after long periods of abstinence (e.g. Solowij, 1995), but others offer conflicting evidence. Pope, Gruber, Hudson, Huestis and Yurgelun-Todd (2001) examined the performance of 108 long-term heavy cannabis users throughout a month of abstinence. Users showed memory impairments for at least 7 days, but by 28 days of abstinence they were not significantly different to controls. The authors concluded that the cannabis-related deficits are reversible with abstinence. It is difficult to examine the effects of cannabis, as it remains in the body for some time after ingestion, so it can be difficult to differentiate between acute effects and residual effects in the short term (days and weeks). Furthermore, heavy cannabis users often differ from controls in terms of lifestyle and other attributes that may well affect cognitive performance. Reviewing the research in the area, Pope, Gruber and Yurgelun-Todd (1995) concluded that there is clear evidence for a short-term (12–24 hours) residual effect on memory, but that evidence is inconclusive for longer-term effects. However, the age at which cannabis use begins may be important as regards long-term damage. Ehrenreich *et al.* (1999) examined the performance of 99 cannabis users (they were not using other drugs and had no history of abusing other drugs) on various measures of attention. Cannabis use early in life was the most important predictor of impaired performance. These findings, and others, suggest that exposure to cannabinoids during early puberty can interfere with brain development and cause long-lasting neurological alterations.

Conclusions

Cannabis use has deleterious effects on memory and attention and cannabis users show clear cognitive impairments relative to controls. There is concern that cannabis use may cause neurological damage resulting in persistent cognitive deficits, but the evidence is currently inconclusive. However, the evidence does suggest that early use of cannabis may cause long-term cognitive problems. Overall, we can conclude that:

- Cannabis use impairs memory, particularly short-term memory, and attention.
- It is unclear whether these impairments are long term.

8.7 Ecstasy

Ecstasy is the everyday name for the synthetic amphetamine derivative MDMA (3,4-methylenedioxymethamphetamine). It achieved popularity at the end of the 1980s and has been strongly associated with "rave" culture. Ramsey, Partridge and

Byron (1999) estimated that approximately 10% of UK 15- to 29-year-olds have tried ecstasy (Table 8.4). Ecstasy tablets often contain substances other than, or in addition to, MDMA, including amphetamines and amphetamine derivatives, caffeine, ketamine, codeine and ephedrine (Parrott, 2001). The subjective effects of ecstasy are powerful and are characterised by positive emotions and euphoria. MDMA acts as an agonist for a group of neurotransmitters known as the mono-amines (serotonin, dopamine, noradrenaline). This group of neurotransmitters is important in mood and emotion; some antidepressants work by inhibiting their re-uptake. MDMA massively increases the release of serotonin and blocks mono-amine re-uptake, and this seems to be the neurochemical basis for the euphoria experienced by users. There are also physiological effects: an increase in heart and respiration rates, disruption of thermoregulation (the body's ability to regulate its temperature). Hyperthermia has been the cause of a number of ecstasy-related deaths, usually exacerbated by hot and crowded dance venues. Many ecstasy users report mood disturbance, particularly feeling low or depressed, in the days following ecstasy use (Curran, 2000). This has been linked to ecstasy-induced deple-tion of serotonin and there is currently concern about the potential long-term depressive effects. Animal studies have clearly demonstrated that ecstasy is a neurotoxin and damages serotoninergic neurons. This damage could have potentially very far-reaching consequences in terms of human depression. However, the laboratory studies have tended to use extremely high doses, so it is unclear how applicable these findings are (Cole, Sumnall, & Grob, 2002).

Table 8.4 Percentage of adults in England and Wales who had ever used ecstasy, amphetamines and cocaine in 1998

16–24 year olds	25–34 year olds	35–44 year olds
• 11% have used ecstasy at least once • 21% have used amphentamines at least once • 7% have used cocaine at least once	• 6% have used ecstasy at least once • 13% have used amphetamines at least once • 5% have used cocaine at least once	• 2% have used ecstasy at least once • 7% have used amphetamines at least once • 2% have used cocaine at least once

Source: Drugscope (2000).

Ecstasy and cognition

In recent years, a good deal of research has focused on the effects of ecstasy on human cognitive performance (see Parrott, 2001, for a review). A few studies have examined the acute effects of ecstasy in laboratory conditions, but obviously there are serious ethical problems with this. Most studies have been concerned with the effects of chronic use and have compared the cognitive performance of ecstasy users and non-users: these studies are fundamentally correlational in nature. It must be remembered ecstasy users are a self-selected sample and probably differ from non-users in other ways. People who use ecstasy often use other drugs as well, particularly cannabis, but some use a wide range of others, including cocaine, amphetamines and ketamine. This makes it difficult not only to choose a suitable control group but also to separate the effects of ecstasy from those of other recreational drugs used. Some studies have used control groups of legal drug users, others cannabis users and still others polydrug users (see Parrott, 2001). Level of ecstasy consumption is usually based on participants' self-reports and this can be problematic, particularly given the variations in MDMA levels in ecstasy tablets. A further problem is lifestyle differences between experimental groups: ecstasy users often have very disrupted sleep patterns and may spend long periods constantly awake, so discrepancies in performance between users and control groups may be due to these differences, rather than variations in drug use. There is also the issue of the appropriate washout period (the number of drug-free days before testing) and this is currently a matter of debate (Parrott, 2001). In general, studies have found no differences between ecstasy users and non-users on simple measures of performance such as reaction time (e.g. Parrott & Lasky, 1998). Vigilance, visual scanning and attention also show few differences (e.g. Rodgers, 2000). However, deficits associated with ecstasy have been reported in two important aspects of cognition: memory and central executive function.

Memory and executive function

Many studies have reported memory impairments in chronic ecstasy users. Deficits have been reported in verbal recall (e.g. Morgan, 1999), working memory (Wareing, Fisk, & Murphy, 2000), prospective memory and central executive function (Heffernan, Jarvis, Rodgers, Scholey, & Ling, 2001). Morgan, McFie, Fleetwood and Robinson (2002) reported impaired working memory and verbal recall in both current and ex-users of ecstasy, suggesting long-term damage. These deficits were predicted by the amount of ecstasy use. Given that cannabis use is strong associated with memory problems and that ecstasy users are often also cannabis users, several studies have attempted to disentangle the effects of the two on memory. It has been suggested that the frequently reported negative effects of ecstasy on memory are actually due to cannabis (Croft, Mackay, Mills, & Gruzeiler, 2001). However, Gouzoulis-Mayfrank *et al.* (2000) found that ecstasy and cannabis users did worse than cannabis-only users and non-drug users, and Rodgers *et al.* (2001) found ecstasy and cannabis use to predict different kinds of memory deficits, as mentioned earlier.

In general, most empirical evidence suggests that ecstasy impairs cognition and some findings suggest that it causes serious and long-lasting harm. Recently, however, these interpretations have been challenged. In an article in *The Psychologist*, Cole *et al.* (2002) expressed concern that the media and some researchers report a causal relationship between ecstasy and cognitive impairment that has not in fact been established. They stated that "telling the 'Chemical Generation' that they are brain damaged when they are not creates a public health problem" (p. 467). Their critique was based on the well-recognised methodological problems. The samples used are often self-selected and unrepresentative and it is particularly difficult to select appropriate control groups. While attempts can be made to control for polydrug use statistically, to try to separate the effects of ecstasy from other drugs, observed cognitive deficits may in fact be *caused* by simultaneous polydrug use. Furthermore, it is difficult to correlate degree of impairment and amount of ecstasy consumed given that the huge variations in MDMA content of ecstasy tablets makes it very difficult to calculate dosage on the basis of self-report. Cole *et al.* (2002) also expressed concern that studies that find no effects of ecstasy are simply not published.

Conclusions

The evidence reviewed strongly suggests that ecstasy has deleterious effects on memory and executive function. Ecstasy is considered by some to be a neurotoxin that can cause irreversible neurological damage and long-term cognitive problems. A good deal of animal work supports this view. Groups of ecstasy users do tend to perform significantly worse than non-users on tests of memory. However, the research with human participants has been essentially correlational in nature and a clear cause and effect relationship has yet to be established. Other factors, particularly lifestyle factors, may be at least partly responsible for the observed differences. Once again, there is a real need for more research to answer these questions. Specifically, we can conclude that:

- Animal work demonstrates that ecstasy damages serotonergic neurons.
- Ecstasy users show reliable impairments in memory and central executive function.
- A clear cause and effect relationship has yet to be demonstrated in humans.

8.8 Cocaine and amphetamines

Although chemically very different, cocaine and the amphetamines have similar effects on the central nervous system and behaviour and so are dealt with in one section. Cocaine is a CNS stimulant that is extracted chemically from the coca leaf. The coca plant is native to South America and the leaves have been chewed for at least a thousand years (Snyder, 1996). Pure cocaine was first isolated in Germany in 1860 and thereafter was widely used throughout Europe and America, often in drinks and tonics. Sigmund Freud was one of the first researchers to investigate its effects and he recommended it as a cure for morphine addiction. However, this treatment often resulted in cocaine psychosis and became unacceptable (Snyder, 1996).

Amphetamines are all synthetic drugs, with the exception of ephedrine, which is extracted from the herb *ma huang*. Ephedrine was originally extracted to treat asthma and synthetic derivatives were developed because *ma huang* was scarce (Snyder, 1996). The subjective effects of cocaine are euphoria, feelings of power, increased well-being and self-belief, mental clarity, increased energy and endurance, and little need for sleep or food. Both cocaine and amphetamines can cause "stimulant psychosis". This psychotic state is similar to schizophrenia and sufferers often experience auditory hallucinations and feelings of paranoia.

Like caffeine, both cocaine and the amphetamines act as adrenergic agonists and increase the availability of the neurotransmitters dopamine and noradrenaline, both by increasing release and by blocking re-uptake. This action increases both CNS and ANS arousal. The increased noradrenergic activity in the cortex is responsible for alertness, and noradrenergic activity probably underpins the euphoric effects too (Snyder, 1996). The increase in dopamine release is thought to explain stimulant psychosis: an excess of or over-sensitivity to dopamine is linked to schizophrenia.

Stimulants and cognition

Acute effects of cocaine and amphetamines have been examined in drug abusers, and occasionally in participants with no history of drug use. Amphetamines tend to increase alertness and improve reaction time under some conditions. Servan, Carter, Bruno and Cohen (1998) found amphetamines to improve reaction time in a task of selective attention and concluded that this was due to the drugs' effects on dopamine activity in cognitive rather than motor processing. While acute doses of cocaine are associated with powerful subjective effects, the effects on performance are inconsistent.

In general, amphetamine and cocaine abusers show cognitive deficits relative to controls. Ornstein *et al.* (2000) found amphetamine abusers to have significant impairments on a range of tasks, including spatial working memory, pattern recognition memory and shifting attention. Chronic amphetamine users also show impairments in decision making (Rogers *et al.*, 1999) and executive function. Deficits in memory and linguistic ability have been reported in those receiving treatment for cocaine abuse (Butler & Frank, 2000). The deficits shown by cocaine and amphetamine abusers are similar to those shown by patients with frontal and pre-frontal cortical damage (Robbins & Everitt, 1999). There is evidence to suggest a positive association between level of cocaine use and level of cognitive impairment (Bolla, Rothman, & Cadet, 1999).

Prenatal exposure to cocaine has been associated with cognitive deficits in later life. Animal work suggests that prenatal exposure can cause long-term memory damage (e.g. Morrow, Elsworth, & Roth, 2002) and exposure in early infancy can impair spatial learning (Melnick, Kubie, Laungani, & Dow-Edwards, 2001). However, Held, Riggs and Dorman (1999) conducted a meta-analysis of the published research on the effects of prenatal cocaine exposure on human infants and found reliable effects only for motor performance and abnormal reflexes.

Conclusions

Acute administration of cocaine and amphetamines tends to improve reaction time in laboratory conditions. Chronic stimulant use and abuse is associated with cognitive deficits, particularly in executive function and decision making, but also in memory and language. It is unclear whether these effects reflect long-term neurological damage. We can conclude that:

- Chronic use of cocaine and amphetamines is associated with deficits in decision making and executive function that resemble those of frontal and prefrontal cortical damage
- Prenatal exposure to cocaine may cause permanent neurological damage, but more research is needed.

Summary

Social drugs and cognition

- Social drugs such as caffeine, alcohol and nicotine have significant effects on cognitive performance.
- Nicotine tends to improve cognitive performance.
- Caffeine tends to increase alertness and speed, particularly under suboptimal conditions.
- Alcohol tends to impair cognitive performance.
- The cognitive effects of social drugs play an important role in promoting and maintaining their use.
- Interactions between the social drugs are complex and have not been well investigated.
- Methodological variations have made it difficult to compare studies directly.

Illegal drugs and cognition

- There is evidence that users of cannabis, ecstasy and the stimulant drugs show cognitive impairments relative to controls.
- Some drugs such as ecstasy may cause neurological damage that produces cognitive deficits, though further research is required to confirm this.
- Cannabis use is strongly associated with short-term memory and attention problems.
- Ecstasy use is associated with deficits in memory and executive function.
- Stimulant abuse is also linked to impaired executive function and to poor decision making.
- Research into drug effects is fraught with methodological difficulties as much of the research is correlational, so it is difficult to establish causal relationships.
- The high frequency of polydrug use also makes it difficult to clearly identify the effects of a single drug.

Further reading

Cole, J., Sumnall, H.R., & Grob, C.S. (2002). Sorted: ecstasy facts and fiction. *The Psychologist*, *15*, 464–467.

McKim, W.A. (1997). *Drugs and behaviour: An introduction to behavioural pharmacology*, 3rd edn. Englewood Cliffs, NJ: Prentice-Hall.

Snel, J., & Lorist, M.M. (Eds.) (1998). *Nicotine, caffeine and social drinking: Behaviour and brain function*. Amsterdam: Harwood Academic.

Chapter 9

Intuitive statistics, judgements and decision making

9.1 Introduction

The notion of probability is fundamental to many forms of human endeavour. Although its relevance to such activities as gambling or games of chance is widely acknowledged, it actually underpins many or even most forms of human reasoning. For example, in courts of law, a defendant is usually found guilty or innocent on the basis of a balance of probability. That is, the jury must decide, as reasonable people who have examined the evidence, whether the defendant is likely to be innocent or guilty. Absolute certainty is rarely available, so instead the jury only has to decide guilt or innocence "beyond reasonable doubt". That is, they must decide in which direction the balance of probability lies.

Similarly, in scientific work, just about everything that we know about the world is based upon observation of patterns and regularities. We then take those patterns to imply certain things about the probability of such events occurring again in the future. For example, the sun has risen on every morning of the author's life, so it probably will do so tomorrow. However, we can never be absolutely certain that this will be the case. This type of inference in which we base future predictions upon regularities in the past is referred to as *inductive* reasoning. Inductive reasoning characterises most of scientific thought and gives rise to scientific method. This is the method of hypothesis and test in which evidence is sought in the world for predictions deriving from scientific theories and models. In sciences such as psychology, scientists test their findings explicitly against probabilities – in this case, the probability of those findings being just a "chance" event. If such a probability is less than 1 in 20, then it is usually deemed *not* to be a chance finding.

On a more mundane level, probability pervades our daily activities, since whenever we make a decision we implicitly make some assessments of probability. For example, in deciding to do a university degree, all sorts of assumptions are made concerning the probabilities of various costs and benefits. A younger person, probably doing their degree to further their career, is betting that the rigours imposed by university study will pay off in the long run, for example in terms of salary, and also betting that they will live long enough to benefit from those gains. Thus, for the younger student a strategy of "deferred gratification" may be appropriate. For the older student, however, deferred gratification is likely to be inappropriate. He or she may instead be betting that the intrinsic benefits of doing a degree, such as following up a long-held interest, are more likely to lead to desired outcomes than are other activities such as travel and leisure.

Gregory (1972) suggested, in the context of visual perception, that the perceiver acts as a "intuitive scientist" generating and testing hypotheses concerning the visual world against reality until a satisfactory interpretation of that scene is achieved. An inappropriate interpretation gives rise to a range of phenomena termed "visual illusions". That is, an interpretation that is systematically in error is accepted. These errors result from the application of normally adaptive visual procedures, such as constancy scaling, to the generation of hypotheses that should be rejected but which, for whatever reason, are not. Analogous illusions may result from the application of default modes of handling uncertainties and probability in everyday life. To give a concrete example: My knee hurts so I visit a local health food store where I am recommended a product that is "good for" arthritic conditions.

I take the product in accordance with the instructions on the label and my knee stops hurting. Would I then be justified in recommending the product to other people suffering from sore knees?

The reader is probably trained in experimental design, so the answer to the foregoing question does not need to be laboured. Clearly, one person using a product is not an experiment that can be generalised. There is no control group and no blinding to take account of any placebo effect. However, the main point for the purposes of the present chapter is that the seeming co-occurrence of taking product and remission of symptoms may simply be an example of coincidence. That is, the pairing of treatment and "cure" may be a purely chance event. Much of the theory of statistical inference is concerned with the elimination of this possibility, so that we can know whether or not an effect of some kind of intervention really can be attributed to that intervention rather than to chance factors.

In real life, of course, we only rarely have the opportunity to conduct well-designed experiments that test out the justifiability of beliefs we arrive at as a result of exposure to regularities in the world. As well as between self-administered treatments and outcomes, such pairings might also be between characteristics of people and their membership of certain groups, between types of gambling behaviour and winning or losing at games, between dreams and subsequent events, and between taking risks and aversive consequences. In the absence of the possibility of formal experimentation, the cognitive system falls back on default methods for handling the statistical information inherent in these pairings in ways that enable beliefs to be formed or supported. These default methods are likely to have their origins in evolution rather than (necessarily) in rationality, and the purpose of the present chapter is to outline examples of such methods as well as their consequences for human belief and behaviour in a number of domains, including gambling, social judgement, paranormal belief, decision making and attitude to risk.

9.2 Definitions of probability

Probability may be defined in a number of ways. Manktelow (1999) suggests three definitions. The first of these is in terms of frequencies. Thus, if I stand at a street corner and count both the number of passing cars and the number of passing cars that happen to be red, then it may be possible for me to arrive at an estimate of the probability of the next car being red. Defined in this way, in terms of frequencies, the probability of an event A, written P(A), is the frequency of event A divided by the frequency of all types of events in which A could have occurred. That is:

P(next car red) = Number of red cars counted / Total number of cars counted

Of course it is not always possible to carry out a frequency count of the kind described above. Under such circumstances, we may instead use the second definition of probability. This is based on possibility. The probability of an event A is now the total number of ways that A can occur divided by the total number of possible outcomes. We can apply this definition readily to familiar probability assessments, such as estimating the probability of winning the UK national lottery (which involves choosing 6 from 49 numbers). Computing the chances of a winning combination would take several thousand human lifetimes if we did this purely by frequency counting. However, if we work out the probability of a particular sequence coming up by enumerating possibilities, it is quite simple to assess the probability. Thus, there is only one way in which a particular sequence can come up and that is by all of those six numbers being chosen (providing we ignore the actual order in which they are called). Again ignoring the order in which individual numbers are called within a sequence, the total number of sequences that can possibly come up is approximately 14,000,000. Hence:

$$P(\text{winning lottery}) = 1/14,000,000 \text{ (approximately)}$$

This ratio illustrates one of the problems that people have in handling probabilities, namely the requirement to handle very large or small numbers. What does a probability of 1 in 14,000,000 mean? Actually it means that to reasonably expect to win the lottery once, you would need to compete every week for 250,000 years (in which time you would have spent £250,000 pounds and lived for twice as long as modern humans are thought to have been in existence). One might conclude then that a rational choice would be to proceed no further with such a venture.

The third and final way of estimating probability is by use of subjective estimates. This is what bookmakers do when they offer odds on a horse winning a race. Here, however, matters are complicated by the fact that the probability is expressed in monetary terms, where the odds on the horse winning actually represents something more like the amount that the bookie can afford to pay you if his probability estimate is wrong, while still making a profit! Subjective estimates of this kind underlie much of intuitive decision making (not to say anxiety, if people overestimate the probability of adverse events). Although subjective probability estimation may be the greyest area of probability, there exist ways of making subjective estimates more reliable by modifying them in light of data. The statistician Bayes called the subjective estimate the "prior" and showed how this could be modified to give the "posterior" probability. Unfortunately, however, much research on human probability judgement indicates that humans are fairly poor Bayesian estimators – that is, they are fairly poor at making these kinds of modifications to subjective probabilities (Kahnemann, Slovic, & Tversky, 1982).

The law of large numbers

Most psychology students are intuitively aware of the law of large numbers. They use it every time they write at the end of one of their laboratory reports, "more participants required". By this they mean that there really is a difference or effect, but it is rather weak and requires a large sample for it to be illustrated. More generally, the law of large numbers states that a sample will only resemble, or be representative of, a population if the former is sufficiently large (often referred to as the sample having a sufficiently large n). A small sample may have similar characteristics (mean and standard deviation) as the population but in most cases will not. Fortunately, small samples are not entirely useless, since the central limit theorem of statistics tells us something about the distribution of means of samples and this result forms the basis of much of statistical testing.

The law of large numbers offers a way of understanding the relationship between frequency-based and possibility-based definitions of probability by showing that both definitions are fundamentally equivalent. Given a big enough number of observations from which to estimate frequency, the probability value yielded comes closer and closer to the "true" value based on possibility. However, just as it is not always feasible to conduct a long enough study of frequencies (as with the lottery), so it may not be possible to enumerate all of the possibilities available. Consider the probability of being knocked down in the London traffic. It is simply not possible to enumerate all of the combinations of events that may bring this about. Thus, our estimates in the latter case would be based upon frequencies of, say, accidents per pedestrian mile.

One of the misconceptions surrounding the law of large numbers concerns its relation to what is often referred to as the "law of averages". The law of large numbers allows us to believe that a particular proportion will be evident given a sufficiently large n. However, other proportions may come up in the short run. Consider the case of tossing a fair coin four times. We would not be unduly alarmed if no heads came up in so short a run, or even in a run of 10 tosses. If after an initial run of 10 heads there are even numbers of heads and tails for the next 1000 tosses, this would give us a 510/500 split and a probability of heads of P(head) = 510/1010 = 0.505, which is quite satisfactorily close to 0.5. All the law of large numbers in fact requires in this case is that P(head) comes arbitrarily close to 0.5 given a sufficiently large n. The number n of trials that is required is not, however, specified.

9.3 A little bit of theory 1: independent events

Whichever definition of probability we apply, one thing is clear, the event(s) we are interested in can never be more frequent than the possible events, since they will occur only on some occasions but not on others. Hence, the lowest value that a probability can be is zero. This value indicates that the event has not occurred (frequency count) or cannot occur (possibility analysis). Again, if the event of interest happens all of the time, then the ratio of the number of times that this happens to the number of total events is 1, since those numbers are equal.

Probability, then, when expressed mathematically, is a fairly simple matter of a number between 0 and 1. A probability of 0 means that one can be certain that an event will not happen. A value of 1 indicates that it certainly will happen. More usually we have number in between 0 and 1, indicating that the event happens some of the time. The nearer the probability of an event is to 1, the more often we can expect that event to occur. We can also express probabilities as percentages by multiplying them by 100. Thus, a probability of 0.413 is a 41.3% chance of a particular outcome happening.

An important notion in dealing with probability is that of *independent events*. These are events that have no (known) bearing upon each other. Examples would be tossing a (fair) coin, or producing children of either gender. Having a boy (or girl) does not influence the gender of the next child in any known way, so any of the following sequences of first and second children may occur with equal probability: boy–boy, boy–girl, girl–boy, girl–girl.

It is not a difficult exercise to estimate the probability of the first child being a boy using the possibility approach. There are two possible outcomes – boy or girl – but only one outcome that involves having a boy. The probability of a boy is, therefore:

$$P(boy) = \tfrac{1}{2} = 0.5$$

In this case, there is no need to do a frequency count to establish the probability of boys and girls being born in labour wards. (However, if one were to do such a thing, it would be found that actually the probability of having a boy is very slightly higher than that of having a girl. This may be nature's way of compensating for the fact that boys tend to have more accidents and illnesses and therefore have higher death rates in infancy. Recently, medical advances and lack of wars have prolonged this slight inequality into adulthood, though in old age the longevity of females ensures that the balance is ultimately redressed, first to equality and then strongly in favour of females.)

If we assume that P(boy) = P(girl) = 0.5, then what is the probability of each of the combinations of genders of first and second born children? A basic rule for combining the probabilities of independent events is that the probabilities *multiply*. Thus, the probability of a conjunction – that is, of event A AND event B – is:

$$P(A \text{ AND } B) = P(A) \times P(B)$$

Therefore,

$$P(boy \text{ AND } girl) = P(boy) \times P(girl)$$
$$= 0.5 \times 0.5$$
$$= 0.25$$

Exactly the same consideration applies to each of the other combinations, so we get:

$$P(BB) = P(BG) = P(GB) = P(GG) = 0.25$$

We may also see how disjunctions are handled in probability theory. *Disjunctions* involve an OR relationship rather than the AND of conjunctive relationships and we wish to compute the probability of event A OR event B. Since the four combinations BB, BG, GB, GG represent all that can happen if one has two children, we may be absolutely certain that one of these combinations of events will occur. Thus,

$$P(BB \text{ OR } BG \text{ OR } GB \text{ OR } GG) = 1$$

Of course, this is exactly what we get if we add up the probabilities of each of the possibilities

$$0.25 + 0.25 + 0.25 + 0.25 = 1$$

This now illustrates the rule for disjunctions of independent events – the probabilities add together (giving a total that is always less than or equal to 1) providing that the events are mutually exclusive. Some events, such as having a life-threatening illness, are not mutually exclusive, since some unfortunate individuals have more than one such disease. If we summed the probabilities of having such diseases, then the answer would come to more than 1 if we did not make some adjustment for this.

9.4 Heuristics and biases 1: representativeness, confirmation bias, the gambler's fallacy and the conjunction fallacy

Kahneman *et al.* (1982) identified a number of heuristics – rules that people apply in handling probabilities – that serve to introduce errors, biases and fallacies into their thinking. One of these, the representativeness heuristic, follows readily from misapplication, or misunderstanding, of the law of large numbers. *Representativeness* essentially is a belief in a "law of small numbers" that leads people to believe that a very limited finding has some ability to represent a wider population. Another is the "gambler's fallacy". This is the belief that nature will somehow "straighten up" a run that goes counter to intuition, such as 10 successive heads in coin tossing, in the short term (such as by generating an equivalent run of tails). Tversky and Kahneman (1971) have referred to such beliefs as almost implying a rather touching faith in inanimate objects' abilities to act with "memory and moral sense".

First, consider the notion of independence itself. How often do people say things like, "Well we've got three girls so the next one must be a boy"? Of course, the probability of the next child being a particular gender is totally unaffected (so far as we know) by that of the last child. The probability of a boy or girl remains essentially 50 : 50. This means, however, that the parents' erroneous prediction is confirmed half of the time, presumably encouraging belief in nature's willingness to "even things up". This situation may further encourage *confirmation bias* – that is, people's tendency to look for information that confirms their beliefs and to ignore other information that may contradict those beliefs (Wason, 1968).

Trying to predict the gender of a child from that of other members of a family is also an example of the *gambler's fallacy*. This fallacy is the type of thinking in which a gambler says to him or herself, "Well, I'd better keep going because my run of bad luck has to end soon" or, alternatively, "I'd better stop soon, my run of good luck cannot go on forever". Of course, the outcome of the next gamble, assuming that the game is fair, is entirely unaffected by previous outcomes and nature is entirely unconcerned with the gambler's bank balance of good and bad luck just as it is with the gender make-up of families.

The *conjunction fallacy* arises as a consequence of the way in which probabilities of independent events combine. The probability of a conjunction can never be greater than the probability of the events making it up. This is because both of the latter probabilities are numbers less than 1, and when they are multiplied together the answer must be less than each (for example, $\frac{1}{4} \times \frac{1}{2} = \frac{1}{8}$). These two facts about independent events – that they do not affect each other and that the probability of conjunctions must always be less than the probabilities of the events themselves – enabled Kahneman and Tversky (1973) to illustrate the fallacy using the following example:

The Linda problem

Imagine somebody called Linda who is "31 years old, single, outspoken and very bright. As a student, she was deeply involved with issues of discrimination and social justice, and also participated in anti-nuclear demonstrations".

What do you think is Linda's most likely current situation? Is she:

(a) a bank clerk,
(b) a feminist, or
(c) a bank clerk who is a feminist?

When asked to rank the options (a), (b) and (c) in order of likelihood, some 89% of participants thought (c) was more likely than (b). However, since (c) is a conjunction, we know on purely mathematical grounds that this has to be the least likely alternative. It seems that participants use some other, and less accurate, basis for probability estimation than simple enumeration of possibility. In this case, the representativeness heuristic may be responsible for the participants' erroneous responses, since their responding may be made on the basis of Linda being representative of a very small group of women – feminists who are also career women – and reasoning is with regard to this limited population rather than the population as a whole.

9.5 Heuristics and biases 2: randomness, availability, adjustment/anchoring, illusory correlation, regression to the mean, flexible attribution, sunk-cost bias

Many examples of erroneous use of probability information derive from the difficulties that humans have in dealing with concepts of randomness and chance. *Randomness* is an article of faith in statistical science and actually forms the basis of many of our most important scientific theories. Both modern physics and evolutionary theory, for example, explicitly acknowledge the role of random, or chance, factors. It is not merely lay people, however, who have difficulty in dealing with these ideas. One of the founders of modern physics, Albert Einstein, once famously remarked that he could not believe that "God played dice with the universe" (although such a belief may not be a very attractive thought, it could nevertheless be true!).

Given a set of events that are equally likely, such as having a boy or girl or getting a head or tail when tossing a fair coin, then which event actually occurs is a matter of chance, just as is which atom in a piece of radioactive uranium that "decides" to emit its radioactive particle at any particular time. It is difficult even to program a computer to simulate the random selection processes at work in these sort of situations, since any computer algorithm used to generate "random" numbers must operate in a mechanical and deterministic way. Since the computer itself is a machine, any number generated must be determined by the previous state of the machine – that is, the last number produced. Since, however, the first number is usually input as a "seed", by definition subsequent numbers cannot be truly random. Hence computer-generated random numbers are often referred to as "pseudo-random" numbers and truly random numbers can only be obtained by some analogue process, such as picking numbered balls from a bag, that may be used in a lottery situation. Evidence suggests that humans are fairly poor at simulating random behaviour, for example in generating random number sequences (Ayton, Hunt, & Wright, 1989), and this has implications for games such as lotteries.

We have seen how a small sample can be erroneously taken to be representative of a larger population. A corollary to this is the *availablity* heuristic. In this case, the sample, or an individual, taken as representative is simply the one(s) that can be brought to mind readily so that the heuristic works essentially on the basis of "If I can think of it, then it must be important". Thus, somebody may in all seriousness claim that cigarette smoking is not harmful because their Uncle Sid smoked 50 cigarettes a day and lived to be 93. Unusual yes, but it tells us absolutely nothing about smoking and health, as Uncle Sid is unlikely to be representative of much. Perhaps he just had genetic resilience to lung cancer. The true picture can only come from examining a large sample that is representative of the population as a whole.

The phenomenon of *illusory correlation*, illustrated by Chapman and Chapman (1969), shows how people can believe that two things go together when in fact they do not. Tversky and Kahneman (1974) suggested that judgements of how frequently two events go together may depend on availability. If thinking of one kind of event encourages thinking of the other, then the belief that the two go together in the world may be reinforced. This phenomenon has been widely applied in social psychology in order to explain stereotyped judgements in which membership of, say, one racial group is taken to imply a lot of other attributes. For example, Rasmussen, Turner and Esgate (2003) found that judgements made in the extremely sparse knowledge domain provided by head and shoulder photographs of unknown black or white individuals posing as athletes prompted biased judgements concerning, for example, natural ability or access to advanced training facilities.

The *anchoring and adjustment* heuristic can be illustrated by consideration of the following. Which of the following two calculations yields the larger answer?

$$8 \times 7 \times 6 \times 5 \times 4 \times 3 \times 2 \times 1$$

or

$$1 \times 2 \times 3 \times 4 \times 5 \times 6 \times 7 \times 8$$

It is not difficult to see, when the two sequences are presented togther in this way, that the answer is the same in both cases. However, Tversky and Kahnemen (1974) found that the first is often perceived as being larger when the sums are presented separately. Participants typically gave an estimated answer of 2250 for the first sum versus 512 for the second (in fact, the correct answer is 40,320). Because, however, the first sequence starts with a larger number, it appears to yield a larger outcome. We can say that the sequences in each sum are each anchored by different values and those anchors create the illusion that sequences may yield different answers. This was further illustrated by Tversky and Kahneman (1983), who asked people to estimate the number of African countries in the United Nations. Participants were initially given a random number and asked whether the number of countries was larger or smaller than the random number. Those given a high initial value produced higher estimates than did those given a low number. In general terms, when people make judgements concerning magnitudes, the initial values to which they are exposed will bias their judgement. In general, then, when people make judgements concerning magnitudes, the initial values to which they are exposed are likely to bias their judgement.

In addition, for purely mathematical reasons, when two variables are not perfectly correlated, extreme values on one variable tend to yield less extreme values on the other variable. Thus very tall or short or intelligent parents tend to produce offspring who are somewhat less extreme on those variables. Thus, extreme values tend to regress back towards the mean. The *regression to the mean* heuristic is concerned with the failure to appreciate this statistical fact and to assume that high values will continue to be associated with equally high or higher ones.

9.6 Applications 1: lotteries, unremarkable coincidences, paranormal belief, unproven treatments

The lottery

Hill and Williamson (1998) point out that gambling games such as the lottery are structured so that players should not expect to win. This may be summarised by saying that the expected utility of the game is low, that people perhaps play more for reasons of the excitement and arousal produced than for any expectation of winning (Griffiths, 1991). Studies have suggested that manipulation of arousal and mood by, for example, music will induce people to continue betting for longer in a casino, to buy more in a shop, and to continue exercising in a gymnasium for longer than they would do otherwise. Moreover, the lottery is a game of chance in which draws cannot be predicted or influenced in any known way by the players, all of whom stand an equal chance of winning with a single combination irrespective of skill. Wagenaar (1988) suggests that the explanation for lottery participation may lie less in players being interested in the properties of lotteries than in the "fair play" situation of an equal chance to win a highly desirable prize for a low outlay. This, taken together with excitement and arousal factors, may partially account for continued participation in a game with low expected utility.

Faulty intuitive statistics, however, are also likely to be relevant. Hill and

Williamson (1998) applied the heuristics and biases approach (Kahneman *et al.*, 1982) to an analysis of lotteries. However, it should be pointed out that since heuristics and biases are many, and since several may be applied to a particular situation, they can have less predictive than explanatory value (Wagenaar, 1988). Biased perception of randomness and also the gambler's fallacy may be linked to elements of choice and probability estimation in the lottery situation, as may availability and illusory correlation. Representativeness and availability, as well as other factors such as the illusion of control, flexible attribution and the sunk-cost bias, may be implicated in the persistence of gambling on the lottery.

Because the UK national lottery (which will hereafter be referred to as "the lottery") is discussed at length in this section, a brief description of its features is first presented. Playing the lottery involves selecting six numbers plus a bonus selection from 49 possibilities made up of the digits 1 to 49. A jackpot win occurs if all six numbers correspond to the winning combination, chosen twice a week by chance procedures involving numbered balls being randomly selected by an analogue, mechanical process. Smaller wins occur if three or more numbers are correct, and five plus the bonus ball results in a substantial prize. Players may choose to make multiple selections for a single draw, or to club together with others in so-called syndicates.

Failure to appreciate the nature of randomness is likely to affect number selection. Haigh (1995) suggested that players are inclined to avoid selections that include adjacent or nearly adjacent numbers. That is, a mistaken concept of randomness may be operating such that players assume that their choices should be equally spread throughout the available 49 number range, for example one from each 10 digit interval. Players may therefore be trying to predict winning combinations by simulating randomness in an entirely inappropriate way. Because of this mistaken idea of randomness and the resulting underestimation of deviation in what is seen as random, many combinations are not considered. As a result, huge numbers of possible combinations are not chosen by anyone. This may result in rollovers – that is, in draws in which no winner emerges – at a far more frequent rate than would be expected on the basis of mathematical analysis. Confirming this, calculation indicates that four rollovers would have been expected in the first 130 weeks of the lottery's operation, during which time some 18 actually occurred (Hill and Williamson, 1998).

Conversely, the fact that many players choose the same combinations results in sharing of prizes on weeks when such a combination wins. The motive behind number selection for the truly sophisticated player then becomes one of selecting a very "unusual" sequence of numbers. To this end, people choose apparently very unusual sequences to include adjacent values. In the extreme case, these would include sequences such as 1, 2, 3, 4, 5, 6. Unfortunately, however, this particular sequence is the most popular sequence of numbers of all among UK lottery players. Some 30,000 players made this selection for the 63rd draw, a double rollover with a £12.8 million jackpot (Hill & Williamson, 1998). The strategy is therefore totally counter-productive in maximising winnings, since, had that selection won in the 63rd draw, each of the 30,000 winners would have received only £1400! Moreover, 1, 2, 3, 4, 5, 6 is in any case a very unlikely candidate for a winning combination, since mathematical analysis indicates that the probability of (any) six adjacent numbers being drawn is just 1 in 6000 draws, in contrast to the 1 in approximately 2 draw expectation of (any) adjacent pair of numbers being drawn.

Some players may wish to make use of evidence from previous draws to assess the likelihood of numbers turning up in the winning combination. For example, each number is expected to be drawn an approximately equal number of times. While the law of large numbers tells us that this may well be true in the very long run, in the short run few predictions can be made. Attempting to predict current games from past occurrences of numbers is therefore an application of the gambler's fallacy. That is, chance is wrongly conceived as being fair and predictable – that is, as a self-correcting process that will inevitably and rapidly restore equilibrium. Such a view is explicitly encouraged by media TV coverage that parades the "form" of any particular number as part of the weekly draw. Usually this is along the lines of "and the next ball is number 23, which has appeared in 17 out of the last 42 weeks". This information may be entertaining, but is also completely useless as a basis for prediction.

Players may also be influenced by the availability of important numbers such as birthdays. This may result in disproportionately many selections of numbers less than 31. Haigh (1995) suggests that lottery players are unwilling to choose numbers, and certainly unwilling to choose several numbers, above 40. Thus, selections that come readily to mind may be favoured on the basis of the availability heuristic. Equally, the personal meaning of such numbers is significant and they may be perceived as being "lucky". This could be evidence of an illusory correlation – that is, of a purely imaginary link between certain numbers and desirable outcomes. Moreover, the introduction of a "lucky dip" facility into the UK lottery, which enables players to have random combinations of numbers selected for them by machine, appears to have had little impact on playing behaviour (Hill & Williamson, 1998), with only around 12% of selections being made in this way. Players are therefore reluctant to alter the non-random strategies that they already use, in ways that might maximise possible wins, even when offered the opportunity to do so.

Other factors influence persistence on the lottery in the face of the inevitable losses. One such is representativeness. Media coverage of winners and their transformed lives, as well as the "It could be you" slogan, create an impression that the very small subgroup of winners may actually be representative of players as a whole. The lack of coverage given to losers also influences the availability of such information. Gabouy, Radouceur and Bussieres (1989) suggest that many players know that lotteries have low or negative expected utility but they want to win, so keep buying tickets. Similarly, Cornish (1989) suggests that people persist with gambling even if they know they will probably not win because they feel comfortable with the form of gambling, feel competitive and involved, and believe the game involves some exercise of skill. The last of these observations suggests that an illusion of control may be operating. Because players may choose their own lucky or favoured numbers, many may feel that they have more control over the outcome and that they may win one day. Near misses, in which two or more selected numbers come up in the winning combination, or in which three correctly chosen numbers result in a small prize, may produce some of the excitement normally reserved for a win and so reinforce playing behaviour (Griffiths, 1991). Similarly, a sunk-cost bias may operate. This phenomenon, sometimes termed the "Concorde effect", refers to the tendency to continue with a project once a certain level of resource has been committed. Since some 60% of UK lottery players choose the same combination of numbers each week, it may be that for them some degree of commitment to their numbers has been made and this, possibly combined with the gambler's fallacy, may encourage a belief that their sequence must come up *one* day.

Unremarkable coincidences

A further problem that people have in dealing with probability concerns the appreciation of coincidence. This is not helped by the tendency of certain (otherwise admirable) psychologists, notably Freud and Jung, to rule out almost completely the possibility that coincidence may occur as a result of chance factors. Instead, they sought to attribute almost all coincidences with deep, and usually hidden, meanings. How often do people try to guess somebody's star sign or other attribute? ("I've got it – you're a Libra"). Do we need to be impressed by this? Of course not, there are only 12 star signs and the chances of guessing correctly are therefore 1/12 = 0.083. This does not even meet the criterion for statistical significance ($p < 0.05$). What about the probability of two or more people in a group having the same star sign? (". . . and to think we're the only two *Libras* in this small group of people"). In fact, the number of people required for such coincidences to occur is actually quite low. If instead of looking for *certainty* that such a coincidence will occur, one instead contents oneself with it being 50% likely (i.e. as likely to happen as not), then the numbers required are quite easy to work out.

The reasoning is simple. The probability of somebody not having the same star sign as somebody else is 11/12. If the group has a third member, then the probability of him or her not sharing a star sign with the other two is 10/12. The probability of a fourth member not sharing a star sign with either of the other two is 9/12. Since these are independent events, the probability of none of them having a common star sign is the product of multiplying all of those probabilities together. This is 0.573. This means that there is a probability of 0.427 that two of the people will share a star sign. Thus, it is almost as likely as not that in a group of four people, two of them will share a star sign.

If we consider birthdays, then we get the even more surprising result that we need only 23 people in a group (about the average-sized seminar group at the author's university) in order to be 50% likely that two of those people will share a birthday. With 30 people, as may be found on the average rugby pitch, it is in fact 70% likely that two people will share a birthday. Note, however, that this does not specify which people or which day – just that such a pairing is as likely as not. As Dawkins (1998) points out, somebody could make a good living going around rugby pitches on Sunday mornings offering to take bets on exactly this outcome. Most people will underestimate the probability of such a coincidence occurring and the bookmaker could expect statistically to win on seven out of ten occasions.

Belief in the paranormal

Blackmore and Troscianko (1985) suggested that belief in the paranormal may imply some misjudgement of probability. Blackmore (1984) found in a telephone survey of students that 25% of respondents claimed to have experienced telepathy and 36% expressed beliefs in extrasensory perception. Of these, 44% cited their own experience as the main reason for their belief. Blackmore suggested that there are only two possible reasons for this. One is that the students have indeed experienced the paranormal, and the other is that they have not but that their beliefs are based on a misinterpretation of normal events as paranormal. An example is the pre-cognitive (or predictive) dream. If one dreams one night that a particular car crashes outside of one's home, and then the next day such a crash actually occurs, then the probability of this pairing is judged to be so low that some explanation other than "just chance" is required. That is, an unmeasurable probability is judged to be too low to be construed as "just coincidence". As the birthday example given above illustrates, however, humans may have a tendency to systematically underestimate the probability of coincidences. The mathematician J.A. Paulos (1988) considers the probability of the pre-cognitive dream as a case in point. Assume the probability of a dream matching some aspect of subsequent events as being a low 1 in 10,000. The probability of not having such a matching dream in a year is then 1/10,000 to the power 365 (i.e. multiplied by itself 365 times), which equals 0.964. That is, 96.4% of people who dream every night will not have a matching dream. However, this of course also means that 3.6% of dreamers do have a matching dream and given that this is 3.6% of a very large number, a substantial number of dreams could therefore be seen as pre-cognitive. If only a few of these are interpreted in this way, belief in pre-cognitive dreams may be reinforced.

Kahneman and Tversky (1973) have shown that heuristics used to judge probability may give rise to serious errors. Moreover, people show confidence in their erroneous judgements, even in the face of contrary evidence (Einthorn & Hogarth, 1978). Errors in judgement of probability could give rise to paranormal beliefs if people, for example, underestimated the probability of a coincidence. Schmeidler and McConnell (1958) coined the unflattering terms "sheep" and "goats" for those inclined to believe and disbelieve, respectively, in paranormal phenomena. Another mechanism is selective forgetting, or errors in the recall of probabilities. In the dream example, one might only remember dreams that come true and forget the others, a form of confirmation bias. Alternatively, one might forget one's own predictions. Fischoff and Beyth (1975) asked people to estimate the likelihood of certain events and then, unexpectedly, to recall their own prediction and the actual outcomes. People seldom perceived having been surprised at the actual outcome, regardless of whether these were what they were expecting or not. Another mechanism is the illusion of control. We have seen the importance of this in the persistence of gambling behaviour such as in lotteries. In the present context, people who perceive themselves to be in control of essentially uncontrollable events when no other mechanism is apparent, may then attribute such control to paranormal phenomena such as mind control. Langer (1975) found that the illusion of control was greatest when participants thought that the experimental task demanded some degree of skill. Langer and Roth (1975) found that this was enhanced by early success on the task and showed that there was a tendency for participants to remember a higher number of successes than there had been. In an extrasensory perception (ESP) task, Ayeroff and Abelson (1976) concluded that people behave in a chance situation as though it were a skill situation to the extent that skill-related cues were present. It may be that for a believer, an ESP task is a skill situation, so it may be perfectly natural for him or her to display a greater illusion of control in such circumstances.

Blackmore and Troscianko (1985) conducted a series of experiments to distinguish between "sheep" (believers in the paranormal) and "goats" (non-believers) in terms of their treatment of probability. In the first task, schoolgirls were told that a hat contained a large number of pieces of paper with the digits 1, 2, 3, 4, 5 on them in equal proportion and were asked to write down a list of 20 numbers in the order that they might be drawn from the hat. That is, they were asked to generate 20 random digits. The number of doubles (i.e. the same number produced twice in succession) in each list produced was counted. Calculation indicated that four pairs were to be expected by chance. Since people are generally poor at generating random number sequences, and produce fewer doubles than would be expected on mathematical grounds (as we saw in the case of the lottery), it was predicted that sheep would produce fewer doubles than goats as a result of their failure to appreciate the role of chance events. Sheep or goat status was determined by a questionnaire concerning paranormal phenomena. Secondly, participants were presented with 12 examples of random mixtures of boys and girls invited to a party. In each case, they were asked to assess whether the choice of boys and girls was biased or unbiased using a semantic differential from 1 to 5. Sheep were predicted to give higher ratings of biasedness, again as a result of the failure to appreciate chance factors. Thirdly, participants were presented with eight examples of coin tossing and asked whether the coin was biased or not. The proportions of heads were 50% and 75% and the numbers of tosses 4, 12, 20 or 60. It was predicted that the goats would be more sensitive to varying sample size. All findings were in the predicted directions, though non-significantly so, with the exception of the result for doubles, which reached statistical significance. Blackmore and Troscianko (1985) concluded that goats may indeed be better able to handle probabilistic information and take account of chance events than sheep, and that this may influence the paranormal beliefs held by the latter.

The illusion of control was examined in a further experiment in which participants took part in a computer game in which they tried to make a coin fall as heads or tails with control exerted via a push button. On half of the trials the button actually influenced outcomes and on the other half it did not. Participants' perceived degrees of control, remembered number of hits, and estimates of belief in paranormal phenomena were recorded. The main prediction was that the sheep would feel that they had exerted greater control than the goats, whether or not this was the case. Other predictions were that goats would be better able to distinguish between control and chance conditions and that sheep would remember a higher hit score than goats. The results showed that the sheep indeed had higher perceived control, though the other predictions were not confirmed. However, when asked to judge the number of hits obtained by chance (by imagining just doing the task without visual feedback), the sheep seriously underestimated the effects of chance. This strengthens the view that a chance level of performance could serve to bolster belief in paranormal phenomena.

Unproven medical treatments

Similar considerations of the role of coincidence to those made in the case of paranormal beliefs may be made regarding belief in the ability of uncorroborated treatments to alter the course of disease. Health food and other shops do a brisk trade in supplements for which all sorts of claims are made, while overt quacks have been known to peddle fraudulent medical treatments with remarkable success (at least as measured by the willingness of people to pay for their services). Paulos (1988) describes why people may find it so easy to be taken in by a quack. The knowingly fraudulent operator takes advantage of the natural ups-and-downs of the natural disease cycle, preferably getting involved while the patient is getting worse. There are only three possible outcomes – the patient gets better, stays the same or gets worse. In two of those cases, the quack may take credit for a desirable outcome – either he stabilised the patient's condition or caused him or her to improve. Thus, there is a 2/3 probability that the quack will be (seen to be) successful. Moreover, these two out of every three cases will be the ones remembered as "miracles". In line with confirmation bias, the others will be discounted as "he did his best but it was too late". Thus, purely taking advantage of the laws of chance and an ability to enumerate outcomes enables a fraudster to make a good living provided the "patient" remains unable to distinguish between normal events in the disease cycle, chance coincidences and the effects of "treatments".

9.7 A little bit of theory 2: conditional probability

Conditional probability may be expressed as the probability that something will occur given that something else has occurred. By definition, such events are therefore *not* independent events. Consider the case of somebody being able to speak English. If they live in England this is very high, say 0.95. If, on the other hand, they are merely humans living somewhere on planet Earth, then the probability that they can speak English is much lower, say 0.4. In these cases, we can express the conditional probabilities as (i) the probability that the person speaks English given that they live in England and (ii) the probability that they speak English given that they are human. Conditional probabilities are written $P(A|B)$, which is read "the probability of A given B". Thus,

P(X speaks English | X is English) = 0.95

9.8 Heuristics and biases 3: neglect of base rates

The following is another example from Kahneman and Tversky (1973):

The taxicab problem

A taxi is involved in an accident at night. In the city there are two taxicab firms. One of the firms has green taxis, while the other has blue taxis. Altogether, 85% of the taxis in the city are green. A witness identifies the taxi involved as being blue. In tests involving the witness in identifying cab colours at night, she correctly identified the colour of the cab 80% of the time. Should we believe her testimony?

This question actually concerns conditional probability. To believe the witness, we need to estimate the probability that the cab was blue, given that the witness says that it was blue. There is a way of working out this probability mathematically using Bayes' rule, but it is somewhat complex. Instead, a simpler version is presented that involves enumerating possibilities.

Imagine that there are 100 cabs in the city, of which 85 are green and 15 are blue. The witness says that the taxi was blue but is right only 80% of the time. Enumerating all of the possibilities, if she sees each of the 15 blue cabs, then she will be correct in identifying their colour on 12 occasions (80% of 15). On the other hand, if she sees all 85 green cabs, then she will misjudge their colour and identify them as blue on 17 occasions (20% of 85). Thus, there are 29 (12 + 17) ways in which she can identify a cab as blue. Of these, only 12 are correct (i.e. those which actually are blue). The conditional probability that the cab is blue when she says that it is blue is, therefore:

P(cab is blue | witness says it is blue) = Number of times she says "blue" correctly / Number of times she says "blue"
= 12 / 29
= 0.41

Thus, the witness was *probably* wrong, since the probability that the cab was blue given that she says it was blue is less than 0.5.

Kahneman and Tversky (1973) presented problems such as the above to their participants. A robust finding was that the participants ignored the base rate. In the above example, the base rate reflects the overwhelming probability of a cab being green given that 85% of the cabs in the city are that colour. The *neglect of base rates* heuristic is also evident in the sophisticated lottery player who tries to evaluate the conditional probability of having to share his winnings with others when choosing a sequence of numbers, but completely ignores the absolutely dismal probability of ever actually winning!

On the theoretical level, Gigerenzer and his colleagues (e.g. Gigerenzer, 1995) have claimed that Tversky and Kahneman have taken a very pessimistic view of human judgement and decision making given their emphasis on errors resulting from the application of heuristics. In the case of base rates, Gigerenzer (1995) has shown that people are much better able to take base rates into account when this information is presented as frequencies rather than as probabilities. As we will see in a subsequent section, the way in which problems are worded, or framed, has a considerable effect on outcomes, and for most people probability is in any case an unnatural and difficult concept. Re-framing problems in terms of frequencies, a much more natural concept that forms the basis for counting, may have very desirable effects in limiting the errors caused by heuristics. Additionally, and as has already been noted, the criticism has been levelled that heuristics are more descriptive than explanatory or predictive and may therefore be of limited value in modelling human behaviour (Wagenaar, 1988).

9.9 Applications 2: social judgement, stereotyping, prejudice, attitude to risk, medical diagnosis

Social judgement, stereotyping and prejudice

One of the more disturbing findings made by Kahneman and Tversky's line of research was that the processes underlying neglect of base rates may actually resemble those involved in social phenomena such as prejudice. In a clever experiment, Hewstone, Benn and Wilson (1988) provided an exact analogue of the cabs problem to participants, this time phrased in terms of crime and the colour of residents. They made the alarming discovery that white participants were more inclined to take account of base rate data if the witness reported that the assailant was white, thereby producing a lower probability estimate of that suspect's guilt. Thus, base rate data may be used selectively to justify judgements based on pre-existing stereotypes in ways that bolster prejudices.

The better-than-average (BTA) effect is a related phenomenon in social judgement, which concerns the finding that many people when asked to rate themselves or members of their group on a variety of dimensions (for example, academic ability, social skill, susceptibility to certain diseases) see themselves as being superior to almost all others (Klar & Giladi, 1997). BTA has two major expressions: IBTA ("I am better than the group average") and EBTA ("Everybody is better than the group average"). The last of these is clearly statistical nonsense. By definition, the group members must cluster around both sides of the group average and cannot all have scores that are above the group average. Explanations for the BTA effect emphasise either the cognitive difficulty of making such comparisons, which may result in pseudo-comparisons being made that limit cognitive demands, or the emergence of in-group/out-group biases as a result of the simple act of categorising individuals into social groups.

Attitude to risk

In the context of risks such as susceptibility to disease, the BTA finding is referred to as unrealistic optimism. That is, some individuals believe themselves to be in some way "immune" from, or at least at reduced risk of, the adverse consequences of risk taking when compared with others, even though there is no basis for such a belief. Individuals may wish to take risks for reasons perhaps connected to personality variables, such as sensation-seeking or paratelic dominance. As with gambling behaviour, excitement and arousal factors may predominate in the decision to engage in particular activities, especially in extreme sports such as bungee-jumping where the thrill promised is unlikely to be gained from consideration of the risks involved. Individuals engaging in these activities may therefore find it convenient to underestimate the risks associated with certain activities. This underestimation is also important in health-related behaviour such as cigarette smoking, drug or alcohol use, and sexual or driving behaviour, though it must be acknowledged that behaviours such as smoking may also be motivated by physical or psychological addiction.

As well as unreasonable optimism, individuals may also make use of psychological ruses such as the availability heuristic (for example, by recalling the relative who was a smoker but reached a great age), be fatalistic, or think that something else will get them first, since the time-course of smoking-related effects is so long, or perhaps by believing that they think that they will give up smoking in time. An example of unreasonable optimism in the case of smokers was provided by McKenna, Warburton and Winwood (1993), who asked smokers to rate the likelihood of future negative events that fell into one of three categories: smoking-related, health-related and health-unrelated. They rated the likelihood of these events happening to themselves, to the average smoker and to the average non-smoker. Results showed that both smokers and non-smokers rated their own likelihood of negative events as being less than for both the average smoker and the average non-smoker. However, while smokers rated their own risk as being higher for both smoking-related and other health-related problems, they rated their own risk as lower than that of the average smoker. Thus, the smokers exhibited a classic optimism bias, which, given the very severe risks associated with smoking, McKenna *et al.* described as being at "the limits of optimism".

Risk theorists (Adams, 1995) provide a measure of risk that combines the probability of an outcome with the importance of that outcome. Thus, a game that carried a 99.999% chance of losing £1 would not be seen as very risky (this is, of course, exactly what lottery players do). Even though the probability of winning is so poor, losing a pound is not a great concern to most people, especially if they enjoy the game. The greatest risk is when the odds are against you and the potential loss is high. This is why smoking is such a poor risk. The smoker risks extremely unattractive outcomes that increase inexorably with exposure to tobacco. The risks may be summed up in slogans such as the following: "Smoking kills more people than all other drugs, legal and illegal, including alcohol, put together". Why, then, would anyone take such a risk? Similarly, when 10 people die each day on the roads of the UK, why does anyone imagine that car driving is a suitable arena for risk-taking? The answers to such questions are complex, but biases such as unreasonable optimism, combined with others such as the relative non-availability of images of the adverse consequences of such behaviours, are likely to be implicated.

Adams (1995) puts forward an additional concept of *risk compensation* that may be very important. In the context of motor transport, this concerns the intractability of the consequences of inappropriate driving behaviour and what Adams claims is the limited ability of technological solutions to counter this fact. In fact, he claims that such solutions may actually make matters worse. Technological solutions such as seatbelts, safety cages, door bars, crash helmets, and so on, have limited the consequences of accidents for many road users but done little to reduce overall numbers of accidents and perhaps just transferred their consequences to those who do not have this technology (ultimately to third-world pedestrians and cyclists). Adams argues that technological solutions may actually make driving behaviour worse, since the driver perceives increased invulnerability that he or she can choose to benefit from either in terms of a safety benefit, mainly accruing to other road users, or a performance benefit, mainly accruing to themselves. In many cases, it is the latter benefit that is extracted with the result that safety improvements may actually be making drivers more inclined to take risks. Similar considerations may apply to behaviours such as smoking. Smokers may believe that they are compensating for one risk by paying more attention to taking exercise or eating well, or perhaps believe that future medical solutions may limit the adverse health effects of their behaviour.

Medical diagnosis

Medical diagnosis provides another example where base rates are frequently ignored. Most diagnostic tests produce both misses (do not detect people who are ill) and false alarms (produce a positive test result for people who are well). In addition, the actual base rate of disease prevalence is often very low. Kahneman and Tversky (1973) presented examples like the following to participants:

False-positive in medical diagnosis

Fred has a test for prostate cancer. The test shows positive in 90% of people who have the disease. It also produces false-positives in 20% of well people. People of Fred's age with symptoms like his have the disease 1% of the time. His test comes back positive. Should he be worried?

The writer imagines that the majority of readers would be very worried if they were in Fred's shoes. However, applying a line of reasoning exactly analogous to that applied to the taxicab problem yields a conditional probability that Fred has the disease, given that he has a positive test result, of only 0.043. That is, he almost certainly does *not* have the disease. This is a statistical consequence of the prevalence rate of the disease in his age group and the false-positive rate of the test. Unfortunately, doctors can be extremely poor at communicating this sort of information to patients, who, as a consequence, experience much avoidable anxiety. To save patients from the distress caused by a false alarm, however, doctors some-times refuse patients' apparently neurotic requests for diagnostic tests in cases where the disease is unlikely. While in most cases this practice is justified, it is perhaps worse to be a miss (someone with an illness who is not diagnosed) than to be a false alarm (someone without the illness who produces a positive test result). This dilemma illustrates some of the complexity of medical decision making and it may be noted in passing that statistical procedures, such as discriminant analysis and logistic regression, were developed at least in part to try to deal with these sorts of problems.

9.10 Decision making: framing effects, risk aversion, overconfidence, hindsight bias

In making decisions, such as whether or not to continue with or cease a risky activity, a number of factors influence the outcome. One such factor is the way in which a problem is posed. Tversky and Kahneman (1981) presented such problems to participants in various ways to examine the effect of framing a problem in particular ways. An example of this is the "Asian disease" problem, which was posed to participants in the following ways before asking them to decide on which treatment programme to select:

The Asian disease problem

Version 1: An outbreak of an unusual Asian disease is likely to kill 600 people. Two programmes are available to deal with the disease. Programme A would save 200 people. Programme B would result in a one-third probability that 600 people would be saved and a two-thirds probability that no-one would be saved.

Version 2: An outbreak of an unusual Asian disease is likely to kill 600 people. Two programmes are available to deal with the disease. If Programme A were used, 400 people would die. If Programme B were used, there would be a one-third probability that no-one would die but a two-thirds probability that everybody would.

It is easy to see that these two versions of the problem are almost identical, the only difference being whether it is stated that lives are saved or lives are lost. The remarkable finding was that this difference had a large impact on responding, with 72% of participants preferring Programme A when Version 1 was presented but 78% of the participants choosing Programme B when Version 2 was presented. It appears that if Programme A was presented as a sure gain, participants avoided taking the risks implicated in Programme B, a phenomenon that Kahneman and Tversky referred to as *risk aversion*. With Version 2, however, when presented with a sure loss, participants were more inclined to take a risk in order to save lives. Risk aversion influences decision making, then, to the extent that a risk may be more readily taken to avoid adverse consequences but not to gain desirable ones. *Framing effects* of this kind may well form the basis for more mundane consumer decisions such as those to buy a product described as 80% fat-free rather than as

20% fat (Johnson, 1987), a finding enthusiastically exploited by processed food manufacturers and supermarkets.

Background information can also be implicated in decision making. In another problem, Tversky and Kahneman (1981) asked participants to imagine that they were buying goods in a store that cost $140 in total (one item being $125 and the other $15). They were then told that another store sold the same items for $5 less and were asked whether they would be willing to travel to that store to save the $5. Tversky and Kahneman found that the result depended upon which item was cheaper. If it was the $15 item, then participants were more likely to travel but would not do so to save $5 on the $125 item. Even though the financial consequences are the same in both cases, the 33% saving on the $15 item was perceived by the participants to be somehow more worthwhile. Similarly, when asked whether they would buy a $10 theatre ticket after arriving at the theatre and finding that they had either lost their original ticket or lost a $10 note, participants were more inclined to buy a ticket in the latter case. Again, the financial consequence is the same in both cases, but background factors have a disproportionate effect on the actual decision made.

Lichtenstein, Fischoff and Phillips (1982) found that people are often *overconfident* in decisions that they make. Thus, when asked for a response to a two-item multiple-choice question, participants claiming 100% confidence in their answers were actually correct about 80% of the time. This finding was influenced both by the difficulty of problems (i.e. overconfidence being lowest for easy questions and highest for "trick" questions) as well as by gender (i.e. males were more over-confident). Fischoff (1977) gave one group of participants a number of general knowledge questions and asked them to choose the correct answer as well as to give a probability that they were right. A second group was given the correct answer and asked to give a probability that they would have given that answer. Probabilities were higher in the second case, a finding referred to as *hindsight bias*. As has often been said, hindsight is always 20/20 vision! Of course, simulations of decision making as provided by artificial laboratory tasks of the kind described may be criticised for lacking ecological validity. In the real world, decisions such as whether or not to marry, change one's job or buy a house are in many cases very hard, with substantial influences from emotion, anxiety and a host of other sources. The implications of a decision in the real world are often extremely serious in ways that cannot be modelled in laboratory tasks involving artificial choice of a treatment programme for a disease or multiple-choice item selection. Theories of decision making are beyond the scope of this chapter, but some theories have attempted to incorporate these affective elements. An example is the regret theory of Loomes and Sugden (1982), which suggests a role for anticipated emotions in decision making. Decision making may therefore be influenced by a balance between the anticipated regret occasioned by making the wrong decision and the anticipated gratification that would have resulted from making the correct decision.

9.11 Applications 3: a couple of brainteasers

The despicable Dr Fischer's bomb party

In his novel *Dr Fischer of Geneva, or the Bomb Party*, Graham Greene (1980) describes a situation in which guests were invited to pull crackers from a barrel after being told that they contained large cheques. One cracker, however, contained a bomb. There were six guests and six crackers, but one guest chose to withdraw from the game altogether. The point of the novel was to provide a psychological analysis of human greed. Guests had the option of either withdrawing entirely or staying, but in the latter case they had to pull a cracker. One guest dashed to the barrel and pulled out a cracker that contained a cheque. Other guests protested that their chances had been shortened by this action and jostled for prime positions in the queue to pull crackers. Which position in the queue should the guests favour? Ayton (1994) put this problem to participants and asked them which position in the queue they would favour. The result is shown in Table 9.1. Clearly the first, second and last positions are favoured.

Table 9.1 Proportions of individuals preferring each position in the queue at Dr Fischer's party

First	Second	Third	Fourth	Fifth	Sixth	No preference
40%	12%	4%	0%	0%	42%	3%

A little analysis, however, reveals that the chances of being blown up are actually independent of position in the queue, provided that the bomb has not gone off. To show this, consider the first to go. He or she has a 1 in 6 chance of being blown up. What of the second to go? This guest now has a 1 in 5 chance of being blown up. However, that is not the probability of he or she being killed, since we must take into account the fact that this occurs in conjunction with the first guest *not* being blown up. This occurs with a probability of 5/6. We must therefore multiply 1/5 by 5/6 to compute the probability of the second guest being blown up. This turns out to be 1/6, which is exactly the same as the probability of the first guest being killed. By exactly the same argument, all of the guests have a probability of 1/6 of being blown up, regardless of position in the queue.

Why is this so difficult to see? Clearly, Greene (1980) did not see the solution and neither did any of the doctor's guests. Nor did Ayton's (1994) participants. This is therefore an example of a probabilistic illusion that we should be able to account for in terms of the heuristics and biases discussed in this chapter. We could interpret the finding in terms of neglect of base rates (individuals are only considering the probability of being blown up without taking account of the previous guest's survival). We might also think in terms of availability – perhaps the participants are failing to consider the possibility that the bomb will explode early in the game. For some, a strategic choice might be made to go last – if the bomb had not already exploded, then they would refuse to pull the last cracker (though by having a guest leave early, Greene put temptation in even the last guest's way, since two crackers would still be available).

The Monty Hall problem

In a TV show hosted by Monty Hall, a contestant is given a choice of three doors. Behind one is a sports car and behind another is a goat. After the contestant has chosen a door, the host opens one of the other doors to reveal the goat. He then asks the contestant whether he wishes to open his or her original choice of door or to switch to the other door. Should they stick or switch?

If the reader is a bit perplexed, he or she need not worry. This problem does have a solution but even PhD statisticians typically have a blind spot for it when first confronted with the problem. The most usual response is that it makes no difference whether you stick or switch – the odds are 50/50 of winning the car no matter which door is opened. However, this is not the correct answer – you actually have a better chance of winning if you switch.

The following explanation, over which the reader is left to muse, is adapted from the one presented in the book *In Code* by the young Irish mathematician Sarah Flannery (2000):

Solution to the Monty Hall problem

Yes, you should switch. Get someone to help you simulate the game using three mugs (to act as the doors) and a matchstick (to act as the car). Close your eyes and get your helper to hide the matchstick under one of the mugs at random. Open your eyes, choose a mug and let your helper reveal a mug with nothing under it. Play the game many times and count how often you win by switching and by not switching.

More formally, imagine two players, the first always staying with the selected door and the second always switching. Then, in each game, exactly one of them wins. Since the winning probability for the strategy "don't switch" is one-third, the winning probability for the second strategy "switch" must be two-thirds. Therefore, switching is the way to go as you double your chance of winning.

Summary

- A number of vulnerabilities in processing of probability information have been outlined, such as people's tendency to base judgements on a small, unrepresentative sample of information.
- A failure to understand independent events or the probability of conjunctions makes people prey to a number of systematic errors in handling probabilities intuitively.

- People typically have great difficulty in appreciating randomness, even when trying to generate random sequences of numbers when competing in a lottery.
- Conditional probabilities are particularly difficult to handle as a result of the tendency to under-utilise base-rate information.
- Bias in the utilisation of probabilistic information can lead to prejudiced judgements, erroneous perceptions of risk, or people being unduly impressed by the occurrence of unremarkable coincidences.
- Puzzles such as the Bomb Party or Monty Hall problems suggest that even sophisticated people can fail to fully appreciate probabilities present within a situation.

Further reading

Adams, J. (1995). *Risk*. London: UCL Press. An up-to-date account of risk written by a leader in the field.

Bernstein, P.L. (1996). *Against the gods*. Chichester, UK: Wiley. An account of the story of risk and risk perception, including a good chapter on the work of Kahneman and Tversky.

Manktelow, K. (1999). *Reasoning and thinking*. Hove, UK: Psychology Press. A thorough introduction to the psychology of thinking, reasoning and problem solving, including a detailed coverage of many of the topics covered here.

Paulos, J.A. (1988). *Innumeracy: Mathematical illiteracy and its consequences*. Harmondsworth, UK: Penguin. A brilliant, highly readable introduction to common errors in statistical inference.

Auditory perception

10.1 Introduction

In this chapter, the nature of auditory perception is considered. First, the nature of sound and of the human auditory system is described before comparisons are drawn between perception in the auditory and in the visual modalities. A historic account of the development of the study of auditory perception is then presented, including the psychophysical, Gestalt, ecological and auditory scene analysis approaches. This is followed by an account of more recent research, including research into sound localisation, perception of speech and non-speech sounds, attention and distraction, and the interaction between the auditory and other sensory modalities. Applications of auditory perceptual research are then described, including the use of sound in computer interface design, sonification of large data sets, design of auditory warnings, machine speech recognition, and forensic applications including earwitness testimony.

10.2 Sound, hearing and auditory perception

What is sound?

Sound is caused by vibrations in the air, which, in turn, are caused by an event involving the movement of one or more objects. The pattern of air vibrations is determined by the materials and actions involved in the event. Dense objects, like stone, make different vibrations than less dense materials, such as wood, and slow scraping movements make different patterns of vibrations from those caused by impacts. Our ears and brains have evolved to pick up these air vibrations caused by objects and events and interpret them as sound.

The air vibration that impinges upon our ears can vary in many ways, but always in the two dimensions of intensity and time. The pattern of vibration may therefore be represented as a (acoustic) waveform, where this can be thought of as a graph of intensity against time. Intensity here refers to the amount of energy transmitted by the wave, where this is evident as the pressure (sound pressure level) exerted by the sound wave as it travels through the air. High peaks in the waveform indicate high levels of intensity and we experience this as relatively louder sound. A greater number of peaks or troughs per second is referred to as higher frequency and this we experience as a higher pitch. Intensity and frequency are thus physical attributes that can be measured, while loudness and pitch are psychological attributes of sounds that result from the perceptual processing by the ears and brain. Since we are capable of registering a very wide range of intensities, the familiar decibel scale uses logarithms of a function of the sound pressure level rather than absolute pressure levels as an index of loudness.

Figure 10.1 shows the waveforms of a pencil falling on a table top, a mouth-organ playing an "A" note, the author saying "hello", and the author saying "hello" while another person (female) is simultaneously saying "goodbye". Although these may all be considered to be quite simple auditory stimuli, Figure 10.1 shows that they nevertheless have quite complex waveforms.

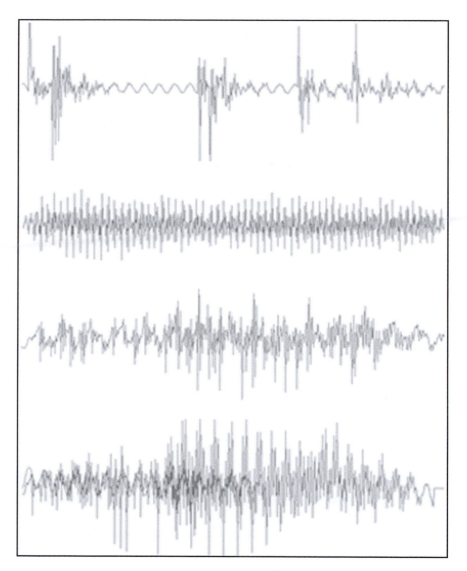

Figure 10.1 (From top to bottom) The waveforms of a pencil falling onto a table top, a mouth-organ playing the note of A, the author saying "hello", and the author saying "hello" at the same time as a woman says "goodbye"

Researchers have developed a way of looking at sounds that gives us more information than the two dimensions of the waveforms shown in Figure 10.1. The sound spectrogram enables us to display sounds using the three dimensions of frequency, time and intensity. Figure 10.2 shows spectrograms of the same speech recorded for Figure 10.1. The vertical axis displays frequency information with

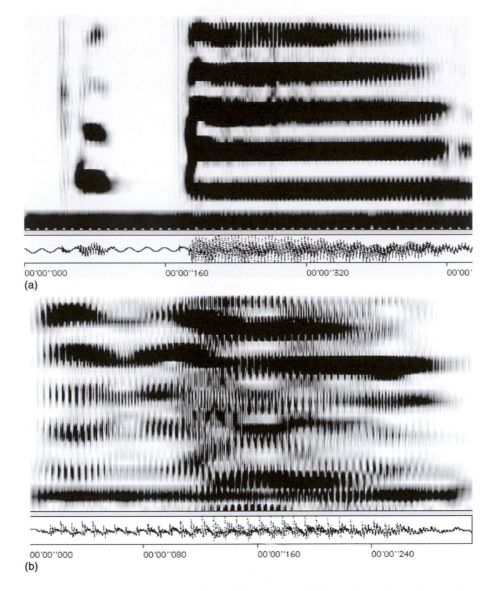

Figure 10.2 Spectrograms of (a) the author saying "hello" and (b) the author saying "hello" at the same time as a woman says "goodbye"

marks high up on the graph being higher in frequency. The horizontal axis is time and the shading of the marks represents intensity, darker patches having more energy than lighter ones. The sound spectrogram enables sounds to be represented in a systematic way.

What is the auditory system?

The auditory system operates in three phases: reception, transduction and perception. Sound energy first impacts upon the eardrums and sets up sympathetic vibrations. These induced vibrations enable the sound energy to be transmitted to the inner ear, where it is transduced into neural impulses. Finally, those neural impulses are transmitted to the brain via the auditory nerve so that the brain can interpret the pattern of impulses as sounds having certain attributes. In effect, the ear acts rather like a sound spectrogram. It analyses the incoming acoustic waveform into frequency and intensity information ready for perceptual processing and interpretation by the brain.

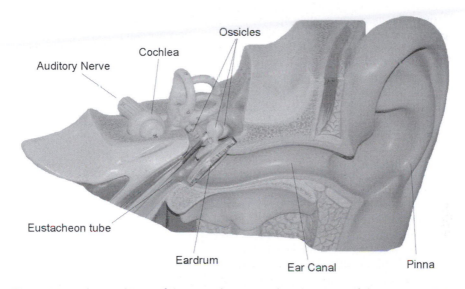

Figure 10.3 The workings of the ear. The external ear consists of the pinna and the ear canal. The middle ear consists of the eardrum (also known as the tympanum) and the ossicles (or ear bones). The inner ear is made up of the cochlea and the auditory nerve. The cochlea is a coiled tube-like structure filled with fluid and an array of sensitive hair cells attached to a vibration-sensitive membrane. The balance system, or vestibular system, is also part of the cochlea and consists of three circular tubes filled with fluid and hair cells that transduce the movements of the head into nerve impulses

One could say that hearing begins when one *feels* the air vibrations on the thin skin membranes of the eardrums. On the inner side of each eardrum is a chain of three of the smallest bones in the body, called the ossicles. These in turn are vibrated, as sympathetic vibrations are set up in the eardrum, and hence the air vibrations are transformed into a mechanical vibration of a slightly different kind. Auditory stimulation is actually a special case of mechanical vibration. The body has many other systems – for example, special receptor cells in the skin – capable of detecting and transducing mechanical vibration. These are generally referred to as mechanoreceptors. Vibrational energy that we experience as sound is simply vibrational energy within a certain frequency band. Some other creatures, notably spiders, use mechanical vibration (of their webs) as their main sensory input and so may, in a literal sense, be said to hear (or even see) "with their feet".

In the auditory system, the last of the ossicles vibrates onto a smaller membrane covering the end of a fluid-filled coiled canal called the cochlea. Inside the cochlea, these vibrations are transformed into electrical impulses by a highly efficient and sensitive structure of membranes and tiny receptor cells called hair cells. The hair cells, like all hair cells in the body, have receptor nerve cells that fire (emit an action potential or electrical impulse) when the hairs are displaced. At one end of the cochlea the nerve endings fire in synchrony with the incoming high-frequency vibrations, while at the other end the nerve endings pick up the lower frequencies. In this way, the incoming sounds are transformed into neural firings representing the frequency–intensity changes over time. However, since we can perceive a far greater range of sound frequencies than the membranes of the inner ear can vibrate to, complex combinations of inputs from regions of the cochlea are required to trans-duce those extra frequencies. This is referred to as the "volley principle". Outputs from the receptors are transmitted along nerve fibres that become gathered together as nerve bundles. These are ultimately rolled into the auditory nerve. Stimulation travels along this nerve through to the midbrain and on to several subcortical structures before finally synapsing on to cortical structures in the brain where higher-level interpretation is carried out.

At this point, we must be wary of describing auditory perception as a bottom-up process. There are feedback loops that can affect the perceptual process. For example, when some sounds get too loud, hair cells in the inner ear change their receptive properties to adjust to the increased energy being received. There are also top-down influences at the perceptual and cognitive levels of processing, especially in speech perception. As in visual perception, the effect of context can also be important. These influences are partly indicative of the integrated nature of perception within the broader processing of cognition. For example, when you are aware of hearing a sound, you usually have little trouble recognising it, identifying where it came from, how it was made, and also understanding any meaning attached to it. Each of these aspects of hearing can involve attention, learning and memory, among other processes. If the sounds are speech sounds, then language processes are also involved. The same is also true of music, another example of highly structured symbolic processing of sound. The perception of sound ultim-ately includes some cognitive processing and this implies that we need to adopt a cognitive approach in which *sensory* information processing is contiguous with *symbolic* information processing.

Seeing and hearing

There are several similarities between auditory and visual perception. One is the problem of perceptual constancy. Both systems manage to deal with widely varying sensory information, and give us remarkably stable perceptions. For example, when you see a person walking towards you, you correctly conclude that the person is not growing in size, even though the retinal image could simplistically be interpreted in such a way. Similar constancies are evident in auditory perception, but are perhaps more fundamental when one considers that the acoustic signal is linear and is usually made up of more than one sound event. Not only does a sound vary slightly every time it is produced, but it is also mixed with other sounds to produce an even more complex waveform and it is this that hits the ear. Thus, the figure-ground problem, first described by the Gestalt psychologists, is thus as important in auditory perception as it is in visual perception.

Like the visual system, the auditory system also has identifiable "what" and "where" pathways (see Groome *et al.*, 1999) that process the location of a sound in parallel to recognition of its meaning. For the visual system, however, recognising an object usually also implies determination of where it is, while for audition it is possible to recognise a sound without being aware of its precise location. In a sense, in humans at any rate, the auditory system may function in the *service* of the visual system when we need to locate something; the visual system takes priority when we need to work out where something is with hearing offering only supplementary information (Kubovy & van Valkenburg, 2001).

Perhaps as a consequence of the primacy of vision to humans, "visuo-centrism" has become evident in research, as more studies have examined visual than auditory perception. When we are asked to explain something, we can more easily do this using pictures, and "knowing" or "understanding" is usually described using visual metaphors such as "I see . . ." (Lakoff & Johnson, 1999). The subject matter for visual research is often fairly easy to present to people. With hearing, on the other hand, it is much more difficult to get hold of a stimulus and pass it about so that we can all "look" at it under the same conditions. Visual stimuli can be made invariant over time. We can draw pictures to use in simple experiments and we can present visual illusions on paper fairly easily. However, sounds are *always* variant over time. As a result, auditory researchers have had to wait longer for technology to become available that will allow for the construction and control of stimuli for experiments. It is only within the last 50 years that accurate audio recordings have been of high enough quality for this purpose, and only within the last 15–20 years has technology been widely available for the digital synthesis, recording and editing of sound.

10.3 Approaches to studying auditory perception

Psychophysics

Early research into auditory perception was influenced by psychophysics. Scientists such as Georg Ohm and Hermann von Helmholtz tried to identify the limits of perception in well-controlled laboratory situations. Examples of the type of questions asked are: What is the quietest sound one can hear? What is the smallest difference in intensity or pitch that one can detect between two tones? The experimental approach was reductionist in character and with an underlying assumption that, in order to understand how complex sounds are perceived, one should begin with "simple" stimuli. Thus, sine-wave tones (often called "pure" tones) were most often used.

Psychophysicists viewed the ear as an analytical instrument. They presumed that it split complex signals into simple components that were then sent to the brain to be reassembled. Hence, if all the data on how we deal with pure tones could be collected, then the laws governing how our auditory system analyses complex sounds could be delineated. In the last 150 years or so, much has been learnt about the physics of sound transmission both outside and inside our ears, but this work is by no means complete.

There have been some excellent practical applications of this approach to research, such as the design of hearing aids, the development of recording techniques, and the improvements in the acoustics of concert halls and theatres. But we must also recognise its limits. Modern hearing aid research is now concentrating on using techniques from artificial intelligence to amplify select frequency bands at different times and situations. Traditional hearing aids are very limiting in "busy" situations, like restaurants and pubs, as they amplify all sounds and not just the voice of the person to whom one is talking.

The limitations of the psychophysical approach are also apparent in a number of simple laboratory observations. Some listeners, when presented with a pure tone, often report hearing harmonics. Harmonics are multiples of a frequency, and occur in all naturally produced sounds. For example, if you strike the middle A key on a piano, the spectrum of the note would have a fundamental frequency of 440 Hz (i.e. lowest frequency) and also harmonics made up of multiples of 440 Hz, which are 880, 1320, and so on (see Figure 10.4). If the ear presents to our brains the information that a sound consists solely of a 440 Hz pure tone, we should not perceive any harmonics. But some people report that they do. It is also possible to synthesise a complex tone that consists of harmonics without the fundamental frequency (see Figure 10.4). Again, people will often report hearing the missing fundamental when, in theory, they shouldn't (Warren, 1982).

The observation that the auditory system does not work by deconstructing and then reconstructing sounds in an almost mechanical way should not come as a surprise to us. The same is true for the visual system. Gunnar Johansson (1985) puts it eloquently in a paper on visual perception: "what is simple for the visual system is complex for our mathematics and what is mathematically simple is hard to deal with for the visual system" (cited by Jenkins, 1985, p. 120). Most researchers in auditory perception would agree that the same is true of the auditory system. One simple assumption may be at the root of this: that a pure tone is a simple sound. In terms of acoustics or physics, this may be true. But in perceptual terms it is not necessarily true (Jenkins, 1985; Baker, 1996). One may reflect upon the fact that until modern times the auditory system had probably never heard a pure sine-wave in isolation.

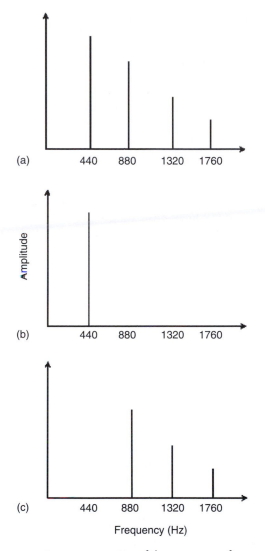

Figure 10.4 Diagrammatic representation of the spectrum of a mouth-organ playing the note of middle A. The figure shows the most intense frequencies. (a) A fundamental frequency of 440 Hz and its harmonics. Other frequencies will be present but at much lower intensities. (b) The spectrum of a pure tone at 440 Hz which has no intense harmonics. (c) A synthesised tone made up of harmonics with a missing fundamental. The missing fundamental does not occur in nature, but our auditory system perceives it as a rich 440 Hz tone nevertheless; in effect, we infer the fundamental frequency

Gestalt psychology

The Gestalt psychologists reacted against the reductionism of psychophysics and concentrated instead on how we perceive parts of a pattern to make a whole. Although many of their examples were explicitly about visual patterns (see Groome *et al.*, 1999), virtually all of their principles are applicable to hearing and the case of figure-ground separation has already been discussed.

Consider the case of the principle of continuation in the context of the two sounds depicted by Figure 10.5. Sound pattern A will be heard as two beeps of the same pitch separated by a small period of silence: beep–beep. Sound pattern B, on the other hand, has two possible perceptions. It could be heard as the same two beeps in A but separated by a buzz of white noise: beep–buzz–beep; or, alternatively, the perception could be of a single long beep continuing to sound through the background of a buzz.

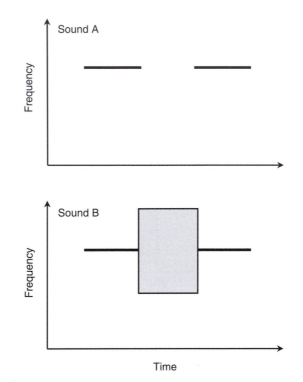

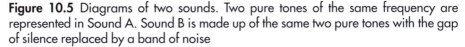

Figure 10.5 Diagrams of two sounds. Two pure tones of the same frequency are represented in Sound A. Sound B is made up of the same two pure tones with the gap of silence replaced by a band of noise

For most people, sound pattern B is usually heard as a single beep continuing through an overlaid buzz. Why does this happen? A Gestalt psychologist might argue that the auditory system is expecting the beeps to continue, in line with the principle of good continuation, and so our perceptual system 'constructs' this perception from that expectation. However, as with their work in visual perception, a criticism often levelled against Gestalt psychologists concerns their descriptive rather than explanatory agenda. Such criticism centres on the vague character of how the principles of grouping work in practice. For example, if one tried to build a working computer model to group sounds in accordance with Gestalt principles, it would be necessary to define concepts such as continuity, proximity and similarity in much more detail and with much more rigour. It would then be necessary to specify exactly how *near* (as a measured quantity) one sound has to be to another for them to be grouped together as part of a single stimulus.

Gibson's ecological approach

Like the Gestalt psychologists, Gibson's (1966) work was mostly on vision. His initial research was aimed at defining the visual cues fighter pilots use to land their planes. The ecological approach to perception that he developed in this context treated the organism as an integrated biological system. It was therefore necessary to take into account *all* of the senses, including auditory perception, when attempting to understand behaviour.

In many ways, the most attractive feature of Gibson's approach is his suggestion that there are certain invariant properties in the environment that perceptual systems may take advantage of. The invariant properties of any stimulus will be available even though other properties may be varying and can help maintain the perceptual constancy of an object. This would explain, for example, how we are able to recognise a friend's voice over the telephone, or when they have a cold, or are whispering. In each of these cases, there are quite noticeable changes in the acoustic structure of the sound (as viewed, for example, on a spectrogram). Despite these acoustic variations, however, we are still able to recognise and understand people's voices.

Similarly, Shepard (1981) has argued that the perceptual system should be able to detect "psychophysical complementarity". He reasoned that because we have evolved in a world that contains regularities, our perceptual systems must have evolved ways of taking advantage of those regularities. In particular, regularities may only be evident when the individual or source of sound is in motion, something that ecologically may be considered to be the normal state of affairs. Consequently, the ecological approach advocates that experiments should be devised that will tell us whether the perceptual systems really do make use of invariant features. The ecological approach has been very influential in shaping some basic auditory perception research and has drawn together the previously opposed approaches of Gestalt psychology and psychophysics. Like the Gestalt approach, it emphasises the holistic nature of pattern perception but simultaneously is underlined by a need for "measurement" that mirrors the concerns of psychophysicists.

Auditory scene analysis

Bregman (1990) has described the central task faced by research into auditory perception as finding out how parts of the acoustic wave are assigned to perceptual objects and events. He takes an ecological position by asserting that this has to be done in the context of the "normal acoustic environment", where there is usually more than one sound happening at a time. Our ears receive these sounds as a compound acoustic signal. The auditory system must somehow "create individual descriptions that are based on only those components of the sound which have arisen from the same environmental event" (Bregman, 1993, p. 11). He has coined the term "auditory scene analysis" for this process, after Marr's approach to visual perception, and it combines aspects of both Gestalt psychology and ecological psychology.

Glancing again at the spectrogram in Figure 10.2, which shows the author saying "hello" at the same time as someone else is saying "goodbye", the problem faced by the auditory system can be appreciated. The task is to take apart the signal by allocating the different patches of acoustic energy to one perceptual stream for my voice, and separating it from another stream that corresponds to the other voice. At any one point in time, the auditory system will have to decide which bits of acoustic energy belong together. Such grouping needs to be carried out simultaneously. The auditory system will also have to decide which bits of acoustic energy spread across time should be sequentially grouped together. Bregman explains that this is accomplished through the use of heuristics based on Gestalt grouping principles. A heuristic is a procedure which is perhaps not guaranteed to solve a problem, but which will more than likely lead to a good solution. He proposes that some of these heuristics are innate and some are learnt.

If we adopt the Gestalt principle of good continuation to explain the perception of the sounds depicted in Figure 10.5, it may be surmised that the auditory system has produced two perceptual streams of sound: one long tone and one noise. We hear the tone continuing through the noise because our auditory system is inferring that this is what is expected to happen to sounds in the usual run of things. Thus, it is working on the basis of the heuristic that says "it is very rare for one sound to start at exactly the same time as another sound stops". From this it concludes that it is much more likely that the tone is continuing through the noise, and so a percept is constructed to reflect this. Research into auditory scene analysis aims to uncover and explore the nature of such heuristics employed by the auditory system.

Ciocca and Bregman (1987) have explored the grouping principles of continuation and proximity in a series of experiments. They presented to their listeners varied patterns of tone glides and noise bands based on the pattern in Figure 10.5. Examples of the patterns that they used are depicted in Figure 10.6. All of the glides before and after the noise were varied for their rate of glide and the frequency at which they abutted the noise. Note that some were rising or falling as "continuations" of the previous glides, and some were near in frequency to the point at which one glide entered and another left. Listeners were asked how clearly they could hear the tone continuing through the noise for the different configurations of glide tones. The best perceptions of hearing a tone through the noise were based on a perception of good continuation – that is, A1–B9, A2–B5, A3–B1. This was followed by the perceptions based on proximity (e.g. A1–B2), where the glide was heard as falling and rising in pitch through the noise. Ciocca and Bregman's results clearly showed that the listeners heard the glides continuing through the noise only for the "plausible" continuations of the glides. This is referred to as the

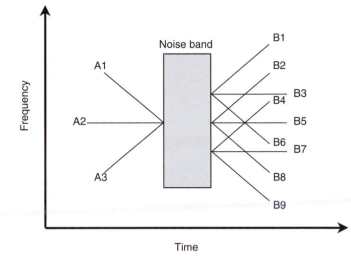

Figure 10.6 Diagrammatic representation of the stimuli used by Ciocca and Bregman (1987). Each presentation consisted of one of three possible tone-glides A, followed by a burst of noise and then one of nine possible tone-glides B

"restoration effect". Such experiments are strong evidence that the auditory system uses various heuristics to integrate sequential acoustic information into streams. Thus, the auditory scene is somehow being processed as a whole, ahead of the actual perception. The auditory system has to take into account the glide *following* the noise before "backtracking in time" to complete the perception of a glide continuing *through* the noise.

Bregman and Pinker (1978) presented the repeated pattern of tones shown in Figure 10.7 to listeners. There are two possible organisations for this pattern (they are shown in the bottom Panel of Figure 10.7): either a fast-beating, high-pitched stream of A + B tones alternating with a slow-beating, low-pitched tone C; or a single tone A alternating with a complex tone BC. In different presentations of this pattern to their participants, Bregman and Pinker adjusted the frequency of tone A, and tone C, and also controlled the timing of tone C relative to tone B. They found that the positions of these tones determined the perceptual organisation of the patterns heard. If tone A was perceived to be "near" in frequency to tone B, it was integrated into a single stream separated from tone C – a heuristic based on frequency proximity operating on the sequential organisation. If tone C started and finished at the same time as tone B, a heuristic based on temporal similarity operated on the *synchronous* organisation that integrated them into the same stream as the complex BC alternating with A. Considering their study as a whole, they demonstrated that heuristics act in competition with one another. Thus, tones A and C compete to be grouped with B, the success of which depends on their proximity in time and frequency.

In an attempt to quantify the frequency distances the auditory system uses in such situations, Baker, Williams and Nicolson (2000) have replicated and extended

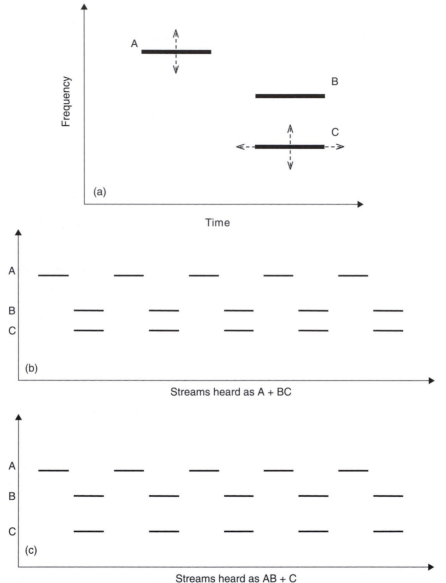

Figure 10.7 Diagrammatic representation of the repeated tonal pattern used by Bregman and Pinker (1978). Each presentation consisted of several successive repetitions of the pattern shown in (a), which was perceived as one of two streams (A + BC or AB + C) dependent on the proximity of tones A and C to tone B, as represented in (b) and (c)

the study of Bregman and Pinker (1978). Such information will be needed to develop a working model of heuristics in computer applications of auditory scene analysis. They found that the competition effects were always apparent, but that when tone C was held constant, the frequency distances did not appear to be straightforward. The distances were not based on either a musical scale or on any metric used by the cochlea in its analysis of sound into frequency–intensity information. Clearly, further research is needed in this area.

Ellis (1995) has summarised the difficulties apparent in trying to get computers to do auditory scene analysis (CASA). He described the "hard problems" faced by software engineers to "build computer models of higher auditory functions". Most of these are beyond the scope of this chapter, but the applications are both interesting and challenging. He identified at least three main applications for CASA: a sound-scene describer, a source-separator and a predictive human model. The sound-scene describer would model our ability to convert an acoustic signal into both verbal and symbolic descriptions of the sound source. These could be used for the deaf and hard of hearing to describe an auditory environment using text-based visual displays able to display messages such as "there is someone talking behind you" or "there is high wind noise". It could also be used to automatically index film soundtracks to build databases for searching film archives. The source-separator would be an "unmixer", taking a sound mixture and outputting it to several channels, each one made up of the sounds from a single source. This would be useful in the restoration of audio recordings to delete unwanted sounds such as a cough at a concert. Additionally, this would assist in the design of hearing aids able to help focus attention in complex auditory environments. Finally, a predictive human model would depend on a very full understanding of auditory perception, but would help in the perfection of hearing aids and the synthesis of sounds for entertainment purposes, such as fully realistic three-dimensional sound.

10.4 Areas of research

Localisation

There are three sources of information that our auditory systems use to localise sound: amplitude differences, time differences and spectral information. When a sound comes from the left of a person's head, it will hit the left eardrum with slightly more energy and will arrive slightly earlier in time than at the right eardrum (see Figure 10.8). The distinction between these cues has been known for many years (since Lord Raleigh identified them in 1877) and they form the basis for what is termed the duplex theory of sound localisation. In general, low frequencies (below 1.5 kHz) are localised as a result of analysis of temporal differences, while high frequencies (above 3 kHz) are localised as a result of analysis of intensity differences.

We are much better at locating sounds in the horizontal plane than the vertical plane (Mills, 1963). When a sound is directly in front of us, or above the midline of our heads, or directly behind us, there are no amplitude and time differences between the two ears (see Figure 10.8). In these circumstances, the auditory system

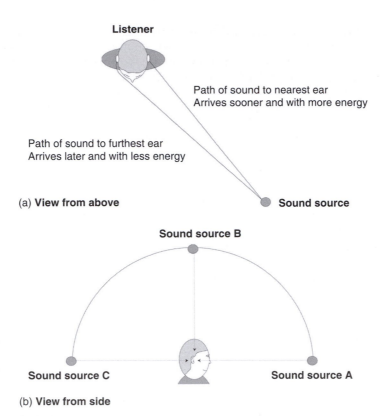

Figure 10.8 (a) In the horizontal plane, time and amplitude differences are used for localisation. (b) In the vertical plane, spectral cues are used. Note that in the vertical plane, time and amplitude differences between the ears will be non-existent

uses the changes made to the sound by the shape of the pinnae (i.e. the external ear), and to some extent the shape and reflecting properties of the head and shoulders. The spectrum of the sound will be changed according to its vertical position. Some frequencies are slightly amplified while others are attenuated. Sounds that cover a wide range of frequencies are therefore more easily located than are narrow-band sounds.

Overall, humans are fairly good at locating sounds, but we do have our limitations. We are much better at locating an object by sight than by sound, but usually we can locate by sound alone with an accuracy of about five degrees (Makous & Middlebrooks, 1990). This accuracy can increase to within two degrees when the sound source is moving and is broadband (like a white noise) rather than a single tone (Harris & Sergeant, 1971). These findings have implications for the design of, for example, telephone rings and emergency vehicle sirens. The former can be hard to localise if more than one telephone is present, while drivers need to localise the source of the latter to determine whether or not they need to pull over to let an emergency vehicle pass.

A note of caution needs to be made when considering the accuracy of localisation research, however, because discrepancies exist between the findings of different studies. For example, Blauert (1969) and Hebrank and Wright (1974) reported different frequency ranges as critical for listeners to discriminate the vertical position of a sound effectively. In addition, Perrett and Noble (1995) have shown that restricting the number of stimuli and the response options available to listeners can affect the outcome of localisation experiments. The laboratory situation therefore needs to be carefully thought out in audition research, and the accuracy of measurement seems difficult to reconcile with our ability to locate sounds with great facility even in noisy environments.

Traditionally, most of the research done in this area has used a psychophysical approach. Guski (1990) pointed out that many studies are carried out under non-ecological conditions using, for example, artificial sounds in an anechoic room presented to a participant whose head is in a fixed position and to whom only a restricted range of responses may be available. He cites research that shows how auditory localisation improves markedly with free head movement (Fisher & Freedman, 1968), the use of natural sound sources (Masterton & Diamond, 1973), or with sound-reflecting walls (Mershon & King, 1975; Mershon et al., 1989). All of these findings emphasise the optimal functioning of the auditory system under ecologically valid conditions.

Guski's own research supports such criticisms. In 1990, Guski proposed that because humans have evolved with ground-reflecting surfaces throughout most of evolutionary history, and that side- and ceiling-reflecting surfaces are relatively new phenomena, we should be better at locating sounds with a sound-reflecting surface on the ground than to either the left or right, or above, or one not being present at all. To test this hypothesis, he presented sounds in an anechoic room with a single sound-reflecting aluminium surface of 1×2 m, which was placed in different positions (left, right, above and below). His findings supported the hypothesis that auditory localisation is better with the reflecting surface on the floor than in other positions. The most ecologically "unrealistic" position for the reflecting surface was on the ceiling and this produced the highest number of localisation errors.

Non-speech sounds

A purely psychophysical approach to auditory perception can be criticised for not dealing with truly realistic or complex sounds. However, it was only by using pure tones that the early researchers showed that the ear does not simply function to register intensity and frequency changes over time. Originally, it was thought that loudness and pitch were the subjective dimensions of sound that should correlate directly with the physical dimensions of intensity and frequency. However, it was soon realised that our perceptual, or phenomenal, experiences depend on the interaction of several characteristics of the stimulus, as well as the listener's psychological state and context.

For example, low-frequency tones that have the same intensity as higher-frequency tones actually sound quieter. Textbooks of acoustical theory present graphs showing curves of "equal loudness". In these the relationships between perceived loudness and frequency are delineated at various decibel levels. In addition, duration is relevant. Tones of around 50 msec duration need to have about twice as much energy to sound as loud as tones of 100 msec. Timbre also appears to be a multidimensional property. Timbre can be defined as the "colour" of a sound we might use to describe a voice or musical instrument. For example, a Spanish guitar has a different timbre than a mouth-organ. Traditionally, it has been thought that timbre is an independent perceptual quality in much the same way as pitch and loudness once were. It was proposed that timbre was indicated by the spectral or harmonic properties of a sound. That for a Spanish guitar and a mouth-organ playing an A note, the harmonics would have the same frequency values (hence denoting an A note), but the relative amplitudes of the harmonics would be different (see Figure 10.9). However, it is clear that both the attack and decay of the notes are as important as the frequency spectrum (Handel, 1989) for the perception of timbre.

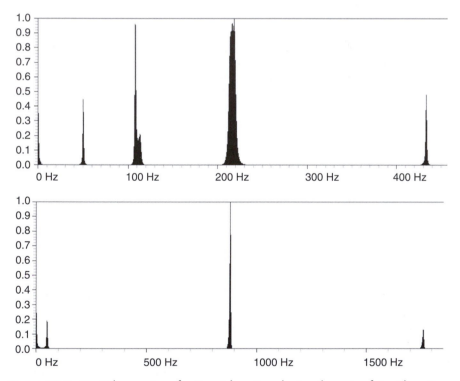

Figure 10.9 (Top) The spectra of a Spanish guitar playing the note of A with a strong harmonic at 220 Hz, and (bottom) the spectra of a mouth-organ playing the note of A with a strong harmonic at 880 Hz. Both sounds are perceived as the same musical note, as they are harmonically related by simple ratios of their spectra

With this in mind, one can understand that searching for acoustic structures of the different perceptual qualities of sounds is a difficult endeavour. Van Derveer

(1979) recorded naturally occurring sounds like people walking up and down stairs, crumpling paper bags, whistling, jangling keys and hammering nails. She found that her listeners were able to identify each sound with a high degree of accuracy. She then asked her participants to group similar sounds together in any way they thought appropriate. So, for example, the sounds of the keys jingling and jingling coins were grouped together, as were shuffling cards, crumpling bags, and crumpling and tearing up paper. Van Derveer found that listeners tend to classify sounds according to the gross temporal patterning, or rhythm, as well as on the basis of the continuity of the sounds. This was in preference to use of, for example, pitch information. So, the jingling keys and coins were judged as similar because of the irregular metallic sounds they produced. The cards and paper were grouped together because of the crackling sound that was continuous through the events. Other researchers have supported the conjecture that it is the temporal structure of sound that is important for the perception of non-speech sounds (e.g. Warren & Verbrugge, 1984). Many researchers are sympathetic to the view that this is an important feature of speech perception also.

Repp (1987) made recordings of 20 people clapping their hands. He was interested in whether listeners could identify the clapper and the configuration of their hands when they clapped, and on which possible acoustic properties they may have based these perceptions. He analysed the recordings of the claps, and reduced them to a collection of different spectral features. So, for example, one person's clap may be made up from 60% of spectral feature one, 20% of feature two, and so on, while another person's clap could be described by a different mix of spectral features. It was assumed that the different physical features of each clap would causally determine the spectral features. Thus, claps made with cupped palms were identifiable using spectrograms with a lot of low-frequency energy, and claps made with fingers to palm contact contained a lot of middle-frequency energy. The 20 clappers were also asked to listen to the recordings of the claps and identify each one. They could not judge the identity of each clapper, other than themselves, very well at all, although they fared much better at identifying the clap configurations. Interestingly, they were quite consistent at identifying some claps as being those of males or females, but this did not necessarily correlate with the true sex of the clapper. Presumably, listeners were relying on stereotyped images of what the clap of a male and of a female would sound like.

In a similar study, Li, Logan and Pastore (1991) investigated the ability of listeners to judge the sounds of people walking. Again, recordings were made of people of different heights and gender, and these were analysed for their spectral content. They also found that the participants were able to judge gender, in this case fairly accurately. However, to control for the type of shoes worn, walkers were again recorded wearing gender-appropriate and gender-inappropriate shoes. In this condition, listeners identified the walker's gender according to the shoe type rather than the walker's gait. Top-down influences thus appeared once again to encourage stereotypical judgements.

The interpretation of sound sequences also depends on context. Ballas, Howard and Kolm (1982) presented environmental sounds in sequences to listeners, and found that listeners tried to make sense of the sequences for themselves. For example, the perception of a metallic clang sound was sometimes judged to be a car crashing when it was presented with the sound of a valve closing and a long noise burst; at other times, it was interpreted as a factory-machine sound when combined with a water drip sound and noise burst. Ballas and Howard (1987) have subsequently hypothesised that we continually attempt to construct meanings for the sounds we hear, and draw parallels with similar linguistic processes found in speech perception.

Speech perception

Speech sounds seem to be quite different from non-speech sounds. Whereas non-speech sounds sometimes only indicate to us that some objects have moved somewhere in the environment, when we listen to speech we do not linger on the actual sounds being made by the speaker's vocal apparatus, but instead we seem to fly straight to the meaning of the message. A major problem in speech perception research, however, is the exact nature of the "objects" implicated in the acoustic signal. When the first sound spectrograms were available, there was some optimism that once we could objectively represent and measure the complex speech waveform visually, then it would be a simple matter of finding the invariants for each speech sound from which the spectrogram could be readily decoded into words. However, speech is much more complex than such an agenda implies.

One of the first findings in speech research was that there were very few "gaps" between the words spoken in normal speech. In fact, it is quite possible to locate lengths of silence in the middle of words that are longer than those between words. Speech is not made up of discrete words in the same way as in printed text. The gaps are perceptual illusions we place on our interpretation of the acoustic speech signal. This is apparent when one listens to someone talking in a foreign language that is not understood. It is almost impossible to write down the speech sounds and then demarcate the gaps between the words intended by the speaker. Word separation is thus fundamental to understanding spoken language.

There are further problems at the level of each speech sound. These are termed "phonemes" and are often considered to be the smallest perceptual unit in speech, although some researchers contend that the syllable is another possibility. In terms of phonemes, a word like CAT is made up of the three phonemes [k], [a] and [t], and a word like SHED is made up of the three phonemes [sh], [e] and [d]. Phonemes are usually defined according to the way in which their sounds are produced by the position and movements of the vocal apparatus – tongue, lips, jaws and vocal cords – though there is of course some noticeable variation between different speakers of the same language. Thus, the spectrograms for a New Zealander and a Scot saying the same word may be dramatically different and the difference between the speech of children, women and men differs from one another in pitch because of the difference between the length of their vocal cords (deeper or lower voices are produced by longer and more slowly vibrating vocal cords).

Not only is there variation between speakers, there is also variation of the speech signal for the same phonemes from the same speaker. The acoustic signal for the [k] in "cat" is not the same as the [k] in "school" or in "neck". If you were to record someone saying each of these words, you could not simply splice the [k] sounds out of each word and swap them around and then hear the original words unchanged. The speech sounds preceding and following each [k] have an effect on its production and acoustic structure, so that when replaced into a different phonemic context the perception is not of a natural [k] phoneme. Even isolating each [k] sound is not a straightforward task, because some of the sound's perceptual information is anticipated by any preceding speech sounds and also lingers to overlap any following one. This phenomenon is referred to as "coarticulation" (Liberman, 1970).

The incredible complexity involved in the speech signal, and the apparent ease and speed with which we hear and understand speech – at up to 10 phonemes a second in some cases (Liberman, Cooper, Shankweiler, & Studdert-Kennedy, 1967) – has urged some researchers to suggest that speech is processed by a dedicated and specialised processing system. This notion is further supported by evidence from research into categorical perception. Categorical perception refers to the way in which some sounds are perceived categorically regardless of any gradual variation on some of the parameters available to perception. A lot of the research done in this area has used the syllables [ba] and [pa]. These sounds are both produced in the same way apart from the timing of the vibration of the vocal cords. Both phonemes begin with closed lips being opened and the release of air from the mouth outwards. These sounds are called bilabial plosives by phoneticians. The [b] is differentiated from the [p] only by the timing of the vocal cords vibrating after the opening of the lips (see Figure 10.10). The timing of the vocalisation (or voicing) is called the voice onset time (VOT). With speech synthesisers, it is possible to manipulate the length of the VOT and run controlled experiments.

Lisker and Abramson (1970) asked listeners to identify and name such synthetic phonemes and found that there was very little overlap in their perception. The consonants were identified as [b] (with VOT below 25 msec) or [p] (with VOT above 25 msec) most of the time, except when the VOT was around 25 msec. This distinctive boundary for the perception of the voiced and unvoiced consonants suggested that the phonemes were perceived categorically. This conclusion has been supported by discrimination experiments. But when the VOT is within the range of a category, listeners are very poor at distinguishing between the phonemes. For example, a [b] that has a VOT of 10 msec is not perceived as being different from one with a VOT of 20 msec. When the VOT varies across the boundary, discrimination is easier (for example, a [b] with a VOT of 20 msec and one with a VOT of 30 msec).

However, the conclusion that speech was processed by a specialised system separate from non-speech is an over-simplification (see Pisoni & Luce, 1986, for a review). It is clear that categorical perception is evident for non-speech sounds (see Cutting & Rosner, 1976; Pisoni, 1977), and is apparent in monkeys, chinchillas and dogs, which may be assumed not to possess a speech processing centre in their brains! It would appear that we are able to process even complex sounds very efficiently, and we may use categories to do this even with non-speech sounds.

Categorical processing suggests that we may have evolved ways of processing sounds efficiently by being able to ignore some of the many features available in the acoustic signal. There are also quite a few top-down effects that help us to become even more efficient, for example by using context to extract meaning, especially

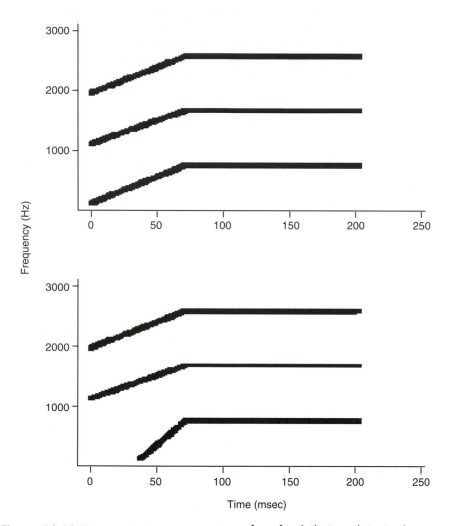

Figure 10.10 Diagrammatic spectrograms of artificial [ba] and [pa] phonemes synthesised with three formants. The diagrams show the onset of the voicing in the fundamental frequency. In (a) the voicing of the fundamental frequency occurs at 0 msec latency and is perceived as a "ba" speech sound. In (b) the voicing occurs 35 msec after the beginning of the speech and is perceived as a "pa" speech sound

when listening to speech. Warren (1970) has demonstrated a phonemic restoration effect that underlines the importance of context in speech perception. He presented the sentence "The state governors met with their respective legislatures convening in the capital city" to listeners and replaced the middle *s* in "legislatures" with a 120 msec tone. Interestingly, only 5% of listeners reported hearing the tone, but they could not identify where in the sentence they had heard it.

An extension of this study also reported some remarkable findings. Warren and Warren (1970) presented listeners with variations of the same sentence with the same phoneme replaced by a noise burst:

It was found that the –eel was on the axle.
It was found that the –eel was on the shoe.
It was found that the –eel was on the orange.
It was found that the –eel was on the table.

The participants reported hearing the words *wheel, heel, peel* and *meal* in each sentence, respectively. Remarkably, the perception of the missing phoneme in "–eel" was dependent on the perception of the final word. Evidently, speech perception can involve a backward processing of the phoneme! Once again, the auditory system processes the acoustic signal, waits for any further information that may be useful for inclusion, and then if this is forthcoming at a later point, backtracks in time to influence a percept. This phonemic restoration effect, however, is at a higher level of cognitive and linguistic processing than is evident in the restoration effect shown by Ciocca and Bregman (1987).

Attention and distraction

There seems to be something very different between hearing and vision when it comes to attention. Hearing is often described as an orienting system, the purpose of which is to alert the organism to changes in the environment and make it aware of the direction of a possible attack or food source, where these features of the environment are subject to further processing by the visual system. Most predators like owls, foxes and cats often have very acute hearing for hunting, as do some prey as a defence measure. Acoustic alerts often work better than visual ones, as the receptor organs do not need to be focused on the source and, unlike light, sound is both transmitted in the dark and goes around corners. As humans, we are aware of the alerting or orienting response to sound when confronted with the interfering aspects of unwanted noise when we are trying to concentrate. We are rarely disturbed to the same extent when faced with outlandishly coloured wallpaper or bright daylight from a window (unless the latter, for example, makes a TV or computer unwatchable at normal contrast levels).

The conversion of office layouts to being more open-plan has promoted co-operation and sharing of ideas. However, there can be auditory drawbacks to the open-plan office. Much of the early work into the effects of noise on work performance concentrated on loudness rather than the frequency or timing (Broadbent, 1971). This is evident in law, as a sound has to be considered (and measured) to be "loud" before it is accepted as disturbing. However, even low-intensity sounds can interfere with cognitive processing, and it has been shown that in some circumstances we can find it very difficult to habituate to the interfering effect of disruptive sounds (Jones, 1999). Frequency is also important, with low-frequency sound being particularly disruptive.

Banbury and Berry (1998) showed that general office noise and speech were disrupting to their participants' ability to memorise prose and carry out some mental arithmetic tasks. They showed that this disruption happened regardless of whether the speech contained meaningful content or not. However, they also found that it is possible to become habituated to the disruptive effects of background noise, but that this habituation is fragile, with only a 5 min break needed to restore the disrupting effects of the interfering noise (Banbury & Berry, 1997). What seems to be important is that noise is a relative phenomenon. It is a person's subjective perception of a sound that determines its distracting effect, rather than the measured intensity. This effect is independent of whether the noise is meaningful or unrelated speech, or even non-speech sounds (Banbury & Jones, 1998; Banbury, Jones, & Berry, 1998). Attributions may also be important (e.g. "He's doing it to annoy me", "I've asked him to stop and he's ignoring me").

Dichotic listening tasks are often employed to examine the limits of attending to linguistic messages (see Groome *et al.*, 1999). A typical dichotic listening task often consists of a listener wearing headphones and being asked to attend to spoken messages in one ear while trying to ignore different messages in the other. Most participants are able to attend to only one of the messages, and research often reports that "very little" about the unattended message is processed (e.g. Cherry, 1953; Moray, 1959). However, even though the semantic meaning of the "very little" may not be processed, other characteristics are consciously available to the listener, such as whether the message was a voice or non-speech sound, or whether the speaker was male or female. This suggests that the auditory system processes unattended material, at least non-linguistically. It may be recalled that the acoustic signal that hits the eardrum is a mixture of all the sounds presently in the environment at an audible level, and that all of the sound-mix is available for processing. It is evident that the auditory system may process unattended material for potential inclusion in the attended signal in rather the same way as future material will help formulate the perception of previous sounds in the phonemic restoration effect.

Interaction with the other senses

Few writers on perception have covered all sense modalities, but those who have generally take a philosophical and theoretical approach (e.g. Gibson, 1966; Marks, 1978). However, when one takes an ecological approach to auditory perception, one cannot make much progress without first acknowledging that we do not simply hear things in isolation from the other senses. In fact, our perceptions can be influenced in surprising ways by senses usually thought to make little contribution. People with slight to moderate hearing loss will notice that their ability to understand speech decreases when they cannot see the speaker's face. Several research studies have shown that the speaker's face and lip movement contribute greatly to speech perception (e.g. Rosen, Fourcin, & Moore, 1981), especially when the acoustic signal is degraded. We can conclude from this that the perception of speech sounds is aided by the visual system to some extent.

McGurk and MacDonald (1976) demonstrated this in an interesting experiment. They used edited video recordings of an individual uttering speech sounds and dubbed different sounds onto the audio track. They used the sounds "ba", "da" and "ga" and found that when they presented the visual images of the talker saying "ga" with the audio track of "ba", 80% of pre-school children and 98% of adults reported hearing "da". This effect is astoundingly robust. Even when listeners were told about the editing process, they still reported that they *heard* the sound "da". When asked to close their eyes, listeners hear the true audio recording "ba", and this reverts to a perception of "da" when the eyes view the video again. It is as though the sensory information is secondary to the final perception of the speech sound, that the brain takes both auditory and visual information into account to construct its best guess of the perception. Curiously, this effect is much stronger for syllables than for complete words (Easton & Basala, 1982), which suggests that if more acoustic and semantic information about the speech is available, then visual cues may not be enough to influence perception on their own.

More direct evidence of the interaction of the senses in perception is given by Durgin and Proffitt (1996). They presented random dot patterns of different density, and paired the presentations with tones. When the high-density pattern was displayed, the participants heard a high-pitched tone; when they saw a low-density pattern, they heard a low-pitched tone. After 180 flashed presentations, the researchers found that there was a significant effect of the tone on the perceived density. When the participants were shown a random dot pattern in the presence of a high-pitched tone, they judged the pattern to be of greater dot density than they had before the habituation period.

It would appear from the McGurk effect and from other research that we do not have much direct awareness about the sensory information our perceptual systems use. Warren (1982) points out that quite a number of sightless people are able to avoid colliding with obstacles through the echoes reflected from surfaces, but that they are not aware that they are using hearing to do so. Several studies report that people using echo-location in such a way describe "feeling" the pressure waves of approaching objects on their faces (Supa, Cotzin, & Dallenbach, 1944; Worchel & Dallenbach, 1947). Warren (1982) has suggested that this makes sense when one considers "the hypothesis that we are aware of events correlated with sensory input rather than sensation *per se*" (p. 191).

This point is supported by another intriguing observation that we all experience at various times. Whenever we hear a sound in an enclosed space, our ears sense the echoes from the objects and walls around us (Guski, 1990). These echoes occur within milliseconds and are not the same as the echoes we are aware of when in a large auditorium or in a deep valley which have a longer latency. A specific part of the auditory system suppresses the processing of these "sub-perceptual" echoes and instead we perceive their presence as a quality of the sound source. If you speak in a room with thick curtains and carpets (i.e. no echoes), your voice will be heard with a dull or clipped quality. If you speak in a room with reflective floors and windows, and thus lots of echoes, your voice will appear to have a brighter quality. The acoustic signal of your voice does not actually change, but your auditory system indicates the change in the environment by the quality of the sounds you hear. If you actually heard the echoes, your perception of the sounds would more than likely be blurred. Remarkably, if you listen to a recording of sounds made in an echoic environment such as a cathedral and then play the recording backwards, you will be more aware of the echoes being present.

10.5 Applications of auditory perception research

The applied use of sound

Sounds have long been used in a creative way to add dramatic effect to films and animation. Listening to a "Tom & Jerry" cartoon is an interesting experience with your eyes closed in comparison to having your eyes open. In films, sound and music are used to add to the emotional intent of the director. Romantic moments are often accompanied by soothing violin melodies, and suspense is often increased with the use of staccato, put to memorable effect in the film *Jaws*. In science fiction films, sound effects add to the drama by playing with our imaginations. Space ships and laser guns in space would not make a sound as there is no medium in which acoustic vibrations can travel. However, the illusion works, as not many people have actually been into space. Music and sound effects are also important in computer applications like multimedia, web-based media and games. A more systematically researched application, however, is computer interface design. With the widespread availability of affordable digital technology, applications that make use of sound are becoming more commonplace. These take advantage of the fact that sound is an information-carrying medium and is especially useful in alerting us that something is happening outside our field of vision or attention. After all, this is what our auditory systems were originally designed for. Sound may also be used, however, to convey meaning. For example, sounds can provide positive or negative feedback on actions and Gaver (1986) has argued that sound feedback is essential to tell us what is happening when the event is not visible or when the eyes are busy elsewhere. For example, the word processor I am using often tries to "help" by correcting errors as I make them, such as by capitalising the first letter in a sentence when I have forgotten to press the shift key. When the word processor makes such a correction (usually while I carry on typing, oblivious to its help), it does this with a soft "schlickkkk" sound that tells me that it is up to something.

There are two types of sound used in interface design: auditory icons and earcons. Auditory icons are caricatures of everyday sounds, where the source of the sound is designed to correspond to an event in the interface. For example, opening a folder may be accompanied by the sound of a filing cabinet drawer opening. Auditory icons draw on the user's knowledge of the real world and how it works. Earcons are based on musical motifs, where aspects of a sound (usually a short melody) are designed to represent aspects of the interface. For example, when a folder is opened a musical crescendo is played, and when it is closed a descending sequence of notes is played. Researchers have carried out studies to determine which type of sounds users prefer, usually with mixed results. For example, Jones and Furner (1989) found that users preferred an earcon to denote interface commands like delete or copy but when asked to associate a sound with a command, auditory icons proved to be more popular, probably because of the inherent semantic meaning available in such a sound. Lucas (1994) found no difference in error rates for learning the association between commands and auditory icons and earcons.

Bussemakers and de Haan (2000) found that when auditory icons are linked with congruent or incongruent visuals (e.g. a picture of a dog with a sound of a dog, or a picture of a dog with a sound of a duck), response times to decide about congruence or incongruence were faster than when the pictures were presented with either earcons or silence. Moreover, it appears to be the case that earcons are difficult to design and are frequently ineffective or simply irritating (Brewster, Wright, & Edwards, 1992). Current research is still exploring good design principles for the use of both auditory icons and earcons. Earcons have a potential application in mobile phones to aid the user in navigating the necessary levels of menus and submenus. The addition of musical sounds is a great benefit given the limited nature of the visual information available on screen. With the careful design of musically distinct earcons, listeners are able to accurately recall as many as 25 earcon sounds regardless of their musical ability (Leplâtre & Brewster, 1998). Applying earcons to help navigate phone users through the different levels of menu selection seems to be successful. Leplâtre and Brewster (2000) asked users to complete a set of navigational tasks on a mobile phone simulation with and without earcons accompanying the selection of menu items. Those who had earcons present completed the tasks with fewer keystrokes and completed more tasks successfully. They also improved in performance with practice much faster than those not using earcons.

Sonification

Being able to synthesise sound broadens the number of applications in which sound can be used. It is possible to use sound to help "visualise" quite complex data sets, by using the data to control some of the many different parameters used in sound synthesis. This relatively new technique of data visualisation is called "sonification", and is still a challenge for sound engineers, psychologists and composers alike. The technique is relatively new and there are variations in the way data are converted into sound, although there are some fundamental considerations to be made about this. First, the data have to be time-based, or converted to be time-based, as sound is a dynamic temporal medium. Then a particular type of sound has to be chosen to represent each data set (e.g. water sounds, crunching sounds, metallic sounds). Lastly, the parameter of the sound to be controlled by the data has to be decided upon – will it change the pitch, loudness, timbre, vibrato, position in three-dimensional space, or some other attribute of the sound?

There are some important restrictions in designing the process of sonification. Designers have to be aware of the basic psychophysics of hearing. We have seen already that some dimensions can interact with each other and should not be considered as completely separate dimensions (see also Melara & Marks, 1990). Such perceptual qualities have the potential to distort the visualisation of the data if not taken into account (Neuhoff, Kramer, & Wayand, 2000). The choice of sounds used to represent each data set should also be based on psychological principles of perception so that the streams of data are perceived as separate streams of sound. Gaver's (1993) analysis of the dimensions of natural sounds has been helpful in this respect. Scaletti and Craig (1991) have also argued that sonification comes into its own with complex data sets in addition to normal visualisation techniques, so that the eyes are focused on one or two aspects of the data and the ears listen to other aspects of the data. In addition, the ears are able to detect smaller changes than the eyes, and it is possible to follow two streams of sound, one presented to each ear. But research in this area is still relatively new and the general guidelines for sonifying data are yet to be agreed upon (Walker & Kramer, 1996).

Navigational aids for the visually impaired work on similar principles as data sonification, but instead of numerical data being the input for sound synthesis, a representation of a visual scene is used. A common arrangement is to have a laser rangefinder scan the environment, the output of which is mapped onto one aspect of a sound, usually pitch. A closely allied system is available in some luxury cars to help parking in tight situations. As the user approaches an object, the pitch increases, thus warning of any impending collision. Other systems use a low-resolution camera to view the scene from a headset worn by the visually impaired person (Meijer, 1993). A small computer reads the visual scene and then converts the image into a low-density grey-scale image, made up of black and white pixels, which is then converted into high and low pitches. The scene is played through headphones as a time-changing sound pattern played from the left of the image to the right. Initially, the sounds are confusing and do not represent anything "real" to the listener. However, with practice, a user will be able to remember the sound signatures of certain scenes – for example, an open doorway sounds different to a closed doorway – and begin to use the device to help them *hear* their way around their environment.

Warning sounds

Warning sounds are used in a variety of situations in the modern world. Attempting to improve the efficacy of such sounds in emergencies is obviously an important application of our knowledge of complex sounds and how they are perceived. Such applications may vary from the improvement of auditory signals to alert machine operators, to the improvement of distress signals in emergencies where vision is hampered.

When sounds are used in the design of a warning system, it is important that they are used in the correct way. Norman (1988) has pointed out that in order for them to be used correctly, they have to be designed to be truly useful or people will tend to ignore them. He describes the example of the warning buzzer used in some cars to tell you that the door is open when the keys are in the ignition. The buzzer sounds to get your attention in order to prevent you from locking your keys in the car, and it certainly works. But what happens when this is ignored, for example when you open the door while the car is running to pay your ticket at a car park. In this situation, the buzzer may get your attention, but the significance is changed and you don't act on it. The problem may now arise that the buzzer may not get your attention with as much urgency or meaning as the designer had intended. As an example of bad design, consider the personnel locators that are sometimes used by firefighters to locate colleagues when vision is impeded by smoke. These usually emit high-pitched single tones with frequencies of around 3 kHz. This is not optimal for localisation, since single tones are not particularly easy to locate, and in fact tones of around 3 kHz produce some of the highest errors in localisation

(Stevens & Newman, 1936; Handel, 1989). Using our knowledge of the auditory system's ability to locate sound, it should be possible to make improvements to such a device to lessen any confusion and make location more accurate.

Ambulance sirens have been improved in such a way. Withington (1999) ran an experimental study using 200 participants to improve the localisation of ambulance sirens. The participants were asked to locate the direction of four different siren signals currently in use by emergency services while sitting in a driving simulator surrounded by eight loudspeakers. These sirens were: the traditional "hi-lo" siren synthesised from a two-tone signal (670–1100 Hz, 55 cycles/min); a "pulsar" siren made from a pulsing sound (500–1800 Hz, 70 cycles/min); a "wail", a continuous sound rising and falling (500–1800 Hz, 11 cycles/min); and a "yelp" siren, a continuous and fast warbling sound (500–1800 Hz, 55 cycles/min). Withington found that many of her participants confused the front–back location of the sirens, with many of them making more false localisation judgements than correct ones, a performance level that was worse than chance! She consequently tested a range of new siren signals optimised for alerting and localisation. These were distinctively different from the traditional sirens tested earlier, being synthesised from pulses of rapidly rising frequency sweeps followed by bursts of broadband noise. Participants showed an improvement in their front–back localisation from 56% to 82%, together with an improvement in their left–right accuracy from 79% to 97%.

The design of the signal is aimed towards helping the listener to locate the source ("where") of the signal, although some secondary consideration may be made to indicate the actual nature ("what") of the sound's meaning. For example, in the design of complex machinery needing complex arrays of consoles for their safe running, it would be important to reduce confusion when a siren sounds. This could be done through the use of good design considerations either by reducing the number of audible alarms or making them quite distinct from one another. Patterson (1990) has suggested that the use of frequency, intensity and rate of presentation should be used to define the different meanings of a warning sound. In addition, other aspects of the alarms' acoustic signals can be enhanced, such as the directional characteristics and/or the spectral shape and content, and/or synchronising with a visual signal. For example, if two alarm signals happen at similar times, one could be located high and to the left and the other lower and to the right of a control panel; one could be high in pitch the other lower in pitch; one could vary at the same rate as a fast flashing visual light source, the other with a slowly rotating light source. To all of these one could apply the findings from streaming research (see Bregman, 1990), as well as basic psychophysical knowledge about sound perception (e.g. Haas & Edworthy, 1996), to enhance the perceptual segregation and localisation of alarms.

Machine speech recognition

There are a large number of applications that would benefit from speech recognition by machine. Most of these are concerned with automating commercial procedures such as customer enquiries and bank operations (not to mention the tedium of entering text or numbers by hand at a computer!). Telephone-based enquiry systems have long been available to process simple commands using the beeps a telephone handset makes. Now some telephone information systems that employ speech recognition software are able to understand the meaning of a limited set of spoken commands and even use voice recognition to ensure the identity of the speaker as well. Already, within the last 10 years, many advances have been made, although this has been mainly due to the increased availability of cheaper computing power and developments in software engineering rather than any rapid advances in our understanding of speech recognition. In computer-based applications, speech-to-text dictation has been heralded as the next revolution in the human–computer interface after the acceptance of the Windows environment and mouse. Some manufacturers have even made claims that speech recognition will eventually replace other forms of input, including keyboard and mouse, entirely. This has not yet happened, partly due to our limited understanding of, and thus limited ability to simulate, the complexities of speech perception.

Most speech recognition software consists of two subsystems, an automatic speech recogniser for transcribing the speech sounds into text-based form, and a language understanding system to improve on the recognition of the intended message. The research involved in their development covers all levels of investigation into speech, from acoustic-phonetics and pattern recognition, to psycholinguistics and neuroscience, and also includes many engineering solutions to the problems not immediately solved by human research. Virtually all speech recognition software relies on training the machine to recognise the speaker's pronunciation. Modern systems concentrate on a set of carefully chosen words or phrases that contain widely used phonemes or syllables and which can be generalised to a wider number of words. The speaker's enunciations of these words are then stored as templates to be used against other words held in the system's lexicon. Once training is complete, the system can be used: carefully pronounced speech is translated into possible word-features by the automatic speech recogniser. This is then analysed by the language understanding system against the lexicon and a translation is offered to the speaker.

There are two major approaches used by the automatic speech recognition systems. The acoustic-phonetics approach attempts to recognise the phonemes in the acoustic signal by trying to identify and match features such as formant frequency, and voicing based on perceptual research (Zue, 1985). Other approaches do not rely explicitly on human behaviour but instead use an engineering solution to the problem by applying either mathematical models to match patterns in the acoustics signal (e.g. Huang, Ariki, & Jack, 1990), or by employing artificial intelligence through expert systems (e.g. Mori, Lam, & Gilloux, 1987) or trained neural networks (e.g. Lippmann, 1989).

There has been progress, with software becoming more efficient due to shorter training periods, and some systems are now even able to generalise to other speakers. The accuracy of recognition has also improved, with the number of errors made falling to around 10% under favourable conditions (e.g. speakers reading text in quiet conditions) (Lippmann, 1997). But this success is fragile, as error rates increase dramatically when more "normal" situations are used involving spontaneous speech and background noise (Zue, Cole, & Ward, 1997). In comparing the performance of machine speech recognition with human speech recognition,

Lippmann (1997) has concluded that more research needs to be done on how humans recognise speech at the acoustic-phonetic level in more naturalistic situations. The specific problems are connected with the variation across speakers and within speakers, as well as with boundaries between words (which are often perceptual rather than acoustic). There are also further restrictions, with most systems working well only with low background noise and with one speaker talking at a time, requiring the use of a directional microphone, and having no ability to recognise new words outside of the stored lexicon (Reddy, 1976, 1990).

In an attempt to improve recognition under difficult conditions and also to solve the problem of learning new words, de Sa (1999) has argued for the use of a multimodal speech recogniser. She has persuasively suggested that integrating both visual and auditory information, as illustrated by the McGurk effect, is the norm in human speech recognition and machine recognition would improve by mimicking this. To this end, she has demonstrated a working neural network application that had learnt to distinguish consonant–vowel syllables using both visual information from lip movements and acoustic signals. At the moment, speech recognition by machine has a niche market as an automatic dictation device for people, like dentists and pathologists, who may need to write when their hands are otherwise occupied. As systems improve, more general uses may become common. Perhaps the ultimate system will also include the ability to automatically translate between spoken languages, so that one can talk in one language while the machine transcribes in another.

Forensic applications (earwitnesses)

The forensic application of auditory perception research has mostly focused on phonetics in general, and the ability of earwitnesses in particular. Before discussing this work, let us look at some other applications, including the authenticity of audio recordings, the identification of unclear or degraded recorded utterances, and the identification of speakers from audio recordings. There are two main traditions in speaker identification from an audio recording (French, 1994). American studies have usually relied on a mechanical or spectrographic description of a speaker's utterances, called a "voicegram" or "voiceprint" analysis. Voiceprint analysis has been considered as an identification method for automated cash tills, but it may be that retinal scanning and iris-identification is less variable when measured and hence more reliable. In Britain, the contested evidence has been traditionally analysed by a trained phonetician using their skill and knowledge of speech sounds and language to match identification.

Earwitnesses have been important in the forensic arena since the famous Lindbergh case in 1935, which involved the recognition of a kidnapper's voice saying "Hey Doc – over here" from memory 33 months later. Bruno Hauptman was convicted and sentenced to death on the strength of the earwitness testimony. At the time there was virtually no research available to help the court and the situation does not seem to have changed much in the intervening 60 years, with present-day research being scarce and often unsystematic in comparison to eyewitness research (Wilding, Cook, & Davis, 2000). What research there is tells us that we are fairly good at recognising familiar voices, not very good at all with unfamiliar voices, and that for both types of voice we tend to overestimate our ability to correctly identify the speaker (Künzel, 1994).

In comparison to eyewitnesses in similar situations, earwitnesses are less accurate and are usually overconfident about their judgements (Olsson, Juslin, & Winman, 1998). In fact, research has shown that the confidence one has about how well one can remember a voice before a lineup is not related to the actual recognition accuracy but is related to post-lineup willingness to testify (Van Wallendael, Surace, Parsons, & Brown, 1994). Obviously, witnesses think they are able to recognise voices fairly well, perhaps assuming that their memory is like a tape recording of reality, but are able to reassess this assumption when they are asked to actually put their ability to the test. This is an important distinction to make when one considers the difference between jurors and witnesses. Jurors will infer a higher level of confidence and ability in an earwitness report and may base their decisions on this unrealistic judgement.

McAllister, Bregman and Lipscombe (1988) found that earwitness reports were even more vulnerable to misleading post-event information than eyewitness memory for a car accident scenario. They used a version of Loftus and Palmer's (1974) experiment in which participants were required to estimate the speed of cars involved in a traffic accident. Whispering, voice distinctiveness and the length of the utterance have all been shown to have an effect on voice identification (e.g. Orchard & Yarmey, 1995). Disguising speech by using whispering or muffling drastically reduces identification (Bull & Clifford, 1984). On the other hand, voice distinctiveness can improve identification so much as to possibly bias the recognition in a lineup, and in such a situation the length of the speech utterance has no effect on the efficacy of recognition (Roebuck & Wilding, 1993), which suggests that witnesses can make a best guess by eliminating mismatching voices rather than accurately identifying the correct one, and consequently leading to a false-positive identification (Künzel, 1994). However, in situations with less varied and fewer voices, the length of the utterance is important in helping improve identification (Orchard & Yarmey, 1995), presumably in aiding the witness to establish a template for later recognition (Cook & Wilding, 1997a). Repetition of the utterance in the lineup can also help to improve recognition, possibly allowing the listener more opportunity to process the speech in a more careful manner (Wilding *et al.*, 2000).

It appears that the context of the voice recognition can also be important. Cook and Wilding (1997b) report that in conditions in which the face of the voice's owner is present, recognition memory for the voice of a stranger is superior to recognition memory for the voice heard when the face is absent. They termed this phenomenon the "face overshadowing effect". This contrasts with their additional findings that other forms of context (such as another voice, name and personal information) had no effect, and neither did re-presenting the face at the lineup. Wilding *et al.* (2000) have some important things to say about the face overshadowing effect. They point out that voice processing is usually added on to theories of face perception as a separate channel. But their findings that the simultaneous presentation of faces with voices interacts to the detriment of voice recognition runs counter to the expectation that voice is a separate and additional channel of information relevant to face recognition. Presumably, the situation is more complex than at first proposed. Wilding *et al.* (2000) have suggested that we do not use voice recognition to help us identify a person's identity but rather the content of the message. The speech and voice characteristics are primarily extracted to aid speech perception, which is supported by the common-sense notion that knowing a speaker's identity will help in speech processing (Nygaard & Pisoni, 1998). Face recognition is primarily visual, whereas speech comprehension is primarily auditory in character. The face overshadowing effect is presented as evidence that identifying a person is primarily a visual task with auditory processing taking a back seat.

Summary

- Information about intensity and frequency is processed in auditory perception to give us a wide range of subjective perceptual qualities.
- Perceptual constancy is a problem in auditory perception, as the acoustic signal is both linear and can be an aggregate of many different sounds at the same time.
- Psychophysics focuses on measuring the limits of hearing using presumed "simple" tones, whereas Gestalt psychology concentrates on the ability of the auditory system to process patterns into wholes but is vague as to the mechanisms involved.
- Ecological psychology looks for invariants in the acoustic signal, and auditory scene analysis is concerned with how we perceive auditory objects and events in noisy situations via the use of heuristics.
- Researchers have to be careful to design ecologically valid experiments when investigating the abilities of the auditory system.
- For both non-speech and speech sounds, the temporal patterning of sounds is important. Both seem to be processed forward and backward in time before a percept is formed.
- Speech perception involves a high level of top-down processing.
- Auditory aspects of unattended sounds are often processed.
- Auditory perception interacts with other senses.
- Applications of auditory perception research include interface design, sonification, warning design, machine speech recognition and earwitness testimony. These are currently active areas of research and development.

Further reading

Bregman A.S. (1990). *Auditory scene analysis*. Boston, MA: MIT Press. A thorough introduction to auditory scene analysis, written by the most influential research professor in the area. A big read, but exhaustive.

Edworthy S., & Adams A. (1996). *Warning design: A research prospective*. London: Taylor & Francis. A thorough account of the emerging applied psychology of auditory warning design.

Handel, S (1989). *Listening: An introduction to the perception of auditory events*. Boston, MA: MIT Press. An excellent introduction that is readable and learned at the same time. It covers virtually every aspect of hearing you could think of.

Sloboda, J.A. (1985). *The musical mind: The cognitive psychology of music.* Oxford: Oxford University Press. One of the first standard texts on the cognitive psychology of music. Thorough and interesting. I have suggested this as further reading due to my inability to fit in much about music into this chapter.

Reading and dyslexia

11.1 Introduction

The aim of this chapter is to provide a basic description of the processes involved when people read. This model of reading has been painstakingly built up using data collected from people who have acquired dyslexia through some form of brain damage. Other models of acquired dyslexia are discussed and different forms of acquired dyslexia presented. Applied aspects, such as assessment and rehabilitation, are considered. The chapter then discusses the difference between acquired dyslexia and developmental dyslexia, and the difficulties that people with developmental dyslexia can encounter at school and in the workplace.

11.2 Acquired dyslexia

Acquired dyslexia is a disorder of reading that occurs as a result of brain damage. This may be due to a stroke, brain infection or degenerative disorder such as Alzheimer's disease. The study of acquired dyslexia was one of the first areas to be investigated from a cognitive neuropsychological perspective. Much of the work had been done on single case studies, looking at single word processing, and you may well question whether this approach is really representative of the reading process.

Acquired dyslexia is not the same thing as developmental dyslexia. Ewald Jackson and Coltheart (2001) provide a description that clearly outlines the difference. They suggest that someone who has achieved a normal level of skill in reading and later loses that skill shows acquired dyslexia. However, someone who has never been able to perform at a normal level in reading shows developmental dyslexia. In fact, you could have an 80-year-old woman who is a developmental dyslexic and an 8-year-old boy who has acquired dyslexia, because age is not always associated with whether dyslexia is developmental or acquired.

Shallice (1988) and Ellis and Young (1995) have discussed the importance of dissociations in cognitive neuropsychology. A dissociation occurs when a patient performs extremely poorly on task A and at a normal level on task B. Many cognitive neuropsychologists might say that these two tasks are handled by different sets of cognitive processes. However, this dissociation does not necessarily mean that the two tasks require different processing systems. It may be that task A is easier than task B. One way to get around this is to find a double dissociation, where another patient is found who performs at a normal level on task A but poorly on task B (Figure 11.1). This would provide a stronger indication that different cognitive processes were needed for the two tasks. Work on acquired dyslexia has relied heavily on double dissociations, as they have been used as evidence of the existence of separate cognitive subsystems.

11.3 Peripheral and central dyslexia

Peripheral dyslexias are characterised by a deficit in processing visual aspects of the stimulus – for example, letter-by-letter reading (alexia), neglect dyslexia and attentional dyslexia (Table 11.1). Central dyslexias are characterised by an

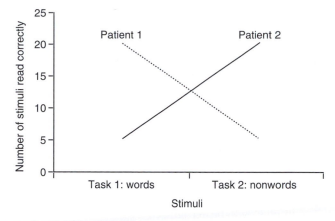

Figure 11.1 A double dissociation

impairment of higher reading functions for example, deep dyslexia, phonological dyslexia, surface dyslexia and reading without meaning. In this chapter, we will concentrate on the central dyslexias.

11.4 Models of acquired dyslexia

Some of the earliest work on acquired dyslexia was that of Dejerine (1892), who described patients with very different patterns of reading impairment. However, there were very few investigations into reading disorders until Marshall and Newcombe's research with dyslexic patients in 1973. They described a patient GR, who produced unusual errors when reading. These errors were semantically related to the target word (e.g. *speak* read as "talk"). They called this disorder "deep dyslexia". They then described patients who were unable to pronounce irregular words such as *yacht*. They called this particular disorder "surface dyslexia".

Table 11.1 Summary of characteristics of the peripheral dyslexias

Letter-by-letter reading (alexia)	Low, laborious reading using a letter-by-letter approach
	Word length effects
	Reading performance not influenced by linguistic factors (noun versus function word, concrete versus abstract word)
	Not influenced by whether a word can be sounded out
Neglect dyslexia	Failure to attend to the first part of a letter string Commonly found in patients with left-sided neglect
Attentional dyslexia	Difficulty reading words presented in text

Marshall and Newcombe (1973) tried to explain their patients' errors using a dual-route model of reading, a typical cognitive neuropsychological model employing boxes and arrows. This is a conceptual framework that has proved extremely useful in subsequent work in the area. Similar models of the reading process were provided by Patterson and Morton (1985) and Ellis and Young (1988), which were widely used in the 1970s and 1980s, and are still relevant today. These models tried to account for the recognition, comprehension and naming of written words in reading.

What are the components that make up a traditional model of reading (Figure 11.2), such as the one described by Ellis and Young (1988), and what do these components do? The function of the *visual analysis system* is to identify the component letters of words and note their positions within the word. Identification here is a purely visual process and does not involve naming the letters. This system ensures that a stimulus will be recognised even if it is presented in different fonts and styles. The *visual input lexicon* will have thousands of representations of words, or it will have if you are a skilled adult reader. A representation will be

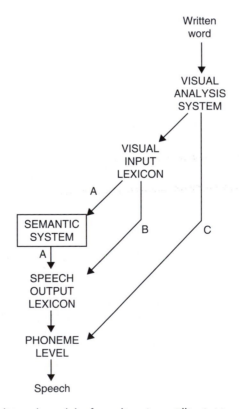

Figure 11.2 A traditional model of reading (e.g. Ellis & Young, 1988). Route A: reading via meaning. Route B: direct non-lexical route. Route C: grapheme–phoneme correspondence route

specifically activated by its own written word. This is the usual route for under-standing a familiar written word. At this stage, the word on the page will be familiar, but the reader will not know what the word means. The word meanings are stored in the next component, the *semantic system*. To get from meaning to the spoken word requires help from the *speech output lexicon*, which stores representa-tions of the spoken form of a word. The retrieved word form activates the *phoneme level*, which allows us to say the word aloud.

In the model, there are three routes to reading. The first is Route A, where a familiar word is recognised, its meaning activated and its word form retrieved from the speech output lexicon. This route is used when a person is "reading via mean-ing". In the model, there is an arrow connecting the visual input lexicon, which recognises familiar written words, to the speech output lexicon, which gives you their pronunciations. This arrow provides a pathway (Route B) by which familiar words can be identified and pronounced quickly, without activating their meanings. Route C is the grapheme–phoneme correspondence route and is used for reading unfamiliar words (e.g. aazvogel, ziggurat) and nonwords, which are unlikely to have representations in the visual input lexicon. Route C will not be very successful in generating a correct reading for irregular words, as it will regularise them. This route is used occasionally by adults, but much more frequently by beginning readers. It is often called the non-lexical route.

New approaches that were complementary to the cognitive neuropsychological one that has just been described started appearing in the late 1980s. They tried to address the problem that there was no neat mapping between the theoretical boxes and arrows approach with specific neurological damage – that is, there did not appear to be any one-to-one correspondence between neural elements and psychological processes.

Computational models of acquired dyslexia

Connectionist models of the reading process have made a great contribution to cognitive neuropsychology in general, and to accounts of acquired dyslexia in par-ticular. These connectionist models are also known as parallel distributed process-ing (PDP) models. The models are made up of a network of interconnected units that can be "taught" to read. Once this has been done, researchers have tried to simulate the performance of acquired dyslexics by destroying a number of connections or units in the connectionist model. In this way, they are causing "lesions" and the data generated by the simulations do appear to show some, but not all, of the characteristics of the different forms of acquired dyslexia. Some of the most successful connectionist models have been reported by Seidenberg and McClelland (1989), Plaut and Shallice (1993), and Coltheart, Langdon and Haller (1995). A typical model is shown in Figure 11.3.

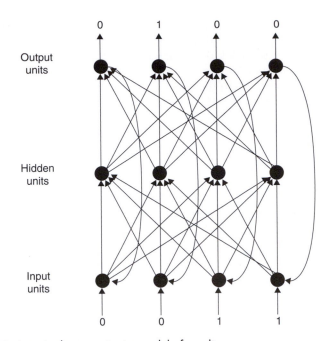

Figure 11.3 A typical connectionist model of reading

11.5 Different forms of acquired dyslexia

Case study: BS

BS was born in 1962. After leaving higher education having completed a business course, he became a marketing manager. He then suffered a cerebral haemorrhage, which left him with a loss of vision in his right visual field, severe receptive and expressive aphasia that subsequently improved, and problems with reading and spelling, which had not improved one and a half years after his stroke. His performance on Raven's Progressive Matrices showed him to be in the top 10% of the population, indicating that his non-verbal intelligence remained unimpaired.

He had no problems recognising, matching and naming single letters. He read 25 of 30 regular words correctly, but only 12 of 30 irregular words. His reading difficulties were improving but he still had problems with irregular words and low-frequency words such as *trough* and abstract words such as *scarce*. The majority of his errors were regularisation errors (e.g. *great* read as "greet"). He was not bad at reading nonwords, but not within normal limits.

For details, see Ellis, Lambon Ralph, Morris and Hunter (2000).

Surface dyslexia

Surface dyslexia is a disorder in which patients basically treat the majority of words as if they are new and unfamiliar. They have great difficulty in reading irregular words. These are words that cannot be pronounced using a phonics strategy of sounding out letters (e.g. *borough*). They do not show the same difficulties when reading regular words and nonwords.

Input surface dyslexia

Marshall and Newcombe (1973) first described this form of acquired dyslexia when they noted the performance of JC and ST. These two patients tended to sound out words that they would previously have been able to read easily. They also tended to make regularisation errors on irregular or ambiguously spelled words. They did not appear to have a semantic impairment, because provided they could say a word correctly, they could understand it and say what it meant. If they misread an irregular word and produced another word instead, then they would understand and define the word based on their mispronunciation. The classic example often quoted is the error that JC made to the word *listen*. The patient misread this as "Liston" and defined it as "that's the boxer". In terms of traditional models of reading, JC and ST have suffered impairments to the visual input lexicon and possibly its connections to the semantic system, and they have been classified by Ellis and Young as input surface dyslexics. Most words are read by the grapheme–phoneme correspondence route (Route C), which is a reasonable explanation of why they are more successful at reading regular words such as *hint* than irregular words such as *yacht*. Some words are still recognised as wholes by the visual input lexicon, so some irregular words can be read.

Central surface dyslexia

Shallice, Warrington and McCarthy (1983) described a patient HTR, another good example of a surface dyslexic. She suffered from a progressive dementing illness, but showed a greater tendency to break words down and assemble a pronunciation as if the word was unknown to her. She was more likely to read regular words aloud correctly than irregular words and she made regularisation errors, treating words as if they were regular when they were not (e.g. reading *gauge* as "gorge" and *come* as "kome"). She was able to read aloud nonwords such as *wull* or *pild*, even though she couldn't read correctly many once-familiar real words. Unlike JC and ST, she did appear to have a semantic impairment, in that she had problems understanding both spoken and written words, together with anomia (i.e. word-finding problems in spontaneous speech).

We can explain HTR's performance using a traditional reading model by saying that she has an impaired semantic system, which has knocked out Route A and left her reliant on Route C. Theoretically, a person with central surface dyslexia should be able to read regular and irregular words using the direct lexical route, B. Evidence to support this comes from Bub, Cancelliere and Kertesz (1985), who described a patient, MP, whose performance on frequent irregular words remained quite good.

Output surface dyslexia

Let us look at another surface dyslexic patient described by Howard and Franklin (1987). MK read regular words better than irregular words and the majority of his errors were regularisations. What is of particular interest is his performance in a lexical decision task, where he performed at 97.5% accuracy, and made no more errors to irregular than to regular words. He could also define regular and irregular words equally well. Where would his locus of impairment be? Using a traditional model of reading, it is suggested that in MK's case, his good performance on the lexical decision task indicates intact representation for regular and irregular words in the visual input lexicon, the early section of Route A, the visual lexical route. The ability to define irregular and regular words shows that MK's semantic representations are also intact. It is only when he has to read the words that there are problems. Whole-word reading would also be difficult if there were difficulties in accessing the pronunciation of words from the speech ouput lexicon. It is therefore suggested that his problem is due to difficulty in retrieving spoken word forms from the speech output lexicon. So like JC, ST and HTR, MK also has to rely on Route C, the grapheme–phoneme correspondence route, which explains his regular word advantage.

Do surface dyslexic patients have the same locus of impairment?

In trying to explain the performance of JC, ST, HTR and MK, there is obviously some impairment to Route A, the visual lexical route between the written word and pronunciation of it. The patients rely on Route C, which involves grapheme–phoneme conversion. There appear to be at least three loci of impairment, because damage at a number of different places in the model might cause an over-reliance on Route C, the grapheme–phoneme correspondence route.

Do the similarities between these surface dyslexics outweigh their differences enough for them to be considered a homogenous category of surface dyslexics? Coltheart and Funnell (1987) have suggested that this is not an easy question to answer. Their view is that within the context of a traditional model of reading, surface dyslexia may be associated with as many as seven distinct types of impairment!

Acquired dyslexia in which there is reading without meaning: evidence for Route B?

Schwartz, Saffran and Marin (1980) described WLP. She was a 62-year-old woman suffering from a progressive senile dementia, which severely impaired her semantic knowledge. This, in turn, affected her speech production and comprehension. What was particularly interesting was her very unusual reading. She appeared to be able to read words that she could not understand. In one task she was shown the written name of an animal, and was required to point to the right picture in a set of four. Her selection was poor, in fact totally random. However, she was able to read animal names aloud with very few errors.

In another task called a semantic categorisation task, she was given a stack of index cards. Each had the name of an animal, colour or body part. She was asked to read each word aloud, then to place the card on one of the three piles according to semantic category. WLP performed this task quite well for common names like *horse*, but her sorting was poor for less frequent names such as *magenta*.

She correctly categorised only 7 of 20 animal names, but was able to read 18 of 20 animal names correctly, including irregular words such as *leopard*. As her illness progressed, she tended to read words almost as if she had never seen them before (e.g. *pint* to rhyme with "hint"). Why is WLP's pattern of performance of any theoretical interest? We have already come across two routes to reading: Route A, the visual lexical route, and Route C, the grapheme–phoneme correspondence route. Reading without meaning cannot be accounted for by using either of these routes.

Schwartz *et al.* (1980) suggested that there must be a third route from print to sound which takes the form of direct, whole-word connections between corresponding representations in the visual lexicon and in the speech output lexicon. This is Route B, a direct non-lexical route from print to sound bypassing the semantic system. The existence of this route would explain how WLP was able to read without meaning. This proposal of direct connections has been widely accepted and used in a number of influential models of reading (e.g. Newcombe & Marshall, 1981; Ellis & Young, 1988).

We will go on to describe forms of acquired dyslexia where there is reading via meaning, namely phonological dyslexia and deep dyslexia.

Case study: CJ

CJ was born in1931, and before he had his stroke he was a policeman. His stroke, at the age of 50, left him with severe receptive and expressive aphasia. When CJ was initially tested by Funnell (1987), his speech comprehension had much improved and his speech was fluent, although rather slow and hesitant. His nonword reading was poor; he could read only 10 of 48 nonwords correctly. Most of his responses were lexicalisation errors, e.g. "wine" as a response to *wune*. He often indicated that he knew he was wrong.

He found producing rhyming words to a target very difficult, e.g. "line" for *pine*. In fact, this task was discontinued because he found it so hard. His performance on other phonological manipulation tasks such as segmentation and blending was also impaired.

When reading words, he showed an imageability effect – that is, he was better at reading high rather than low imageable words. His reading performance did not show a regularity effect, in that he did not perform significantly differently on regular and irregular words. His reading performance also reflected a frequency effect, so he was better at reading high-frequency than low-frequency words.

For details, see Patterson (2000).

Phonological dyslexia

Phonological dyslexia is of interest, as it was predicted theoretically before actual cases were reported. The theory proposed that if some patients with surface dyslexia were reliant on Route C and the grapheme–phoneme correspondence route, and had an impaired visual lexical route (Route A), then there should be some patients who are reliant on Route A and have an impaired Route C. Such a patient was first described by Derousne and Beauvois in 1979. They described RG, who was very good at reading familiar words but very bad at reading nonwords. They named this type of acquired dyslexia "phonological dyslexia". Patterson (1982) described AM, a 62-year-old man who had good auditory comprehension and no major problems with speech production. His comprehension and reading aloud of words was good (95%) but his reading of nonwords was poor (8%). He tended to make lexicalisation errors (e.g. *soof* being read as the word "soot"). And Funnell (1983) described WB, who had similar problems with nonword reading. The suggestion is that words will be dealt with efficiently by the visual input lexicon, but if the letter string is not a word, then there are problems in translating the letter string into a phoneme string because the grapheme–phoneme correspondence route is not working.

Coltheart (1986) has suggested that assembling a pronunciation for an unfamiliar letter string is quite a complex process – it involves graphemic segmentation of the letter string into groups that will map onto single phonemes or syllables, translating those segments into a string of phonemes and, finally, blending the phonemes together into a pronounced word. Because of this complexity, there may be a breakdown at any of these stages for different examples of phonological dyslexics. Coltheart proposed that phonological dyslexics with very similar patterns of performance do not always have the same underlying deficit.

Phonological dyslexia is a fairly mild disorder, in that reading real words is not greatly affected; unlike surface dyslexics, phonological dyslexics have no problem reading irregular words. The lesions associated with phonological dyslexia are considered to be less severe than those associated with deep dyslexia.

Deep dyslexia

Case study: GR

In 1944, GR was a 20-year-old soldier on active service. When falling off a lorry, he accidently shot himself. The bullet entered his brain in front of his left ear and caused damage to his temporal and parietal lobes and the sylvian fissure. This resulted in right-sided hemiplegia and a severe language disorder, whereby he could only use grunts to communicate. His language function improved over time, but his severe difficulties with reading and writing persisted.

Marshall and Newcombe (1966, 1973) noted that he could name only half the letters in the alphabet. His success at reading depended on the grammatical class of the word. Nouns were read better than adjectives, which, in turn, were read more successfully than verbs. He found function words such as *for* and *his* incredibly difficult to read. His most common errors were semantic errors, which neither looked nor sounded like the target word (e.g. "pixie" for *gnome*). These errors indicated that his reading was influenced by the meaning of the word.

For details, see Funnell (2000).

GR was a good example of someone who has deep dyslexia. Deep dyslexia is associated with large perisylvian lesions extending into the frontal lobe, and is linked with Broca's aphasia. It is one of the most interesting forms of acquired dyslexia, as one of the most unusual and characteristic errors that deep dyslexics make is the semantic error. For example, when shown the word *garden*, a deep dyslexic may respond *spade*. Many patients do not even know that they are making semantic errors.

These patients also make a number of other types of reading error, as noted by Coltheart (1980a). They are much better at reading concrete imageable words such as *table* than abstract words such as *justice*. They also show a part-of-speech effect, being better at reading content words (e.g. nouns); they are less good at modifiers such as adjectives and adverbs and worst at function words (e.g. pronouns, prepositions, conjunctions and question words). If they make an error on a function word, it will be another function word (e.g. *was* read as "with"). Coslett (1991) has shown that this part-of-speech effect is fairly robust, as it was still apparent when imageability was controlled for.

Deep dyslexics also produce visual errors, where their response bears a close similarity to the target word (e.g. *signal* read as "single"). They produce morphological errors (e.g. *scolded* read as "scolds"). GR made a most unusual type of reading error, the visual then semantic error. Here the target word *sympathy* was misread as "orchestra". How could this have happened? An initial visual misreading would have produced *symphony*, then a semantic error to this word would have produced "orchestra". Another example of a visual then semantic error was when he read *earl* as "deaf".

One of the most telling impairments that all deep dyslexic patients have is very poor nonword reading, tending to make lexicalisation errors (i.e. reading nonwords as words).

There are several approaches to explaining the performance of deep dyslexics. The first is the use of traditional models of reading, as proposed by Morton and Patterson (1980), Newcombe and Marshall (1980a,b) and Shallice and Warrington (1980). An alternative approach is the right hemisphere hypothesis, supported by Coltheart (1980b, 1983) and others.

If we use traditional models of reading to explain the pattern of performance of people with deep dyslexia, it suggests that deep dyslexics have an impaired Route C, the grapheme–phoneme correspondence route, and therefore they perform poorly on nonwords. It also suggests an impaired Route B, the whole word route (mediated by connections between the visual input lexicon and speech output lexicon), which leaves the deep dyslexic patient totally reliant on the semantic route. In fact, it has been suggested that even Route A, the semantic route, has been impaired. A central semantic impairment would explain the better reading of concrete versus abstract words and the characteristic semantic errors made by deep dyslexics.

The right hemisphere hypothesis, as described by Coltheart (1980b), suggested that the characteristics of deep dyslexia are due to right hemisphere processing, a part of the brain not usually thought to be involved in the reading process. Coltheart pointed out that many deep dyslexic patients had damage in the language areas of the left hemisphere. There was also independent evidence from three different sources. The first was work with split-brain patients, where the two hemispheres had been surgically separated by sectioning the corpus callosum. The second was the pattern of performance in patients who have had a left hemisperectomy. The third strand of evidence came from experiments with normal individuals, in which words were presented to one or other of the cerebral hemispheres. The pattern of performance of these three different groups were considered to be very similar to those of deep dyslexic patients. Zaidel (1982), Gazzaniga (1983) and Patterson and Besner (1984) have criticised this approach as being somewhat limited, and more current brain imaging studies by Price et al. (1998) suggest both left and right hemisphere processing.

Funnell (2000) described a very interesting connectionist model developed by Plaut and Shallice (1993) to simulate the characteristic errors found in deep dyslexia, which has been partially successful.

11.6 Assessment of acquired dyslexia

Greenwald (2000) has provided a comprehensive and detailed account of assessments currently used to assess acquired dyslexia. An initial assessment of acquired dyslexia is often made using the relevant subtests of the Western Aphasia Battery or the Boston Diagnostic Aphasia Examination. More detailed testing is needed to discover the type and the severity of the reading disorder. This could be done using the Psycholinguistic Assessments of Language Processing in Aphasia (PALPA) developed by Kay, Lesser and Coltheart (1992). The PALPA uses stimuli that are controlled for spelling regularity, word frequency, imageability and length, all factors known to have an effect on reading performance. It is also very useful to get a language sample to determine whether expressive language or comprehension has been impaired.

Some of the methods used to assess subcomponents of the normal reading process are listed in Table 11.2. Many of these are included in the PALPA, but also in measures such as the Maryland Reading Battery (Berndt, Haendiges, Mitchum, & Wayland, 1996) and the Johns Hopkins University Dyslexia Battery (Goodman & Caramazza, 1986).

Graphemic knowledge can be assessed by asking the patient to match letters across case and/or font. Another popular task is the lexical decision task, which assesses visual word recognition. Here, the patient is presented with a written word

Table 11.2 Tasks used to assess components of reading

Component of reading	Task
• Visual perception • Visual word recognition • Semantic processsing • Grapheme–phoneme conversion	• Letter matching • Visual lexical decision • Category sorting • Letter sounding

or a nonword and they have to decide if the stimulus they have just seen is a real word or not. The lexical decision list should be made up of equal numbers of words and nonwords. A patient may be asked to make a lexical decision on high-frequency versus low-frequency words, high imageable versus low imageable words, regular versus irregular words and even "regular" nonwords versus "irregular" nonwords. Semantic processing can be assessed by a variety of means. A patient may be required to sort single words into piles on the basis of semantic category. The difficulty of the sorting task can be increased by asking the patient to sort words into close semantic categories (e.g. kitchen equipment versus office equipment). Single word comprehension can be assessed via cross-modality matching, where a word can be matched to one of several pictures.

Grapheme–phoneme conversion can be very simply assessed by getting the patient to sound out letters. In some instances, patients have not been able to sound out the letter that starts their first name! Graphemic knowledge can also be assessed by graphemic parsing – that is, getting the patient to segment printed letter strings into smaller units or segment real word stems from inflections.

There has been some debate as to the extent to which recommendations for treatment can be derived from assessments. Some cognitive neuropsychologists (e.g. Caramazza, 1989) are not very positive about this approach. Others (e.g. Behrmann & Byng, 1992) are more optimistic.

11.7 Rehabilitation

There are many informative descriptions of speech and language therapy used to try and improve patients' reading, for example the work of Coltheart and Byng (1989). A more recent therapy study by Ellis *et al.* (2000) is particularly convincing regarding the ability of assessment to indicate what sort of therapy to embark upon. They wished to assess the usefulness of therapy with BS, a surface dyslexic. Ellis *et al.* were very clear as to what they wanted from their therapy study:

1   Therapy should be based on careful assessment and should be grounded in the understanding of a patient's problems.
2   Positive changes should clearly reflect the effects of therapy, rather than be the result of slow, spontaneous improvement that so often occurs in patients.

3   Any improvements should clearly be due to the effects of therapy, rather than patient motivation or the effect of the people involved in therapy (sometimes referred to as the "charm effect").

4   Therapy should be practical, so that it could be adapted by other therapists in a normal clinical setting.

5   The benefits of therapy should be long-lasting and sustainable after therapy has stopped.

Cross-over treatment design

Ellis *et al.* (2000) used an approach called a "cross-over treatment design". This design was initially developed to show that observed improvements in a patient were due to therapy rather than spontaneous improvement or charm effects. They worked on two difficulties that their patient BS had – naming objects and reading words. A set of 52 pictures that he had trouble naming and a set of 52 words that he had trouble reading were collated. Both sets were divided to create a set of pictures and a set of words that were to be used in therapy sessions, and a set of pictures and a set of words that were not to be used in therapy sessions. We will look at the reading therapy in particular and any improvements it might have had.

A baseline measure of BS's performance on all the pictures and all the words was first conducted. Then, he received a 3 week therapy session on naming a set of 26 pictures. Another measure of all the words and pictures was taken, after which the therapy session for reading the set of words was started. A third full assessment was then conducted, after which BS had a well-deserved break of nearly 3 months, before the fourth and final assessment.

Ellis and his colleagues were convinced that BS's surface dyslexia was of the input type – that is, he had a problem accessing the representations of written words in the visual input lexicon. They hoped that if BS saw a difficult word, and heard it at the same time, that the spoken word would activate its meaning and provide its pronunciation. The therapy involved BS being given a sheet of paper with the 26 words on it and an accompanying audio-cassette tape. He had to look at the first word on the list and try to read it. He then played the tape and heard the word being spoken. If he had read it correctly, he could move on. If he hadn't, he had to look at the word again, repeat the correct pronunciation to himself several times and think about its meaning. In this way, Ellis *et al.* hoped that the links between written word, spoken word and meaning would be re-established.

Four different word orders with accompanying tapes were used to control for order effects. BS was asked to choose a different list each day and spend 20 min working on his own. BS had been allocated 3 weeks for the reading therapy, but after 2 weeks he was confident enough to request that the assessment be brought forward.

It is evident that there was a dramatic improvement in BS's ability to read the treated set of words, from 8 of 26 at assessment 2 to 23 of 26 at assessment 3 (Figure 11.4). There was no significant change in performance for the untreated words over assessments, indicating that the benefits were confined to the treated items, ruling out either spontaneous improvement or general charm effects. What was especially pleasing was that the improvements remained stable; at the fourth

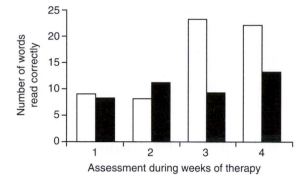

Figure 11.4 Effects of reading therapy on patient BS. □, treated words; ■, untreated words

and final assessment after a break of 11 weeks, his reading of treated words remained improved.

11.8 Developmental dyslexia

We have already noted that acquired dyslexia is *not* the same thing as developmental dyslexia. Someone who has achieved a reasonable level of reading and later loses that skill shows acquired dyslexia. However, someone who has never been able to perform at a reasonable level in reading shows developmental dyslexia. Before we move on to definitions of developmental dyslexia, it would be worthwhile to touch on the debate as to whether there are subtypes of developmental dyslexia that mirror the subtypes of acquired dyslexia described earlier in this chapter.

Masterson (cited in Funnell, 2000) has provided a very interesting summary of the work in this area. Coltheart, Masterson, Byng, Prior and Riddoch (1983) examined the reading and spelling performance of CD, a 16-year-old developmental dyslexic. Her reading age was 4 years below her chronological age and her spelling age was 6 years behind. She was of average IQ, there was no evidence of neurological damage, language problems or social and emotional problems, but she had always had problems with reading and spelling. Their investigation of her reading and spelling performance showed that she had difficulty reading irregular or exception words. Many of her responses to irregular words were regularisation errors. Coltheart *et al.* suggested that her pattern of impairment was similar to that of a surface dyslexic. In the same year, Temple and Marshall (1983) reported the case of HM, who they considered a clear example of developmental phonological dyslexia, as her reading was similar to that of previous cases of acquired phonological dyslexia. Bryant and Impey (1986) criticised both of these studies for not taking into account the reading strategies of children learning to read normally. They found features typical of surface dyslexia, including poor reading of irregular words, and regularisation errors were also present in their group of normal readers. Temple (1987) swiftly countered with a criticism of Bryant and Impey's poor reading age match.

Masterson describes further reports of developmental surface dyslexia (Masterson, 1984; Temple, 1985), the possibility of an orthographic processing deficit in developmental dyslexia (Seymour & Evans, 1993) and Castles and Coltheart's (1993) attempt to provide evidence for a clear distinction between developmental surface dyslexia and developmental phonological dyslexia. Although there is evidence of developmental dyslexia that may have parallels with subtypes of acquired dyslexia, there is still little consensus on this matter.

11.9 Definitions of developmental dyslexia

There are problems in defining developmental dyslexia, both in the school setting and in the workplace. There are several reasons for this. First, there is no agreement among experts, such as psychologists, neurologists and educationalists, as to what causes it. Miles (2001) suggests a physical basis, and that in some cases of dyslexia a genetic basis might well be plausible. Researchers are very measured in their approach to causation, indicating an interaction between different genes, different physical bases and environmental influences. Another reason is that with a lack of consensus on cause, there is equal confusion about definition. Fitzgibbon and O'Connor (2002) point out "that dyslexia remains a condition with numerous definitions but no generally agreed best definition" (p. 2).

The educational setting has depended upon several psychometric indicators of dyslexia, such as a mismatch between verbal IQ and performance IQ on tests like the Weschler Intelligence Scale for Children and the Weschler Adult Intelligence Scale. These tests can only be administered by psychologists who have appropriate training and experience. It is not enough to depend on these test scores alone; psychologists also need to look at performance on other tests to get an all-round picture of the difficulties that a child or adult faces.

The mismatch or discrepancy approach is reflected in discrepancy type definitions such as that provided by Thomson and Watkins (1990). They define dyslexia as being a severe difficulty with the written form of language, independent of intellectual, cultural or emotional causes. They characterise it by the individual's standards of reading, writing and spelling being well below those expected based on intelligence and chronological age.

A recent report of the Working Party of the Division of Educational and Child Psychology of the British Psychological Society (1999) was titled "Dyslexia, Literacy and Psychological Assessment". It contained a working definition that purported to separate description from causal explanations: "Dyslexia is evident when accurate and fluent word reading and/or spelling develops very incompletely or with great difficulty. This focuses on literacy learning at the word level and implies the problem is severe and persistent despite appropriate learning opportunities. It provides the basis for a staged process of assessment through teaching" (p. 20). This definition did not find favour with Fitzgibbon and O'Connor (2002). They considered that the definition was so general it could be applied to any child who had poor literacy skills, regardless of how they came about. They also pointed out that many children diagnosed as dyslexic have standards of reading, writing and spelling that are lower than they should be, compared with their intelligence, but are still considered average.

11.10 Dyslexia in the school setting

Most mainstream schools emphasise the importance of literacy for academic success. However, acquiring that literacy competence is difficult for dyslexic children, as the English language is a very complex one. It makes many demands on working memory and phonology, and requires a good knowledge of an often confusing orthographic system. This does not mean that all dyslexic children have below average levels of literacy, as they can still overcome their dyslexic difficulties.

Fitzgibbon and O'Connor (2002) suggested that there are many factors that can have an effect on the progress of a dyslexic child (see Table 11.3). The individual ability of the child, his or her motivation and the effort made to acquire literacy skills are very important. These will be influenced by the learning environment of the child, both at home and at school. An able dyslexic child will learn to read, write and spell at an average level and will not necessarily pose a problem for teachers. However, parents may consider the discrepancy between attainment levels and ability levels extremely worrying.

Table 11.3 Factors that can affect a dyslexic child in school

- Ability level of child
- Strategies for compensating
- Learning environment
- Early diagnosis
- False beliefs of others
- Information technology

Many dyslexic children try to overcome the difficulties they face in school using a variety of strategies. They may try and compensate by making above average efforts and working much harder than their peers in an attempt to keep up with their class. Parents may try and support their child's efforts with extra tuition.

A supportive learning environment can be very helpful in encouraging a dyslexic child. Many teachers use multi-sensory methods, knowing that this can be helpful to dyslexic children. They encourage listening skills, demonstrations and do not overburden the class with too much information and too many words in too short a space of time. Their lesson plans provide clear structure and children build on things they have already learned and are encouraged to review previous work. Different strategies for note taking and revision are encouraged, including mind mapping.

Teachers are flexible in their approach in that they are prepared to vary the pace of presentation in class, go over something several times, or break down pieces of information into smaller units. Teachers will make sure that there is enough time left at the end of the lesson for the class to note down homework and to plan what is needed for the next session. These seemingly obvious adjustments can make a huge difference to a dyslexic child failing in the school system.

Early diagnosis is an important factor in how well a child does at school. In many cases, a child's failure is seen as evidence of their low ability, and little support may be given. In other cases, a child who has poor reading, writing and spelling may be diagnosed as being dyslexic. However, few of those who do not show a below average performance will be detected. Once a child is diagnosed, then learning strategies can be encouraged and support provided in the classroom and at home.

False beliefs about all dyslexic children being of low intelligence and having very poor literacy skills lead to the equally inaccurate view that dyslexic children will not go far academically or get good jobs. Negative feedback from school and home can further damage their confidence and desire to do well. It is vital for teachers and parents to make sure that these myths are seen to be generalisations and are not applicable to every dyslexic child.

Information technology provides a very practical solution to problems faced by dyslexic students. Dyslexia software programs can provide support for students who have particular problems with spelling. Touch-typing can be helpful to students who spend a long time over course work. Voice-activated software and text-to-speech software are useful in a job that requires a great deal of reading and writing.

11.11 Dyslexia in the workplace

When we think of dyslexia, we usually think about it in a school setting. However, dyslexia is a life-long condition that also affects the lives of adults. The effects of dyslexia change as the person gets older. If a child has problems with spelling, then it is important to provide remediation in that area, as it is considered a key skill within the education system. Poor spelling in an adult dyslexic may not have such a great impact on their ability to do their job successfully.

The issue of whether or not dyslexia is a disability is a contentious one. Legally, dyslexia is considered a disability in several pieces of UK legislation, in particular the Disability Discrimination Act (1995). This Act defines disability as a "physical or mental impairment which has a substantial and long term adverse effect on a person's ability to carry out normal day-to-day activities". Although it has been criticised for being rather narrow in scope, it does provide some dyslexic adults with protection from unfair discrimination, especially if they are considered by the employment tribunal to be severely dyslexic. It should be noted that there are some occupations not covered by the Act (for example, the police, the armed forces and the prison service), but this may change in the future.

Fitzgibbon and O'Connor (2002) provided a conservative estimate that 10% of the workforce in the UK is dyslexic. If this is the case, employers need to review their working practices and organisational culture. Workers should have access to psychological assessment services that can help with diagnosis, assessments are required in the workplace to make adjustments for employees who are known to be dyslexic, and dyslexia awareness training should be made available for managers and supervisors. Of course, under the Disability Discrimination Act (Section 6:1), employers are obliged to make "reasonable adjustment" for their disabled employees. The Act specifically notes that: "Where a) any arrangement made by or on behalf of an employee, or b) any physical feature of premise occupied by the employer, places the disabled person concerned at a substantial disadvantage in comparison with persons who are not disabled, it is the duty of the employer to take such steps as is reasonable, in all the circumstances of the case, for him to have to take in order to prevent the arrangements or feature having that effect".

This may well prove rather problematic on several counts. There are going to be many legal discussions as to what "reasonable adjustment" means in the context of a small employer. Also, in the majority of cases, when an employee alleges unfair discrimination, it is the employee who has to prove that they have been unfairly discriminated against (i.e. the burden of proof falls upon them). It is clear that litigation will increase if more thought is not given to the difficulties faced by dyslexic people in the workplace.

Summary

- Acquired dyslexia has been explained using traditional cognitive neuropsychological models of reading. Connectionist models of reading have also made a contribution in accounting for acquired dyslexia.
- Surface dyslexics tend to read using the grapheme–phoneme correspondence route, as they have an impaired visual lexical route. There is evidence that they can still use the direct lexical route. Surface dyslexics may well have different loci of impairment.
- There have been examples of patients being able to read without meaning, which can be seen as evidence of a direct lexical route, which bypasses the semantic system.
- Phonological dyslexia and deep dyslexia are forms of acquired dyslexia in which there is reading for meaning, using the visual lexical route. The grapheme–phoneme correspondence route is not working. Phonological dyslexia is considered to be a fairly mild disorder compared with deep dyslexia.
- The impaired normal systems hypothesis and the right hemisphere hypothesis have both been used to account for deep dyslexia.
- There has been some debate as to the extent to which recommendations for treatment for patients with acquired dyslexia can be derived from assessments.
- Developmental dyslexia is not the same thing as acquired dyslexia. Someone who has never been able to perform at a reasonable level in reading shows developmental dyslexia.
- Some of the factors that can affect a dyslexic child in a school setting are the ability of the child, strategies for compensating, the learning environment, an early diagnosis, the false belief of others and appropriate use of information technology.

- About 10% of the workforce in the UK is dyslexic, so it is essential that employers are able to make "reasonable adjustment" for people with dyslexia in the workplace under the Disability Discrimination Act (1995).

Further reading

Coslett, H.B. (2000). Acquired dyslexia. In M. Farah & T. Feinberg (Eds.), *Patient-based approaches to cognitive neuroscience*. Cambridge, MA: MIT Press. A clear account of both peripheral and central dyslexias.

Ellis, A.W., & Young, A.W. (1995). Reading: a composite model for word recognition and production. In *Human cognitive neuropsychology: A textbook with readings*. Hove, UK: Psychology Press. A classic text.

Funnell, E. (Ed.) (2000). *Case studies in the neuropsychology of reading*. Hove, UK: Psychology Press. A very accessible text with some fascinating case studies described by leading names in the field.

Greenwald, M. (2000). The acquired dyslexias. In S. Nadeau, L. Gonzalez Rothi, & B. Crosson (Eds.), *Aphasia and language: Theory to practice*. New York: Guilford Press. A detailed account of the clinical subtypes of acquired dyslexia, with a great deal of information on diagnosis and treatment. It is a useful reference book.

Applied aspects of reading

Barlett, D., & Moody, S. (2000). *Dyslexia in the workplace*. London: Whurr Publishers. This book draws on semi-structured interviews to illustrate the effects of dyslexia on emotional and behavioural development.

Fitzgibbon, G., & O'Connor, B. (2002). *Adult dyslexia: A guide for the workplace*. Chichester, UK: Wiley. This text provides practical advice for employers on how to create a dyslexia-friendly working environment and details of laws on anti-discrimination and dyslexia.

Morgan, E., & Klein, C. (2000). *The dyslexic adult in a non-dyslexic world*. London: Whurr Publishers. A description of those who struggled through school and who did not have their dyslexic difficulties diagnosed until later in life.

Useful organisations

Adult Dyslexia Organisation, 336 Brixton Road, London SW9 7AA, UK: http://www.futurenet.co.uk/charity/ado/index.html
British Dyslexia Association, 98 London Road, Reading RG1 5AU, UK: http://www.bda-dyslexia.org.uk
Dyslexia Institute, 133 Gresham Road, Staines, Middlesex TW18 2AJ, UK: http://www.dyslexia-inst.org.uk

References

Adams, J. (1995). *Risk*. London: UCL Press.

Adams, J.A. (1971). A closed loop theory of motor control. *Journal of Motor Behaviour, 3*, 111–150.

Adan, A. (1993). Circadian variations in psychological measures: a new classification. *Chronobiologia, 20*, 145–161.

Algan, O., Furedy, J.J., Demigoren, S., Vincent, A., & Pogun, S. (1997). Effects of tobacco smoking and gender on interhemispheric cognitive function: performance and confidence measures. *Behavioural Pharmacology, 8*, 416–428.

Allen, G.A., Mahler, W.A., & Estes, W.K. (1969). Effects of recall tests on long-term retention of paired associates. *Journal of Verbal Learning and Verbal Behaviour, 8*, 463–470.

Allen, P., Towell, N., Pike, G., & Kemp, R. (1998). Why Gary Lineker shouldn't turn to crime: recognising EFITs of famous faces. Paper presented to the *British Psychological Society Conference*, Brighton, 26–29 March.

Allport, D.A., Antonis, B., & Reynolds, P. (1972). On the division of attention: a disproof of the single channel hypothesis. *Quarterly Journal of Experimental Psychology, 24*, 225–235.

Alm, H., & Nilsson, L. (1994). Changes in driver behaviour as a function of hands-free mobile phones: a simulator study. *Accident Analysis and Prevention, 26*, 441–451.

Altman, J., Everitt, B.J., Glautier, S. *et al.* (1996). The biological, social and clinical bases of drug addiction: commentary and debate. *Psychopharmacology, 125*, 285–345.

Altmann, E.M. (2001). Near-term memory in programming: a simulation-based analysis. *International Journal of Human–Computer Studies, 54*, 189–210.

Altmann, E.M., & Trafton, J.G. (1999). Memory for goals: an architectural perspective. In *Proceedings of the Twenty First Annual Conference of the Cognitive Science Society*. Hillsdale, NJ: Erlbaum.

Ameri, A. (1999). The effects of cannabinoids on the brain. *Pharmacology, Biochemistry and Behaviour, 64*, 257–260.

Anderson, K.J. (1994). Impulsivity, caffeine and task difficulty: a within-subjects test of the Yerkes-Dodson Law. *Personality and Individual Differences, 16*, 813–829.

REFERENCES

Anderson, M.C. (2001). Active forgetting: evidence for functional inhibition as a source of memory failure. *Journal of Aggression, Maltreatment, and Trauma, 4,* 185–210.

Anderson, M.C., Bjork, R.A., & Bjork, E.L. (1994). Remembering can cause forgetting: retrieval dynamics in long-term memory. *Journal of Experimental Psychology: Learning, Memory, and Cognition, 20,* 1063–1087.

Anderson, M.C., Bjork, R.A., & Bjork, E.L. (2000). Retrieval-induced forgetting: evidence for a recall-specific mechanism. *Journal of Experimental Psychology: Learning, Memory, and Cognition, 7,* 522–530.

Anderson, M.C., & Neely, J.H. (1996). Interference and inhibition in memory retrieval. In E.L. Bjork & R.A. Bjork (Eds.), *Memory: Handbook of perception and cognition.* New York: Academic Press.

Arnaud, M.J. (1984). Products of metabolism of caffeine. In P.B. Dews (Ed.), *Caffeine.* Berlin: Springer-Verlag.

Arnold, M.E., Petros, T.V., Beckwith, B.E., Coons, G., & Gorman, N. (1987). The effects of caffeine, impulsivity and sex on memory for word lists. *Physiology and Behaviour, 41,* 25–30.

Ashcraft, M.H. (1995). Cognitive psychology and simple arithmetic: a review and summary of new directions. *Mathematical Cognition, 1,* 3–34.

Ashcraft, M.H., Donley, R.D., Halas, M.A., & Vakali, M. (1992). Working memory, automaticity, and problem difficulty. In J.I.D. Campbell (Ed.), *The nature and origins of mathematical skills.* Advances in Psychology #91. Amsterdam: North-Holland.

Ashcraft, M.H., & Kirk, E.P. (2001). The relationships among working memory, math anxiety, and performance. *Journal of Experimental Psychology: General, 130,* 224–237.

Asso, D. (1983). *The real menstrual cycle.* New York: Wiley.

Asso, D. (1987). Cyclical variations. In M.A. Baker (Ed.), *Sex Differences in Human Performance.* New York: Wiley.

Atkinson, R.C. (1975). Mnemotechnics in second language learning. *American Psychologist, 30,* 821–828.

Atwood, M.E., & Polson, P.G. (1976). A process model for water jug problems. *Cognitive Psychology, 8,* 191–216.

Auebeeluck, A., & Maguire, M. (2002). The Menstrual Joy Questionnaire items alone can positively prime reporting of menstrual attitudes and symptoms. *Psychology of Women Quarterly, 26,* 160–162.

Aust, R., Sharp, C., & Goulden, C. (2002). Prevalence of drug use: key findings from the 2001/2002 British Crime Survey. *Home Office Research Findings, 18,* 1–6. Available at: http://www.homeoffice.gov.uk/rds/pdfs2/r182.pdf (retrieved 22 January 2004).

Ayeroff, F., & Abelson, R.P. (1976). Belief in personal success at mental telepathy. *Journal of Personality and Social Psychology, 34,* 240–247.

Ayton, P. (1994) The bomb party probability illusion. Poster presented at JDM, St Louis.

Ayton, P., Hunt, A.J., & Wright, G. (1989). Psychological conceptions of randomness. *Journal of Behavioural Decision Making, 2,* 221–238.

Ayton, P., & McClelland A. (1997). The despicable Doctor Fischer's (Bayesian) bomb party. *Teaching Mathematics and its Applications, 6,* 179–183.

Baddeley, A.D. (1982). *Your memory: A user's guide.* New York: Macmillan.

Baddeley, A.D. (1986). *Working memory.* Oxford: Oxford University Press.

Baddeley, A.D. (1996). Exploring the central executive. *Quarterly Journal of Experimental Psychology, 49A,* 5–28.

Baddeley, A.D. (1997). *Human memory: Theory and practice* (revised edition). Hove, UK: Psychology Press.

Baddeley, A.D., & Hitch, G.J. (1974). Working memory. In G.H. Bower (Ed.), *The psychology of learning and motivation: Advances in research and theory* (Vol. 8). New York: Academic Press.

Baddeley, A.D., & Logie, R.H. (1999). Working memory: the multiple-component model. In A. Miyake & P. Shah (Eds.), *Models of working memory: Mechanisms of active maintenance and executive control*. Cambridge: Cambridge University Press.

Baddeley, A.D., & Longman, D.J.A. (1978). The influence of length and frequency of training sessions on the rate of learning to type. *Ergonomics, 21*, 627–635.

Baddeley, A.D., & Wilson, B. (1988). Comprehension and working memory: a single case neuropsychological study. *Journal of Memory and Language, 27*, 479–498.

Bahrick, H.P., Bahrick, P.O., & Wittlinger, R.P. (1975). Fifty years of memory for names and faces: a cross-sectional approach. *Journal of Experimental Psychology: General, 104*, 54–75.

Baker, D., Pryce, G., Croxford, J.L. *et al.* (2000). Cannabinoids control spasticity and tremor in a multiple sclerosis model. *Nature, 404*, 84–87.

Baker, K.L. (1996). Auditory perception: between psychophysics and speech. *International Journal of Psychology, 31*, 51.

Baker, K.L., Williams, S.M., & Nicolson, R.I. (2000). Evaluating frequency proximity in stream segregation. *Perception and Psychophysics, 62*, 81–88.

Baker, M.A. (1987). Sensory functioning. In M.A. Baker (Ed), *Sex differences in human performance*. New York: Wiley.

Baker, S., & Marshall, E. (1988). Chernobyl and the role of psychologists – an appeal to reason. *The Psychologist: Bulletin of the British Psychological Society, 1*, 107–108.

Ballas, J.A., & Howard, J.H. (1987). Interpreting the language of environmental sounds. *Environment and Behaviour, 19*, 91–114.

Ballas, J.A., Howard, J.H., & Kolm, C. (1982). Listener descriptions of isolated and patterned acoustic transients. *Psychological Documents, 12*, 3(ms. #2469).

Banbury, S., & Berry, D. (1997). Habituation and dishabituation to speech and office noise. *Journal of Experimental Psychology: Applied, 3*, 1–16.

Banbury, S., & Berry, D. (1998). Disruption of office-related tasks by speech and office noise. *British Journal of Psychology, 89*, 499–517.

Banbury, S., & Jones, D.M. (1998). Auditory distraction in the workplace: a review of the implications from laboratory studies. In M.A. Hanson (Ed.), *Contemporary Ergonomics*. London: Taylor & Francis.

Banbury, S., Jones, D.M., & Berry, D.C. (1998). Extending the "irrelevant sound effect": the effects of extraneous sound on performance in the office and on the Flight deck. In *Proceedings of the 7th International Congress on Noise as a Public Health Problem*, Sydney, NSW.

Banerji, M.R., & Crowder, R.C. (1989). The bankruptcy of everyday memory. *American Psychologist, 44*, 1185–1193.

Barnard, P.J. (1985). Interacting cognitive subsystems: a psycholinguistic approach to short-term memory. In A.Ellis (Ed.), *Progress in the psychology of language* (Vol. 2). London: Erlbaum.

Barnard, P.J. (1991). Bridging between basic theories and the artefacts of human–computer interaction. In J.M. Carroll (Ed.), *Designing interaction: Psychology at the human computer interface*. Cambridge: Cambridge University Press.

Barnard, P.J. (1999). Interacting cognitive subsystems: modelling working memory phenomena within a multiprocessor architecture. In A. Miyake & P. Shah (Eds.), *Models of working memory: Mechanisms of active maintenance and executive control*. Cambridge: Cambridge University Press.

Bartlett, D., & Moody, S. (2000). *Dyslexia in the workplace*. London: Whurr.

REFERENCES

Bartlett, F.C. (1932). *Remembering*. Cambridge: Cambridge University Press.

Baumeister, R.F. (1984). Choking under pressure: self-consciousness and paradoxical effects of incentives on skilful performance. *Journal of Personality and Social Psychology, 46*, 610–610.

Baumeister, R.F., & Showers, C.J. (1986). A review of paradoxical performance effects: choking under pressure in sports and mental tests. *European Journal of Social Psychology, 16*, 361–383.

Behrmann, M., & Byng, S. (1992). A cognitive approach to the neurorehabilitation of acquired language disorders. In D.I. Margolin (Ed.), *Cognitive Neuropsychology in Clinical Practice*. Oxford University Press: New York.

Bennett, P.J. (1986). Face recall: a police perspective. *Human Learning: Journal of Practical Research and Applications, 5*, 197–202.

Berndt, R.S., Haendiges, A.N., Mitchum, C.C., & Wayland, S.C. (1996). An investigation of non-lexical reading impairments. *Cognitive Neuropsychology, 13*, 762–801.

Berry, D., & Broadbent, D.E. (1984). On the relationship between task performance and associated verbalisable knowledge. *Quarterly Journal of Experimental Psychology, 36A*, 209–231.

Biederman, I., Cooper, E.E., Fox, P.W., & Mahadevan, R.S. (1992). Unexceptional spatial memory in an exceptional memorist. *Journal of Experimental Psychology: Learning, Memory, and Cognition, 18*, 654–657.

Bjork, R.A. (1999). Assessing our own competence: heuristics and illusions. In D. Gopher & A. Koriat (Eds.), *Attention and performance XVII. Cognitive regulation of performance: Interaction of theory and application*. Cambridge, MA: MIT Press.

Bjork, R.A., & Bjork, E.L. (1992). A new theory of disuse and an old theory of stimulus fluctuation. In A. Healey, S. Kosslyn, & R. Shiffrin (Eds.), *From learning processes to cognitive processes: Essays in honour of William K. Estes* (Vol. 2). Hillsdale, NJ: Erlbaum.

Bjork, R.A., & Geiselman, R.E. (1978). Constituent processes in the differentiation of items in memory. *Journal of Experimental Psychology: Human Learning and Memory, 4*, 344–361.

Black, S.L., & Koulis-Chitwood, A. (1990). The menstrual cycle and typing skill: an ecologically valid study of the "raging hormones" hypothesis. *Canadian Journal of Behavioural Science, 22*, 445–455.

Blackmore, S. (1984). A postal survey of OBEs and other experiences. *Journal of the Society for Psychical Research, 52*, 225–244.

Blackmore, S., & Troscianko, T. (1985). Belief in the paranormal: probability judgements, illusory control, and the "chance baseline shift". *British Journal of Psychology, 76*, 459–468.

Blauert, J. (1969). Sound localisation in the median plane. *Acustica, 22*, 205–213.

Bolla, K.I., Rothman, R., & Cadet, J.L. (1999). Dose-related neurobehavioural effects of chronic cocaine use. *Journal of Neuropsychiatry and Clinical Neurosciences, 11*, 361–369.

Bonnefond, A., Muzet, A., Winter-Dill, A.-S. *et al.* (2001). Innovative working schedule: introducing one short nap during the night shift. *Ergonomics, 44*, 937–945.

Bonnet, M.H., & Arnaud, D.L. (1994). The use of prophylactic naps and caffeine to maintain performance during a continuous operation. *Ergonomics, 37*, 1009–1020.

Boon, J.C., & Noon, E. (1994). Changing perspectives in cognitive interviewing. *Psychology, Crime and Law, 1*, 59–69.

Bourne, L.E., & Archer, E.J. (1956). Time continuously on target as a function of distribution of practice. *Journal of Experimental Psychology, 51*, 25–33.

Bower, G.H. (1967). A multi-component theory of the memory trace. In K.W. Spence and J.T. Spence (Eds.), *The psychology of learning and motivation* (Vol. 1). New York: Academic Press.

Bower, G.H. (1970). Imagery as a relational organiser in associative learning. *Journal of Verbal Learning and Verbal Behaviour, 9*, 529–533.

Brace, N., Pike, G., & Kemp, R. (2000). Investigating E-FIT using famous faces. In A. Czerederecka, T. Jaskiewicz-Obydzinska, & J. Wojcikiewicz (Eds.), *Forensic psychology and law*. Krakow: Institute of Forensic Research Publishers.

Bregman, A.S. (1990). *Auditory scene analysis*. Cambridge, MA: MIT Press.

Bregman, A.S. (1993). Auditory scene analysis: hearing in complex environments. In S. MacAdams and E. Bigand (Eds.), *Thinking in sound: The cognitive psychology of human audition*. Oxford: Clarendon Press.

Bregman, A.S., & Pinker, S. (1978). Auditory streaming and the building of timbre. *Canadian Journal of Psychology, 32*, 19–31.

Brewster, S.A., Wright, P.C., & Edwards, A.D.N. (1992). A detailed investigation into the effectiveness of earcons. In G. Kramer (Ed.), *Auditory Display, Sonification, Audification and Auditory Interfaces: Proceedings of the First International Conference on Auditory Display*. Santa Fe, NM: Addison-Wesley.

Brice, C., & Smith, A. (2001). The effects of caffeine on simulated driving performance, subjective alertness and sustained attention. *Human Psychopharmacology: Clinical and Experimental, 16*, 523–531.

Brigham, J.C., & Wolfskeil, M.P. (1983). Opinions of attorneys and law enforcement personnel on the accuracy of eyewitness identifications. *Law and Human Behavior, 7*, 337–349.

British Psychological Society (1999). *Dyslexia, literacy and psychological assessment*. Report of the Working Party of the Division of Educational and Child Psychology. Leicester: BPS.

Broadbent, D.E. (1958). *Perception and communication*. Oxford: Pergamon Press.

Broadbent, D.E. (1971) *Decision and stress*. London: Academic Press.

Broadbent, D.E. (1980). The minimisation of models. In A.J. Chapman & D.M. Jones (Eds.), *Models of man*. Leicester: British Psychological Society.

Broadbent, D.E. (1982). Task combination and the selective intake of information. *Acta Psychologica, 50*, 253–290.

Broadbent, D.E., Cooper, P.F., Fitzgerald, P., & Parkes, K.R. (1982). The Cognitive Failures Questionnaire (CFQ) and its correlates. *British Journal of Clinical Psychology, 21*, 1–16.

Broman, M. (2001). Spaced retrieval: a behavioural approach to memory improvement in Alzheimer's and related dementias. *NYS-Psychologist, 13*, 31–34.

Broverman, D.M., Klaiber, E.L., & Vogel, W. (1980). Gonadal sex hormones and cognitive functioning. In J.E. Parsons (Ed.), *The psychobiology of sex differences and sex roles*. New York: McGraw-Hill.

Broverman, D.M., Vogel, W., Klaiber, E.L. *et al.* (1981). Changes in cognitive task performance across the menstrual cycle. *Journal of Comparative and Physiological Psychology, 95*, 646–654.

Brown, R., & Kulik, J. (1977). Flashbulb memories. *Cognition, 5*, 73–99.

Brown, R., & McNeill, D. (1966). The "tip-of-the-tongue" phenomenon. *Journal of Verbal Learning and Verbal Behaviour, 5*, 325–337.

Bruce, V., Henderson, Z., Greenwood, K. *et al.* (1999). Verification of face identities from images captured on video. *Journal of Experimental Psychology: Applied, 5*, 339–360.

Bruce, V., & Young, A. (1986). Understanding face recognition. *British Journal of Psychology, 77*, 305–327.

Bryant, P., & Impey, L. (1986). The similarities between normal readers and developmental and acquired dyslexics. *Cognition, 24*, 121–137.

Bub, D., Cancelliere, A., & Kertesz, A. (1985). Whole-word and analytic translation of spelling to sound in a non-semantic reader. In K.E. Patterson, J.C. Marshall, & M. Coltheart

(Eds.), *Surface dyslexia: Neuropsychological and cognitive studies of phonological reading*. London: Erlbaum.

Bull, R., & Clifford, R. (1984). Earwitness voice recognition accuracy. In G.L. Wells and E.F. Loftus (Eds.), *Eyewitness testimony: Psychological perspectives*. Cambridge: Cambridge University Press.

Burian, S.E., Ligouri, A., & Robinson, J.H. (2002). Effects of alcohol on risk taking during simulated driving. *Human Psychopharmacology: Clinical and Experimental, 17,* 141–150.

Bussemakers, M.P., & de Haan, A. (2000). When it sounds like a duck and it looks like a dog ... Auditory icons vs. earcons in multimedia environments. In P.R. Cook (Ed.), *Proceedings of the 6th International Conference on Auditory Display*. Atlanta, GA: International Community for Auditory Display.

Butler, L.F., & Frank, E.M. (2000). Neurolinguistic function and cocaine abuse. *Journal of Medical Speech Language Pathology, 8,* 199–212.

Buzan, T. (1974). *Use your head*. London: BBC Books.

Byrne, M.D., & Bovair, S. (1997). A working memory model of a common procedural error. *Cognitive Science, 21,* 31–62.

Camp, C.J., & McKittrick, L.A. (1992). Memory interventions in Alzheimer's type dementia populations: methodological and theoretical issues. In R.L. West & J.D. Sinnott (Eds.), *Everyday memory and ageing: Current research and methodology*. New York: Springer-Verlag.

Campbell, J.I.D. (1994). Architectures for numerical cognition. *Cognition, 53,* 1–44.

Campbell, J.I.D., & Clark, J.M. (1992). Cognitive number processing: an encoding-complex perspective. In J.I.D. Campbell (Ed.), *The nature and origins of mathematical skills*. Advances in Psychology #91. Amsterdam: North-Holland.

Candel, I., Jelicik, M., Merckelbach, H., & Wester, A. (2003). Korsakoff patients' memories of September 11, 2001. *Journal of Nervous and Mental Disease, 191,* 262–265.

Caramazza, A. (1989). Cognitive neuropsychology and rehabilitation: an unfulfilled promise? In X. Seron & G. Deloche (Eds.), *Cognitive approaches in neuropsychological rehabilitation*. Hillsdale, NJ: Erlbaum.

Card, S.K., Moran, T.P., & Newell, A. (1983). *The psychology of human–computer interaction*. Hillsdale, NJ: Erlbaum.

Casagrande, M., Violani, C., Curcio, G., & Bertini, M. (1997). Assessing vigilance through a brief pencil and paper letter cancellation task (LCT): effects of one night of sleep deprivation and time of day. *Ergonomics, 40,* 613–630.

Castles, A., & Coltheart, M. (1993). Varieties of developmental dyslexia. *Cognition, 24,* 121–137.

Chandler, P., & Sweller, J. (1992). The split-attention effect as a factor in the design of instruction. *British Journal of Educational Psychology, 62,* 233–246.

Chapman, L.J., & Chapman J.P. (1969). Illusory correlation as an obstacle to the use of valid diagnostic signs. *Journal of Abnormal Psychology, 74,* 271–280.

Chase, W.G., & Ericsson, K.A. (1981). Skilled memory. In J.R. Anderson (Ed.), *Cognitive skills and their acquisition*. Hillsdale, NJ: Erlbaum.

Chase, W.G., & Ericsson, K.A. (1982). Skill and working memory. In G.H. Bower (Ed.), *The psychology of learning and motivation* (Vol. 16). New York: Academic Press.

Cherry, E.C. (1953). Some experiments on the recognition of speech with one and with two ears. *Journal of the Acoustical Society of America, 25,* 975–979.

Chincotta, D., Underwood, G., Ghani, K.A., Papadopoulou, E., & Wresinski, M. (1999). Memory span for Arabic numerals and digit words: evidence for a limited capacity visuo-spatial storage system. *Quarterly Journal of Experimental Psychology, 52A,* 325–351.

Chrisler, J.C., Johnston, I.K., Champagne, N.M., & Preston, K.E. (1994). Menstrual joy: the construct and its consequences. *Psychology of Women Quarterly, 18*, 375–388.

Christie, D.F., & Ellis, H.D. (1981). Photofit constructions versus verbal descriptions of faces. *Journal of Applied Psychology, 66*, 358–363.

Chu, S., & Downes, J.J. (2000). Long live Proust: the odour-cued autobiographical memory bump. *Cognition, 75*, B41–B50.

Ciocca, V., & Bregman, A.S. (1987). Perceived continuity of gliding and steady-state tones through interrupting noise. *Perception and Psychophysics, 42*, 476–484.

Clark, H.H., & Clarke, E.V. (1977). *Psychology and language*. New York: Harcourt Brace Jovanovich.

Clark, J.M., & Campbell, J.I.D. (1991). Integrated versus modular theories of number skills and acalculia. *Brain and Cognition, 17*, 204–239.

Clifford, B.R., & Davies, G.M. (1989). Procedures for obtaining identification evidence. In D.C. Raskin (Ed.), *Psychological methods in criminal investigation and evidence*. London: Routledge.

Clifford, B.R., & George, R. (1996). A field investigation of training in three methods of witness/victim investigative interviewing. *Psychology, Crime and Law, 2*, 231–248.

Clifford, B.R., & Gwyer, P. (1999). The effects of the cognitive interview and other methods of context reinstatement on identification. *Psychology, Crime and Law, 5*, 61–80.

Cole, J., Sumnall, H.R., & Grob, C.S. (2002). Sorted: ecstasy facts and fiction. *The Psychologist, 15*, 464–467.

Collins, P., Maguire, M., & O'Dell, L. (2002). Smokers' representations for their own smoking: a Q-methodological study. *Journal of Health Psychology, 7*, 641–652.

Coltheart, M. (1980a). Deep dyslexia: a review of the syndrome. In M. Coltheart, K.E. Patterson, & J.C. Marshall (Eds.), *Deep dyslexia*. London: Routledge & Kegan Paul.

Coltheart, M. (1980b). Deep dyslexia: a right hemisphere hypothesis. In M. Coltheart, K.E. Patterson, & J.C. Marshall (Eds.), *Deep dyslexia*. London: Routledge & Kegan Paul.

Coltheart, M. (1983). The right hemisphere and disorders of reading. In A.W. Young (Ed.), *Functions of the right cerebral hemisphere*. London: Academic Press.

Coltheart, M. (1986). Cognitive neuropsychology. In M. Posner & O.S.M. Marin (Eds.), *Attention and performance XI*. Hillsdale, NJ: Erlbaum.

Coltheart, M., & Byng, S. (1989). A treatment for surface dyslexia. In X.Seron & G. Deloche (Eds.), *Cognitive approaches to neuropsychological rehabilitation*. Hillsdale, NJ: Erlbaum.

Coltheart, M. & Funnell, E. (1987). Reading and writing: one lexicon or two? In D.A. Allport, D.G. MacKay, W. Prinz, & E. Scheerer (Eds.), *Language perception and production: Shared mechanisms in listening, reading and writing*. London: Academic Press.

Coltheart, M., Langdon, R., & Haller, M. (1995). Simulation of acquired dyslexias by the DRC model, a computational model of visual word recognition and reading aloud. In *Proceedings of the 1995 Workshop on Neural Modelling of Cognitive and Brain Disorders*. College Park, MD: University of Maryland.

Coltheart, M., Masterson, J., Byng, S., Prior, M., & Riddoch, J. (1983). Surface dyslexia. *Quarterly Journal of Experimental Psychology, 35A*, 469–495.

Connors, E., Lundregan, T., Miller, N., & McEwan, T. (1996). *Convicted by juries, exonerated by science: Case studeis in the use of DNA evidence to establish innocence after trial*. Alexandria, VA: National Institute of Justice.

Conway, M.A. (1991). Cognitive psychology in search of meaning: the study of autobiographical memory. *The Psychologist, 4*, 301–305.

Conway, M.A. (1994). *Flashbulb memories*. Hove, UK: Psychology Press.

Conway, M.A., Anderson, S.J., Larsen, S.F. *et al.* (1994). The formation of flashbulb memories. *Memory and Cognition, 22*, 326–343.

Conway, M.A., Turk, D.J., Miller, S.L. *et al.* (1999). A positron-emission tomography (PET) study of autobiographical memory retrieval. *Memory, 7,* 679–702.

Cook, S., & Wilding, J. (1997a). Earwitness testimony: never mind the variety, hear the length. *Applied Cognitive Psychology, 11,* 95–111.

Cook, S., & Wilding, J. (1997b). Earwitness testimony 2: voices, faces and context. *Applied Cognitive Psychology, 11,* 527–541.

Corfitsen, M.T. (1994). Tiredness and visual reaction time among young male nighttime drivers: a roadside survey. *Accident Analysis and Prevention, 26,* 617–624.

Corfitsen, M.T. (1996). Enhanced tiredness among young impaired male nighttime drivers. *Accident Analysis and Prevention, 28,* 155–162.

Cornish, D.B. (1989) *Gambling: A review of the literature*. London: HMSO.

Coslett, H.B. (1991). Read but not write "idea": evidence for a third reading mechanism. *Brain and Language, 40,* 425–443.

Coslett, H.B. (2000). Acquired dyslexia. In M.J. Farah & T.E. Feinberg (Eds.), *Patient-Based Approaches to Cognitive Neuroscience*. Cambridge, MA: MIT Press.

Courneya, K.S., & Carron, A.V. (1992). The home advantage in sport competitions: a literature review. *Journal of Sport and Exercise Psychology, 14,* 13–27.

Craig, A., & Condon, R. (1985). Speed–accuracy trade-off and time of day. *Acta Psychologia, 58,* 115–122.

Craig, A., Davies, D.R., & Matthews, G. (1987). Diurnal variation, task characteristics and vigilance performance. *Human Factors, 29,* 675–684.

Craik, F.I.M. (1977). Depth of processing in recall and recognition. In S. Dornik (Ed.), *Attention and performance VI*. New York: Raven Press.

Craik, F.I.M. (2002). Levels of processing: past, present . . . and future? *Memory, 10,* 305–318.

Craik, F.I.M., Anderson, N.D., Kerr, S.A., & Li, K.Z.H. (1995). Memory changes in normal ageing. In A.D. Baddeley, B.A. Wilson, & F.N. Watts (Eds.), *Handbook of memory disorders*. Chichester, UK: Wiley.

Craik, F.I.M., & Lockhart, R.S. (1972). Levels of processing: a framework for memory research. *Journal of Verbal Learning and Verbal Behaviour, 11,* 671–684.

Craik, F.I.M., & Tulving, E. (1975). Depth of processing and the retention of words in episodic memory. *Journal of Experimental Psychology: General, 104,* 268–294.

Croft, R.J., Mackay, A.J., Mills, A.T.D., & Gruzeiler, J.G.D. (2001). The relative contributions of ecstasy and cannabis to cognitive impairment. *Psychopharmacology, 153,* 373–379.

Crovitz, H.F., & Schiffman, H. (1974). Frequency of episodic memories as a function of their age. *Bulletin of the Psychonomic Society, 4,* 517–518.

Curci, A., Luminet, O., Finkenauer, C., & Gisle, L. (2001). Flashbulb memories in social groups: a comparative test–retest study of the memory of French President Mitterand's death in a French and a Belgian group. *Memory, 9,* 81–101.

Curran, V. (2000). Is MDMA (ecstasy) neurotoxic in humans? An overview of evidence and methodological problems in research. *Neuropsychobiology, 42,* 34–41.

Cutler, B.L., Penrod, S.D., & Dexter, H.R. (1990). Juror sensitivity to eyewitness identification evidence. *Law and Human Behavior, 14,* 185–191.

Cutler, B.L., Penrod, S.D., & Martens, T.K. (1987). The reliability of eyewitness identification: the role of system and estimator variables. *Law and Human Behavior, 11,* 233–258.

Cutler, W.B., & Garcia, C.R. (1980). The psychoneuroendocrinology of the ovulatory cycle of woman. *Psychoneuroendocrinology, 5,* 89–111.

Cutting, J.E., & Rosner, B.S. (1976). Discrimination functions predicted from categories in speech and music. *Perception and Psychophysics, 20,* 87–88.

Dalton, K. (1960). Effect of menstruation on schoolgirls' weekly work. *British Medical Journal, i,* 326–328.

Dalton, K. (1968). Menstruation and examinations. *Lancet, 11*, 1386–1388.

Daneman, M., & Carpenter, P.A. (1980). Individual differences in working memory and reading. *Journal of Verbal Learning and Verbal Behaviour, 19*, 450–466.

Dark, V.J., & Benbow, C.P. (1991). Differential enhancement of working memory with mathematical versus verbal precocity. *Journal of Educational Psychology, 83*, 48–60.

Das, M., & Chattopadhyay, P.K. (1982). Arousal in menstruation: a study with some CNS measures. *Indian Journal of Clinical Psychology, 9*, 99–104.

Davidson, P.S.R., & Glisky, E.L. (2002). Is flashbulb memory a special instance of source memory? Evidence form older adults. *Memory, 10*, 99–111.

Davies, G.M., Van der Willik, P., & Morrieson, L.J. (2000). Facial composite production: a comparison of mechanical and computer-driven systems. *Journal of Applied Psychology, 85*, 119–124.

Dawkins, R. (1998). *Unweaving the rainbow*. London: Penguin.

De Bene, R., & Moe, A. (2003). Presentation modality effects in studying passages: are mental images always effective? *Applied Cognitive Psychology, 17*, 309–324.

Dehaene, S. (1992). Varieties of numerical abilities. *Cognition, 44*, 1–42.

Dehaene, S., Bossini, S., & Giraux, P. (1993). The mental representation of parity and number magnitude. *Journal of Experimental Psychology: General, 122*, 371–396.

Dehaene, S., & Cohen, L. (1995). Towards an anatomical and functional model of number processing. *Mathematical Cognition, 1*, 83–120.

Dejerine, J. (1892). Contribution a l'etude anatomo-pathologique et clinique des differentes varietes de cecite verbale. *Compte Rendu Hebdomadaire des Seances et Memoires de la Societe de Biologie, 4*, 61–90.

Dekle, D.J., Beale, C.R., Elliott, R., & Huneycutt, D. (1996). Children as witnesses: a comparison of lineup versus showup identification methods. *Applied Cognitive Psychology, 10*, 1–12.

Delaney, J., Lupton, M.J., & Toth, E. (1987). *The curse: A cultural history of menstruation*. Urbana, IL: University of Illinois Press.

Dempster, F.N. (1987). Effects of variable encoding and spaced presentations on vocabulary learning. *Journal of Educational Psychology, 79*, 162–170.

Dempster, F.N. (1988). The spacing effect: a case study of the failure to apply the results of psychological research. *American Psychologist, 43*, 627–634.

Department for Education and Employment (1997). *Disability Discrimination Act 1995: The Employment Provisions and Small Employers: A Review*. London: DfEE.

Department of Health (1998). *Smoking Kills: A White Paper on Tobacco*. London: Stationery Office.

Derousne, J., & Beauvois, M.F. (1979). Phonological processes in reading: data from alexia. *Journal of Neurology, Neurosurgery and Psychiatry, 42*, 1123–1132.

De Sa, V. (1999). Combining unimodal classifiers to improve learning. In H. Ritter, H. Cruse, & J. Dean (Eds.), *Prerational intelligence: Adaptive behavior and intelligent systems without symbols and logic* (Vol. 2). Dordrecht: Kluwer Academic.

Dix, A., Finlay, J., Abowd, G., & Beale, R. (1998). *Human–computer interaction* (2nd edn.). Harlow, UK: Prentice-Hall.

Dodge, R. (1982). Circadian rhythms and fatigue: a discrimination of their effects on performance. *Aviation, Space and Environmental Medicine, 53*, 1131–1136.

Dodson, C., & Reisberg, D. (1991). Indirect testing of eyewitness memory: the (non) effect of misinformation. *Bulletin of the Psychonomic Society, 29*, 333–336.

Doty, R.L., Snyder, P.J., Huggins, G.R., & Lowry, L.D. (1981). Endocrine, cardiovascular and psychological correlates of olfactory sensitivity changes during the human menstrual cycle. *Journal of Comparative and Physiological Psychology, 95*, 45–60.

Drugscope (2000). *UK drug situation: UK report to the European Monitoring Centre for Drugs and Drug Addiction* (*EMCDDA*). Available at: http://www.drugscope.org.uk/druginfo/ trends/ukdrugsit2000.pdf (retrieved 31 May 2003).

Dryenfurth, I., Jewelewicz, R., Waren, M., Ferin, M., & Vande Wiele, R.L. (1974). Temporal relationships of hormonal variables across the menstrual cycle. In M.M. Ferin, F. Halberg, M. Richart, & R.C. VandeWiele (Eds.). *Biorhythms in human reproduction*. New York: Wiley.

Durgin, F.H., & Proffitt, D.R. (1996). Visual learning in the perception of texture: simple and contingent aftereffects of texture density. *Spatial Vision, 9*, 423–474.

Dye, L. (1992). Visual information processing and the menstrual cycle. In J.T.E. Richardson (Ed.), *Cognition and the menstrual cycle*. New York: Springer-Verlag.

Easterbrook, J.A. (1959). The effect of emotion on cue utilisation and the organisation of behaviour. *Psychological Review, 66*, 183–201.

Easton, R.D., & Basala, M. (1982). Perceptual dominance during lipreading. *Perception and Psychophysics, 32*, 562–570.

Ebbinghaus, H. (1885). *Uber das Gedachtnis: Untersuchugen zur experimentellen Psychologie*. Leipzig: Dunker & Humbolt.

Ehrenreich, H., Rinn, T., Kunert, H.J. *et al.* (1999). Specific attentional dysfunction in adults following early start of cannabis use. *Psychopharmacology, 142*, 295–301.

Einthorn, H.J., & Hogarth, R.M. (1978). Confidence in judgement: persistence of the illusion of validity. *Psychological Review, 85*, 395–416.

Ellis, A.W., Lambon Ralph, M.A., Morris, J., & Hunter, A. (2000). Surface dyslexia: description, treatment, and interpretation. In E. Funnell (Ed.), *Case studies in the neuropsychology of reading*. Philadelphia, PA: Psychology Press.

Ellis, A.W., & Young A.W. (1988). *Human cognitive neuropsychology*. Hove, UK: Erlbaum.

Ellis, A.W., & Young, A.W. (1995). *Human cognitive neuropsychology: A textbook with readings*. Hove, UK: Psychology Press.

Ellis, D. (1995). Hard problems in computational auditory scene analysis. Posted to the AUDITORY email list, August. Available at: http://web.media.mit.edu/~dpwe/writing/ hard-probs.html (retrieved 5 July 2004).

Ellis, H.D., Davies, G.M., & Shepherd, J.W. (1978). A critical examination of the Photofit system for recalling faces. *Ergonomics, 21*, 297–307.

Engle, R.W., Kane, M.J., & Tuholski, S.W. (1999). Individual differences in working memory capacity and what they tell us about controlled attention, general fluid intelligence, and functions of the prefrontal cortex. In A. Miyake & P. Shah (Eds.), *Models of working memory: Mechanisms of active maintenance and executive control*. Cambridge: Cambridge University Press.

Epting, L.K., & Overman, W.H. (1998). Sex sensitive tasks in men and women: a search for performance fluctuations across the menstrual cycle. *Behavioural Neuroscience, 112*, 1304–1317.

Er, N. (2003). A new flashbulb memory model applied to the Marmara earthquake. *Applied Cognitive Psychology, 17*, 503–517.

Ewald Jackson, N., & Coltheart, M. (2001). *Routes to reading success and failure: Towards an integrated cognitive psychology of atypical reading*. Philadelphia, PA: Psychology Press.

Farris, E. (1956). *Human ovulation and fertility*. New York: Pitman.

Fenigstein, A., Scheier, M.F., & Buss, A.H. (1975). Public and private self-consciousness: assessment and theory. *Journal of Consulting and Clinical Psychology, 43*, 522–527.

Fenner, J., Heathcote, D., & Jerrams-Smith, J. (2000). The development of wayfinding competency: asymmetrical effects of visuo-spatial and verbal ability. *Journal of Environmental Psychology, 20*, 165–175.

Fischoff, B. (1977). Hindsight is not equal to foresight: the effect of outcome knowledge on judgement under uncertainty. *Journal of Experimental Psychology: Human Perception and Performance, 1*, 288–299.

Fischoff, B., & Beyth, R. (1975). "I knew it would happen". Remembered probabilities of once-future things. *Organisational Behaviour and Human Performance, 13*, 1–16.

Fisher, H.G., & Freedman, S.J. (1968). The role of the pinna in auditory localization. *Journal of Auditory Research, 8*, 15–26.

Fisher, R.P., & Geiselman, R.E. (1992). *Memory-enhancing techniques for investigative interviewing: The cognitive interview.* Springfield, IL: Charles C. Thomas.

Fisher, R.P., Geiselman, R.E., & Amador, M. (1990). A field test of the cognitive interview: enhancing the recollections of actual victims and witnesses of crime. *Journal of Applied Psychology, 74*, 722–727.

Fisher, R.P., Geiselman, R.E., Raymond, D.S., Jurkevich, L.M., & Warhaftig, M.L. (1987). Enhancing enhanced eyewitness memory: refining the cognitive interview. *Journal of Police Science and Administration, 15*, 291–297.

Fitts, P.M., & Posner, M.I. (1967). *Human performance.* Belmont, CA: Brooks/Cole.

Fitzgibbon, G., & O'Connor, B. (2002). *Adult dyslexia: A guide for the workplace.* Chichester, UK: Wiley.

Flannery, S. (2000). *In code: A mathematical journey.* London: Profile.

Flin, R., Boon, J., Knox, A., & Bull, R. (1992). The effect of a five-month delay on children's and adults' eyewitness memory. *British Journal of Psychology, 83*, 323–336.

Folkard, S., & Monk, T.H. (1980). Circadian rhythms in human memory. *British Journal of Psychology, 71*, 295–307.

Fowler, F.D. (1980). Air traffic control problems: a pilot's view. *Human Factors, 22*, 645–653.

Frankenhauser, M., Myrsten, A.L., & Post, B. (1970). Psychophysiological reactions to cigarette smoking. *Scandinavian Journal of Psychology, 11*, 237–245.

French, P. (1994). An overview of forensic phonetics with particular reference to speaker identification. *Forensic Linguistics, 1*, 169–181.

Freud, S. (1905/1953). Three essays on sexuality. In J. Stracey (Ed.), *The standard edition of the complete psychological works of Sigmund Freud.* London: Hogarth Press.

Freud, S. (1938). Psychopathology of everyday life. In A.A. Brill (Ed.), *The writings of Sigmund Freud.* New York: Modern Library.

Freudenthal, D. (2001). Age differences in the performance of information retrieval tasks. *Behaviour and Information Technology, 20*, 9–22.

Fritz, C.O., Morris, P.E., Bjork, R.A., Gelman, R., & Wickens, T.D. (2000). When further learning fails: stability and change following repeated presentation of text. *British Journal of Psychology, 91*, 493–511.

Fruzzetti, A.E., Toland, K., Teller, S.A., & Loftus, E.F. (1992). Memory and eyewitness testimony. In M. Gruneberg & P. Morris (Eds.), *Aspects of memory: The practical aspects.* London: Routledge.

Fuerst, A.J., & Hitch, G.J. (2000). Separate roles for executive and phonological components of working memory in mental arithmetic. *Memory and Cognition, 28*, 774–782.

Funnell, E. (1983). Phonological processes in reading: new evidence from acquired dysgraphia. *British Journal of Psychology, 74*, 159–180.

Funnell, E. (2000). Deep dyslexia. In E. Funnell (Ed.), *Case studies in the neuropsychology of reading.* Hove, UK: Psychology Press.

Gabouy, A., Ladouceur, R., & Bussieres, O. (1989). Structures des lotteries et comportements des joueurs. *Revue de Psychologie Appliquee, 39*, 197–207.

Gallagher, M., & Colombo, P.J. (1995). Ageing: the cholinergic hypothesis of cognitive decline. *Current Opinion in Neurobiology, 5*, 161–168.

Galton, F. (1879). Psychometric experiments. *Brain, 2*, 149–162.

Galton, F. (1883). *Enquiries into human faculty and its development*. London: Macmillan.

Gandelman, R. (1983). Gonadal hormones and sensory function. *Neuroscience and Behavioural Reviews, 7*, 1–17.

Garcia-Larrea, L., Perchet, C., Perren, F., & Amendo, E. (2001). Interference of cellular phone conversations with visuomotor tasks: an ERP study. *Journal of Psychophysiology, 15*, 14–21.

Garland, D.J., Stein, E.S., & Muller, J.K. (1999). Air traffic controller memory: capabilities, limitations and volatility. In D.J. Garland & J.A. Wise (Eds.), *Handbook of aviation human factors: Human factors in transportation*. Mahwah, NJ: Erlbaum.

Gates, A.I. (1917). Recitation as a factor in memorising. *Archives of Psychology, 6* (whole of issue 40).

Gathercole, S.E., & Baddeley, A.D. (1993). *Working memory and language*. Hove, UK: Erlbaum.

Gaver, W.W. (1986) Auditory icons: using sound in computer interfaces. *Human–Computer Interaction, 2*, 167–177.

Gaver, W.W. (1989). The SonicFinder: an interface that uses auditory icons. *Human–Computer Interaction, 4*, 67–94.

Gaver, W.W. (1993). What in the world do we hear? An ecological approach to auditory event perception. *Ecological Psychology, 5*, 1–29.

Gazzaniga, M.S. (1983). Right hemisphere language following brain bisection: a 20 year perspective. *American Psychologist, 38*, 525–537.

Geary, D.C., & Widaman, K.F. (1992). Numerical cognition: on the convergence of componential and psychometric models. *Intelligence, 16*, 47–80.

Geiselman, R.E. (1999). Commentary on recent research with the cognitive interview. *Psychology, Crime and Law, 5*, 197–202.

Geiselman, R.E., & Fisher, R.P. (1997). Ten years of cognitive interviewing. In D.G. Payne & F.G. Conrad (Eds.), *Intersections in basic and applied memory research*. Mahwah, NJ: Erlbaum.

Geiselman, R.E., Fisher, R.P., MacKinnon, D.P., & Holland, H.L. (1985). Eyewitness memory enhancement in the police interview: cognitive retrieval mnemonics versus hypnosis. *Journal of Applied Psychology, 70*, 401–412.

Geiselman, R.E., Fisher, R.P., MacKinnon, D.P., & Holland, H.L. (1986). Eyewitness memory enhancement in the cognitive interview: cognitive retrieval mnemonics versus hypnosis. In L.S. Wrightsman & C.E. Wyllis (Eds.), *On the witness stand: Controversies in the courtroom* (Vol. 2). Thousand Oaks, CA: Sage.

Gibling, F., & Bennett, P. (1994). Artistic enhancement in the production of Photo-FIT likenesses: an examination of its effectiveness in leading to suspect identification. *Psychology, Crime and Law, 1*, 93–100.

Gibson, J.J. (1966). *The senses considered as perceptual systems*. Boston, MA: Houghton-Mifflin.

Gibson, J.J. (1979). *The ecological approach to visual perception*. Boston, MA: Houghton-Mifflin.

Gigerenzer, G. (1995). On narrow norms and vague heuristics: a reply to Kahneman and Tversky (1995). *Psychological Review, 103*, 592–596.

Gilbert, R.M. (1984). Caffeine consumption. In G.A. Spiller (Ed.), *Methylxanthine beverages and foods: Chemistry, consumption and health effects*. New York: Liss.

Gilovich, T., Wang, R.F., Regan, D., & Nishina, S. (2003). Regrets of action and inaction across cultures. *Journal of Cross-Cultural Psychology, 34*, 61–71.

Gitomer, D.H. (1988). Individual differences in technical troubleshooting. *Human Performance, 1*, 111–131.

Glenberg, A.M., & Adams, F. (1978). Type 1 rehearsal and recognition. *Journal of Verbal Learning and Verbal Behaviour, 17*, 455–463.

Glenberg, A.M., & Lehman, T.S. (1980). Spacing repetitions over 1 week. *Memory and Cognition*, *8*, 528–538.

Godden, D., & Baddeley, A.D. (1975). Context-dependent memory in two natural experiments: on land and under water. *British Journal of Psychology*, *66*, 325–331.

Gold, D.R., Rogacz, S., Bock, N. *et al.* (1992). Rotating shift-work, sleep and accidents related to sleepiness in hospital nurses. *American Journal of Public Health*, *82*, 1011–1014.

Goodman, R., & Caramazza, A. (1986). *The Johns Hopkins University Dyslexia Battery*. Unpublished manuscript, Johns Hopkins University, Baltimore, MD.

Gordon, B.N., Baker-Ward, L., & Ornstein, P.A. (2001). Children's testimony: a review of research on memory for past experiences. *Clinical Child and Family Psychology Review*, *4*, 157–181.

Gordon, H.W., Corbin, E.D., & Lee, P.A. (1986). Changes in specialised cognitive function following changes in hormones levels. *Cortex*, *22*, 399–415.

Gouzoulis-Mayfrank, E., Dauman, J., Tuchtenhagen, F. *et al.* (2000). Impaired cognitive performance in drug free users of recreational ecstasy (MDMA). *Journal of Neurology, Neuorsurgery and Psychiatry*, *68*, 719–725.

Graham, H. (1994). Gender and class as dimensions of smoking behaviour in Britain: insights from a survey of mothers. *Social Science and Medicine*, *38*, 691–698

Green, D.L., & Geiselman, R.E. (1989). Building composite facial images: effects of feature saliency and delay of construction. *Journal of Applied Psychology*, *74*, 714–721.

Greene, G. (1980). *Dr. Fischer of Geneva, or the bomb party*. London: The Bodley Head.

Greenspoon, J., & Ranyard, R. (1957). Stimulus conditions and retroactive inhibition. *Journal of Experimental Psychology*, *53*, 55–59.

Greenwald, M. (2000). The acquired dyslexias. In S. Nadeau, L. Gonzalez Rothi, & B. Crosson (Eds.), *Aphasia and language: Theory to practice*. New York: Guilford Press.

Gregory, R.L. (1972). Seeing as thinking. *Times Literary Supplement*, 23 June.

Griffiths, M.D. (1991). The psychobiology of the near miss in fruit machine gambling. *Journal of Psychology*, *125*, 347–357.

Griffiths, R.R., & Woodson, P.P. (1988). Caffeine and physical dependence: a review of human and laboratory animal studies. *Psychopharmacology*, *94*, 437–451.

Groeger, J.A. (1997). *Memory and remembering*. Harlow, UK: Longman.

Groeger, J.A. (2000). *Understanding driving: Applying cognitive psychology to a complex everyday task*. Hove, UK: Psychology Press.

Groome, D.H. (1999). Memory. In D.H. Groome *et al.*, *An introduction to cognitive psychology: Processes and disorders*. Hove, UK: Psychology Press.

Groome, D.H. (2003). Psychological and physiological aspects of panic disorder: the relationship between the psycho and the physio. In *Proceedings of the First International Conference on Panic Attacks and Panic Disorder*. Available at: http://anxiety-panic-.com/conference/c2003.htm

Groome D.H., Dewart, H., Esgate, A., Gurney, K., Kemp, R., & Towell, N. (1999). *An introduction to cognitive psychology: Processes and disorders*. Hove, UK: Psychology Press.

Groome, D.H., & Levay, L. (2003). The effect of articulatory suppression on free recall of auditory images, visual images, written words, and spoken words. In *Proceedings of the Annual Conference of the British Psychological Society*. Leicester: BPS.

Groome, D.H., & Soureti, A. (2004). PTSD and anxiety symptoms in children exposed to the 1999 Greek earthquake. *British Journal of Psychology*, *95*, 387–397.

Gruneberg, M.M. (1978). The feeling of knowing: memory blocks and memory aids. In M.M. Gruneberg & P.E. Morris (Eds.), *Aspects of memory*. London: Methuen.

Gruneberg, M.M. (1987). *Linkword French, German, Spanish, Italian, Greek, Portuguese*. London: Corgi Books.

Gruneberg, M.M., & Jacobs, G.C. (1991). In defence of Linkword. *The Language Learning Journal, 3*, 25–29.

Gruneberg, M.M., & Morris, P.E. (1982). Applying memory research. In M. Gruneberg & P. Morris (Eds.), *Aspects of memory, Vol. 1: The practical aspects*. London: Routledge.

Gruneberg, M.M., Morris, P.E., & Sykes, R.N. (1991). The obituary on everyday memory and its practical applications is premature. *American Psychologist, 46*, 74–76.

Guski, R. (1990). Auditory localization: effects of reflecting surfaces. *Perception, 19*, 819–830.

Haas, E.C., & Edworthy, J. (1996). Designing urgency into auditory warnings using pitch, speed and loudness. *Computing and Control Engineering Journal, 7*, 193–198.

Haber, R.N., & Myers, B.L. (1982). Memory for pictograms, pictures, and words separately and all mixed up. *Perception, 11*, 57–64.

Haberlandt, K. (1997). *Cognitive psychology* (2nd edn.). Needham Heights, MA: Allyn & Bacon.

Haigh, J. (1995). Inferring gamblers' choice of combinations in the National Lottery. *Bulletin of the Institute of Mathematics and its Applications, 31*, 132–136.

Hain, P. (1976). *Mistaken identity: The wrong face of the law*. London: Quartet Books.

Hameleers, P.A.H.M., Van Boxtel, M.P.J., Hogervorst, E. *et al.* (2000). Habitual caffeine consumption and its relation to memory, attention, planning capacity and psychomotor performance across multiple age groups. *Human Psychopharmacology: Clinical and Experimental, 15*, 573–581.

Hampson, E. (1990). Variations in sex-related cognitive abilities across the menstrual cycle. *Brain and Cognition, 14*, 26–43.

Hampson, E., & Kimura, D. (1988). Reciprocal effects of hormone fluctuations on human perceptual and motor skills. *Behavioural Neuroscience, 102*, 456–459.

Handel, S. (1989) *Listening: An introduction to the perception of auditory events*. Boston, MA: MIT Press.

Harris, J.D., & Sergeant, R.L. (1971). Monaural/binaural minimum audible angles for a moving sound source. *Journal of Speech and Hearing Research, 14*, 618–629.

Hartley, L.R., Arnold, P.K., Smythe, G., & Hansen, J. (1994). Indicators of fatigue in truck drivers. *Applied Ergonomics, 25*, 143–156.

Hartley, L.R., Lyons, D., & Dunne, M. (1987). Memory and the menstrual cycle. *Ergonomics, 30*, 111–120.

Hausmann, M., Slabbekoorn, D., Van Goozen, S.H.M., Cohen-Kettenis, P.T., & Guentuerkuen, O. (2000). Sex hormones affect spatial abilities during the menstrual cycle. *Behavioural Neuroscience, 114*, 1245–1250.

Hay, J.F., & Jacoby, L.L. (1996). Separating habit and recollection: memory slips, process dissociations, and probability matching. *Journal of Experimental Psychology: Learning, Memory and Cognition, 22*, 1323–1335.

Healy, D. (1987). Rhythm and blues: neurochemical, neuropharmacological and neuropsychological implications of a hypothesis of circadian rhythm dysfunction in affective disorders. *Psychopharmacology, 93*, 271–285.

Heard, K.V., & Chrisler, J.C. (1999). The Stereotypic Beliefs about Menstruation Scale. In D. Berg (Ed.), *Looking forward, looking back: The place of women's everyday lives in health research*. Scottsdale, AZ: Society for Menstrual Cycle Research.

Heathcote, D. (1994). The role of visuo-spatial working memory in the mental addition of multi-digit addends. *Current Psychology of Cognition, 13*, 207–245.

Hebrank, J., & Wright, D. (1974). Spectral cues used in the localisation of sound sources on the median plane. *Journal of the Acoustical Society of America, 56*, 1829–1834.

Heffernan, T.M., Jarvis, H., Rodgers, J., Scholey, A.B., & Ling, J. (2001). Prospective memory, everyday cognitive failure and central executive function in recreational users of ecstasy. *Human Psychopharmacology: Clinical and Experimental, 16*, 607–612.

Held, J.R., Riggs, M.L., & Dorman, C. (1999). The effect of prenatal cocaine exposure on neurobehavioural outcome: a meta-analysis. *Neurotoxicology and Teratology*, *21*, 619–625.

Herrmann, D., Raybeck, D., & Gruneberg, M. (2002). *Improving memory and study skills: Advances in theory and practice*. Ashland, OH: Hogrefe & Huber.

Hertel, P.T. (1992). Improving memory and mood through automatic and controlled procedures of mind. In D.J. Herrmann, H. Weingartner, A. Searleman, & C.L. McEvoy (Eds.), *Memory improvement: Implications for memory theory*. New York: Springer-Verlag.

Hewstone, M., Benn, W., & Wilson, A. (1988). Bias in the use of base rates: racial prejudice in decision-making. *Cognition*, *18*, 161–176.

Higbee, K. (1977). *Your memory: How it works and how to improve it*. Englewood Cliffs, NJ: Prentice-Hall.

Hill, E., & Williamson, J. (1998). Choose six numbers, any numbers. *The Psychologist*, *11*, 17–21.

Hill, S.Y., & Ryan, C. (1985). Brain damage in social drinkers? Reasons for caution. In M. Galanter (Ed.), *Recent developments in alcoholism* (Vol. 3). New York: Plenum Press.

Hitch, G.J. (1978). The role of short-term working memory in mental arithmetic. *Cognitive Psychology*, *10*, 302–323.

Hitch, G.J. (1980). Developing the concept of working memory. In G. Claxton (Ed.), *Cognitive psychology: New directions*. London: Routledge & Kegan Paul.

Ho, H.-Z., Gilger, J.W., & Brink, T. (1986). Effects of menstrual cycle on spatial information processes. *Perceptual and Motor Skills*, *63*, 743–751.

Holliday, R.E. (2003). Reducing misinformation effects in children with cognitive interviews: dissociating recollection and familiarity. *Child Development*, *74*, 728–751.

Homa, D., Haver, B., & Schwartz, T. (1976). Perceptibility of schematic face stimuli: evidence for a perceptual Gestalt. *Memory and Cognition*, *4*, 176–185.

Hope, J.A., & Sherrill, J.M. (1987). Characteristics of skilled and unskilled mental calculators. *Journal of Research in Mathematics Education*, *18*, 98–111.

Horne, J.A., & Ostberg, C.O. (1977). Individual differences in human circadian rhythm. *Biological Psychology*, *5*, 179–190.

Hornstein, S.L., Brown, A.S., & Mulligan, N.W. (2003). Long-term flashbulb memory for learning of Princess Diana's death. *Memory*, *11*, 293–306.

Horowitz, M.J. (1976). *Stress response syndromes*. New York: Aronson.

Horswill, M.S., & McKenna F.P. (1999). The effect of interference on dynamic risk-taking judgements. *British Journal of Psychology*, *90*, 189–200.

Howard, D., & Franklin, S. (1987). Three ways for understanding written words, and their use in two contrasting cases of surface dyslexia. In D.A. Allport, D. MacKay, W. Prinz, & E. Scheerer (Eds.), *Language perception and production: Common processes in listening, speaking, reading and writing*. London: Academic Press.

Howard, J.H., & Howard, D.V. (1997). Learning and memory. In A.D. Fisk & W.A. Rogers (Eds.), *Handbook of human factors and the older adult*. San Diego, CA: Academic Press.

Howe, M.L., & Courage, M.L. (1997). The emergence and early development of autobiographical memory. *Psychological Review*, *104*, 499–523.

Huang, X.D., Ariki, Y., & Jack, M.A. (1990) *Hidden Markov models for speech recognition*. Edinburgh: Edinburgh University Press.

Huguenard, B.R., Lerch, F.J., Junker, B.W., Patz, R.J., & Kass, R.E. (1997). Working memory failure in phone-based interaction. *ACM Transactions on Computer–Human Interaction*, *4*, 67–102.

Hull, C.L. (1943). *The principles of behaviour*. New York: Appleton-Century-Crofts.

Hunter, J.M.L. (1979). Memory in everyday life. In M.M. Gruneberg & P.E. Morris (Eds.), *Applied problems in memory*. New York: Academic Press.

Hyde, T.S., & Jenkins, J.J. (1969). The differential effects of incidental tasks on the organisation of recall of a list of highly associated words. *Journal of Experimental Psychology*, *82*, 472–481.

Hyman, I.E., & Loftus, E.F. (2002). False childhood memories and eyewitness memory errors. In M.L. Eisen (Ed.), *Memory and suggestibility in the forensic interview*. Mahwah, NJ: Erlbaum.

Istavan, J., & Matarazzo, J.D. (1984). Tobacco, alcohol and caffeine use: a review of their interrelationships. *Psychological Bulletin*, *95*, 301–326.

James, J.E. (1994). Does caffeine enhance or merely restore degraded psychomotor performance? *Neuorpsychobiology*, *30*, 124–125.

Jarvis, M.J. (1993). Does caffeine intake enhance absolute levels of cognitive performance? *Psychopharmacology*, *110*, 42–52.

Jeannerod, M. (1997). *The cognitive neuroscience of action*. Oxford: Blackwell.

Jenkins, J.J. (1985). Acoustic information for objects, places and events. In W.H. Warren & R.E. Shaw (Eds.), *Persistence and change: Proceedings of the First International Conference on Event Perception*. Hillsdale, NJ: Erlbaum.

Jerabek, I., & Standing, L. (1992). Imagined test situations produce contextual memory enhancement. *Perceptual and Motor Skills*, *75*, 400.

Jerrams-Smith, J., Heathcote, D., & White, L. (1999). Working memory span as a usability factor in a virtual community of elderly people. In L. Brooks and C. Kimble (Eds.), *Information systems: The next generation*. Maidenhead, UK: McGraw-Hill.

Johnson, R.D. (1987). Making judgements when information is missing: inferences, biases, and framing effects. *Acta Psychologica*, *98*, 377–389.

Jones, D. (1999). The cognitive psychology of auditory distraction: the 1997 BPS Broadbent Lecture. *British Journal of Psychology*, *90*, 167–187.

Jones, R.A. (2001). Proust's contribution to the psychology of memory: the reminiscences from the standpoint of cognitive science. *Theory and Psychology*, *11*, 255–271.

Jones, S.D., & Furner, S.M. (1989). The construction of audio icons and information cues for human–computer dialogues. In T. Megaw (Ed.), *Contemporary ergonomics: Proceedings of the Ergonomics Society's 1989 Annual Conference*. London: Taylor & Francis.

Kahneman, D., Slovic, P., & Tversky, A. (Eds.) (1982). *Judgement under uncertainty: Heuristics and biases*. Cambridge: Cambridge University Press.

Kahneman, D., & Tversky, A. (1973) On the psychology of prediction. *Psychological Review*, *80*, 237–251.

Kalyuga, S., Chandler, P., & Sweller, J. (1999). Managing split-attention and redundancy in multimedia instruction. *Applied Cognitive Psychology*, *13*, 351–371.

Kapardis, A. (1997). *Psychology and law: A critical introduction*. Cambridge: Cambridge University Press.

Kassin, S.M., Ellsworth, P.C. and Smith, V.L. (1989). The "general acceptance" of psychological research on eyewitness testimony: a survey of the experts. *American Psychologist*, *44*, 1089–1098.

Kassin, S.M., Tubb, V.A., Hosch, H.M., & Memon, A. (2001). On the "general acceptance" of eyewitness testimony research. *American Psychologist*, *56*, 405–416.

Kay, H. (1955). Learning and retaining verbal material. *British Journal of Psychology*, *46*, 81–100.

Kay, J., Lesser, R., & Coltheart, M. (1992). *Psycholinguistic Assessments of Language Processing in Aphasia (PALPA)*. Hillsdale, NJ: Erlbaum.

Kebbell, M.R. (2000). The law concerning the conduct of lineups in England and Wales: how well does it satisfy the recommendations of the American Psychology-Law Society? *Law and Human Behavior, 24,* 309–315.

Kebbell, M., & Milne, R. (1998). Police officers' perceptions of eyewitness performance in forensic investigations. *Journal of Social Psychology, 138,* 323–330.

Kebbell, M.R., Milne, R., & Wagstaff, G.F. (1999). The cognitive interview: a survey of its forensic effectiveness. *Psychology, Crime and Law, 5,* 101–115.

Keele, S.W. (1986). Motor control. In K.R. Boff, L.Kaufman, & J.P. Thomas (Eds.), *Handbook of perception and performance.* New York: Wiley.

Kelemen, W.L., & Creeley, C.E. (2001). Caffeine (4 mg/kg) influences sustained attention and delayed free recall but not memory predictions. *Human Psychopharmacology: Clinical and Experimental, 16,* 309–319.

Kemp, R., McManus, C., & Pigott, T. (1990). Sensitivity to the displacement of facial features in negative and inverted images. *Perception, 19,* 531–543.

Kemp, R., Pike, G.E., & Brace, N.A. (2001). Video based identification procedures: combining best practice and practical requirements when designing identification systems. *Psychology, Public Policy and Law, 7,* 802–807.

Kemp, R., Towell, N., & Pike, G. (1997). When seeing should not be believing: photographs, credit cards and fraud. *Applied Cognitive Psychology, 11,* 211–222.

Kerr, J.S., & Hindmarch, I. (1991). Alcohol, cognitive function and psychomotor performance. *Reviews on Environmental Health, 9,* 117–122.

Kerr, J.S., & Hindmarch, I. (1998). The effects of alcohol alone or in combination with other drugs on information processing, task performance and subjective responses. *Human Psychopharmacology: Clinical and Experimental, 13,* 1–9.

Kerr, J.S., Sherwood, N., & Hindmarch, I. (1991). Separate and combined effects of the social drugs on psychomotor performance. *Psychopharmacology, 104,* 113–119.

Kieras, D.E., & Meyer, D.E. (1997). An overview of the EPIC architecture for cognition and performance with application to human–computer interaction. *Human–Computer Interaction, 12,* 391–438.

Kieras, D.E., Meyer, D.E., Mueller, S., & Seymour, T. (1999). Insights into working memory from the perspective of the EPIC architecture for modelling skilled perceptual-motor and cognitive human performance. In A. Miyake & P. Shah (Eds.), *Models of working memory: Mechanisms of active maintenance and executive control.* Cambridge: Cambridge University Press.

Kimura, D. (1996). Sex, sexual orientation and sex hormones influence human cognitive function. *Current Opinion in Neurobiology, 6,* 259–263.

Kimura, D., & Hampson, E. (1994). Cognitive pattern in men and women is influenced by fluctuations in sex hormones. *Current Directions in Psychological Science, 3,* 57–61.

Klaiber, E.L., Broverman, D.M., Vogel, W., Kennedy, N.J., & Marks, P. (1982). Estrogens and CNS function: EEG, cognition and depression. In R.C. Friedman (Ed.), *Behaviour and the menstrual cycle.* New York: Marcel Dekker.

Klar, Y., & Giladi, E. (1997). No-one in my group can be below the group's average: a robust positivity bias in favour of anonymous peers. *Journal of Personality and Social Psychology, 73,* 885–901.

Knapp, B. (1963). *Skill in Sport.* London: Routledge.

Kneller, W., Memon, A., & Stevenage, S. (2001). Simultaneous and sequential lineups: decision processes of accurate and inaccurate eyewitnesses. *Applied Cognitive Psychology, 15,* 659–671.

Koehn, C.E., & Fisher, R.P. (1997). Constructing facial composites with the Mac-A-Mug Pro system. *Psychology, Crime and Law, 3,* 209–218.

Koehnken, G., & Maass, A. (1988). Eyewitness testimony: false alarms or biased instructions? *Journal of Applied Psychology, 73*, 363–370.

Koehnken, G., Milne, R., Memon, A., & Bull, R. (1999). The cognitive interview: a meta-analysis. *Psychology, Crime and Law, 5*, 3–27.

Koelega, H.S. (1998). Effects of caffeine, nicotine and alcohol on vigilance performance. In J. Snel & M.M. Lorist (Eds.), *Nicotine, caffeine and social drinking: Behaviour and brain function*. Amsterdam: Harwood Academic.

Koriat, A., & Goldsmith, M. (1996). Memory metaphors and the real-life/laboratory controversy: correspondence versus storehouse conceptions of memory. *Behavioural and Brain Sciences, 19*, 167–188.

Kubovy, M., & Van Valkenburg, D. (2001). Auditory and visual objects. *Cognition, 80*, 97–126.

Künzel, H. (1994). On the problem of speaker identification by victims and witnesses. *Forensic Linguistics, 1*, 45–57.

Kurzthaler, I., Hummer, M., Miller, C. *et al.* (1999). Effect of cannabis use on cognitive functions and driving ability. *Journal of Clinical Psychiatry, 60*, 395–399.

Kyllonen, P.C. (1996). Is working memory capacity Spearman's g? In I. Dennis & P. Tapsfield (Eds.), *Human abilities: Their nature and measurement*. Hillsdale, NJ: Erlbaum.

Kyllonen, P.C., & Christal, R.E. (1990). Reasoning ability is (little more than) working memory capacity. *Intelligence, 14*, 389–433.

Kyllonen, P.C., & Stephens, D.L. (1990). Cognitive abilities as determinants of success in acquiring logic skill. *Learning and Individual Differences, 2*, 129–160.

Lahtinen, V., Lonka, K., & Lindblom-Ylanne, K. (1997). Spontaneous study strategies and the quality of knowledge construction. *British Journal of Educational Psychology, 67*, 13–24.

Lakoff, G., & Johnson, M. (1999). *Philosophy in the flesh: The embodied mind and its challenge to western thought*. New York: Basic Books.

Lamberty, G.J., Beckwith, B.E., & Petros, T.V. (1990). Posttrial treatment with ethanol enhances recall of prose narratives. *Physiology and Behaviour, 48*, 653–658.

Lamble, D., Kauranen, T., Laasko, M., & Summala, H. (1999). Cognitive load and detection thresholds in car following situations: safety implications for using mobile (cellular) telephones while driving. *Accident Analysis and Prevention, 31*, 617–623.

Landauer T.K., & Bjork, R.A. (1978). Optimal rehearsal patterns and name learning. In M.M. Gruneberg, P.E. Morris, & R.N. Sykes (Eds.), *Practical aspects of memory*. London: Academic Press.

Lane, J.D., & Rose, J.E. (1995). Effects of daily caffeine intake on smoking behaviour in the natural environment. *Experimental and Clinical Psychopharmacology, 3*, 49–55.

Lang A.J., Craske M.G., & Bjork R.A. (1999). Implications of a new theory of disuse for the treatment of emotional disorders. *Clinical Psychology: Science and Practice, 6*, 80–94.

Langer, E.J. (1975). The illusion of control. *Journal of Personality and Social Psychology, 32*, 311–328.

Langer, E.J., & Roth, J. (1975). Heads I win, tails it's chance: the illusion of control as a function of the sequence of outcomes in a purely chance task. *Journal of Personality and Social Psychology, 32*, 951–955.

Larsson, A.S., Granhag, P.A., & Spjut, E. (2003). Children's recall and the cognitive interview: do the positive effects hold over time? *Applied Cognitive Psychology, 17*, 203–214.

Laughery, K.R., & Fowler, R.H. (1980). Sketch artists and Identikit procedures for recalling faces. *Journal of Applied Psychology, 65*, 307–316.

Le Houezec, J. (1998). Pharmacokinetics and pharmacodynamics of nicotine. In J. Snel & M.M. Lorist (Eds.), *Nicotine, caffeine and social drinking: Behaviour and brain function*. Amsterdam: Harwood Academic.

Leippe, M.R. (1995). The case for expert testimony about eyewitness memory. *Psychology, Public Policy and Law, 1*, 909–959.

Lemaire, P., Abdi, H., & Fayol, M. (1996). The role of working memory resources in simple cognitive arithmetic. *European Journal of Cognitive Psychology, 8*, 73–103.

Leplâtre, G., & Brewster, S.A. (1998). An investigation of using music to provide navigation cues. In S.A. Brewster & A.D.N. Edwards (Eds.), *Proceedings of the Fifth International Conference on Auditory Display*. Glasgow: British Computer Society.

Leplâtre, G., & Brewster, S.A. (2000). Designing non-speech sounds to support navigation in mobile phone menus. In P.R. Cook (Ed.), *Proceedings of the 6th International Conference on Auditory Display*. Atlanta, GA: International Community for Auditory Display.

Levi, A.M., & Lindsay, R.C.L. (2001). Lineup and photo spread procedures: issues concerning policy recommendations. *Psychology, Public Policy and Law, 7*, 776–790.

Levin, E.D. (1992). Nicotinic systems and cognitive function. *Psychopharmacology, 108*, 417–431.

Levin, E.D., & Torry, D. (1996). Acute and chronic nicotine effects on working memory in aged rats. *Psychopharmacology, 123*, 88–97.

Li, X., Logan, R.J., & Pastore, R.E. (1991). Perception of acoustic source characteristics: walking sounds. *Journal of the Acoustical Society of America, 90*, 3036–3049.

Liberman, A.M. (1970). The grammars of speech and language. *Cognitive Psychology, 1*, 301–323.

Liberman, A.M., Cooper, F.S., Shankweiler, D.S., & Studdert-Kennedy, M. (1967). Perception of the speech code. *Psychological Review, 74*, 431–461.

Lichtenstein, S., Fischoff, B., & Phillips, L.D. (1982). Calibration of probabilities: the state of the art to 1980. In D. Kahneman, P. Slovic, & A. Tversky (Eds.), *Judgement under uncertainty: Heuristics and biases*. Cambridge: Cambridge University Press.

Lieberman, H.R. (1992). Caffeine. In A.P. Smith & D.M. Jones (Eds.), *Handbook of human performance* (Vol. 2). London: Academic Press.

Lieberman, H.R., Tharion, W.J., Shukitt-Hale, B., Speckman, K.L., & Tulley, R. (2002). Effects of caffeine, sleep loss and stress on cognitive performance and mood during U.S. Navy SEAL training. *Psychopharmacology, 164*, 250–261.

Lieberman, H.R., Wurtman, R.J., Emde, G.G., Roberts, C., & Coviella, I.L.G. (1987). The effects of low doses of caffeine on human performance and mood. *Psychopharmacology, 92*, 308–312.

Liebert, R.M., & Morris, L.W. (1967). Cognitive and emotional components of test anxiety: a distinction and some initial data. *Psychological Reports, 20*, 975–978.

Light, L.L., Kayra-Stuart, F., & Hollander, S. (1979). Recognition memory for typical and unusual faces. *Journal of Experimental Psychology: Human Learning and Memory, 5*, 212–228.

Lindsay, R.C., & Wells, G.L. (1985). Improving eyewitness identifications from lineups: simultaneous versus sequential lineup presentation. *Journal of Applied Psychology, 70*, 556–564.

Linton, M. (1975). Memory for real-world events. In D.A. Norman & D.A. Rumelhart (Eds.), *Explorations in cognition*. San Francisco, CA: Freeman.

Lippmann, R.P. (1989). Review of neural networks for speech recognition. *Neural Computation, 1*, 1–38.

Lippmann, R.P. (1997). Speech recognition by machines and humans. *Speech Communication, 22*, 1–15.

Lisker, L., & Abramson, A.S. (1970). The voicing dimension: some experiments in comparative phonetics. In *Proceedings of the 6th International Congress of Phonetic Sciences*. Prague: Academia.

Lockhart, R.S., & Craik, F.I.M. (1990). Levels of processing: a retrospective commentary on a framework for memory research. *Canadian Journal of Psychology, 44*, 87–112.

Loftus, E.F. (1975). Leading questions and the eyewitness report. *Cognitive Psychology, 7*, 560–572.

Loftus, E.F. (1979). *Eyewitness testimony*. Cambridge, MA: Harvard University Press.

Loftus, E.F., & Burns, T. (1982). Mental shock can produce retrograde amnesia. *Memory and Cognition, 10*, 318–323.

Loftus, E.F., & Greene, E. (1980). Warning: even memory for faces may be contagious. *Law and Human Behaviour, 4*, 323–334.

Loftus, E.F., Levidow, B., & Duensing, S. (1992). Who remembers best? Individual differences in memory for events that occurred in a science museum. *Applied Cognitive Psychology, 6*, 93–107.

Loftus, E.F., Miller, D.G., & Burns, H.J. (1978). Semantic integration of verbal information into a visual memory. *Journal of Experimental Psychology: Human Learning and Memory, 4*, 19–31.

Loftus, E.F., & Palmer, J.C. (1974). Reconstruction of automobile destruction: an example of the interaction between language and memory. *Journal of Verbal Learning and Verbal Behavior, 13*, 585–589.

Loftus, E.F., & Zanni, G. (1975). Eyewitness testimony: the influence of the wording of a question. *Bulletin of the Psychonomic Society, 5*, 866–888.

Logie, R.H. (1993). Working memory and human–machine systems. In J.A. Wise, V.D. Hopkin, & P. Stager (Eds.), *Verification and validation of complex systems: Human factors issues*. Berlin: Springer-Verlag.

Logie, R.H. (1995). *Visuo-spatial working memory*. Hove, UK: Erlbaum.

Logie, R.H., & Baddeley, A.D. (1987). Cognitive processes in counting. *Journal of Experimental Psychology: Learning, Memory and Cognition, 13*, 310–326.

Logie, R.H., Baddeley, A.D., Mane, A., Donchin, E., & Sheptak, R. (1989). Working memory and the analysis of a complex skill by secondary task methodology. *Acta Psychologica, 71*, 53–87.

Logie, R.H., Gilhooly, K.J., & Wynn, V. (1994). Counting on working memory in arithmetic problem solving. *Memory and Cognition, 22*, 395–410.

Loke, W.H. (1993). Caffeine and automaticity in encoding prelexical tasks: theory and some data. *Human Psychopharmacology, 8*, 77–95.

Loke, W.H., Hinrichs, J.V., & Ghoneim, M.M. (1985). Caffeine and diazepam: separate and combined effects on mood, memory and psychomotor performance. *Psychopharmacology, 87*, 344–350.

Loomes, G., & Sugden, R. (1982). Regret theory: an alternative theory of rational choice under uncertainty. *Economic Journal, 92*, 805–824.

Lorayne, H., & Lucas, J. (1974). *The memory book*. London: W.H. Allen.

Lorenzetti, R., & Natale, R. (1996). Time of day and processing strategies in narrative comprehension. *British Journal of Psychology, 87*, 209–221.

Lorist, M. (1998). Caffeine and information processing in man. In J. Snel & M.M. Lorist (Eds.), *Nicotine, caffeine and social drinking: Behaviour and brain function*. Amsterdam: Harwood Academic.

Lorist, M.M., Snel, J., Kok, A., & Mulder, G. (1994). Influence of caffeine on selective attention in well-rested and fatigued subjects. *Psychophysiology, 31*, 525–534.

Lucas, D. (1984). Everyday memory lapses. Unpublished PhD thesis, University of Manchester.

Lucas, P. (1994). An evaluation of the communicative ability of auditory icons and earcons. In G. Kramer and S. Smith (Eds.), *Proceedings of the Second International Conference on Auditory Display*. Santa Fe, NM: Addison-Wesley.

Luria, A.R. (1975). *The mind of a mnemonist*. Harmondsworth, UK: Penguin.

Luus, C.A.E., & Wells, G.L. (1994). The malleability of eyewitness confidence: co-witness and perseverance effects. *Journal of Applied Psychology*, *79*(5), 714–723.

MacDonald, S., Uesiliana, K., & Hayne, H. (2000). Cross-cultural and gender differences in childhood amnesia. *Memory*, *8*, 365–376.

MacLeod, M.D. (2000). The future is always brighter: temporal orientation and psychological adjustment to trauma. In V. Violanti, D. Paton, & C. Dunning (Eds.), *Alternative approaches to debriefing*. Springfield, IL: Charles C. Thomas.

MacLeod, M.D. (2002). Retrieval-induced forgetting in eyewitness memory: forgetting as a consequence of remembering. *Applied Cognitive Psychology*, *16*, 135–149.

MacLeod, M.D., & Macrae, C.N. (2001). Gone today but here tomorrow: the transient nature of retrieval-induced forgetting. *Psychological Science*, *12*, 148–152.

Macrae, C.N., & MacLeod, M.D. (1999). On recollections lost: when practice makes imperfect. *Journal of Personality and Social Psychology*, *77*, 463–473.

Maguire, E.A., Henson, R.N.A., Mummery, C.J., & Frith, C.D. (2001). Activity in prefrontal cortex, not hippocampus, varies parametrically with the increasing remoteness of memories. *Neuroreport: For Rapid Communication of Neurosciences Research*, *12*, 441–444.

Maguire, M.S., & Byth, W. (1998). The McCollough effect across the menstrual cycle. *Perception and Psychophysics*, *60*, 221–226.

Makous, J.C., & Middlebrooks, J.C. (1990). Two dimensional sound localisation by human listeners. *Journal of the Acoustical Society of America*, *87*, 2188–2200.

Malpass, R.S., & Devine, P.G. (1981). Eyewitness identification: lineup instructions and the absence of the offender. *Journal of Applied Psychology*, *66*, 482–489.

Mandler, G. (1968). Organisation and memory. In K.W. Spence & J.T. Spence (Eds.), *The psychology of learning and motivation* (Vol. 2). New York: Academic Press.

Mandler, G., & Pearlstone, Z. (1966). Free and constrained concept learning and subsequent recall. *Journal of Verbal Learning and Verbal Behaviour*, *5*, 126–131.

Mandler, G., Pearlstone, Z., & Koopmans, H.S. (1969). Effects of organisation and semantic similarity on a recall and recognition task. *Journal of Verbal Learning and Verbal Behaviour*, *8*, 410–423.

Mangan, G.L., & Golding, J.F. (1983). The effects of smoking on memory consolidation. *Journal of Psychology*, *115*, 65–77.

Manktelow, K. (1999). *Reasoning and thinking*. Hove, UK: Psychology Press.

Marcus, N., Cooper, M., & Sweller, J. (1996). Understanding instructions. *Journal of Educational Psychology*, *88*, 49–63.

Marks, L.E. (1978). *The unity of the sense: Interrelations among the modalities*. New York: Academic Press.

Marshall, J.C., & Newcombe, F. (1966). Syntactic and semantic errors in paralexia. *Neuropsychologia*, *4*, 169–176.

Marshall, J.C., & Newcombe, F. (1973). Patterns of paralexia: a psycholinguistic approach. *Journal of Psycholinguistic Research*, *2*, 175–199.

Martens, R., Vealey, R.S., & Burton, D. (Eds.) (1990). *Competitive anxiety in sport*. Champaign, IL: Human Kinetics.

Masters, R.S.W. (1992). Knowledge, knerves and know-how: the role of explicit versus implicit knowledge in the breakdown of a complex skill under pressure. *British Journal of Psychology*, *83*, 343–358.

Masters, R.S.W., Polman, R.C.J., & Hammond, N.V. (1993). Reinvestment: a dimension of personality implicated in skill breakdown under pressure. *Personality and Individual Differences*, *14*, 655–666.

Masterson, J. (1984). Surface dyslexia and its relationship to developmental disorders of reading. *Visible Language, 18*, 388–396.

Masterson, J. (2000). Developmental surface dyslexia. In E. Funnell (Ed.), *Case studies in the neuropsychology of reading*. Hove, UK: Psychology Press.

Masterton, B., & Diamond, I.T. (1973). Hearing: central neural mechanisms. In E.C. Carterette and M.P. Friedman (Eds.), *Handbook of perception* (Vol. 3). New York: Academic Press.

Matthews, G., Coyle, K., & Craig, A. (1990). Multiple factors of cognitive failure and their relationship with stress vulnerability. *Journal of Psychopathology and Behavioural Assessment, 12*, 49–64.

Mathews, G., Davies, D.R., Westerman, S.J., & Stammers, R.B. (2000). *Human performance: Cognition, stress and individual differences*. Hove, UK: Psychology Press.

Matthews, G.A., & Harley, T.A. (1993). Effects of extraversion and self-report arousal on semantic priming: a connectionist approach. *Journal of Personality and Social Psychology, 65*, 435–456.

McAllister, H.A., Bregman, N.J., & Lipscombe, T.J. (1988). Speed estimates by eyewitnesses and earwitnesses: how vulnerable to postevent information? *Journal of General Psychology, 115*, 25–35.

McCann, U.D., Mertl, M., Eligulasvili, V., & Ricaurte, G.A. (1999). Cognitive performance in (+/–)3,4-methylenedioxymethamphetamine (MDMA "ecstasy") users: a controlled study. *Psychopharmacology, 143*, 417–425.

McClean, J.F., & Hitch, G.J. (1999). Working memory impairments in children with specific arithmetic learning difficulties. *Journal of Experimental Child Psychology, 74*, 240–260.

McDougal, S.J.P., & Gruneberg, M. (2002). What memory strategy is best for examinations in psychology? *Applied Cognitive Psychology, 16*, 451–458.

McGurk, H., & MacDonald, J. (1976). Hearing lips and seeing voices. *Nature, 264*, 746–748.

McKenna, F. (1983). Accident proneness: a conceptual analysis. *Accident Analysis and Prevention, 15*, 65–71.

McKenna, F.P., Warburton, D.M., & Winwood, M. (1993). Exploring the limits of optimism: the case of smokers' decision making. *British Journal of Psychology, 84*, 389–394.

McKim, W.A. (1997). *Drugs and behaviour: An introduction to behavioural pharmacology*, 3rd edn. Englewood Cliffs, NJ: Prentice-Hall.

McLeod, P. (1977). A dual-task response modality effect: support for multiprocessor models of attention. *Quarterly Journal of Experimental Psychology, 29*, 651–667.

Meijer, P.B.L. (1993). An experimental system for auditory image representations. *IEEE Transactions on Biomedical Engineering, 39*, 112–121 (reprinted in the 1993 *IMIA Yearbook of Medical Informatics*).

Melara, R.D., & Marks, L.E. (1990). Interaction among auditory dimensions: timbre, pitch, and loudness. *Perception and Psychophysics, 482*, 169–178.

Melnick, S.M., Kubie, J.L., Laungani, R., & Dow-Edwards, D.L. (2001). Impairment of spatial learning following preweaning cocaine exposure in the adult rat. *Neurotoxicology and Teratology, 23*, 445–451.

Memon, A., Wark, L., Bull, R., & Koehnken, G. (1997). Isolating the effects of the cognitive interview techniques. *British Journal of Psychology, 88*, 179–197.

Memon, A., & Wright, D.B. (1999). Eyewitness testimony and the Oklahoma bombing. *The Psychologist, 12*, 292–295.

Mershon, D.H., Ballenger, W.L., Little, A.D., McMurtry, P.L., & Buchanan, J.L. (1989). Effects of room reflectance and background noise on perceived auditory distance. *Perception, 18*, 403–416.

Mershon, D.H., & King, L.E. (1975). Intensity and reverberation as factors in the auditory perception of egocentric distance. *Perception and Psychophysics, 18*, 409–415.

Meyer, D.E., & Kieras, D.E. (1997). A computational theory of executive cognitive processes and multiple-task performance: Part 1. Basic mechanisms. *Psychological Review, 104*, 3–65.

Miles, T. (2001) Reflections and research. In M. Hunter-Carsch (Ed.), *Dyslexia: A psychosocial perspective*. London: Whurr Publishers.

Miller, G.A. (1956). The magical number seven, plus or minus two: some limits on our capacity for processing information. *Psychological Review, 63*, 81–97.

Miller, L.S., & Miller, S.E. (1996). Caffeine enhances initial but not extended learning in a proprioceptive-based discrimination task in non-smoking moderate users. *Perceptual and Motor Skills, 82*, 891–898.

Mills, A.W. (1963). Auditory perception and spatial relations. *Proceedings of the International Congress on Technology and Blindness, 2*, 111–139.

Millsaps, C.L., Azrin, R.L., & Mittenberg, W. (1994). Neuropsychological effects of chronic cannabis use on the memory and intelligence of adolescents. *Journal of Child and Adolescent Substance Abuse, 3*, 47–55.

Milne, R., & Bull, R. (1999). *Investigative interviewing: Psychology and practice*. Chichester, UK: Wiley.

Milne, R., & Bull, R. (2002). Back to basics: a componental analysis of the original cognitive interview mnemonics with three age groups. *Applied Cognitive Psychology, 16*, 743–753.

Milne, R., & Bull, R. (2003). Does the cognitive interview help children to resist the effects of suggestive questioning? *Legal and Criminological Psychology, 8*, 21–38.

Mogford, R.H. (1997). Mental models and situation awareness in air traffic control. *International Journal of Aviation Psychology, 7*, 331–341.

Monk, T.H. (1982). The arousal model of time of day effects in human performance efficiency. *Chronobiologia, 9*, 49–54.

Monk, T.H., Weitzman, E.D., Fookson, J.E. *et al.* (1983). Task variables determine which biological clock controls circadian rhythms in performance. *Nature, 304*, 543–544.

Moos, R. (1968). The development of a Menstrual Distress Questionnaire. *Psychosomatic Medicine, 30*, 853–860.

Moray. N. (1959). Attention in dichotic listening: affective cues and the influence of instruction. *Quarterly Journal of Experimental Psychology, 11*, 56–60.

Morgan, E., & Klein, C. (2000). *The dyslexic adult in a non-dyslexic world*. London: Whurr Publishers.

Morgan, M.J. (1998). Recreational use of "ecstasy" (MDMA) is associated with elevated impulsivity. *Neuropsychopharmacology, 19*, 252–264.

Morgan, M.J. (1999). Memory deficits associated with recreational use of "ecstasy" (MDMA). *Psychopharmacology, 152*, 230–248.

Morgan, M.J., McFie, L., Fleetwood, L.H., & Robinson, J.A. (2002). "Ecstasy" (MDMA): are the psychological changes associated with its use reversed by prolonged abstinence? *Psychopharmacology, 159*, 294–303.

Mori, R.D., Lam, L., & Gilloux, M. (1987). Learning and plan refinement in a knowledge-based system for automatic speech recognition. *IEEE Transactions on Pattern Analysis Machine Intelligence, 9*, 289–305.

Morris, L.W., & Liebert, R.M. (1970). Relationships of cognitive and emotional components of test anxiety to physiological arousal and academic performance. *Journal of Consulting and Clinical Psychology, 35*, 332–337.

Morris, P.E., & Fritz, C.O. (2002). The improved name game: better use of expanding retrieval practice. *Memory, 10*, 259–266.

Morris, R.B., & Walter, L.W. (1991). Subtypes of arithmetic-disabled adults: validating childhood findings. In B.P. Rourke (Ed.), *Neuropsychological validation of learning disability subtypes*. New York: Guilford Press.

Morrow, B.A., Elsworth, J.D., & Roth, R.H. (2002). Prenatal cocaine exposure disrupts non-spatial, short-term memory in adolescent and adult male rats. *Behavioural Brain Research, 129*, 217–223.

Morrow, D. M., Lee, A., & Rodvold, M. (1993). Analysis of problems in routine controller–pilot communication. *International Journal of Aviation Psychology, 3*, 285–302.

Morton, J., & Patterson, K.E. (1980). A new attempt at an interpretation, or, an attempt at a new interpretation. In M. Coltheart, K.E. Patterson, & J.C. Marshall (Eds.), *Deep dyslexia*. London: Routledge & Kegan Paul

Mousavi, S., Low, R., & Sweller, J. (1995). Reducing cognitive load by mixing auditory and visual presentation modes. *Journal of Educational Psychology, 87*, 319–334.

Nadeau, S., Gonzalez Rothi L., & Crosson, B. (2000). *Aphasia and language: Theory to practice*. New York: Guilford Press.

Naire, J.S. (1983). Associative processing during rote rehearsal. *Journal of Experimental Psychology, 9*, 3–20.

Neisser, U. (1976). *Cognition and reality*. San Francisco, CA: Freeman.

Neisser, U. (1982). Memorists. In U. Neisser (Ed.), *Memory observed: Remembering in natural contexts*. San Francisco, CA: Freeman.

Neisser, U. (1996). Remembering as doing. *Behavioural and Brain Sciences, 19*, 203–204.

Neisser, U., & Harsch, N. (1992). Phantom flashbulbs: false recollections of hearing the news about *Challenger*. In E. Winograd & U. Neisser (Eds.), *Affect and accuracy in recall: Studies of "flashbulb" memories*. New York: Cambridge University Press.

Nelson, K. (1988). The ontogeny of memory for real events. In U. Neisser & E. Winograd (Eds.), *Remembering reconsidered: Ecological and traditional approaches to the study of memory*. Cambridge: Cambridge University Press.

Nelson, K., & Ross, G. (1980). The generalities and specifics of long-term memory in infants and young children. In M. Perlmutter (Ed.), *Children's memory: New directions for child development*. San Francisco, CA: Jossey-Bass.

Neuhoff, J.G., Kramer, G., & Wayand, J. (2000). Sonification and the interaction of perceptual dimensions: can the data get lost in the map? In P.R. Cook (Ed.), *Proceedings of the 6th International Conference on Auditory Display*. Atlanta, GA: International Community for Auditory Display.

Newcombe, F., & Marshall, J.C. (1980a). Response monitoring and response blocking in deep dyslexia. In M. Coltheart, K.E. Patterson, & J.C. Marshall (Eds.), *Deep dyslexia*. London: Routledge & Kegan Paul.

Newcombe, F., & Marshall, J.C. (1980b). Transcoding and lexical stabilization in deep dyslexia. In M. Coltheart, K.E. Patterson, & J.C. Marshall (Eds.), *Deep dyslexia*. London: Routledge & Kegan Paul.

Newcombe, F., & Marshall, J.C. (1981). On psycholinguistic classifications of the acquired dyslexias. *Bulletin of the Orton Society, 31*, 29–46.

Newcombe, N.S., Drummey, A.B., Fox. N.A., Lie, E., & Ottinger-Alberts, W. (2000). Remembering early childhood: how much, how, and why (or why not). *Current Directions in Psychological Science, 9*, 55–58.

Newell, A. (1990). *Unified theories of cognition*. Cambridge, MA: Harvard University Press.

Newlands, P.J., George, R.C., Towell, N.A., Kemp, R.I., & Clifford, B.R. (1999). An investigation of description quality from real-life interviews. *Psychology, Crime and Law, 5*, 145–166.

Nichols, J.M., & Martin, F. (1998). Social drinking, memory and information processing. In J. Snel & M.M. Lorist (Eds.), *Nicotine, caffeine and social drinking: Behaviour and brain function*. Amsterdam: Harwood Academic.

Nicolson, P. (1992). Menstrual cycle research and the construction of female psychology. In J.T.E. Richardson (Ed.), *Cognition and the menstrual cycle*. Berlin: Springer-Verlag.

Niessen, C., Eyferth, K., & Bierwagen, T. (1999). Modelling cognitive processes of experienced air traffic controllers. *Ergonomics, 42*, 1507–1520.

Niessen, C., Leuchter, S., & Eyferth, K. (1998). A psychological model of air traffic control and its implementation. In F.E. Riter & R.M. Young (Eds.), *Proceedings of the Second European Conference on Cognitive Modelling*. Nottingham, UK: Nottingham University Press.

Noon, E., & Hollin, C.R. (1987). Lay knowledge of eyewitness behaviour: a British survey. *Applied Cognitive Psychology, 1*, 143–153.

Norman, D.A. (1981). Categorisation of action slips. *Psychological Review, 88*, 1–15.

Norman, D.A. (1988). *The psychology of everyday things*. New York: Basic Books.

Nygaard, L.C., & Pisoni, D.B. (1998). Talker specific learning in speech perception. *Perception and Psychophysics, 60*, 355–376.

Oatley, K. (1974). Circadian rhythms and representations of the environment in motivational systems. In D.G. McFarland (Ed.), *Motivational control systems analysis*. London: Academic Press.

Oborne, D.J., & Rogers, Y. (1983). Interactions of alcohol and caffeine on human reaction time. *Aviation, Space and Environmental Medicine, 54*, 528–534.

O'Brien, D. (1993). *How to develop a perfect memory*. London: Pavillion Books.

Olsson, N., Juslin, P., & Winman, A. (1998). Realism of confidence in earwitness versus eyewitness identification. *Journal of Experimental Psychology: Applied, 4*, 101–118.

Orchard, T.L., & Yarmey, A.D. (1995). The effects of whispers, voice-sample duration, and voice distinctiveness on criminal speaker identification. *Applied Cognitive Psychology, 9*, 249–260.

Ornstein, T.J., Iddon, J.L., Baldacchino, A.M. *et al.* (2000). Profiles of cognitive dysfunction in chronic amphetamine and heroin abusers. *Neuropsychopharmacology, 23*, 113–126.

Owens, D.S., MacDonald, I., Tucker, P. *et al.* (1998). Diurnal trends in mood and performance do not parallel alertness. *Scandinavian Journal of Work, Environment and Health, 24* (suppl. 3), 109–114.

Paivio, A. (1965). Abstractness, imagery, and meaningfulness in paired-associate learning. *Journal of Verbal Learning and Verbal Behaviour, 4*, 32–38.

Paivio, A. (1971). *Imagery and verbal processes*. New York: Holt, Rinehart & Winston.

Paivio, A. (1991). Dual coding theory: retrospect and current status. *Canadian Journal of Psychology, 45*, 255–287.

Parker, E.S., Parker, D.A., & Brody, J.A. (1991). Specifying the relationship between alcohol use and cognitive loss: the effects of frequency of consumption and psychological distress. *Journal of Studies on Alcohol, 52*, 366–373.

Parkin, A.J. (1983). The relationship between orienting tasks and the structure of memory traces: evidence from false recognition. *British Journal of Psychology, 74*, 61–69.

Parkin, A.J., & Hunkin, N.M. (2001). British memory research: a journey through the 20th century. *British Journal of Psychology, 92*, 37–52.

Parlee, M.B. (1974). Stereotypical beliefs about menstruation: a methodological note on the Moos MDQ and some new data. *Psychosomatic Medicine, 36*, 229–240.

Parlee, M.B. (1983). Menstrual rhythms in sensory processes: a review of fluctuations in vision, olfaction, audition, taste and touch. *Psychological Bulletin, 93*, 539–548.

Parrott, A.C. (2001). Human psychopharmacology of ecstasy (MDMA): a review of 15 years of empirical research. *Human Psychopharmacology: Clinical and Experimental, 16*, 557–577.

Parrott, A.C., & Craig, D. (1992). Cigarette smoking and nicotine gum (0, 2 and 4 mg): effects upon four visual attention tasks. *Neuropsychobiology, 25*, 34–43.

Parrott, A.C., & Lasky, J. (1998). Ecstasy (MDMA) effects on mood and cognition: before, during and after a Saturday night dance. *Psychopharmacology*, *139*, 261–268.

Patterson, K. (1982). The relation between reading and phonological coding: further neuropsychological observations. In A.W. Ellis (Ed.), *Normality and pathology in cognitive functioning*. London: Academic Press.

Patterson, K. (2000). Phonological alexia: the case of the singing detective. In E. Funnell (Ed.), *Case studies in the neuropsychology of reading*. Hove, UK: Psychology Press.

Patterson, K.E., & Besner, D. (1984). Is the right hemisphere literate? *Cognitive Neuropsychology*, *1*, 315–341.

Patterson, K.E., & Morton, J. (1985). From orthography to phonology: an attempt at an old interpretation. In K.E. Patterson, J.C. Marshall, & M. Coltheart (Eds.), *Surface dyslexia: Neuropsychological and cognitive studies of phonological reading*. London: Erlbaum.

Patterson, R.D. (1990). Auditory warning sounds in the work environment. *Philosophical Transactions of the Royal Society of London*, *327*, 485–492.

Paulos, J.A. (1988). *Innumeracy: Mathematical illiteracy and its consequences*. London: Penguin.

Payne, D.G. (1987). Hyperamnesia and reminiscence in recall: a historical and empirical review. *Psychological Bulletin*, *101*, 5–27.

Perrett, S., & Noble, W. (1995). Available response choices affect localization of sound. *Perception and Psychophysics*, *57*, 150–158.

Perry, E.K., Perry, R.H., Smith, C.J. *et al.* (1986). Cholinergic receptors in cognitive disorders. *Canadian Journal of Neuroscience*, *13*, 521–527.

Pihl, R.O., Assaad, J.-M., & Bruce, K.R. (1998). Cognition in social drinkers: the interaction of alcohol with nicotine and caffeine. In J. Snel & M.M. Lorist (Eds.), *Nicotine, caffeine and social drinking: Behaviour and brain function*. Amsterdam: Harwood Academic.

Pike, G., Kemp, R., Brace, N., Allen, J., & Rowlands, G. (2000). The effectiveness of video identification parades. *Proceedings of the British Psychological Society*, *8*, 44.

Pillemer, D.B., Goldsmith, L.R., Panter, A.T., & White, S.H. (1988). Very long-term memories of the first year in college. *Journal of Experimental Psychology: Learning, Memory and Cognition*, *14*, 709–715.

Pillemer, D.B., & White, S.H. (1989). Childhood events recalled by children and adults. In H.W. Reese (Ed.), *Advances in Child Development and Behaviour*. San Diego, CA: Academic Press.

Pisoni, D.B. (1977). Identification and discrimination of the relative onset time of two component tones: implications for voicing perception in stops. *Journal of the Acoustical Society of America*, *61*, 1352–1361.

Pisoni, D.B., & Luce, P.A. (1986). Speech perception: research, theory, and the principle issues. In E.C. Schwab & H.C. Nusbaum (Eds.), *Pattern recognition by humans and machines, Vol. 1: Speech perception*. London: Academic Press.

Plaut, D.C., McClelland, J.L., Seidenberg, M.S., & Patterson, K. (1996). Understanding normal and impaired word reading: computational principles in quasi-regular domains. *Psychological Review*, *96*, 523–568.

Plaut, D.C., & Shallice, T. (1993). Deep dyslexia: A case study of connectionist neuropsychology. *Cognitive Neuropsychology*, *10*, 377–500.

Poole, D.A., & Lindsay, D.S. (2001). Children's eyewitness reports after exposure to misinformation from parents. *Journal of Experimental Psychology: Applied*, *7*, 27–50.

Pope, H.G., Gruber, A.J., Hudson, J.I., Huestis, M.A., & Yurgelun-Todd, D. (2001). Neuropsychological performance in long-term cannabis users. *Archives of General Psychiatry*, *58*, 909–915.

Pope, H.G., Gruber, A.J., & Yurgelun-Todd, D. (1995). The residual effects of cannabis: the current status of research. *Drug and Alcohol Dependence*, *38*, 25–34.

Price, C.J., Howard, D., Patterson, K. *et al.* (1998). A functional neuroimaging description of two deep dyslexic patients. *Journal of Cognitive Neuroscience, 10*, 303–315.

Pritchard, W.S., & Robinson, J.H. (1998). Effects of nicotine on human performance. In J. Snel & M.M. Lorist (Eds.), *Nicotine, caffeine and social drinking: Behaviour and brain function*. Amsterdam: Harwood Academic.

Provost, S.C., & Woodward, R.E. (1991). Effects of nicotine gum on repeated administration of the Stroop test. *Psychopharmacology, **104***, 536–540.

Rabbitt, P.M.A., & Vyas, S.M. (1980). Selective anticipation for events in old age. *Journal of Gerontology, 35*, 913–919.

Ramsey, M., Partridge, B., & Byron, C. (1999). Drug misuse declared in 1998: key findings from the British Crime Survey. *Home Office Research Findings, 93*, 1–4. Available at: http://www.homeoffice.gov.uk/rds/pdfs2/r182.pdf (retrieved 22 January 2004).

Rasmussen, J. (1982). Human errors: a taxonomy for describing human malfunction in industrial installations. *Journal of Occupational Accidents, 4*, 311–333.

Rasmussen, R., Turner, D., & Esgate, A. (2003) On your marks, get stereotyped, go! Novice coaches and Black stereotypes in sprinting. *Journal of Sports Sciences, 21*, 358.

Raugh, M.R., & Atkinson, R.C. (1975). A mnemonic method for learning a second language vocabulary. *Journal of Educational Psychology, 67*, 1–16.

Read, J.D., Connolly, D., & Turtle, J.W. (2001). Memory in legal contexts: remembering events, circumstances, and people. In R.A. Schuller & J.R.P. Ogloff (Eds.), *Introduction to cognitive psychology and law: Canadian perspectives*. Toronto: University of Toronto Press.

Reason, J. (1979). Actions not as planned: the price of automaticity. In G. Underwood & R. Stevens (Eds.), *Aspects of consciousness, Vol. 1: Psychological issues*. Chichester, UK: Wiley.

Reason, J. (1984a). Absent-mindedness. In J. Nicholson & H. Beloff (Eds.), *Psychology survey 5*. Leicester: British Psychological Society.

Reason, J. (1984b). Absent-mindedness and cognitive control. In J. Harris & P. Morris (Eds.), *Everyday memory, actions and absent-mindedness*. London: Academic Press.

Reason, J. (1987). The Chernobyl errors. *Bulletin of the British Psychological Society, 40*, 201–206.

Reason, J. (1988). Stress and cognitive failure. In S. Fisher & J.T. Reason (Eds.), *Handbook of life stress, cognition, and health*. Chichester, UK: Wiley.

Reason, J. (1990). *Human error*. Cambridge: Cambridge University Press.

Reason, J. (1992). Cognitive underspecification: its variety and consequences. In B.J. Baars (Ed.), *Experimental slips and human error: Exploring the architecture of volition*. New York: Plenum Press.

Reason, J., Manstead, A.S.R., Stradling, S., Baxter, J., & Campbell, K. (1990). Errors and violations on the roads: a real distinction? *Ergonomics, 33*, 1315–1332.

Reason, J., & Mycielska, (1982). *Absent-minded? The psychology of mental lapses and everyday errors*. Englewood Cliffs, NJ: Prentice-Hall.

Reddy, D.R. (1976). Speech recognition by machine: a review. *Proceedings IEEE, 64*, 501–531.

Reddy, D.R. (1990). Speech recognition by machine: a review. In A. Waibel and K.F. Lee (Eds.), *Readings in speech recognition*. San Mateo, CA: Morgan Kaufmann.

Reder, L.M. (1987). Strategy selection in question answering. *Cognitive Psychology, 19*, 90–134.

Reder, L.M., & Anderson, J.R. (1982). Effects of spacing and embellishment for the main points of a text. *Memory and Cognition, 10*, 97–102.

Redgrove, J. (1971). Menstrual cycles. In W. Colquhoun (Ed.), *Biological rhythms and human performance*. New York: Academic Press.

Repp, B.H. (1987). The sound of two hands clapping: an exploratory study. *Journal of the Acoustical Society of America, 81*, 1100–1109.

Revell, A.D. (1988). Smoking and performance: a puff-by-puff analysis. *Psychopharmacology*, *96*, 563–565.

Richardson, J.T.E. (1989). Student learning and the menstrual cycle: premenstrual symptoms and approaches to studying. *Educational Psychology*, *9*, 215–238.

Richardson, J.T.E. (1992). Memory and the menstrual cycle. In J.T.E. Richardson (Ed.), *Cognition and the menstrual cycle*. Berlin: Springer-Verlag.

Robbins, T.W., & Everitt, B.J. (1999). Interaction of the dopaminergic system with mechanisms of associative learning and cognition: implications for drug abuse. *Psychological Science*, *10*, 199–201.

Rodgers, J. (2000). Memory ability among recreational users of ecstasy. *Psychopharmacology*, **151**, 19–24.

Rodgers, J., Buchanan, T., Scholey, A.B. *et al.* (2001). Differential effects of ecstasy and cannabis on self-reports of memory ability: a web-based study. *Human Psychopharmacology: Clinical and Experimental*, *16*, 619–625.

Rogers, R.D., Everitt, B.J., Baldacchino, A. *et al.* (1999). Dissociable deficits in decision-making cognition of chronic amphetamine abusers, opiate abusers, patients with focal damage to the prefrontal cortex and tryptophan-depleted normal volunteers: evidence for monoaminergic mechanisms. *Neuropsychopharmacology*, *20*, 322–339.

Roebuck, R., & Wilding, J. (1993). Effects of vowel variety and sample length on identification of a speaker in a line up. *Applied Cognitive Psychology*, *7*, 475–481.

Roediger, H.L., & Neely, J.H. (1982). Retrieval blocks in episodic and semantic memory. *Canadian Journal of Psychology*, *36*, 213–242.

Roger, D., & Nesshoever, W. (1987). The construction and preliminary validation of a scale for measuring emotional control. *Personality and Individual Differences*, *8*, 527–534.

Rosa, R.R., & Bonnet, M.H. (1993). Performance and alertness on 8 h and 12 h rotating shifts at a natural gas utility. *Ergonomics*, *36*, 1177–1193.

Rosen, S.M., Fourcin, A.J., & Moore, B.C.J. (1981). Voice pitch as an aid to lipreading. *Nature*, *291*, 150–152.

Rothkopf, E.Z., & Coke, E.U. (1963). Repetition interval and rehearsal method in learning equivalences from written sentences. *Journal of Verbal Learning and Verbal Behaviour*, *2*, 406–416.

Rubin, D.C., Rahal, T.A. & Poon, L.W. (1998). Things learned in early adulthood are remembered best. *Memory and Cognition*, *26*, 3–19.

Rubin, D.C., Wetzler, S.E., & Nebes, R.D. (1986). Autobiographical memory across the lifespan. In D.C. Rubin (Ed.), *Autobiographical memory*. Cambridge: Cambridge University Press.

Ruble, D.N. (1977). Premenstrual symptoms: a reinterpretation. *Science*, *197*, 291–292.

Ruble, D.N., Brooks-Gunn, J., & Clark, A. (1980). Rersearch on menstrual related changes: alternative perspectives. In J.E. Parsons (Ed.), *The psychobiology of sex differences and sex roles*. New York: McGraw-Hill.

Ryan, L., Hatfield, C., & Hofstetter, M. (2002). Caffeine reduces time-of-day effects on memory performance in older adults. *Psychological Science*, *13*, 68–71.

Ryback, R.S. (1971). The continuum and specificity of the effects of alcohol on memory. *Quarterly Journal of Studies on Alcoholism*, *32*, 215–216.

Salthouse, T.A., & Babcock, R.L. (1991). Decomposing adult age differences in working memory. *Developmental Psychology*, *27*, 763–776.

Satinder, K.P., & Mastronardi, L.M. (1974). Sex differences in figural aftereffects as a function of phase of the menstrual cycle. *Psychologia*, *17*, 1–5.

Saunders, J., & MacLeod, M.D. (2002). New evidence on the suggestibility of memory: the role of retrieval-induced forgetting in misinformation effects. *Journal of Experimental Psychology*, *8*, 127–142.

Scaletti, C., & Craig, A.B. (1991). Using sound to extract meaning from complex data. In E.J. Farrell & T.J. Watson (Eds.), *Proceedings of the SPIE Conference 1459, Extracting Meaning from Complex Data: Processing, Display, Interaction II*. San Jose, CA: Society of Photo Optical.

Schachtel, E.G. (1947). On memory and childhood amnesia. *Psychiatry, 10*, 1–26.

Schmeidler, G.R., & McConnell, R.A. (1958). *ESP and personality patterns*. Westport, CT: Greenwood.

Schmidt, D.M., & Bjork, R.A. (1992). New conceptualisations of practice: common principles in three paradigms suggest new concepts for training. *Psychological Science, 3*, 207–217.

Schmidt, R.A. (1975). A schema theory of discrete motor skill learning. *Psychological Review, 82*, 225–260.

Schmidt, R.A., & Lee, T.D. (1999). *Motor control and learning: A behavioural emphasis* (2nd edn.). Champaign, IL: Human Kinetics.

Schmolk, H., Buffalo, E.A., & Squire, L.R. (2000). Memory distortions develop over time: recollections of the O.J. Simpson trial verdict after 15 and 32 months. *Psychological Science, 11*, 39–45.

Schneider, W., & Shiffrin, R.M. (1977). Controlled and automatic human information processing: I. Detection, search and attention. *Psychological Review, 84*, 1–66.

Schulkind, M.D., Hennis, L.K., & Rubin, D.C. (1999). Music, emotion, and autobiographical memory: they're playing your song. *Memory and Cognition, 27*, 948–955.

Schwartz, M.F., Saffran, E.M., & Marin, O.S.M. (1980a). Fractionating the reading process in dementia: evidence for word-specific print-to-sound associations. In M. Coltheart, K.E. Patterson, & J.C. Marshall (Eds.), *Deep dyslexia*. London: Routledge & Kegan Paul

Schwartz, R.H. (1991). Heavy marijuana use and recent memory impairment. *Psychiatric Annals, 21*, 80–82.

Searleman, A., & Herrmann, D. (1994). *Memory from a broader perspective*. New York: McGraw-Hill.

Seidenberg, M.S., & McClelland, J.L. (1989). A distributed developmental model of word recognition and naming. *Psychological Review, 96*, 523–568.

Servan, S.D., Carter, C.S., Bruno, R.M., & Cohen, J.D. (1998). Dopamine and the mechanisms of cognition: Part II. d-amphetamine effects in human subjects performing a selective attention task. *Biological Psychiatry, 43*, 723–729.

Seymour, P.H.K., & Evans, H.M. (1993). The visual (orthographic) processor and developmental dyslexia. In D.M. Willows, R.S. Kruk, & E. Corcos (Eds.), *Visual processes in reading and reading disabilities*. Hove, UK: Erlbaum.

Shaffer, L.S. (1975). Multiple attention in continuous verbal tasks. In P.M.A. Rabbitt & S. Dornic (Eds.), *Attention and performance V*. London: Academic Press.

Shah, P., & Miyake, A. (1996). The separability of working memory resources for spatial thinking and language processing: an individual differences approach. *Journal of Experimental Psychology: General, 125*, 4–27.

Shah, P., & Miyake, A. (1999). Models of working memory: an introduction. In A. Miyake & P. Shah (Eds.), *Models of working memory: Mechanisms of active maintenance and executive control*. Cambridge: Cambridge University Press.

Shallice, T. (1988). *From neuropsychology to mental structure*. Cambridge: Cambridge University Press.

Shallice, T., & Warrington, E. K. (1980). Single and multiple component central dyslexic syndromes. In M. Coltheart, K.E. Patterson, & J.C. Marshall (Eds.), *Deep dyslexia*. London: Routledge & Kegan Paul.

Shallice, T., Warrington, E.K., & McCarthy, R. (1983). Reading without semantics. *Quarterly Journal of Experimental Psychology, 35A*: 111–138.

Sharps, M.J., & Pollit, B.K. (1998). Category superiority effects and the processing of auditory images. *Journal of General Psychology, 125*, 109–116.

Shaw, J.S., Bjork, R.A., & Handal, A. (1995). Retrieval-induced forgetting in an eyewitness-memory paradigm. *Psychonomic Bulletin and Review, 2*, 249–253.

Shepard, R.N. (1981). Psychophysical complementarity. In M. Kubovy & J.R. Pomerantz (Eds.), *Perceptual organisation*. Hillsdale, NJ: Erlbaum.

Sherwood, N., Kerr, J.S., & Hindmarch, I. (1992). Psychomotor performance in smokers following single and repeated doses of nicotine gum. *Psychopharmacology, 108*, 432–436.

Shiffrin, R.M., & Schneider, W. (1977). Controlled and automatic human information processing: II. Perceptual learning, automatic attending, and a general theory. *Psychological Review, 84*, 127–190.

Shute, V.J. (1991). Who is likely to acquire programming skills? *Journal of Educational Computing Research, 7*, 1–24.

Sierra, M., & Berrios, G.E. (2000). Flashbulb and flashback memories. In G.E. Berrios & J.R. Hodges (Eds.), *Memory disorders in psychiatric practice*. New York: Cambridge University Press.

Simon, D.A., & Bjork, R.A. (2001). Metacognition in motor learning. *Journal of Experimental Psychology: Learning, Memory and Cognition, 27*, 907–912.

Slater, A. (1995). Saving money on ID parades. *Policing, 11*, 203–231.

Sloboda, J.A., Davidson J.W., & Howe M.J.A. (1994). Is everyone musical? *The Psychologist, 7*, 349–354.

Smith, A., Sturgess, W., & Gallagher, J. (1999). Effects of a low dose of caffeine given in different drinks on mood and performance. *Human Psychopharmacology: Clinical and Experimental, 14*, 473–482.

Smith, A.P. (1998). Effects of caffeine on attention: low levels of arousal. In J. Snel & M.M. Lorist (Eds.), *Nicotine, caffeine and social drinking: Behaviour and brain function*. Amsterdam: Harwood Academic.

Smith, A.P. and Miles, C. (1986). Effects of lunch on selective and sustained attention. *Neuropsychology, 16*, 117–120

Smith, A.P., Rusted, J.M., Eaton-Williams, P., & Hall, S.R. (1991). The effects of caffeine, impulsivity and time of day on performance, mood and cardiovascular function. *Journal of Psychopharmacology, 5*, 120–128.

Smith, A.P., Rusted, J.M., Eaton-Williams, P., Savory, M., & Leathwood, P. (1990). Effects of caffeine given before and after lunch on sustained attention. *Neuropsychobiology, 23*, 160–163.

Smith, S.M., Glenberg, A.M., & Bjork, R.A. (1978). Environmental context and human memory. *Memory and Cognition, 6*, 342–353.

Smyth, M.M., Collins, A.F., Morris, P.E., & Levy, P. (1994). *Cognition in action* (2nd edn.). Hove, UK: Erlbaum.

Snyder, S.H. (1996). *Drugs and the brain*. New York: Scientific American Library.

Solowij, N. (1995). Do cognitive impairments recover following cessation of cannabis use? *Life Sciences, 56*, 2119–2126.

Sommer, B. (1992). Cognitive performance and the menstrual cycle. In J.T.E. Richardson (Ed.), *Cognition and the menstrual cycle*. Berlin: Springer-Verlag.

Spelke, E.S., Hirst, W.C., & Neisser, U. (1976). Skills of divided attention. *Cognition, 4*, 215–230.

Spielberger, C.D., Gorsuch, R.L., & Luschene, R.E. (1970). *Manual for the State–Trait Anxiety Inventory (STAI)*. Palo Alto, CA: Consulting Psychologists Press.

Sporer, S. L., Penrod, S., Read, D., & Cutler, B. (1995). Choosing, confidence, and accuracy: a meta-analysis of the confidence–accuracy relation in eyewitness identification studies. *Psychological Bulletin, 118*, 315–327.

Steblay, N.M. (1992). A meta-analytic review of the weapon focus effect. *Law and Human Behavior*, *16*, 413–424.

Steblay, N.M. (1997). Social influence in eyewitness recall: a meta-analytic review of lineup instruction effects. *Law and Human Behavior*, *21*, 283–297.

Steblay, N., Dysart, J., Fulero, S., & Lindsay, R.C.L. (2001). Eyewitness accuracy rates in sequential and simultaneous lineup presentations: a meta-analytic comparison. *Law and Human Behavior*, *25*, 459–473.

Stein, E.S., & Garland, D. (1993). Air traffic controller working memory: considerations in air traffic control tactical operations. *Technical Report DOT/FAA/CT–TN 93/37*. Atlantic City, NJ: Federal Aviation Administration.

Steptoe, A., & Fidler, H. (1987). Stage fright in orchestral musicians: a study of cognitive and behavioural strategies in performance anxiety. *British Journal of Psychology*, *78*, 241–249.

Steptoe, A., Malik, F., Pay, C. et al. (1995). The impact of stage fright on student actors. *British Journal of Psychology*, *86*, 27–39.

Stevens, S.S., & Newman, E.B. (1936). The localization of actual sources of sound. *American Journal of Psychology*, *48*, 297–306.

Stinson, V., Devenport, J.L., Cutler, B.L., & Kravitz, D.A. (1996). How effective is the presence-of-counsel safeguard? Attorney perceptions of suggestiveness, fairness, and correctability of biased lineup procedures. *Journal of Applied Psychology*, *81*, 64–75.

Streufert, S., & Pogash, R. (1998). Limited alcohol consumption and complex task performance. In J. Snel & M.M. Lorist (Eds.), *Nicotine, caffeine and social drinking: Behaviour and brain function*. Amsterdam: Harwood Academic.

Streufert, S., Pogash, R., Miller, J. et al. (1995). Effects of caffeine deprivation on complex human functioning. *Psychopharmacology*, *118*, 377–384.

Supa, M., Cotzin, M., & Dallenbach, K.M. (1944). Facial vision: the perception of obstacles by the blind. *American Journal of Psychology*, *57*, 133–183.

Sweller, J., Chandler, P., Tierney, P., & Cooper, M. (1990). Cognitive load as a factor in the structuring of technical material. *Journal of Experimental Psychology: General*, *119*, 176–192.

Talarico, J.M., & Rubin, D.C. (2003). Confidence, not consistency, characterises flashbulb memories. *Psychological Science*, *14*, 455–461.

Tanaka, J.W., & Farah, M.J. (1993). Parts and wholes in face recognition. *Quarterly Journal of Experimental Psychology A*, *2*, 225–245.

Tekcan, A.I., & Peynircioglu, Z.F. (2002). Effects of age on flashbulb memories. *Psychology and Aging*, *17*, 416–422.

Temple, C.M. (1985). Surface dyslexia: variations within a syndrome. In K.E. Patterson, J.C. Marshall, & M.Coltheart (Eds.), *Surface dyslexia: Neuropsychological and cognitive studies of phonological reading*. Hove, UK: Erlbaum.

Temple, C.M. (1987). The nature of normality, the deviance of dyslexia and the recognition of rhyme: a reply to Bryant & Impey (1986). *Cognition*, *27*, 103–108.

Temple, C.M., & Marshall, J. (1983). A case study of developmental phonological dyslexia. *British Journal of Psychology*, *74*, 517–533.

Thomas, M.H., & Wang, A.Y. (1996). Learning by the keyword mnemonic: looking for long-term benefits. *Journal of Experimental Psychology: Applied*, *2*, 330–342.

Thomson, M.E., & Watkins, E.J. (1990). *Dyslexia: A teaching handbook*. London: Whurr Publishers.

Thorndike, E.L. (1914). *The psychology of learning*. New York: Teachers College Press.

Tindall-Ford, S., Chandler, P., & Sweller, J. (1997). When two sensory modes are better than one. *Journal of Experimental Psychology: Applied*, *3*, 257–287.

Turner, M.L., & Engle, R.W. (1989). Is working memory capacity task dependent? *Journal of Memory and Language, 28,* 127–154.

Tulving, E. (1962). Subjective organisation in free recall of "unrelated" words. *Psychological Review, 69,* 344–354.

Tulving, E. (1972). Episodic and semantic memory. In E. Tulving & W. Donaldson (Eds.), *Organisation and memory.* New York: Academic Press.

Tulving, E. (1974). Cue-dependent forgetting. *American Scientist, 62,* 74–82.

Tulving, E. (1976). Ecphoric processes in recall and recognition. In J. Brown (Ed.), *Recall and recognition.* New York: Wiley.

Tulving, E., & Pearlstone, Z. (1966). Availability versus accessibility of information in memory for words. *Journal of Verbal Learning and Verbal Behaviour, 5,* 381–391.

Tulving, E., & Thomson, D.M. (1973). Encoding specificity and retrieval processes in episodic memory. *Psychological Review, 80,* 352–373.

Tversky, A., & Kahneman, D. (1971). Belief in the law of small numbers. *Psychological Bulletin, 6,* 105–110.

Tversky, A., & Kahneman, D. (1974). Judgement under uncertainty: heuristics and biases. *Science, 185,* 1124–1131.

Tversky, A., & Kahneman, D. (1981). The framing of decisions and the psychology of choice. *Science, 211,* 453–458.

Tversky, A., & Kahneman, D. (1983). Extensional versus intuitive reasoning: the conjunction fallacy in probability judgement. *Psychological Review, 90,* 239–315.

Underwood, B.J. (1969). Attributes of memory. *Psychological Review, 76,* 559–573.

USDHHS (1988). *The health consequences of smoking: Nicotine addiction.* A report of the Surgeon General. Washington, DC: US Government Printing Office.

Ussher, J. (1989). *The psychology of the female body.* London: Routledge.

Ussher, J. (1992). The demise of dissent and the rise of cognition in menstrual cycle research. In J.T.E. Richardson (Ed.), *Cognition and the menstrual cycle.* New York: Springer-Verlag.

Valentine, T., & Heaton, P. (1999). An evaluation of the fairness of police line-ups and video identifications. *Applied Cognitive Psychology, 13*(spec. issue), S59–S72.

Van der Stelt, O., & Snel, J. (1998). Caffeine and human performance. In J. Snel & M.M. Lorist (Eds.), *Nicotine, caffeine and social drinking: Behaviour and brain function.* Amsterdam: Harwood Academic.

Van Derveer, N.J. (1979). Ecological acoustics: human perception of environmental sounds. *Dissertation Abstracts International, 40/09B,* 4543 (University Microfilms #8004002).

Van Wallendael, L.R., Surace, A., Parsons, D.H., & Brown, M. (1994). "Earwitness" voice recognition: factors affecting accuracy and impact on jurors. *Applied Cognitive Psychology, 8,* 661–677.

Varma, V.K., Malhotra, A.K., Dang, R., & Das, K. (1988). Cannabis and cognitive functions: a prospective study. *Drug and Alcohol Dependence, 21,* 147–152.

Vash, C.L. (1989). The spacing effect: a case study in the failure to apply the results of psychological research (Comment). *American Psychologist, 44,* 1547.

Victor, M. (1992). The effects of alcohol on the nervous system. In J.H. Mendelson & N.K. Mello (Eds.), *Medical diagnosis and treatment of alcoholism.* New York: McGraw-Hill.

Wagenaar, W.A. (1986). My memory: a study of autobiographical memory over six years. *Cognitive Psychology, 18,* 225–252.

Wagenaar, W.A. (1988). *Paradoxes of gambling behaviour.* Hove, UK: Psychology Press.

Waldfogel, S. (1948). The frequency and affective character of childhood memories. *Psychological Monographs: General and Applied, 62* (whole issue).

Walker, A. (1992). Men's and women's beliefs about the influence of the menstrual cycle on academic performance: a preliminary study. *Journal of Applied Social Psychology*, *22*, 896–909.

Walker, A.E. (1997). *The menstrual cycle*. London: Routledge.

Walker, N.B., & Kramer, G. (1996). Mappings and metaphors in auditory displays: an experimental assessment. In *Proceedings of the Third International Conference of Auditory Display*. Available at: http://www.icad.org/websiteV2.0/Conferences/ICAD96/proc96/walker5.htm (retrieved 5 July 2004).

Warburton, D.M. (1995). The effects of caffeine on cognition with and without caffeine abstinence. *Psychopharmacology*, *119*, 66–70.

Warburton, D.M., & Wesnes, K. (1984). Drugs as research tools in psychology: cholinergic drugs and information processing. *Neuropsychobiology*, *11*, 121–132.

Ward, T. (1997). A note of caution for clinicians using the paced auditory serial addition task. *British Journal of Clinical Psychology*, *36*, 303–307.

Wareing, M., Fisk, M., & Murphy, J.E. (2000). Working memory deficits in current and previous users of MDMA ("ecstasy"). *British Journal of Psychology*, *91*, 181–188.

Warren, R.M. (1970). Perceptual restorations of missing speech sounds. *Science*, *167*, 392–393.

Warren, R.M. (1982). *Auditory perception: A new synthesis*. New York: Pergamon Press.

Warren, R.M., & Warren, R.P. (1970). Auditory illusions and confusions. *Scientific American*, *223*, 30–36.

Warren, W.H., & Verbrugge, R.R. (1984). Auditory perception of breaking and bouncing events. *Journal of Experimental Psychology: Human Perception and Performance*, *10*, 704–712.

Wason, P.C. (1968). Reasoning about a rule. *Quarterly Journal of Experimental Psychology*, *20*, 273–281.

Waterhouse, J., Reilly, T., & Atkinson, G. (1997). Jet-lag. *Lancet*, *350*, 1609–1614.

Wells, A., & Matthews, G. (1994). *Attention and emotion: A clinical perspective*. Hove, UK: Erlbaum.

Wells, G.L. (1978). Applied eyewitness-testimony research: system variables and estimator variables. *Journal of Personality and Social Psychology*, *36*, 1546–1557.

Wells, G.L. (1993). What do we know about eyewitness identification? *American Psychologist*, *48*, 553–571.

Wells, G.L. (2001). Police lineups: data, theory, and policy. *Psychology, Public Policy and Law*, *7*, 791–801.

Wells, G.L., Rydell, S.M., & Seelau, E.P. (1993). The selection of distractors for eyewitness lineups. *Journal of Applied Psychology*, *78*, 835–844.

Wells, G.L., Small, M., Penrod, S. *et al.* (1998). Eyewitness identification procedures: recommendations for lineups and photospreads. *Law and Human Behaviour*, *22*, 603–647.

Wesnes, K., & Revell, A. (1984). The separate and combined effects of nicotine and scopolamine on human information processing. *Psychopharmacology*, *84*, 5–11.

Wesnes, K., & Warburton, D.M. (1983). Effects of smoking on rapid information processing performance. *Neuropsychobiology*, *9*, 223–229.

Wesnes, K., & Warburton, D.M. (1984). Effects of scopolamine and nicotine on human rapid information processing performance. *Psychopharmacology*, *82*, 147–150.

West, R., French, D., Kemp, R., & Elander, J. (1993). Direct observation of driving, self-reports of driver behaviour, and accident involvement. *Ergonomics*, *36*, 557–567.

White, N.M. (1998). Cognitive enhancement: an everyday event? *International Journal of Psychology*, *33*, 95–105.

Whitfield, D., & Jackson, A. (1982). The air traffic controller's picture as an example of a mental model. In G. Johansen & J.E. Rijnsdorp (Eds.), *Proceedings of the IFAC Conference on Analysis, Design and Evaluation of Man–Machine Systems*. London: Pergamon Press.

Wickens, C.D. (1992). *Engineering psychology and human performance* (2nd edn.). New York: HarperCollins.

Wickens, C.D. (2000). *Engineering psychology and human performance* (3rd edn.). Englewood Cliffs, NJ: Prentice-Hall.

Wilding, J., Cook, S., & Davis, J. (2000). Sound familiar? *The Psychologist, 13*, 558–562.

Wilding, J.M., & Valentine, E.R. (1994). Memory champions. *British Journal of Psychology, 85*, 231–244.

Wilkins, A., & Baddeley, A.D. (1978). Remembering to recall in everyday life: an approach to absent-mindedness. In M. Grunenberg, P. Morris, & R. Sykes (Eds.), *Practical aspects of memory*. London: Academic Press.

Williams, D.G. (1980). Effects of cigarette smoking on immediate memory and performance in different kinds of smoker. *British Journal of Psychology, 71*, 83–90.

Williams, J.M.G., Watts, F.N., McLeod, C., & Mathews, A. (1988). *Cognitive Psychology and Emotional Disorders*. New York: Wiley.

Williams, S.J., Wright, D.B., & Freeman, N.H. (2002). Inhibiting children's memory of an interactive event: the effectiveness of a cover-up. *Applied Cognitive Psychology, 16*, 651–664.

Wilson, B.A., Baddeley, A.D., Evans, J., & Shiel, A. (1994). Errorless learning in the rehabilitation of memory-impaired people. *Neuropsychological Rehabilitation, 4*, 307–326.

Wincour, G., & Hasher, L. (1999). Aging and time-of-day effects on cognition in rats. *Behavioural Neuroscience, 113*, 991–997.

Wing, A., & Baddeley, A.D. (1980). Spelling errors in handwriting. In U. Frith (Ed.), *Cognitive processes in spelling*. London: Academic Press.

Withington, D. (1999). Localisable alarms. In N.A. Stanton & J. Edworthy (Eds.), *Human factors in auditory warnings*. Aldershot: Ashgate Publishing.

Worchel, P., & Dallenbach, K.M. (1947). "Facial vision": perception of obstacles by the deaf-blind. *American Journal of Psychology, 60*, 502–553.

Wright, D.B., Loftus, E.F., & Hall, M. (2001). Now you see it, now you don't: inhibiting recall in the recognition of scenes. *Applied Cognitive Psychology, 15*, 471–482.

Wright, D.B., Self, G., & Justice, C. (2000). Memory conformity: exploring misinformation effects when presented by another person. *British Journal of Psychology, 91*, 189–202.

Wright, D.B., & Stroud, J. (1998). Memory quality and misinformation for peripheral and central objects. *Legal and Criminological Psychology, 3*, 273–286.

Wright, K. (2002). Times of our lives. *Scientific American, 287*, 41–47.

Wright, P. (1981). The instructions clearly state: can't people read? *Applied Ergonomics, 12*, 131–141.

Wright, P., & Crow, R.A. (1973). Menstrual cycle: effects on sweetness preference in women. *Hormones and Behaviour, 4*, 387–391.

Wundt, W. (1874). *Grundzuge der Physiologischen Psychologie* (*Principles of physiological psychology*). Berlin: Springer-Verlag.

Yarmey, A.D. (2001). Does eyewitness memory research have any probative value for the courts? *Canadian Psychology, 42*, 92–100.

Yen, S.C.C., Vandenberg, G., Tsai, C.C., & Parker, D.C. (1974). Ultradian fluctuations of gonadotrophins. In M.M. Ferin, F. Halberg, M. Richart, & R.C. Vande Wiele (Eds.), *Biorhythms in human reproduction*. New York: Wiley.

Yerkes, R.M., & Dodson, J.D. (1908). The relation of strength of stimulus to rapidity of habit formation. *Journal of Comparative Neurology and Psychology, 18*, 459–482.

Young, A.W., Hay, D.C., McWeeny, K.H. *et al.* (1985). Matching familiar and unfamiliar faces on internal and external features. *Perception, 14,* 737–746.

Young, A.W., Hellawell, D., & Hay, D.C. (1987). Configurational information in face perception. *Perception, 16,* 747–759.

Young, R.W. (1978). Visual cells, daily rhythms and vision research. *Vision Research, 18,* 573–578.

Yule, W. (1999). *Post-traumatic stress disorders: Concepts and therapy.* New York: Wiley.

Zaidel, E. (1982). Reading by the disconnected right hemisphere: an aphasiological perspective. In Y. Zotterman (Ed.), *Dyslexia: Neuronal, cognitive and linguistic aspects.* Oxford: Pergamon Press.

Zaragoza, M.S., & Lane, S.M. (1998). Processing resources and eyewitness suggestibility. *Legal and Criminological Psychology, 3,* 294–300.

Zeef, E., Snel, J., & Maritz, B.M. (1998). Selective attention and event related potentials in young and old social drinkers. In J. Snel & M.M. Lorist (Eds.), *Nicotine, caffeine and social drinking: Behaviour and brain function.* Amsterdam: Harwood Academic.

Zhang, J., & Norman, D.A. (1994). Representations in distributed cognitive tasks. *Cognitive Science, 18,* 87–122.

Zue, V.W. (1985). The use of speech knowledge in automatic speech recognition. *Proceedings IEEE, 73,* 1602–1615.

Zue, V., Cole, R., & Ward, W. (1997). Speech recognition. In R.A. Cole, J. Mariani, H. Uszkoreit, A. Zaenen, & V. Zue (Eds.), *Survey of the state of the art in human language technology.* Cambridge: Cambridge University Press.

Subject index

Author index